Museum Documentation Systems: Developments and Applications

edited by

Richard B. Light, D. Andrew Roberts and Jennifer D. Stewart
Museum Documentation Association

Butterworths
London Boston Durban Singapore Sydney Toronto Wellington

First published 1986

© Butterworth & Co. (Publishers) Ltd, 1986

British Library Cataloguing in Publication Data
Museum documentation systems : developments and
     applications.
     1. Museum registration methods—Data processing
     I. Light, Richard B. II. Roberts, D.A.
     III. Stewart, Jennifer D.
     069.5'2'02854   AM139
     ISBN 0-408010815-0

Library of Congress Cataloging in Publication Data

Main entry under title:
Museum documentation systems.
     Bibliography: p.
     Includes index.
     1. Museum registration methods—Addresses, essays, lectures. 2.
Museums—Data processing—Addresses, essays, lectures. I. Light, Richard
B. II. Roberts, D. Andrew (David Andrew) III. Stewart, Jennifer D.
AM139.M77 1985   069.5'2   85-11003
ISBN 0-408-10815-0

Printed and bound in Great Britain by Anchor Brendon Ltd., Tiptree, Essex

Foreword

Geoffrey D. Lewis
President, International Council of Museums
Director, Department of Museum Studies, University of Leicester

Information technology is having a profound effect on society. Like the so-called agricultural revolution of prehistory and the comparatively recent industrial revolution it is bringing greater efficiency and new opportunities which, appropriately used, can only raise standards and benefit mankind. As with those previous major developments, this new technology can have a profound effect on the environment into which it is introduced. Its application to museums and their documentation systems is no exception. It provides a powerful tool in the service of museums with a capability to harness information, manipulate it and transmit it on a scale not previously conceived. Museums adopting these techniques will inevitably change in character. Whether for better or worse will depend much on an understanding of the purpose of museums, the theory behind the subject disciplines represented in their collections and, of course, the particular technology being used.

This book provides an authoritative review of the current state of the application of information technology to museum documentation. It has been written by the practitioners themselves who give an insight into some of the theoretical considerations of their work as well as the practical advantages to be gained from it. In a sense this book is already a history of this fast developing subject and will stand as such for many years to come. More importantly, however, it embodies the collective experience of many who have pioneered this field in many different parts of the world. It is therefore an indispensible source for those now developing museum documentation systems and from which it can be anticipated that new horizons will increasingly be seen.

Indeed as heavily labour-intensive institutions, museums should be exploring to the full the benefits that can accrue from these new techniques. That the emphasis so far has been on museum documentation is understandable. Some work is now proceeding in developing more general management systems for the museum situation and in applying the 'new' technology either as an interface between visitor and exhibit or for promotional purposes. There are many other applications yet to be developed.

In the meantime we should be particularly grateful to the editors of this work and their collaborators for sharing their experience with us. Museum staff are not noted for the publication of the theory and practice of their work and, indeed, there is some evidence to suggest that this reluctance has retarded museum development. This enterprise will ensure that this is not the case in the development of museum documentation systems.

Preface and acknowledgments

In the last two decades, museums throughout the world have become conscious of the importance of the documentation of collections. It is now widely recognized that the standard of documentation plays a fundamental part in determining the ability of a museum to utilize and preserve the collections in its care. This book is an introduction to the documentation systems and procedures used on a national scale and within individual institutions in 11 different countries.

The contributors were selected by the editors to provide a representative cross-section of some of the major documentation developments that are now taking place. The emphasis varies from statements of principle to practical descriptions of working systems.

As is inevitable when compiling a book of this nature, the individual chapters were completed during an eighteen-month period. Most refer to the state of developments in late 1982 or early 1983. The views expressed are those of the authors and do not necessarily reflect those of the institutions concerned.

The editors would like to thank each contributor for their work during the preparation of this volume. With original papers from 11 countries with eight different languages, communications problems of various kinds have had to be overcome. The editors would also like to acknowledge the help of Jacqueline Hilary (who translated Chapters 23 and 24) and support by their colleagues and the Executive Committee of the Museum Documentation Association. The author of Chapter 17 wishes to thank Dr M.D. Crane for information concerning the history of Bristol City Museum and Art Gallery. The figures and tables in each chapter are reproduced by permission of the institutions concerned.

Contents

List of contributors

Mr Michel Aubert,
Chef du Service Informatique,
Ministère de la Culture,
4, rue de la Banque,
75002 Paris,
France

Mr John C. Baker, BA, AMA, DPA,
Senior Museums Officer (Applied Art),
Sunderland Museum and Art Gallery,
Tyne and Wear County Museums,
Borough Road, Sunderland, SR1 1PP
England

Mr Göran Bergengren,
Curator,
Nordiska museet,
S-115 21 Stockholm,
Sweden

Mr Tàmas Bezeczky,
Archaeologist,
Hungarian National Museum,
Múzeum körút 14-16, 1370 Budapest VIII,
Hungary

Mr John Buchanan,
Registrar,
The Metropolitan Museum of Art,
Fifth Avenue at 82nd Street,
New York, N.Y., 10028,
USA

Mrs Noemi Castillo-Tejero,
Head, Seccion de Maquinas Electrónicas,
Museo Nacional de Antropologia,
Calzada M. Gandhi,
Mexico 5, D.F.,
Mexico

Ms Betsy Comstock,
Consultant,
Canadian Heritage Information Network,
National Museums of Canada,
Ottawa, Ont. K1A 0M8,
Canada

Mr Charles J.T. Copp,
Assistant Curator, Natural History,
City of Bristol Museum and Art Gallery,
Queen's Road, Bristol BS8 1RL,
England

Dr Jonathan L. Cutbill,
Head, Information Retrieval Section,
National Maritime Museum,
Romney Road, Greenwich,
London SE10 9NF,
England

Mr Istvan Éri,
Director,
Institute of Conservation and Methodology of Museums,
Könyves Kalman krt 40,
H-1476 Budapest 100,
Hungary

Professor Oreste Ferrari,
Director,
Instituto Centrale per il Catalogo e la Documentazione,
Ministero per i Beni Culturali e Ambientali,
Piazza di Porta Portese, 1,
00153 Rome,
Italy

Dr Anthony Fletcher,
Keeper, Documentation and Information Retrieval,
Leicestershire Museums, Art Galleries and Records Service,
96 New Walk,
Leicester LE1 6TD,
England

Dr T. Gary Gautier,
Chief, ADP Section,
National Museum of Natural History,
Smithsonian Institution,
Washington, D.C., 20560,
USA

Ms Heidi Henricksson,
Nordiska museet,
S-115 21 Stockholm,
Sweden

Mr Richard B. Light, BA,
Deputy Secretary,
Museum Documentation Association,
Duxford Airfield,
Duxford, Cambridgeshire CB2 4QR,
England

Mr Tom Loy,
Assistant Curator,
Head, Collections Management Section,
Archaeology Division,
British Columbia Provincial Museum,
Provincial Buildings,
Victoria, B.C. V8V 1X4,
Canada

Mr David McCutcheon,
Principal Research Fellow,
Department of Scientific Research and Conservation,
The British Museum,
London WC1B 3DG,
England

Mrs Paulette Olcina,
Head, Unesco-ICOM Documentation Centre,
Maison de l'Unesco,
1, rue Miollis,
75732 Paris 15,
France

Mr Charles W. Pettitt, MSc, MIBiol,
Secretary,
Federation of Natural Sciences Collection Research,
The Manchester Museum,
University of Manchester,
Oxford Rd., Manchester M13 9PL,
England

Ms Dominique Piot,
Service Informatique,
Cellule Recherche,
Ministère de la Culture,
4, rue de la Banque,
75002 Paris,
France

Ms Eloise Ricciardelli,
Registrar,
The Museum of Modern Art,
11 West 53rd Street,
New York, N.Y. 10019,
USA

Mr D. Andrew Roberts, MSc, MIInfSc,
Secretary,
Museum Documentation Association,
Duxford Airfield,
Duxford, Cambridgeshire CB2 4QR,
England

Ms Lenore Sarasan,
Willoughby Associates Limited,
2800 Sheridan Place,
Evanston, Ill. 60201,
USA

Ms Judith L. Schulman,
Registrar/DARIS,
Founders Society Detroit Institute of Arts,
5200 Woodward Avenue,
Detroit, Mich. 48202,
USA

Dr Jacob Sher,
Informatic Department,
Hermitage Museum,
Dvortzovaja emb 34,
191065 Leningrad,
USSR

Ms Jane Sledge,
Chief, Museum Services,
Canadian Heritage Information Network,
National Museums of Canada,
Ottawa, Ont. K1A 0M8,
Canada

Mr Roger B.N. Smither, BA,
Keeper, Department of Information Retrieval,
Imperial War Museum,
Lambeth Road,
London SE1 6HZ,
England

Mr Charles A.B. Steel, BSc, AMA, FLS,
Principal Keeper (Support Services),
Portsmouth City Museums Service,
City Museum and Art Gallery,
Museum Road,
Old Portsmouth   PO1 2LJ
England

Ms Sheila M. Stone, MA, AMA,
Keeper of Archaeology,
St. Albans Museums, Verulamium Museum,
St. Michael's,
St. Albans, Herts AL3 4SW,
England

Mrs Sonja Tanner-Kaplash,
Registrar,
Royal Ontario Museum,
100 Queen's Park,
Toronto, Ont. M5S 2C6,
Canada

Dr Jan P. van de Voort,
Director,
Stickling MARDOC,
Scheepmakershaven 48,
3011 VC Rotterdam,
The Netherlands

Mr David Vance,
President,
Museum Computer Network, Inc.,
Department of Computer Science,
State University of New York,
Stony Brook, N.Y. 11794,
USA

Ms Terese Varveris,
Advisor, Australian Gallery Directors' Council,
37-25 75th Street,
Jackson Heights,
New York. N.Y. 11372,
USA

Professor Frank Willett, MA, FRSE,
Director,
Hunerian Museum and Art Gallery,
The University of Glasgow,
Glasgow G12 8QQ,
Scotland

Chapter 1

Introduction

The phrase 'museum documentation system' refers to the procedures used by museums to manage information concerning their collections or of relevance to their curatorial functions. The primary aims of such a system include aiding the control and use of collections and ensuring the preservation of information about the cultural and environmental heritage. It may incorporate facilities to help locate items, manage internal movements and external loans, apply insurance procedures, undertake audit and stockchecks, aid the preparation of publications and lectures, provide sources for research, assist the development of displays and exhibitions, and include provision for long-term storage and access to data.

Its scope may extend to the documentation of physical collections (objects, bibliographic items, archival material and audio-visual material) and information assets such as details of conservation and record photographs, people, places, events and activities. When documenting an object, the information accumulated by the museum may include its history prior to its acquisition, details of its subsequent incorporation into the collections, physical description and classification, use for display or as a loan and its movement while in the institution. Similarly, for a place, the information may include details of its location and history, environmental significance and management status.

The system may be developed, maintained and used by either specialized documentation staff or general curatorial officers within the museum. Help may also be provided by staff of outside organizations or service agencies.

The physical system may be based on either manual or automated facilities which may also have been developed by the museum itself or be supported by an outside agency, such as a cooperative group or a national museum service.

Many of the most ambitious advances in the use of automated systems have taken place in Canada. The National Museums of Canada has been responsible for an unprecedented investment in central computer facilities on behalf of museums throughout the country. The role of the Canadian Heritage Information Network and the application of its facilities by two users is described in Chapters 2-4.

The project at the British Columbia Provincial Museum (Chapter 3) has concentrated on processing information about archaeological collections and sites in the province. Work at the Royal Ontario Museum (Chapter 4) has been concerned with the inventory and location control of the art and archaeology collections during a major rebuilding programme.

Two of the major themes in the development of documentation in United States museums have been the growing use of computers and the role of registrars. The history of the adoption of computers and the coordinating work of the Museum Computer Network are reviewed in Chapter 5.

Chapters 6, 8, 9 and 10 describe schemes which make extensive use of computers, at the National Museum of Natural History, the Museum of Modern Art, the Detroit Institute of Arts and the Dallas Museum of Fine Arts. The first of these examples illustrates the importance now attached to a comprehensive inventory of the collections for internal control purposes and to enable the museum to demonstrate accountability to outside authorities. In these museums and the Metropolitan Museum of Art (Chapter 7), a registrar's department plays a key part in ensuring that basic records are prepared and maintained, assisting curatorial staff in the collection-holding departments.

Two of these contributions note that there has been an emphasis on computer systems, rather than the records which these systems are designed to manipulate. As a counter to this bias, Chapter 10 also describes the importance of a rigorous system analysis exercise prior to any decision concerning a change of system.

The final contribution from the American continent concerns developments in Mexico (Chapter 11). The National Museum of Anthropology has been active in coordinating the preparation of records about archaeological finds held in museums and private hands throughout the country. The team at the National Museum has designed record cards and terminology manuals to help in this work.

Museums in the United Kingdom have made important changes in their documentation procedures in recent years, including the gradual introduction of computer systems, the appointment of professional documentation staff, the implementation of major recataloguing and inventorying projects and an emphasis on the role of documentation for collections management. Chapter 12 reviews these overall trends and describes the evolution of cooperative schemes. This interest in cooperation can be traced back for nearly 100 years, and has now resulted in the development of a documentation system and support for a central advisory body, the Museum Documentation Association.

Recent work in three of the national museums in the United Kingdom is outlined in Chapters 13-15. The British Museum has recognized the importance of documentation since its formation in the 1750s. During the last decade, it has been planning the most appropriate use of computer-based systems, the first major application of which concerns a project in the Ethnography Department. The initial emphasis of this project is on the inventorying and indexing of the collection. In the British Museum and the Imperial War Museum (Chapter 14), documentation procedures are arranged on a departmental basis, including acquisition and control operations. In the latter museum, a Department of Information Retrieval provides a small central pool of personnel and expertise which can be used to assist the collection-holding departments with particular projects. The National Maritime Museum (Chapter 15) has a similar Information Retrieval Section which supports documentation systems for use by departmental staff. The Museum is involved in a major long-term programme to automate, enhance and utilize the information about its varied collections.

Comparable developments in a cross-section of non-national museums are described in Chapters 16-21. Although each of these museums has been introducing automated systems and most have a member of staff with overall responsibility for the coordination of documentation, the individual contributions illustrate some of the distinct solutions that have been developed to suit local circumstances. In Brighton Art Gallery and Museum (Chapter 16) and Leicestershire Museums, Art Galleries and Records Service (Chapter 18), the museum has turned to its parent local authority for access to computer hardware and systems. Bristol City Museum and Art Gallery (Chapter 17), St Albans Museums (Chapter 19), Tyne and Wear County Museum Service (Chapter 20) and the Hunterian Museum and Art Gallery, University of Glasgow (Chapter 21) have been more closely involved in adopting manual and computer aspects of the system produced by the Museum Documentation Association. In each case, the author describes the overall documentation procedures used by the museum. Some of the contributions refer to recent major recataloguing schemes that have been undertaken with the help of temporary staff funded by a national job creation agency and to pressure from external auditors for effective control over collections.

A number of these museums have important natural science collections. Natural science curators throughout the United Kingdom have now united to establish cooperative registers about collections in museums and private hands. As noted in Chapter 22, this work has been undertaken on an informal basis within regionally-based research units, following pioneering work in north west England.

Chapters 23-28 describe some of the major schemes elsewhere in Europe. In the case of France (Chapter 23) and Italy (Chapter 24), the national museum authorities have been responsible for important developments of computer-based catalogues for research purposes. In France, Directorates of the Ministry of Culture have prepared documentation systems for five disciplines; in Italy, the Ministry of Culture and Environmental Property has been experimenting on a broad scale. Both organizations stress the importance of careful system design and terminology control.

The approach in the Netherlands (Chapter 25) has been similar to that in the United Kingdom, with a number of museums cooperating to prepare new systems and procedures. In the case of maritime museums, the newly-established MARDOC Foundation has been investigating documentation methods and undertaking a survey of maritime collections.

Developments in Sweden are represented by a detailed description of the practical aspects of the documentation system used by the Nordiska Museet (Chapter 26). While noting recent experiments with computer systems, the contribution stresses the value of well-established and effective manual procedures.

The contributions concerning documentation in Hungary (Chapter 27) and the USSR (Chapter 28) both emphasize the coordinating role of the national museum authorities in the overall development of documentation. The Hungarian chapter concentrates on the uniform manual documentation system used for acquisition and cataloguing purposes. In contrast, the Soviet chapter examines the theoretical and practical requirements of an automated system.

The last museum contribution describes a proposal for a documentation system for use by art museums in Australia (Chapter 29). The system incorporates a record card and procedural manual. Various alternative computer systems are being assessed to see which is most appropriate to support the proposed central file of Australian art.

A number of these schemes in individual countries and museums have been influenced by the work of UNESCO, ICOM and the specialized ICOM Committee for Documentation (CIDOC) (Chapter 30). Important developments by these bodies are outlined in the final contribution.

The references cited within each contribution have been combined into a single list at the end of the volume. The bibliographic details are complemented by a brief guide to primary sources of information.

I CANADA

Chapter 2

The Canadian Heritage Information Network

Jane Sledge and Betsy Comstock

Introduction

Canada's National Inventory Programme was one of the most ambitious museum documentation schemes in the world when it was conceived in 1972. The programme was charged with creating a data bank of all the public museum collections in Canada and providing access to it through a computerized national network. The task was formidable, but because the Government of Canada was committed to the programme as part of its National Museum Policy there seemed to be good reason for optimism.

Eight years later, with some 150 museums participating and 1.5 million records in the system's data bank, both the museums and National Inventory staff were beginning to question whether the ambitious goals were attainable. After spending years preparing records for a national computer system, the museums were frustrated by long delays when they tried to enter data and use the system for research and they were finding that many other basic museum needs could not be met.

The original system, which was designed with the expectation that museum records would be more or less static once they were entered, was found to be completely inadequate for the actual working situation where records changed from day-to-day. (For a description of the original system, see Homulos, 1978.) Although data could be searched fairly efficiently, updating was slow. Restrictions in the retrieval process limited the usefulness of the system for research and eliminated the possibility of using it for collections management. To add to the problems, museum records were not nearly as complete or consistent as expected, and this further slowed both data entry and revision.

At this point two events led to a major change in Canada's museum documentation programme. In August 1980, the National Museums of Canada, the government agency responsible for four national museums and various Canada-wide museum services, began a sweeping review of the programme to decide whether it should continue and, if so, how it could be made more effective. And coincidentally, in December 1980, Control Data

Corporation (CDC) approached the National Inventory Programme with an unsolicited proposal for a joint venture.

CDC had been working with The State Hermitage Museum in Leningrad to create a computer system that would make it possible to index and conduct research on The Hermitage's more than 2.5 million works of art. They had designed an information management system called PARIS (Pictorial and Artifact Retrieval and Information System) and were looking for a large network of museums where it could be applied, further developed and refined.

In June 1981, the National Museums of Canada reached its verdict. In the words of the then Secretary-General, Ian Clark, "We concluded that we should continue our efforts to use computer technology to assist the Canadian museum community with its information management problems. We further concluded that, while the original objective of information sharing was solid, there was also a need to use the computer to help museums in their daily management of collections." (Canada. National Museums of Canada, 1982.)

After two successful pilot projects (converting 135 000 extensive records from all five divisions of the National Museum of Man, and 350 000 eight-field records from the Royal Ontario Museum's Location Record Project (Chapter 4)), the PARIS system was officially adopted in April 1982. The National Inventory Programme and Control Data Canada, Ltd., began a seven-year joint project to develop the hardware and software to reach the new goals. The National Inventory Programme was renamed the Canadian Heritage Information Network (CHIN) to reflect its changed character and renewed purpose (Canada. National Museums of Canada, 1982).

Meanwhile, between 1980 and 1983, the Government of Canada was conducting an intensive study of the whole cultural sphere. The Federal Cultural Policy Review Committee (FCPRC) was a key in the study. In its 1982 report, the FCPRC proposed a set of guiding principles which would set the direction for Canadian cultural policy for the next ten years. Among its judgments was that CHIN was of great potential benefit to all heritage activity in Canada. The committee urged that this 'extraordinary' information base be completed with all possible dispatch in order to facilitate collections management, exhibition planning, research and education activities based on heritage collections throughout Canada (Canada. Department of Communications, 1982).

It is expected that CHIN will eventually offer access to some 34 million records on Canadian museum, university and government collections of which the nine million museum records will remain the first priority.

Hardware and software

The computer currently used by CHIN is a Cyber 170, Model 720, located at its headquarters in Ottawa. Museums and other clients gain access to the system by means of telephone lines to any location in Canada where one of 75 terminals has been installed. There are participating museums in each Canadian province and the Northwest Territories and at least one terminal in nearly every major population centre.

The present system can support simultaneous use by 124 terminals. With the addition of a second network processing unit, some 200 additional terminals can be accommodated, depending on the configuration. It is expected that 110 terminals will be connected to the system by the end of 1984 and a further 50 or 60 within two years after that.

The nucleus of PARIS is a data base management system called BASIS, which CDC used as the starting point for extensive museum applications. With BASIS, a large volume of data can be manipulated with a great deal of flexibility. Because BASIS uses natural language, the structure of a data base can closely match the characteristics of individual museums and their collections. Other features of the system include the ability to deal with fields of variable length; online exchange between the user and the computer, with the option to enter and edit data online; good response and search times; a large number of display, printout and report formats; and several levels of data security. (Examples of day-to-day use of the system are provided in Figures 2.1 and 2.2.)

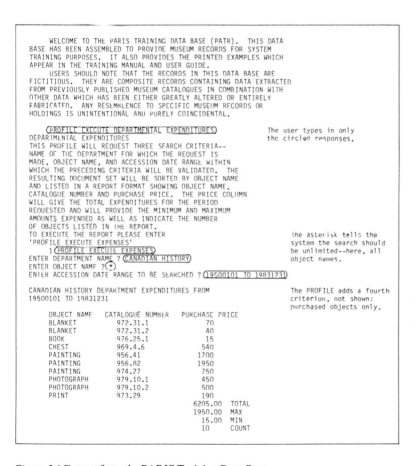

Figure 2.1 Extract from the PARIS Training Data Base

10

```
                                           The asterisk tells the system the
                                           search should not be limited to
                                           "Canadian" (objects known to be
                                           Canadian), but should include
/?PROFILE EXECUTE SUBJECT MATTER SEARCH     "Canadian ?" (objects thought to
ENTER OBJECT NAME ? PAINTING                be Canadian).
ENTER CULTURE ? CANADIAN*
ENTER SUBJECT ? LANDSCAPE
     1 FIND OB=PAINTING AND CU=CANADIAN* AND SUB=LANDSCAPE      The system shows the
*    74    1/    OB=PAINTING                                    number of records that
*    96    2/    CU=CANADIAN* ( 2 TERMS COMBINED)               meet each criterion and
*    33    3/    SUB=LANDSCAPE                                  then the number of records
*    22    4/    OB=PAINTING AND CU=CANADIAN* AND SUB=LANDSCAPE that meet all of the
                                                               criteria. Each result is
                                                               given a set number for
                                                               future retrieval and
CANADIAN LANDSCAPE PAINTINGS                                   study.


         MEDIUM                 ARTIST              CATALOGUE NUMBER
ACRYLIC ON CANVAS         MICHAELS, DAVID           C980.07.15
ACRYLIC ON CANVAS         MILLER, MELANIE           C980.07.16
EGG TEMPERA ON MASONITE   FORRESTALL, CHRISTOPHER   974.2.3
OIL ON BOARD              MACDONALD, J.E.H.         970.11.3
OIL ON CANVAS             HARRIS, LAWREN            962.1.2
OIL ON CANVAS             JACKSON, A.Y.             978.20.2
OIL ON CANVAS             MACDONALD, J.E.H.         980.4.19
OIL ON CANVAS             THOMSON, TOM              916.78
OIL ON CANVAS             THOMSON, TOM              956.41
OIL ON CANVAS             THOMSON, TOM              971.4.2
OIL ON PANEL              COLLIER, ALAN             965.82
OIL ON PANEL              LISMER, ARTHUR            978.20.1
OIL ON PANEL              THOMSON, TOM              927.17
OIL ON PANEL              THOMSON, TOM              936.27
OIL ON PANEL              THOMSON, TOM              970.11.1
OIL ON PANEL              THOMSON, TOM              079.11.2
OIL ON PAPER              STEVENSON, GEORGE         970.15
WATERCOLOUR ON PAPER      CHAVIGNAUD, GEORGE        977.18.15
WATERCOLOUR ON PAPER      HURLEY, ROBERT            971.84
WATERCOLOUR ON PAPER      STEVENSON, GEORGE         970.15.1
WATERCOLOUR ON PAPER      STEVENSON, GEORGE         970.15.12
WATERCOLOUR ON PAPER BOARD FORRESTALL, CHRISTOPHER  975.29.1
```

Figure 2.2 Example of a PARIS search

These procedures can be carried out on a wide range of machines. CHIN has developed microcomputer communications protocols that allow the central computer to accept data from other compatible microcomputer systems and also permit retrieval of PARIS records for additional processing in a micro environment. If other mainframe computers with museum-related data are linked with the CHIN computer, the number of possible combinations and the information available to all participants will greatly increase.

The museum network

CHIN operates the central computer system and carries out its national advisory functions with a staff of 38, not including data entry and computer operators who work under a facilities management contract. Eighteen staff members work as system analysts, programmers and software and communications support officers; 14 work with museums, half as museum consultants and half as a documentation research and training group.

In recent years, there has been increasing emphasis within CHIN on support, both technical and non-technical, including advice to individual museums on documentation problems, education of new users, consultation on information systems for museums and sharing of new applications and information throughout the network. As well, CHIN coordinates and distributes the results of work being done by individual museums for the benefit of all users of the system. Where one museum has an outstanding collection in a specific area and has developed glossaries and standards of documentation, these are shared with the rest of the network.

In addition to Canada's four national museums (the National Gallery of Canada, the National Museum of Man, the National Museum of Natural Sciences and the National Museum of Science and Technology, all in Ottawa), CHIN serves a large network of provincial, university and community museums which vary greatly in size and scope. At one end of the scale are large museums in major centres like the National Museum of Man, which has more than 138 000 records in the system and may eventually add nearly 150 000 archaeological specimen records. It has eight terminals on site. The PARIS system is equally equipped to serve institutions like the Biggar Museum and Gallery in Biggar, Saskatchewan, which has about 3500 records, and the Owens Art Gallery at Mt. Allison University in Sackville, New Brunswick, with some 2500 records. Like many smaller institutions participating in CHIN, these two museums do not yet have their own terminals. They send copies of their records or handwritten work sheets to CHIN. The data entry staff input the data and send printouts back to the museum for correction. After the corrections have been dealt with, CHIN prints catalogue cards by accession number, source or any other field the museum request, and may also provide computer-generated indexes of the museum's records. Finally, there are a number of museums of all sizes, in or near major population centres, which do not have their own terminals but have access to one at a nearby institution. Although CHIN proposed that these museums enter their own data using a neighbouring terminal, most of them are finding that it is more convenient to send data to CHIN for entry because of the competition for terminal time. They use the local terminals only for occasional retrieval of information.

Museums of all sizes see a need for more terminals. In museums that have only one terminal, individual departments are pressing for their own terminals so they can use PARIS as a tool for everyday collections management. Smaller or more remote museums want their own terminals so that they can use the system independently. In the past, CHIN has supplied the terminals to its clients free of charge. As the number of users in each area increases, it is expected that the museums will pay for all terminals. CHIN will use the funds thus saved to acquire equipment which will allow expansion of the network.

Because of the projected size of its network (both geographical size and number of terminals) and the amount and rate of information flowing through it, CHIN has converted to a packet-switching telecommunications service called DATAPAC for communication to and from remote users. (Museums in the Ottawa area do not use DATAPAC.) It is both a method of transmitting data and a means of reducing costs in a large network. The previous system, called Dataroute, used dedicated telephone lines for which CHIN paid a set monthly rate regardless of the amount of use. With DATAPAC, CHIN can develop a much larger terminal network without greatly increasing costs since it will be charged only for the information actually sent down the line in packet units. Supporting this network and tying it together requires flexibility. To do it, CHIN must function within a constant state of change and development. The communication system is an important factor in the support of the network. It allows CHIN to communicate with other computers and computer systems and supports a high degree of interaction. In this sense, the communication system is as important as the software and the hardware of PARIS.

Costs and financial support for documentation

CHIN is one of the services provided to the Canadian museum community by the National Museums of Canada through its National Programmes Branch. About $6.9 million was allocated to the programme between 1972 and 1982.

CHIN's operating cost in the fiscal year 1982-1983 was $1.5 million, not including staff salaries and basic office and administrative costs which are the responsibility of the National Museums Corporation as a whole. Approximately $480 000 was spent on hardware and software rental, $200 000 on line charges for the telecommunications network, $160 000 on maintenance of the system hardware, and $110 000 on travel (which included the cost of bringing museum representatives to CHIN headquarters for training sessions and visits to associated museums by CHIN staff).

CHIN has a specialized format for receipt of computer readable museum data and it absorbs the cost of converting data in this format to PARIS. CHIN also pays the initial cost of training museum staff members. The operating cost for an individual museum, outside the salaries of data entry operators, cataloguers, etc., depends on the number of terminals installed, the additional training needed and the location and size of the museum.

In addition to the services and support provided by CHIN directly, a number of museums have benefitted from other funding programmes that support documentation. The funding comes from many levels: other National Museum programmes; other government sources (federal, provincial and municipal); and by reallocation of funds within individual museum budgets.

Qualifying museums and art galleries receive financial grants and technical services from the Museum Assistance Programmes (MAP), another National Programme of the National Museums of Canada. Under its Registration Assistance Programme, MAP provides grants to museums to encourage them to document their collections or to remodel existing documentation. A museum can apply for funds both to document its collection and to enter its records into the computer system, up to a maximum of five years. In its first ten years, the Registration Assistance Programme allocated about $4.5 million to Canadian museums. Expenditures for Registration Assistance in 1982-1983 were approximately $800 000.

A number of provincial and municipal programmes can also be used for general museum purposes. In Ontario, for example, job creation assistance can be given to students for museum work during the summer.

CHIN itself provides assistance by coordinating summer documentation projects which are funded by the Canadian Employment and Immigration Commission. Since 1977, 137 such projects have been arranged. In 1982, 76 students were hired to prepare basic manual records in 19 local museums, at a cost of $219 860.

As much as five years of funding may be necessary for one department of a large museum to convert its documentation into the computer system, perhaps entering and editing between 15 000 and 30 000 records. In such a case, the external funds would typically be used to pay the salaries of a data entry operator and two cataloguers. Generally speaking, Canadian museums have not been able to computerize their records without outside financial support. However, they have also had to make their own commitment to maintain the system when outside support ceased.

One of the key lessons learned in CHIN's eleven year history is that a museum must be willing to make a long-term commitment, and to enlist the support of all areas of its operation, before it embarks on a major computerization project. A project of this magnitude and complexity requires cooperation at many levels over a number of years. It should not be made solely in response to the requirements of a central agency, or a funding agency or auditor, or because it is supported by one officer. Unless the goals and procedures are agreed upon within a museum in advance, other projects may demand resource allocation and a documentation project may be interrupted or abandoned midway.

When a museum decides to automate its documentation its priorities must shift to reflect this commitment. The Canadian museums which have implemented and used PARIS successfully, for their own benefit and for their colleagues in other parts of the country, have had strong commitments, not only to sharing information and to efficient collections management, but to obtaining outside funding and reallocating the necessary resources from within their own budgets.

CHIN today

CHIN's first regular training session on the PARIS system began in July 1982. By March 1983, 108 staff members from client museums had been trained. They in turn have trained people in their own institutions. A recent client survey showed that more than 1000 people within the Canadian museum community are now able to use the system. About two-thirds of the data from the original system had been converted to PARIS by March 1983. It is expected that the remaining data will be converted by the end of 1983. There are museums at all stages of the conversion process, from improving and completing handwritten records to using PARIS for everyday work. More than 146 000 new records have been entered since PARIS went into operation and approximately 70 000 changes, additions and deletions are made each month to existing records. A large number of museums are taking advantage of the features of the system to clean up existing records, review data standards and enforce rules of syntax.

In the 1970s, lists of data categories (fields) were made up by task forces of specialists from each discipline. In most cases, the fields were direct carry overs from manual documentation systems, which described objects primarily from the curator's point of view. The records for an individual museum's collections were separated by discipline and were included in nationally-shared data bases for each discipline. Eight years of working experience revealed two major problems with the structure of these data bases. First, because of the growing concern for collections management in a wider sense, museums were gradually forcing a greater range of information into the existing fields than they were designed to accommodate. Second, the separation of data bases by discipline created problems in research. For example, the Montreal Museum of Fine Arts, one of Canada's oldest museums, with a very diversified collection, was using three separate data bases (History, Ethnology, and Fine and Decorative Arts). Multi-disciplinary research was extremely slow and cumbersome since it was necessary to search all the data bases to review the collection.

Today, every museum has its own data bases, composed of portions of a common set of data fields. The earlier approach, separate lists of fields for each discipline, has been revised in favour of two basic sets, one for the humanities and the other for the natural sciences. These are, in effect, menus from which museums can select the fields that match their collection requirements. The need for independent data bases for each museum (rather than a single general file) and for dynamic control by museums over their records were two of the factors that influenced the decision to adopt the PARIS system.

At the same time, PARIS has made it possible to break down the data categories used to describe each object and thus to name and define fields more precisely. Many Canadian museums founded in the 19th and 20th centuries have a large number of manufactured objects in their collections. In the original computer system, all the details about the manufacturer of an object were recorded in one field. With the expanded fields in PARIS, the Manufacturer field has been expanded with the addition of a dozen separate related fields: Mailing address, Location address, City, Province/state, Country, Postal code, Founding date, Incorporation date, Liquidation date, Known brand names, Manufacturer remarks and Manufacturer references. Furthermore, with additional fields available, it is possible to record information useful to museum directors, exhibit designers, conservators and registrars as well as curators. The museum is treated as a whole, with a total institutional perspective reflected in the record for each object. There are now 660 fields of information for CHIN's humanities data base and 680 for natural sciences and the number continues to grow.

There is a danger in the unlimited expansion of fields, however. Objectives should be defined in such a way that clearcut results, which support work in progress, can be achieved. One must ask: what is the purpose of the institution? What activities support that purpose? What information is needed to support each of those activities? What information should be computerized? Because data entry is a building process rather than a finished product, it is important to begin with well-defined objectives, and use the results to establish further documentation requirements.

Despite the emphasis in museums today on institutional data bases, the original idea of a shared national inventory has continued to be endorsed and encouraged by users for a variety of reasons. Effort is now being focused on building two national data bases made up of subsets of the humanities and natural science data bases. The national data bases are intended as reference points for the institutional data bases. Proposals for the make-up of the subsets were presented and discussed at a users meeting in the summer of

1983. The most likely approach seems to be to select about 20 key fields from each museum file and incorporate them in the shared data bases. The fields and the amount of data in the national data bases will be analysed, through studies of actual usage, and as a result the data bases will continue to change and evolve.

The continued emphasis on pooling information is another factor which encourages CHIN to maintain a central system with major processing and storage capacity. It is recognized, however, that much of the preliminary work of the individual museums could be carried out on smaller local computers.

The future

Ten years after the start of the original National Inventory Programme, the full potential of the programme is beginning to be realized, as illustrated in Chapters 3 and 4. Canadian museums are already demonstrating that their needs will continue to grow, meeting and even exceeding the possibilities of the existing technology. Two central problems are emerging as the museums computerize their documentation: the need to establish clear lines of responsibility for information within each museum, to ensure that the quality of data will be maintained as the number of users increases; and the need to develop further the standards for recording data. The first is an internal problem for each museum, the second requires cooperation among all the museums to develop shared and disciplinary standards.

In most Canadian museums that have converted from a manual to a computerized information system there has been only one terminal and one person or department has controlled the procedures by which data enters the system. Museum staff are understandably reluctant to expand the number of people who have access to their data, particularly the number who can add to it or change it, until controls are established to protect the quality of the information. This problem is drawing attention to the importance of security procedures as a means to ensure the quality as well as the privacy of information. Several different levels of security have been developed for PARIS using a set of controlled passwords. Each authorized user is assigned a password which provides access to specific data for an authorized use. For example, data bases can be structured so that only the registrar can change the location field. Curatorial staff may be cleared to enter data in some fields but only to read from those which are the responsibility of other museum staff. The desired combination of restrictions can be built into a data base before it is converted to PARIS.

The question of data standards is an intricate one. There are areas where it is important to establish strict guidelines (proper names, dates); areas where disciplinary interests should prevail (for example, archaeologists should define microliths); areas where it is necessary to compile a thesaurus of acceptable terms in order to preserve flexibility and regional variations in language; and areas where the computer system itself needs refinement. While much of the work on data standards must be done by the client museum (they have already agreed to certain standards of syntax), CHIN is studying its original records and other recording systems to learn the patterns used in recording data and to determine where the computer system needs to be more flexible.

Now that the PARIS system is starting to meet basic museum needs such as location and inventory control, production of catalogue cards, accountability for insurance and evaluation, the emphasis is shifting towards refining the applications of the technology, to expand the usefulness of the data bases and to improve the quality of collections management services available to Canadian museums.

While the priorities rest firmly on collections management services, part of CHIN's resources are directed toward investigating the application of new technology. Several components of the National Museums of Canada would like to work with CHIN to produce an interactive videodisc which would tie photographs, slides and perhaps conservation files to the object files. CHIN is also looking at possible tie-ins to word processors and to Canada's Telidon videotext system.

Although the Canadian Heritage Information Network would not have been possible without major technical advances, there is strong feeling here that it is the human resources, the Canadian government's long-term commitment to the project and the integrity and persistence of the people in museums across Canada for more than a decade which have ensured the success of this large documentation effort.

Chapter 3

Collections computerization at the British Columbia Provincial Museum

Tom Loy

Introduction

The British Columbia Provincial Museum was created by Provincial legislation in 1886 and charged to collect and interpret the human and natural history of the province to its residents. Its total collection holdings number approximately 1.5 million specimens which have been collected within the province. Yearly museum attendance averages 1.2 million visitors. At present there are eight curatorial divisions representing Amerindian Linguistics, Ethnology, Archaeology, Modern History, Entomology, Aquatic Zoology, Vertebrate Zoology and Botany. In addition, there are three service divisions — Conservation, Education and Extension, and Exhibits. Approximately 150 full and part-time staff carry out the museum's functions. There is no central Registrar of Collections. Individual collections staff are guided by an overall Museum collections policy and specific divisional collections policies.

The Archaeology Division has been in the process of transferring its registration data into the Canadian Heritage Information Network (CHIN) system for the past nine years (see Chapter 2). The majority of that time has been spent working in conjunction with the national centre on the development and testing of various systems and data entry/retrieval procedures. Production processing into CHIN on a large scale began three years ago. In addition to three divisional registration and collections staff, three assistant registrars and one part-time data entry operator have been hired through the National Museum's Registration Assistance Programme. The assistant registrars and data entry operator primarily have responsibility for transferring registration data into the system, editing and data retrieval. As funding has permitted, portions of the Ethnological collection and Ornithological collections have been entered as well.

Documentation of the archaeological collection

The archaeological collection contains accessions which have been accumulated since the 1880s. Since that time, the variety of registrars and cataloguers and the shifting disciplinary emphasis upon the nature of description in catalogue records has resulted in an aggregate catalogue of variable, and in some cases dubious, quality. At the inception of the computerization process it was determined that the entire collection (then about 90 000 formed artefacts) needed to be re-examined and re-described according to a modern set of standards.

Unlike many other museum disciplines, systems of archaeological taxonomy and terminology have tended to be idiosyncratic and certainly internally inconsistent. Clearly what was needed was a set of objective standards that would guide our re-description of the collection. In conjunction with the National Museum's National Inventory Programme (the progenitor of CHIN) we developed a set of topical entry headings that became the inventory data standard. We then produced a guide to the standardization of information which filled the topical headings. This included the creation of an artefact descriptive syntax based upon objective morphological attributes and the writing of a dictionary of terms suitable for use within the descriptive system (Figure 3.1) (Loy and Powell, 1977).

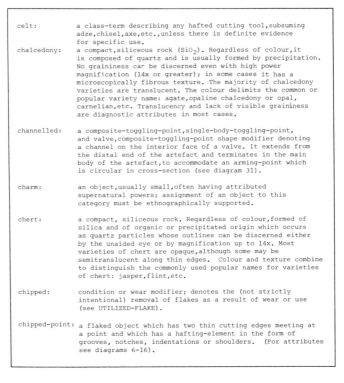

Figure 3.1 Dictionary of terms used when recording archaeological collections

Concurrent with the preparation of standards for the description of collection artefacts, a standardized format for the recording of archaeological sites was developed. This record of sites became part of the National Inventory of Prehistoric Sites and formed the nucleus of the Provincial Site Location File. Site information is linked to artefact collections by the identification of each artefact using a uniform site designation scheme (Borden, 1952; Anon., 1975) as part of the artefact catalogue number.

Our computerized database includes both individual artefact (Figure 3.2) and more general site information. Only in special circumstances are artefacts treated on a lot or batch basis (e.g. trade beads, nails); each artefact is fully described and recorded individually within the system. In addition, the recording strategy for both sites and artefacts is directed toward a net increase of specific information during the re-registration process (e.g. accurate material identification, bibliographic citations).

The documentation process

In July 1982, CHIN initiated its new operating system (PARIS). This system is permitting us to realize the full potential of a computerized database; we have for many years realized that in addition to faster access to collections records, a computerized system will permit the active management of our collections. In the present database, our initial series of 67 information fields describing the artefact, its context and its collection documentation has enlarged to 120 fields which include information about current location, loan, display or other status.

Although the original National Inventory system could not support the collections management function, procedures for collection documentation, storage and process control were implemented by us in anticipation of future system developments. One early example of this strategy is seen in the consolidation of our collection into modular, track-mounted storage units in order to maximize our storage space. Our collection is physically organized in storage by site designation; this means that as collections are made from individual sites, the entire collection must at some point be rearranged to accommodate the new artefacts. To ease this burden, and to control location in the interim, each drawer in the collection is given a unique storage address; with the PARIS system we are now able to accommodate new acquisitions from previously excavated sites at various locations in storage. Control over our storage locations enables us to store artefacts within a site grouping according to special conservation needs, or by similar material or similar artefact type, rather than arbitrarily by consecutive catalogue number. We have thus extended the concept of random access data storage into the collections room.

Whether dealing with our backlog or with newly accessioned professionally excavated site-collections, the procedures followed in computerized registration are essentially the same. The divisional Keeper prepares an inventory of items and drawer addresses; he also assesses the site-collection for storage and specific conservation requirements. The divisional Registrar collates all site contextual documents, organizes site records, prepares a storage inventory list of all photographs, soil, faunal, floral and other analytical samples, and creates primary accession records.

In collaboration with the Senior Collections Technician, Keeper and

DOCUMENT   2

PARIS NUMBER   23236
USER ID   -FORMS-
DATE OF CHANGE   831115
RECORD LANGUAGE   E
INSTITUTION   BCPM
DEAP-ID   BNP1000410881041
DEPARTMENT   ARCHEOLOGY
CATEGORY   ARTIFACT
OBJECT NAME   BOWL
OBJECT STATE   ENTIRE, COMPLETE
LENGTH   32.00
WIDTH   17.20
THICKNESS   10.70
UNIT-LINEAR   CM
DIMENSION REMARKS   LENGTH AND WIDTH ARE APPROXIMATE. DEPRESSION MEASUREMENTS ARE: 13.00 x 13.00 x 7.10 CM.
WEIGHT   6063.0
UNIT-WEIGHT   GM
MATERIAL   STONE, VOLCANIC, BASALT
TECHNIQUE   PECKED-GROUND, ENTIRE, CARVED, INCISED,,Y
DESCRIPTION   BIRD-SHAPED, ENTIRE, DEPRESSION, BODY TOP,, ZOOMORPHIC-CARVED-INCISED, ENTIRE,, ONE END OF THE BOWL
                           EXHIBITS A RAVEN MOTIF HEAD. TWO LARGE EYES HAVE BEEN CARVED ON EITHER SIDE OF THE HEAD, THE BEAK HAS
                           A CARVED LINE ON EITHER SIDE OF IT REPRESENTING THE OPENING. THERE IS A V-SHAPED RIDGE ON THE TOP OF
                           THE HEAD BETWEEN THE 2 EYES. LOWER ON THE BOWL UNDER THE RAVEN HEAD IS A SMALL HAWK-LIKE BEAK WITH A
                           CURVED UNDER END. AT THE OPPOSITE END OF THE BOWL THERE IS A FLAT, ROUGHLY RECTANGULAR PROTRUBERANCE
                           REPRESENTING THE TAIL. THERE ARE SOME INCISED GEOMETRIC LINES ON THE TOP OF THIS REPRESENTING 7 TAIL
                           FEATHERS. THE BACK OF THE LEGS PROTRUDE UNDER THIS. WINGS OF A ROUGHLY HALF MOON SHAPE ARE LATERAL.
                           CARVED ON EACH OF THESE IS AN UPSIDE-DOWN GEOMETRIC FACE, IN PROFILE.
ORIGIN-PROVINCE/TERR   BC
NATURAL REGION   21,S. QUEEN CHARLOTTES; 22.N. QUEEN CHARLOTTES
CURRENT ETHNO AREA   HAIDA
BORDEN NUMBER   FT/FU y
ACCESSION NUMBER   1927-1;4115
OTHER INVENTORY NOS   04545
CATALOGUE NUMBER   13
MUSEUM COLLECTOR   TOLMIE
COLLECTION DATE   1927
SOURCE   NEWCOMBE, W.A.
CURRENT LOC-SITE   BCPM
PHOTO NUMBER   PHOTO
PUBLICATIONS   DUFF, WILSON, "IMAGES STONE B.C.", HANCOCK HOUSE PUBLISHERS LTD.(SAANICHTON, B.C.), 1975, PP.154, 188;
                           STEWART, HILARY, "ARTIFACTS OF THE PACIFIC NORTHWEST", HANCOCK HOUSE PUBLISHERS LTD. (SAANICHTON, B.C.),
                           1973, P.102
REMARKS   SEE ALSO RECORD FOR FT/FU y:13 CAST.

Registrar, the Senior Assistant Registrar for computerization collates all information about the site and its artefacts. The Senior Assistant Registrar then organizes all fields of information into sets according to the nature of their rate of information change. For example, each record will contain a certain amount of invariant information: site designation, bibliographic references, name of site, location, excavation grid bearing, pit locations, stratigraphic and level/layer designation schemes. Additional fields will change at differing rates: for example, the actual level/layer, pit of excavation, artefact class. It is the function of the Senior Assistant Registrar to assess the information and organize a data recording and entry strategy which uses the powerful data editing features of the PARIS system to minimize the number of repetitive keystrokes during data entry.

The actual item registration begins with the signing out of a drawer from storage, the assignment of class and descriptive terminology, and the recording of all item-specific variable data. This information is written on preprinted forms from which it is entered into the system. Batches of individual records are edited according to their content of changing data; the entire collection records are inspected by the Assistant Registrars and final system editing is done. When a drawer of artefacts is re-registered it is returned to the Keeper for return inventory and replacement in storage.

For some years the Assistant Registrars have been responsible for entering their own artefact records into the system. We have found that this procedure keeps the input error-rate low; nevertheless it is an impractical strategy for very large-volume data entry, and a data entry operator has been used as funds have permitted.

Documentation priorities

In our re-description of the collection we have had to set priorities regarding the processing of different types of collections. Highest priority has been given to the most recently excavated collections (i.e. those made by professional archaeologists using modern field techniques). Next highest were those sites that are important to ongoing regional research because they constitute a 'type' or reference collection. Next in ranking are surface collections made by non-professional collectors; these usually have no within-site provenience and often represent only the most recognizable artefact types. Lowest priority are specimens that are only provisionally associated with a known site, or that have no specific site association. These last two categories often provide interesting or spectacular artefact types suitable for display. Regardless of established priorities, any object moving out of the collection for loan or display purposes is re-described and the details entered into the computer.

In addition to objects that are permanently part of our collection, we endeavour to catalogue artefacts that are loaned to us for study purposes: often these artefacts form part of a private collection. By including these objects in our database we hope to be able to more easily track them through the commercial and export antiquities market, and in some cases to encourage donation of the collection at a later date.

Although our main goal at present is to complete the re-description and computerization of our collection data, we are preparing now for the eventual integration of other types of data into the main artefact register. We currently maintain paper inventories of soil, faunal, floral, radio-carbon samples and lithic debitage from excavated sites. We will add these inventories on a box or lot basis to the computerized records pertinent to those samples as an adjunct to the artefact catalogue. In addition to field-collection records we intend to add the results of analytical research (e.g. edge wear, residue studies, material analysis, material identification) to the specimen database.

At present, however, our main interest lies in keeping up with our growing collections. From an initial collection size at the beginning of computerization of about 90 000 formed artefacts, our collection has grown to about 220 000 artefacts of which we have re-described 90 000. In recent years the majority of the division's collections growth has resulted from research or rescue excavation projects. In order to cope with the number of artefacts generated by these projects we have instituted a set of minimum standards for the acceptance of professionally generated collections. These standards are designed to ensure better curatorial care during the fieldwork and to ease the task of computerization of excavation records.

In the past, field notes and artefact catalogues were minimal and of varied quality; as part of the computerization of our records we have designed a suite of recording forms for use in the field (Figure 3.3). In some cases the standard set of recording forms is not appropriate to the specific project; in these cases we work with the project director in designing forms suitable for project needs and that are compatible with rapid processing into computer storage. We have taken the view that good curation and registration begin at the inception of a field project and not just at the museum's door.

The role of documentation

In our opinion, collections management is not simply a more modern phrase with which to replace the venerable term curation. It is the embodiment of a strategy to provide access to and control of the entirety of our collection and its attendant data. The traditional museum catalogue, accessions book and sometimes donor's register cannot serve to quickly answer questions not framed within their mode of organization. Cross-indexed card files, original field records and notes, and all other paper records are used by us as interim documentation methods, not as ends in themselves. Having tried to use automated systems that provide batch-oriented collections documentation, we have come to the conclusion that this approach merely produces a faster card file (a technique that is firmly rooted in the nineteenth century). Having access to the truly interactive PARIS system which can control and use an enormous amount of data directly relevant to research, display and management of our artefacts, we are implementing techniques that will become fundamental in the 21st century. Of prime importance from a museological view is our new ability to track, document and control collections management processes such as accessioning, loans, valuations, casting and conservation treatments and the like.

Of equal importance to the museological tasks is our ability to answer questions about our collections — not only for curatorial research, but as part of a wider public-information responsibility. In designing our data

ARTIFACT RECORDING SHEET   Site _Dc Ru 12_   Artifact # _1055_

1. Excavation Unit _N 104 - E 215_
2. DBD _0.25_ m. 3. (DBD) DBS HAU HASL _0.20_ m.
4. Arb. Level(s) _4_   5. Nat. Layer(s) _A_
6. Measurement to artifact location: (N)/S _1.23_ m. (E)/W _0.94_ m.
7. Quality of Provenience: (2d) 2d level screen gridded site surface
8. Matrix (clastic): gravel_____, sand _X_, silt _X_, clay _?_,
   humus_____, other_____
   coarse_____   medium _X_   fine_____
9. Matrix Colour: general visual _medium brown_
   Munsell code _5YR 3/6_   soggy, wet, (moist) dry
10. Shell: High (%)_____   (medium) (%) _40-50%_, low (%)_____, absent_____
    coarse_____, medium_____, fine _X_
    scattered _X evenly mixed_ lensed_____
11. Artifact material: stone _basalt_, mineral_____, bone_____,
    tooth_____, antler_____, shell_____,
    other_____
12. Manufacture: flaking _X_, grinding_____, sawing_____, pecking_____,
    sectioning_____, other_____
13. Artifact Class: _Chipped-point_
    (try to use defined terms if possible)
14. Condition: A (circle at least one)   B (circle at least one)
    (entire)   (complete)
    fragmented   incomplete
    broken   restored
    fissile   needs conservation work
    eroded by_____
    chipped
    affected by fire   OR can't tell
    patinated   inapplicable
15. Remarks: _possible traces of pitch on hafting element_

16. Assoc. Numbers for: Photos _Colour, Camera 3 - Roll 2B - Frames 12, 13, 14_
    Features _F-21 hearth_   Burials _none_
    Faunal Remains _none_   Matrix Sample _S-107_
17. Recorded/Excavated by _JP_   18. Date _Sept 03, 1979_
    ———————————— NATIONAL INVENTORY ————————————
    Category _artifact_   Class _chipped-point_
    Description _bifacial, m., rectangular shoulders, excurvate blade, convex base_
    Modifiers _flake scars contracting, random, basally thinned_
    Length _8.02_ cm. width _3.15_ cm. thickness _1.21_ cm. weight _12.25_ gm.
    Qual. of Measure _exact_   Date _Dec. 15, 1982_

Figure 3.3 Completed artefact record sheet

recording standards we identified the probable major users of our collection and determined that to be of continued use, our catalogues must be very complete and primarily descriptive. Specific research data are carried in the computerized records, but it is rarely the point of entry into the data base. The greater emphasis is on answering fundamental questions such as what does the artefact look like, what is it made from, where is it from, how old is it, and where is it located in storage? The emphasis here is placed on the very time-consuming early phase of academic research where the researcher attempts to locate objects or collections relevant to specific research projects. Due to its sheer volume and inconsistency our old paper record system discouraged many kinds of enquiry concerning our collections; now we are finding that as we bring major blocks of collections data online the range and variety of enquiries from the public is much greater. To paraphrase Murphy's Third Law: use of a computer documentation system increases proportionately to its completeness and flexibility; or more simply, questions are asked more often as the ability to answer them increases.

In our experience, it is imperative to build in a constant system of review of processes and concepts during the conversion of collections data into the computer. For example, in the early stages of formulation of standards we accepted the notion that all artefacts must be measured at least for length, width, thickness and weight. These appeared to be essential descriptive attributes. We are currently re-evaluating that assumption in light of two considerations. First, individual researchers will want to have specific measurements made according to their particular research design and their landmarks for measurement may not coincide with the generalized specific measures we record. Second, if measurements are done to assist in the unique identification of a specific artefact (which might occur in a situation where the label has disappeared from an artefact), weight alone will suffice. Significant savings in item processing time can be made by dropping linear measures for most artefact types. We have in fact dropped length, width and thickness measures from many artefact types (e.g. amorphous outline flakes, raw material fragments, abrasive stones). Our natural curatorial conservatism has, however, prevented us from dropping the three principal linear measures altogether.

Conclusion

In our programme we made an early decision to structure our data toward museological and curatorial needs as opposed to the more usual problem-oriented academic research model for computer storage of information. Although strictly scientific research is supported by our data base, the era of computer compiled and written dissertations relying upon museum collections is not yet at hand (nor is it likely ever to be) (Loy, 1982). Although conversion to a fully computerized system is not yet complete, the effects of conversion are already being felt through the implementation of standards of description, of standards of field recording, and of systematic collections management functions. These effects act to free museum staff to be more responsive to public and scientific demand and above all to enhance the usefulness of the vast amount of information contained in our collection.

Chapter 4

The Royal Ontario Museum, Toronto

Sonja Tanner-Kaplash

Introduction

The Royal Ontario Museum (ROM) belongs to that generation of encyclopaedic museums with collections which span the earth and life sciences, archaeology and the fine and applied arts. It is the third largest museum on the North American continent, and Canada's most important institution, both in terms of collections and number of specialized staff. The collections are divided between 19 different curatorial departments. Documentation for the nine art and archaeology departments is processed by a centralized Registration Department, while the 10 science departments maintain independent records.

The Art and Archaeology collections, which presently number about 350 000 items, have been expanding at the rate of approximately 300 accessions annually. This means that about 1000 items are added to the collections each year (excluding scientific specimens).

While curatorial departments are responsible for researching acquisitions, and providing catalogue information to the Registration Department, all other documentation of transactions involving the collections are the responsibility of the Registrar's Office. This includes such diverse activities as securing appropriate levels of approval for major gifts and loans, legal transfer of ownership, appraisals for income tax receipts, negotiating loan contracts and completing transportation and customs arrangements for international shipments. In addition, this department is responsible for the more usual duties of assigning accession numbers, the maintenance of donor/vendor files and centralized catalogue files, and most recently, location records and random checks on collection locations.

Museum Expansion and Renovation Project

By the early 1970s, it became clear that the existing three-storey building of approximately 700 000 square feet was totally inadequate for the Museum's present level of operation. In November 1977, the ROM Board of Trustees approved a major Expansion and Renovation Project based upon feasibility studies which recommended on-site expansion and retention of the Museum's convenient central location.

Fortunately, the design of the existing H-shaped building allowed the addition of new structures between the wings. To ensure maximum temperature and humidity control, these were designed as two separate, self-contained units. They were to be joined to the original building by glazed atria, housing bridges and elevators to connect the three, high-ceilinged floors of the old Museum to the six levels of the new construction. One new building was designed as a terraced display area; the second as a Curatorial Centre to house administrative and curatorial offices, laboratories, workrooms and badly needed collection storage space.

In order to proceed on schedule with the extensive renovations to the old building, it was essential to provide suitable interim storage for collections. To this end, construction of the Curatorial Centre began in May 1978. An early decision was taken to retain all collections on the Museum premises. This was not only for reasons of safety, security and conservation, but also to ensure that artefacts and specimens remained accessible to curators, conservators, senior scholars and, indirectly, to the general public, by means of off-site exhibits and loans to other institutions.

Location Record Project

As planning proceeded, it became apparent that documenting the movement of collections would create an enormous additional workload, at a time when Museum staff were already under stress. Given the sheer volume of collections, the time-frame, the necessity for access and the further requirement for an audit trail for security purposes, it was decided that a computerized documentation system was the only solution. While the central registry held accession, disposal and loan records for nine departments, location records had traditionally been a curatorial responsibility. Over the years, various departments had developed different systems, with varying degrees of efficiency and accuracy. Collections were physically numbered with Museum accession numbers, and held in various display or storage areas, clearly identified by holding department.

The Museum had been investigating the automation of records for some time, and a computer services unit was planned for the new facility, but this would not be operational in time to deal with the immediate dislocation of collections. Therefore, it was necessary to look towards other solutions for the short term.

Since 1972, the Canadian federal government, through the National Museums of Canada has provided certain computer services and other assistance to museums through the National Inventory Programme (recently renamed the Canadian Heritage Information Network) and various funding programmes (Chapter 2). In September 1978, the Royal Ontario Museum began its Location Record Project and became the largest user of this service. This was on the understanding that all data generated by the institution would be provided in machine-readable form for future use on in-house equipment. For the immediate future, however, all data will be stored in a data bank located at CHIN headquarters in Ottawa.

The project divided logically into several phases. Each was preceded by a short pilot project, in order to calculate timing, manpower requirements and costs for each step. The Registration Department was augmented by full- or part-time contract staff as required, ranging from three to ten persons at different times. Careful records were kept of Location Record Project staff, hours and production, to verify costing forecasts and facilitate the tracing of errors.

Phase I (September - December 1978)

Phase I called for the creation of a data base from existing documentation. The catalogue card record was selected for this purpose, since it was the most reliable and consistent of the manual records (Figure 4.1). This was arranged in chronological order according to the tripartite accession number (e.g. 981.1.1). While the earliest Museum accessions date from 1885, the total volume of collections had never actually been calculated. Approximate figures were estimated and random drawers of catalogue cards were selected for manual counting. An 'accuracy factor' was then established and applied against the total figure to correct early rough calculations.

```
981.977.20.1-2          CANADIANA DEPARTMENT

             Gift of Mr. Jean Rideau
             Montréal, Quebec

PAIR OF TABLESPOONS, silver; fiddle pattern.  Bright-cut
engraved initials «OC» in script on front of handle.   On
back of handle, maker's marks of «J.T.» twice, interspersed
with two marks apparently representing stretched animal
skin. (Probably Jonathan Tyler, Montreal, 1817).

                  -small surface scratches on both spoons; face
                  of bowl of (2) has a group of about 12
                  scratches about 1.5 cm. in length, resulting
                  in bulge on back of bowl.

L: 22 cm.
```

Figure 4.1 Example of a catalogue card record

Since the Location Record Project was clearly for collections management purposes and not for detailed cataloguing or research, a minimal amount of information was required for each object. Commercial keypunch staff were hired to operate three VDU's in shifts, for 16 hours each day. They were trained to extract only three relevant pieces of information from each catalogue card: the accession number, the holding department, and the object name. In approximately four months, a skeletal record, initially of these three categories, was created for over 300 000 objects.

28

At the end of this phase, a printout was prepared and sorted first by holding department and then by accession number (Figure 4.2). This was bound into volumes for easier storage and handling. Originally, this document was intended for use as a working list for the next phase; however, the time-frame dictated that this second step was actually begun before the end of Phase I.

```
INV2 ROM INVENTORY                                    MAR 19, 1979    PAGE 509
                                    ROM INVENTORY LISTING
                                             FOR
                                    CANADIANA DEPARTMENT
       DEPT    ACCESSION NUMBER     OBJECT NAME
       CD      981.977.12           WATERCOLOUR ...................................
               981.977.13           WATERCOLOUR ...................................
               981.977.14           IRON .........................................
               981.977.15           IRON .........................................
               981.977.16           IRON .........................................
               981.977.17           IRON .........................................
               981.977.18           POSTCARD .....................................
               981.977.19           MEDAL ........................................
               981.977.20.1         TABLESPOON ...................................
               981.977.20.1         TABLESPOON ...................................
               981.977.21           CLOCK ........................................
               982.10.1             SEWING MACHINE .........................
               982.25.1             BOWL .........................................
               982.25.2             MUG ..........................................
               982.25.3             PITCHER ......................................
               982.33.1             DISH .........................................
```

Figure 4.2 Printout at the end of Phase I of Location Record Project

Phase II (November 1978 - May 1979)

Phase II involved an independent physical inventory of all museum collections. For this purpose, four recording teams were used. Each consisted of one preparator to handle artefacts and one recorder to document the results. Each location, such as display cases, shelves or drawers in curatorial offices, laboratories and storage areas, was assigned a unique number. The full location code identified floor, gallery or room, and concluded with the unique number. The development of a consistent, universal system was essential, since the continued use of various departmental location systems could lead to alpha/numeric duplications and other confusing situations. The recording teams completed a separate sheet for each numbered and labelled location, identifying the holding department and listing all the items found there by accession number and brief description. Each team was able to process about 1000 items per day.

Phase III (May 1979 - December 1980)

Phase III was perhaps the most onerous and time-consuming step. The results of the physical inventory were 'matched' with the data base created from the existing documentation in the Registration Department, and a 'first location' was manually added to the printout record. This was then available for later computer input as a fourth category. By now, it was apparent that some recorded items were not found during the physical inventory, while 'extra' items were located. A variety of other difficulties became evident, including duplicate accession numbers, typing errors and 'no such number'. Therefore, a code was created to specifically identify more than 30 different types of error. Records containing one of these errors were identified and flagged for future action. This error code was entered as a new category on the next generation of printouts, bringing to five the total number of categories for each record.

During this phase, all records were proofread and, where possible, verified, corrected or flagged for future attention. Finally, records were recalled one by one on a VDU for corrections and additions. The final result was a printout for each holding department, listing objects by accession number for each individual location.

Phase IV (January 1981 - December 1983)

In order to reduce the handling of collections during the actual move, a system of Movable Storage Units (MSU's) was designed. Many curatorial departments decided upon these as permanent storage units for their new facilities. Each lockable, dust-proof unit featured adjustable slots for drawers of different sizes. Approximately 200 units were fabricated in advance for use during the move.

Gradually, the Museum was closed to the public, and objects from display and storage areas were carefully packed into numbered MSU's. This operation was also undertaken by the same recording teams, using the most recent generation of computer printouts as working copies upon which to manually note a second location for each item. Since these printouts were the *only* location record in existence at that stage, they were treated as high-security documents and signed in and out by all staff. When each volume was completed, second locations were input into the computer as soon as possible.

During the Project, requests for MSU access were made on a standard form processed by the Registration Department. Curatorial staff were accompanied by an authorized key holder, and both parties were identified on the access request form. As different wings of the Museum were handed over to contractors for renovation, MSU's were moved by specially adjusted forklift trucks to other locations, behind temporary walls separating the interim storage areas from construction and renovation activities.

To accommodate the diversity of different storage units already in use at the Museum, it was necessary to devise a flexible and internally expandable location identification for storage areas in the new facility. Generally, objects already packed in MSU's were moved as a group inside their cabinet. Most of the large, irregularly shaped items were transferred individually, or held in temporary areas while existing racking was dismantled and reassembled in the new facility. For these reasons, it was essential to be able to identify a space *before* actual occupation by storage units or artefacts and specimens.

   Identification of the building, floor, curatorial suite and specific storage room was based upon the code devised by the architects for preliminary construction plans. In the storage rooms, each curatorial department agreed to use a 'bank' system (i.e. rows of various storage units divided by aisles). Each vertical unit within the bank was numbered starting, where applicable, at a wall and numbering towards the 'expandible' end of the bank. Within each vertical unit, adjustable shelf or drawer *slots* were numbered, starting at the floor (Figure 4.3). In this way, horizontal units added or reorganized at a later date would not require physical renumbering, or extensive changes to the location record. In addition, items placed on top of cabinets could still have a unique shelf number. Where a vertical unit actually consisted of two stacked cabinets, all horizontal shelves or drawers were through-numbered, bottom to top.

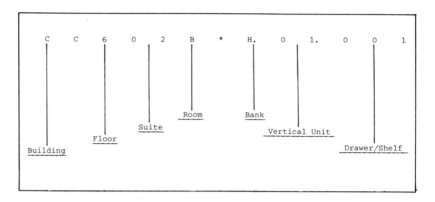

Figure 4.3 Location code system

   The final move into permanent quarters was accomplished by the same recording teams, now assisted by curatorial staff and technicians who were gradually trained to take over the recording function as the teams were needed elsewhere.

   Initially, collection movements were reported to the Registration Department on a form designed for that purpose, and then input by Location Record staff, who also conducted monthly random checks on recorded locations. As the documentation of continuing location changes becomes the responsibility of each curatorial department, a specific staff member is appointed departmental liaison to be responsible for this function.

   During this period, regular inventory checks have been continued and somewhat expanded. Of course, the random check selections are not entirely random, in that certain types of collections are more heavily featured — notably material on incoming loan, high-value collections and recent acquisitions. On a regular, but not absolutely predictable schedule, Location Record staff visit each curatorial department in turn, and meet with the departmental liaison to check the recorded locations of selected items. Items that are not located are reported to the department head immediately and to senior management within five days. These records are then reviewed by the Museum's external auditors on an annual basis.

Figure 4.4 is an example of a printout showing the up-to-date location of a group of sixteen objects. The location code previously described is contained in the page heading and two previous locations are also shown. In this particular example, the entire group has moved as a unit twice; in most instances previous locations might vary considerably.

Certain errors still appear in this generation of printout; clearly the 'object name' listing requires editing for consistency. The 'error code' column (on the extreme left of the page) indicates two items which were never renumbered into the tripartite accession system introduced to the Museum in the 1950s, but still bear, both physically and in the documentation, an 'old' alpha-numeric catalogue number. Near the bottom of the page is one of the many records which could not be verified during Phases II and III. Since the entire data base was originally constructed from existing documentation, in all probability this record will eventually be matched with one of those items that were 'found' during the physical inventory without an accession number physically affixed, and which are still awaiting identification.

Costs

To date, our accomplishments have been rewarding. Our basic premise in undertaking this project was *not* to establish a completely comprehensive catalogue record — a feat that few institutions can perform without enormous cost (Sarasan, 1981) — but rather, to work towards a minimal record for collections management purposes. It is planned to expand the inevitable 'pass through' process for updating locations, to correct and refine existing information and to contribute new data. The ROM skeletal record of approximately 350 000 items has been accomplished within a relatively short period of time and at very reasonable cost — a total of approximately CDN \$83 000 in National Museums of Canada grants, plus an equal contribution by the institution. This figure was expended almost exclusively on salary costs, and does not include computer time, user's costs or rental fees of any kind, since these services were provided free of charge, along with minor program modifications, printing, etc. However, keeping this in mind, as well as the fact that a certain amount of student manpower was available free of charge to the Museum during the summer months, the total actual costs are still below CDN \$300 000 for the period September 1978 to March 1982. With the exception of Phase I, where commercial keypunch operators were recruited on short-term contracts, the Project employed and trained relatively unskilled staff, often recent university graduates without previous work experience.

System maintenance - current status and future directions

As the Museum realizes its goal of full computerization, curatorial departments are being equipped with terminals, initially to record location changes and ultimately to facilitate the addition of other information to the centralized data bank.

By the end of 1983, the Location Record Project was close to termination.

```
5 JUL 82                      ROM CURRENT LOCATION LISTING                              PAGE 414
                                    CC507-B.01.003
```

ERR CODE	DEPT CODE	ACCESSION NUMBER	CATALOGUE NUMBER	OBJECT NAME	PREVIOUS LOCATION 1	PREVIOUS LOCATION 2	WORK AREA	PARIS NUMBER
SP	GR	G590	G590	SMALL SICKLE-SHAPED TOOL	2.16/208.0	2.15 T192825	....	294476
SP	GR	G640	G640	FISH HOOK	2.16/208.0	2.15 T192825	....	294475
	GR	910.130.74	G2505	FISH-HOOK	2.16/208.0	2.15 T192825	....	306899
	GR	910.130.76	G2508	FISH-HOOK	2.16/208.0	2.15 T192825	....	294488
	GR	910.175.128	G494	FISH HOOK	2.16/208.0	2.15 T192825	....	294480
	gr	910.175.228	G578	SICKLE	2.16/208.0	2.15 T192825	....	294479
	GR	910.175.89	G657	SHEARS	2.16/208.0	2.15 T192825	....	294485
	GR	910.175.93	G664	SICKLE	2.16/208.0	2.15 T192825	....	294484
	GR	910.175.94	G665	AXE	2.16/208.0	2.15 T192825	....	294483
	GR	910.175.97	G674	HOOK	2.16/208.0	2.15 T192825	....	294481
	GR	910.94.10	G715	TENACULEM HOOK	2.16/208.0	2.15 T192825	....	306727
	GR	910.94.23	G728	FORCEPS	2.16/208.0	2.15 T192825	....	306910
FO	GR	910.94.44		CATHETER			....	354347
	GR	910.94.5	G710	SPATULA PROBE	2.16/208.0	2.15 T192825	....	306918
	GR	910.94.7	G712	SPOON PROBE	2.16/208.0	2.15 T192825	....	306917
	GR	918.5.177	G4348	FISH HOOK	2.16/208.0	2.15 T192825	....	294477

```
TOTAL RECORDS FOR LOCATION CC507-B.01.003 = 16
```

Figure 4.4 Final printout location listing of a group of objects

All major collection moves and the reorganization of storage areas are complete and the major portion of proofreading, correction and basic editing work on the preliminary data base is finished; the Museum is now ready to move into a new phase of collections management and computer application.

By this time, CHIN had made several changes and improvements to the services offered to client/users, and the Museum was able to secure access to a greatly expanded number of fields for each object record. After extensive discussion and consultation with CHIN personnel, the Museum was able to select and structure available services to accommodate our own particular needs and requirements, and to complement the existing pattern of collection documentation, which had traditionally been a joint venture undertaken by both the Registration Department and the various curatorial departments responsible for the physical safekeeping of Museum objects.

Of the approximately 550 fields now available to the Museum through the expanded CHIN operation, approximately 250 are designated as an 'Administrative Data Base' to be supported by the centralized Registration Department, while the balance comprises the 'Curatorial Data Bases' to be directly supplied with information from each of the nine curatorial departments. In this manner, the familiar structure of the original registration system has been maintained, and the operational department responsible for the initial generation of either administrative or curatorial information will be responsible for contributing these data to the centralized record. Users of each data base have 'read only' access to almost the entire spectrum of fields (since very few fields have been reserved as 'restricted' by the Administrative Data Base). Each data base is maintained as a separate entity, and modifications of any type may only be made to the Administrative Data Base by the Registration Department and to each of the Curatorial Data Bases by the corresponding curatorial department.

One of the most important fields assigned to the Administrative Data Base is that intended for the Museum accession number; therefore, only one information source, the centralized Registration Department, can create an entirely new record. Since individual curatorial departments are still responsible for the physical location of collections, this division of responsibility provides several security features. First, it means that both administrative and descriptive information about an object in the collections cannot be accidentally deleted by the same operator. Second, as curatorial departments become responsible for maintaining their own location records, the new information can be entered directly into the system, thereby avoiding the delays that inevitably occurred when information was provided to the Registration Department and entered by Location Record staff. In addition, curatorial departments may undertake the detailed cataloguing of collections as time and resources permit, and contribute this information to the centralized data base. Finally, the random check procedure, which is still carried out by the Registration Department, ensures that considerable motivation exists for prompt documentation about location changes.

Conclusions

In North America, the question of public accountability has received considerable attention, most particularly since the early 1970s. Increasingly, museum collections are viewed as major assets of public institutions, which are usually registered as charitable organizations. Depending upon the actual articles of incorporation and the structure of the local authority, a museum may come under the jurisdiction and scrutiny of the Public Trustee or the Attorney General. In Ontario, these are two separate functions; in some regions (for example New York State), they are combined.

Clearly, the documentation of collections is closely related to the principal function of the museum; that is, the gathering and maintenance of collections. Adequate documentation can no longer be considered an incidental activity to be undertaken as one of the secondary functions of museums, but has become the principal means by which an institution is able to demonstrate accountability to the public that it serves. To this end, some institutions have published a *Statement of Ethics*, such as that produced by the Royal Ontario Museum in 1982, which clearly sets out the responsibilities of the staff in the area of collections management and documentation and states the intentions of the institution to comply with all relevant federal and provincial legislation, as well as those international conventions to which Canada is signatory (Royal Ontario Museum, 1982).

These concerns for public accountability have gradually come to the forefront in the North American museum community, and have brought about a climate in which resources have been made available for the documentation of museum collections. This position represents a radical change in attitude, compared to the situation ten years ago, and given the economic situation during this period of time, it is a particularly encouraging development. Museums and galleries have gradually come to realize that appropriate collection documentation provides not only legal security and identification of museum collections, but also a firm foundation for curatorial research and ultimately, for the museum's most public role, the exhibition of collections.

II UNITED STATES OF AMERICA

Chapter 5

The Museum Computer Network in context

David Vance

Computers and museums: the United States experience

This is a history of the beginnings — the first two decades — of the use of computer systems to manage, inventory and index public collections in the United States. The Museum Computer Network (MCN) is the story's protagonist, often an actor, always an observer. What follows is drawn from its files and library: its 'memory'.

MCN is a small association of museums. It is the only United States organization devoted to helping museums of every kind and size to take advantage of modern information technology. At present it has 51 members, including six outside this country. Much of the activity reported here has been undertaken by museums that are not members, or were not when they began using a computer.

The United States is a land of independent museums. Data about them come only from questionnaires received by known museums and voluntarily answered, and so are incomplete — to an unknown extent. For what it may be worth, the Official Museum Directory for 1982 lists 5793 United States museums (American Association of Museums, 1981). A 1979-1980 survey of computer use in collections management found 320 museums, zoos, etc., admitting to such activities (Sarasan, 1981; Sarasan and Neuner, 1983). Of these, 137 provided details of 182 separate undertakings. Some of these lie in the past, others in the future. Needless to say, known projects went unreported: questionnaires were not returned.

Ignorance is compounded by initiatives aborted in planning or full operation, the end usually less visible than the beginning. Abrupt halts, a recurring theme of this chapter, stem from finances. In commerce an enterprize is financed by borrowing against expected profits. In the non-profit sector there are, by definition, no profits. New undertakings are financed by begging and, once started, are exceedingly difficult to sustain.

This, therefore, is a history of starts and stops here and there. The Museum Computer Network has been a stable, but never dominant, presence since 1967. The story, however, begins four years earlier.

Development of computing systems

About that time the so-called 'third generation' of computing machinery appeared and, with it, large-scale 'direct access' data devices: machines that can select data from any part of an archive at any time instead of having to 'read' from the beginning, as with magnetic tape. They differ from tape storage as a book differs from a scroll and thus open the way to *indexed* files. The reason for committing museum inventories to magnetic storage is exactly to index them: to cross-reference without keeping multiple card files of the same information. It occurred to many people that computers might now be used for *permanent*, indexed catalogues of museum holdings, not merely for statistical analyses, as in the past.

So it was that in 1963 the Automatic Data Processing Committee was set up at the National Museum of Natural History of the Smithsonian Institution. In the next two years data processing personnel were hired and work began on SIIRS (Smithsonian Institution Information Retrieval System), a forerunner of the better known SELGEM (Squires, 1966). Ironically, SIIRS relied upon tape, not direct access data storage.

Also in 1963, the Institute for Computer Research in the Humanities (ICRH) grew out of the Heights Academic Computing Facility of New York University, a private institution. Both were directed by Professor Jack Heller. ICRH was devoted to research involving large data bases, such as concordances, indexes to periodicals and studies of literary and musical authorship and chronology. The Facility had an IBM 2321 Data Cell Drive with a capacity of 400 million characters online, then the ultimate in direct access. Some data management programs developed there by Heller were christened GRIPHOS (General Retrieval and Information Processor for Humanities Oriented Studies). The United Nations Dag Hammarskjold Library became the principal user and underwriter of GRIPHOS. It was also used and supported for a time by the American Institute of Physics for a bibliographic application. Museum use came later and remained secondary.

For a decade literature on United States museums and computers gave systems more attention than the information they process. It was easy, though mistaken, to perceive American museums divided into five warring camps, corresponding to the five major 'museum' systems described by Chenhall: SELGEM, GRIPHOS, GIPSY, TAXIR and GIS (Chenhall, 1975). All these are general information systems, not peculiar to museums. Only SELGEM was designed for museum use; but it too can handle any kind of itemized records. It is our most widely used system, with scores of applications (see Chapter 6). No more than six institutions ever used GRIPHOS for a museum-like data bank, though it was experimented with by others. Only two still have it and both plan conversion to more current software. GIPSY was used only by the Oklahoma and Missouri Inventories of Ethnological Collections before 1970. TAXIR is used primarily by universities and by some university museums. GIS was an IBM product with one museum-related application, the Flora North America project. The 'big five' never existed. They merely happened to have been used in museums before *Museum Cataloguing in the Computer Age* was written and to appear, as examples, in a work really about cataloguing.

Other software systems used fall into two broad, overlapping categories:

the commercial product and the home-grown. Commercial 'packages' have the advantages of substantial professional support and financial backing, all of which can be withdrawn through corporate failure or replacement on the market by a more competitive product. Home-grown systems (often developed at a nearby university rather than within the museum) offer local control and tailoring to specific needs and equipment but little solid support. A few of the packaged systems in use are MARK IV® at the Carnegie Museum of Natural History (by Informatics, Inc.), INQUIRE® at the Strong Museum, Rochester (by Infodata Systems, Inc.) and FOCUS® at the Yale Center for British Art (by Information Builders, Inc.). The home-grown are legion but two have attracted wide attention and may come into more general use. These are DARIS at the Detroit Institute of Arts (Chapter 9) and 'The Information System' at the Children's Museum, Boston (Mayhew, 1980).

All this was in the future when, in 1965, collection data were first fed into computers in three unrelated projects, at the Smithsonian Institution, at the Museum of Paleontology of the University of California, Berkeley (Rensberger and Berry, 1967) and at the Joe and Emily Lowe Art Gallery (now the Lowe Art Museum) of the University of Miami, Florida (Freundlich, 1966). The last named was our first art museum project. All three data bases are still active.

Also in 1965 the Oklahoma Inventory of Ethnological Collections was funded by the National Science Foundation as the pilot for a national inventory. Computers were not part of the plan; but headquarters were at the University of Oklahoma, Norman, where James W. Sweeney was working on GIPSY (General Information Processing System). Although produced without museum use in mind, this became the first interactive or 'online' system applied to museum data. When GIPSY met the Inventory a threshold was crossed: there was a data bank combining parts of several museum collections. The *Guide to Inventorying Ethnological Collections*, including a controlled vocabulary, was prepared, and trained teams were fielded to capture uniform data (Ricciardelli, 1968; Schneider, 1970). In the end, 44 265 objects from 42 museums in three states were listed (Sweeney, 1970). Funds were not granted to continue the project. Other events of 1965 included the founding of the *Newsletter of Computer Archaeology*, edited by Robert G. Chenhall, and initial planning for the Flora North America project, which would have been completed about 1986 (see below).

TAXIR (TAXonomic Information Retrieval) was begun in 1967 at the Taximetric Laboratory of the University of Colorado, Boulder, by a team headed by David J. Rogers, with Robert C. Brill and George F. Estabrook. An impressive array of scientific applications was reported as early as 1968. TAXIR, now largely an interactive system, is supported at the University of Michigan, Ann Arbor (Brill, 1978). It is a big, well-documented system, noted for speed, economy and reliability, which, however, limits data to a so-called 'flat table', without hierarchical structures. STIRS (Chenhall, 1975) and EXIR are offshoots of TAXIR. TAXIR and its progeny run today at university centres in Brazil, Canada, England and Italy. Recently it was used to control and document a major archaeological excavation in the Tombigbee River Valley, Alabama, via remote terminals in the field (Peebles and Galloway, 1981).

Cooperative schemes

In 1966 staff members of the Metropolitan Museum of Art, New York, got in touch with Heller at ICRH, initially about projects other than cataloguing (Bowles, 1968; Dauterman, 1968). When Heller visited the Museum, William D. Wilkinson, then its Registrar, interested him in the general card catalogue, housed then as now in a bank of wooden file drawers one city block in length. Obviously this was but a subset of the cards in art museums of the city, country and world. Their combined information value must be unimaginable. Yet very little was accessible save by inventory number (Heller, 1968). Within months Heller prepared a $2.5 million proposal for a 'Fine Arts "Data Bank"'. New York museum directors (including some not of art museums) met at the Whitney Museum of American Art in February and March, 1967, to study the proposal. There they formed a 'Museum Computer Network' (MCN) to plan and seek funds.

Seed grants were awarded by the New York State Council on the Arts and the private Old Dominion Foundation. An office was set up at The Museum of Modern Art and Everett Ellin left his post as Assistant Director of the Solomon R. Guggenheim Museum to become the first Executive Director of MCN. The Network quickly expanded to take in the National Gallery of Art, Washington, and nine other great art museums outside New York. International contacts were established when Ellin attended a meeting of the ICOM International Committee on Documentation (CIDOC) in 1968. Since that time MCN has nurtured this and other foreign relations on behalf of U.S. museums and, unofficial though it is, served as a quasi-National Committee on Documentation (Chapter 30).

The 1968 Conference on Computers and their Potential Applications in Museums was sponsored by the Metropolitan Museum of Art with funds from IBM. Twenty-one inventive scholars shared their thoughts, often but not always profoundly foresighted, with several hundred museum people (Metropolitan Museum of Art, 1968). Thomas P. F. Hoving said '... these machines are going to put us on our toes as never before.'

This writer, then Associate Registrar of the Museum of Modern Art, proposed and supervised the creation of a trial data bank to see whether records of different museums could, in fact, merge without the impossible task of recataloguing. Twelve museums opened their files and the ICRH used an early form of GRIPHOS to build and interrogate a union catalogue of 2000 miscellaneous items (Vance, 1970). There was no attempt to revise terminology since we wanted to see how variable it was; but *data categories* (e.g. artist, date, material) were rigorously defined for the first time in art museums. It was and is MCN's position that such definition is the first (but not sufficient) condition for making a union catalogue, which — attainable or not — remains the ultimate goal.

It came as a surprise that this definition was lacking. Examining these museums' files, one invariably found printed cards with labelled 'fields'. Nowhere was there a written definition of even one field label. Often the same label (notably 'provenience') was used by different museums for radically different content. The only way to learn what a label meant was to interrogate the staff, who often disagreed among themselves.

In GRIPHOS a record consists of any number of fields, each of any length, assembled in any order. A field is created by entering a label followed by some content. The record is analogous to a blank card, on which anything may be written. The system uses the labels (which may be letters, numbers or both) to make sense of the records when they are retrieved (Vance, 1977). This could hardly succeed without a standard set of defined labels, which had to be invented. To avoid disputes over terminology, arbitrarily chosen numbers were used instead of words: '70' meant 'attribution' (as defined), '51' 'dimensions', etc. (Vance and Heller, 1971).

On subsequent museum visits staff members were questioned about the actual use of each field until it could be identified with a numerical label already defined, or else determined to represent a new concept requiring definition. Our experiment could not have continued if a high degree of natural, unplanned consistency had not been found to underlie the apparent babel.

The experiment was pronounced a success though, in retrospect, too little had been learned from too small a data bank. Costs of data capture were determined but those of selective retrieval, using GRIPHOS, were underestimated with dire consequences for the future. The folly of giving a computer too much information per item (which should have been obvious even without an experiment) went unnoticed.

The appearance of success led the Metropolitan Museum of Art (Chapter 7), the Museum of Modern Art (Chapter 8) and the Arkansas Archaeological Survey to adopt MCN methods and the GRIPHOS programs for conversion of whole collections, two of art and one of site records (Chenhall, 1969). The Metropolitan's effort was terminated in 1971 for financial reasons.

Other early users of these systems were the Bureau of Historic Sites and Properties of the State of Florida, the International Museum of Photography at George Eastman House, Rochester, and the Yale Center for British Art.

Meanwhile, the Network's fund raising was anything but a success. At the end of 1970 MCN lacked not only money, but staff and offices too. I moved its files and library to the Registrar's Department at the Museum of Modern Art and began to administer the penniless consortium in 'spare' time.

The ICRH, too, had been closed. Heller moved to the State University of New York at Stony Brook and continued work on GRIPHOS, assisted by graduate students and supported, primarily, by the Hammarskjold Library. A second Metropolitan Museum computer conference in 1970 (never published) was sponsored by New York University with a residue of ICRH funds.

Chenhall's 1971 international Archaeological Data Bank Conference at the University of Arkansas was another milestone and lent further impetus to the development of an informal 'computer-and-museum' community of individuals (Chenhall, 1971).

In 1972 MCN became a non-profit corporation, and two years later followed Heller to Stony Brook, helped by a timely grant from the Columbia Broadcasting System. Since that time its main support by far has been the University's contribution of space and services.

The growth of SELGEM (SELf GEnerating Master) began at the Smithsonian in 1968 (Creighton and Crockett, 1971; Neuner, 1976; Humphrey and Clausen, 1977). Thanks to a policy of releasing programs and documentation gratis and because SELGEM is reliable and easy to use, it became the most used system among United States museums. Programs were written in COBOL, originally for the Institution's Honeywell 2015 computer and, once released, have had to be recoded in the COBOL dialects of IBM, Univac, CDC, etc. Institutions with SELGEM versions for different makes and models of machine soon became secondary SELGEM distribution centres. Development and home use of the programs were documented in the series *Smithsonian Institution Information Systems Innovations* and external applications in the occasional *MESH Newsletter.*

Willing as the Institution was to share its programs, it did not envisage turning into a service bureau. Takers were free to use SELGEM as they might see fit but were expected to provide their own system support. Inevitably, however, requests for help were frequent and SELGEM workshop meetings had to accommodate not only the Institution's own staff but numerous guests from the outside world. In an effort to free the Institution of this burden and, at the same stroke, free users of undue dependence, Reginald A. Creighton and others tried in 1976-1977 to establish a permanent user organization, MESH (Museum Exchange of Systems Help) (Creighton and Parsons, 1977). MESH was carefully designed to become financially self-sustaining after a short gestation, for which 'start-up' funds of $114 925 were sought. In the unpublished application for assistance Creighton indicated that over 700 requests for help had been received and 70 institutions had taken SELGEM documentation (not all of these having put the system to use). Presumably these numbers exclude approaches to the secondary distribution centres. There can be no doubt of SELGEM's wide acceptance, but funds for MESH were not forthcoming.

One SELGEM application deserving special mention was the Bicentennial Inventory of American Paintings Executed before 1914, prepared at the National Collection of Fine Arts (now the National Museum of American Art). It is an uncritical but comprehensive index to known works in both private and public collections by artist, present location and ownership and subject matter (Booth, 1972).

Flora North America (FNA) was this country's most ambitious, most thoroughly planned and documented museum computer application (Shetler, 1975). It was to have been a morphological and taxonomic information base for all vascular plants of the United States, Canada and Greenland, with such additional files as the FNA Automated Bibliography, the Type Specimen Register and an index to ongoing botanical research. Under the direction of Stanwyn G. Shetler it went into full operation in 1971 at the National Museum of Natural History. Six years had gone into preparation and completion was expected after fifteen more years of work. Computer programs were based upon IBM's GIS (Generalized Information System). Documentation consisted of a series of *FNA Reports*. In *FNA Report 71* we read that in January, 1973 '... funding for FNA was withdrawn suddenly and FNA was given a maximum of 60 days to get all of its files out of the computer.' (Shetler and Read, 1973; Irwin, 1973).

The Museum Data Bank Coordinating Committee (MDBCC) formed in 1972, its dozen charter members including most of the Americans then deeply concerned with putting computers to work for museums. Robert G.

Chenhall was elected Chairman and soon raised monies that kept MDBCC going for five years. Until 1974 it had a secretariat at the University of Arkansas and Chenhall did considerable consultation on its behalf, while at work on the book that became the principal legacy of those years (Chenhall, 1975). The group then met four times per year. When funds ran low MDBCC did not feel justified in seeking more, in competition with the museums it wanted to help. Since museum projects then afoot could not be literally 'coordinated,' MDBCC changed to Museum Data Bank Committee (MDBC), closed its office and thereafter met semi-annually, with growing membership. Papers read and discussed were published as the twelve *Museum Data Bank Research Reports* and distributed through the facilities of the Strong Museum, Rochester, N.Y. In 1977 MDBC disbanded voluntarily.

The International Species Inventory System (ISIS) was proposed in 1973 by Ulysses S. Seal and Dale G. Makey, sponsored by the American Association of Zoological Parks and Aquariums and quickly established at the Minnesota Zoological Gardens, Minneapolis (Murtfeldt, 1974). One hundred and fifty zoos participated initially and over 50 000 birds and mammals have been catalogued with 'biographies' and pedigrees as available. This animal census and marriage bureau serves many scientific ends, of which the most critical may be protection of the captive 'gene pool' against inbreeding, which amounts sometimes to preservation of a species. (This ISIS is no relation to the ISIS system used by the National Inventory Programme in Canada.)

Since 1977 The Detroit Institute of Arts, helped by the Burroughs Corporation, has developed its own DARIS (Detroit Art Registration Information System) and become the leader among United States art museums (Chapter 9). There is a moderately large Burroughs computer installation in the building, used for general museum business and also for collections management. The first goal was to trace the whereabouts and movements of all 50 000 works of art. Now descriptive catalogue information is being attached to the brief original records. Work has begun towards linking at least nine other museums into the DARIS system to form a Michigan Art Network (Anon., 1981). The Institute is a member of the Museum Computer Network but, like the majority of members, never used GRIPHOS.

At the Field Museum of Natural History, Chicago, individual departments are larger than most museums. The Anthropology collection of about one third of a million objects faced moving to new storage without a current inventory. As early as 1973 the Department thought of creating a computerized index, at first considering the Oklahoma Inventory's methods and program. Costs of data capture were an obstacle. MCN's trial data bank, for example, had cost $1.50 per item, a fraction of which would have been prohibitive. It was not until 1977, with the much postponed move imminent, that Lenore Sarasan solved the problem with AIMS (Chapter 27). Using AIMS, cost per item was less than one percent of MCN's (taking the intervening nine years' inflation into account) (Sarasan, 1979). How could there be such huge improvement? Only a combination of factors, multiplied together, can explain it. First, 20 data fields (on the average) take longer than six. Second, between 1968 and 1977 the cathode ray tube/visual display unit terminal had replaced the abominable keypunch for data entry. Third, most museum records, including all those in MCN's experiment, have to be reorganized on standard forms before input; but records at the Field Museum were an exception to the rule. Finally, and most important, GRIPHOS lacks AIMS's ability to propagate unchanging data fields forward through a series of consecutive records.

Standardization activities

By the mid-1970s interest shifted from fascination with systems to the data itself. Systems were seen at last to be ephemeral and changing whereas museum records, regarded as eternal, would survive to be processed by generation after generation of programs. It was obvious, for example, that GRIPHOS was already obsolescent and could no longer be recommended.

Now the expression 'data standards' sprang into being and instantly achieved cliché status. Although there is no agreement as to what it means, vocabulary control is surely a large component. This became the focus of attention.

The need for standard vocabulary was felt especially among history museums, which had lagged in data banking partly because they were not always able to decide what to call things. Chenhall was now Director of Data Services at the new Strong Museum, Rochester, N.Y. This museum held a vast collection of artefacts (a single legacy) with no documentation at all; and its first Director, Holman J. Swinney, saw electronic data processing as its only hope for building an inventory and index in a finite period of time. A nomenclature for man-made objects became an urgent necessity. It was decided that such an effort should not be undertaken by the staff of a single institution for its own sole benefit. The result was *Nomenclature for Museum Cataloguing: a System for Classifying Man-Made Objects*, prepared by Chenhall with the help of 62 subject specialists from 23 institutions (Chenhall, 1978a). Inevitably such a work has controversial aspects; but the central fact is that American history museums have a common reference for names, where there was none before.

Names of things are important not only for cataloguing objects but equally for indexing pictorial archives. There are, for example, many collections of photographs ranging up to several million images, though the average size is less. Few of these can be considered works of art. They are valuable for what they depict. Recently the problem of indexing image content has received growing attention. A very informal Image Access Society was formed in 1980 to serve as a channel of communication. It has, thus far, met annually.

The name of the Art and Architecture Thesaurus project (AAT) is descriptive. It is a group of scholars working with subject specialists and existing authority lists, as Chenhall did, but now to standardize usage for art and architecture. Library of Congress subject headings have been taken as an existing standard to be adhered to as nearly as possible (Petersen, 1981).

Technological developments

The first microcomputer was marketed in November, 1971. Today these machines are profoundly affecting American museums' view of computer applications. At first they appeared to suffer from limitations that would render them useless for cataloguing and other 'data base' applications. Their greatest weakness was external data storage, first cassette tape and later 'floppy' disks. In keeping with the small price that makes a microcomputer attractive, these media are cheap. However their capacity, speed and reliability are totally inadequate for data base operations. By 1979 true computer disks ('hard disks') were on the market for microcomputers. The usual computing power of these little machines had, by then, far exceeded that of the IBM 360/30 used at ICRH in 1968.

We have seen that investments in machinery, programming and data capture were a major obstacle. Now, with an entire computer installation costing a few thousand dollars and with improvements in economical data capture, the financial barrier is still there, but much lower.

In the summer of 1980 the Museum Computer Network convened the North American Planning Conference at Stony Brook to consider the implications of microcomputers for museums and how best to make use of them (North American Planning Conference, 1980). Some museum catalogues assembled and used with the aid of microcomputers are at the Danforth Museum, Framingham, Mass., the Strecker Museum, Waco, Tex. (Anon., 1978) and the State Museum of Oklahoma, Oklahoma City (Williams, 1981). These collections range from small (Danforth) to moderately large (Oklahoma); but, in every case, the computer is an inexpensive piece of equipment. Many other museums have used microcomputers in conjunction with larger machines or for applications other than cataloguing.

A very young technology, the computer-controlled videodisc, has aroused more interest in the United States museum community than the computer itself (Nyerges, 1982). At the first organizing meeting of the Museum Computer Network, February 20, 1967, it was noted in the minutes that:

'Although there is no existing hardware which will permit the storage and computer-actuated random retrieval of images..., it is hoped that further technological developments in this direction will, in time, permit this important feature to be incorporated in the Data Bank system.'

During the past year or two we have realized that the hardware is here. The videodisc was introduced for entertainment. Its capacity for storing 54 000 images on a side is the requirement for a half-hour program. Some museums have begun using discs for gallery talks and other audio-visual presentations, including fund raising. However, the 54 000 frames can also be used to archive that number of still images and, moreover, can be summoned individually by frame number and held on a monitor screen.

Merely storing such a number of pictures can be useless without a computer and a machine-readable index so that images matching a viewer's unpredictable criteria can be selected out of the mass. A small number of museums have already recorded pictures of a few objects, without computer control, to study image quality and costs. Some others plan fully integrated computer-cum-videodisc 'image banks'; but only one such project on a small scale is known to have succeeded. This one is the Art History Interactive

Videodisc Project at the University of Iowa, Iowa City (Sustik, 1981). The images are 1000 black and white photographs of woodcuts and engravings by Durer and Raimondi, bypassing the issue of colour veracity.

Evolution of MCN's role

The role and goals of the Museum Computer Network have evolved steadily. Certain general ideas are constant: that museums cannot afford duplicate effort or parallel invention; that the logic of indexing collections is independent of content; that each institution must be the primary beneficiary of its own investment and yet that the results of investments in a catalogue must tend in the direction of a universal union index. In other words, logical compatibility is important. This last idea has proved controversial.

MCN has long since abandoned its early hope that GRIPHOS and the Network's standard definitions of data categories, in conjunction with vocabulary standards developed by others, could lead to realization of its goals. Indeed, the appearance of TAXIR, GIPSY and SELGEM showed, before 1970, that United States museums would not adopt common software.

The necessity of financial survival has conditioned the Network's activities. At first it was thought that nominal fees for the use of GRIPHOS, together with grants by private and public foundations, would suffice. They did not. Since 1974 MCN has existed with the help of the State University of New York at Stony Brook, though not without the need for additional general funds. For a time it did continue to rely upon GRIPHOS' earnings and nearly all efforts were directed to the support of users. There was no effort to attract member museums because more GRIPHOS installations could not have been serviced.

By 1978 the system itself could no longer be supported. MCN lacked the resources to adapt it to new operating systems or to new and smaller machines, much less to convert it from antiquated batch processing to online use. In short, GRIPHOS was obsolete. Moreover, it was apparent by then that support of such a system was by no means the best way to serve the whole community of museums.

Since 1979 the Network has served primarily as a focus for the collection, exchange and dissemination of information about applications of information science and technology to the control and use of collections. Every effort has been made to attract both institutional and individual members, including museums committed to any system or none; and members' dues have become the main source of secondary income. Consultation services are also offered.

The principal means of spreading information have been annual conferences, occasional special conferences, programmes presented for annual meetings of the American Association of Museums, the quarterly newsletter *Spectra*, irregular *McNews Extras* (for members only), use of the MCN library and response to enquiries by mail and telephone.

Since one of the most useful items of information for the Network's clientele would be the name, source and cost of a truly adequate software system, the search for one continues. Thus far none has been identified; but there are ever more promising candidates both from commercial sources (often costly) and from the world of hospitals and health services.

On the other hand, there is now such an abundance of excellent, affordable hardware that the reliability and quality of repair services and replacement parts in a given locality have become the main criteria for selection.

Chapter 6

National Museum of Natural History, Smithsonian Institution

T. Gary Gautier

Introduction

The National Museum of Natural History (NMNH), Smithsonian Institution, has used automated methods for collection management since the early 1960s, and now has a well established Automatic Data Processing (ADP) Programme involving all collections. Most new cataloguing is done using computers, and a comprehensive, computerized inventory of the entire collection will be completed by mid-1983. At that time, the Smithsonian will begin moving many collections to its new Museum Support Center (MSC), where computers will play an even greater role in collection management and museum operations. This chapter gives a brief sketch of the museum's information system (Gautier, 1978 and Wilcox, 1980).

Overview of the Museum

NMNH is one of several museums in the Smithsonian Institution, created in 1846. With collections from all over the world containing over 60 million specimens, it is one of the largest natural history museums. In addition to conducting extensive exhibit and education programs for the public, it is a major centre for basic scientific research, employing over one hundred scientists and providing access to its facilities and collections to other scientists and scholars. Administratively, the museum is divided into seven collection/research departments (Anthropology, Botany, Entomology, Invertebrate Zoology, Mineral Sciences, Paleobiology and Vertebrate Zoology), and nine program units (Automatic Data Processing Programme, Exhibits, Education, Building Management, Registrar, Smithsonian Oceanographic Sorting Centre, Handbook of North American Indians, Scientific Event Alert Network and Smithsonian Marine Station at Link Port, Florida). Richard S. Fiske, a volcanologist, is the director of the museum. Part of the museum's budget comes from private sources, but its collection management program and computer systems are funded primarily by the United States government.

48

Collection information system

The care and documentation of the collections is the departments' responsibility, but the ADP Programme and Registrar's Office provide assistance. Each department has a chairman, curator/scientists, museum technicians and specialists and administrative/clerical employees. Since the curators have substantial research duties, most departments have appointed collection managers from the technical staff to oversee day-to-day collection operations, including the capture and computerization of collection data. Cataloguing is done by the departments, who also do most of the work on loans and new accessions. The primary duties of the Registrar's Office are to review registrarial transactions for clerical accuracy and conformance to museum policy, and to maintain the central registrar's files, where all paperwork for loans and accessions is eventually placed.

The ADP Programme is responsible for administering and coordinating ADP and inventory operations across the museum. ADP funds and employees (over 80 people) are dispersed to departments to assist with cataloguing or inventory projects. Each department has one or more teams of museum technicians and clerk/typists (departmental and ADP employees) who prepare and enter data into computer files. Each team has a 'data manager' or 'inventory manager' who is generally responsible for supervising the work, for obtaining supplies such as data sheets, for making daily decisions about data problems and for submitting computer processing requests.

Work procedures vary between the two dozen major collection information projects in the museum due to differences in objectives, available resources, the nature of existing catalogues, indexes and labels and other factors. The general plan is the same, however. Data are captured and entered into a computer file. A variety of reports are then printed or displayed on data-entry terminals for proofreading, and the computer file is corrected. Specimen labels, index cards, indexes and other final reports are then printed.

Most data are first recorded on preprinted data sheets. Where conditions permit, however, data are entered directly from specimen labels or other documents, by typists or technicians. More than 20 data-entry terminals have been placed at strategic locations throughout the museum. An operator selects one of many pre-programmed screen formats, and fills in the labelled fields with the required data. The data-entry computer (located in another building) automatically checks many fields for errors in format, content and spelling, and stops the typist when mistakes are found. Data common to many records can be automatically duplicated, saving much typing time. Some screen formats allow immediate printing of specimen labels and index cards on a printer attached to the terminal.

Data standards are determined by each department, in consultation with the ADP Office. Data definitions and structures are standardized as much as possible across the museum, with allowances being made for differences between collections and between scientific disciplines. Though the total number of possible major data elements is well over 100, most computerized catalogue records contain between 20 and 30 items of data such as catalogue number, accession number, genus, species, country, state, county, number of specimens, stratigraphic position, and bibliographic references for published specimens.

Collection data are processed with SELGEM, an information management system designed and developed by the Smithsonian over the last twelve years (see Chapter 5). SELGEM is a batch-processing system consisting of over forty COBOL programs. Master files are usually stored on tape, but some are processed on disc. The programs perform a wide variety of tasks from routine updating of files to interfacing with other systems that plot distribution maps. A wide variety of standard or customized reports can be printed on microfilm or on any kind of paper with any kind of printer. A typical cataloguing project uses SELGEM to create and correct a master file and to print reports including proofreading reports, specimen labels, catalogue cards and catalogue-ledger pages (for binding later), master lists and taxonomic, geographic or other indexes for ready reference in a catalogue room. Labels for wet specimens are printed on Byron and Weston, Linen Ledger Resistol paper using Qume or Diablo daisy-wheel printers and standard nylon or mylar ribbons. Small labels with fifteen characters per inch horizontally and ten lines per inch vertically can be produced using Qume's 15-pitch print wheel (WP Gothic number 82090). Limited use has also been made of a Xerox-9700 computer printer to produce dry labels with type as small as 6 pt., for labelling small specimens and microscope slides.

SELGEM is run on a mainframe computer (Honeywell 6680) located in another building and managed by the Office of Information Resource Management (OIRM). OIRM is the Smithsonian's computer centre, providing analysis, programming and computing services to all Smithsonian museums, programs and administrative offices. Most fundamental systems development accomplished in the museum has been conducted jointly by the museum and OIRM (formerly Office of Computer Services).

All computer processing for NMNH collections passes through the central office of the ADP Programme, which has a staff of 10 people who specialize in the application of computer methods to collections. This staff provides most of the technical computer assistance needed by the departments, and assists in monitoring ADP/inventory operations. To initiate computer runs (e.g. to update a file), users submit handwritten instructions on a job-request form to the central office, where the computer runs are set up and transmitted via terminals for processing. All printout comes back to the central office, where it is logged out and placed in the appropriate users' mailboxes. Upwards of 400 requests for computer processing are received each month, resulting in over 10 000 computer runs per year. Over half of the routine runs (updates, master lists and standard reports) are completed within twenty-four hours, often the same day. More complex jobs take longer. Complete records (tape numbers, file statistics, processing histories and processing costs) are kept in the ADP Office, augmenting management records of departments.

It costs between one and three dollars on average to prepare and computerize specimen data in typical projects. This includes cost of equipment, supplies, computer time and personnel, and covers all work needed to put a correct record on the computer file and produce labels, index cards and other standard reports. If the data preparation team also reorganizes a collection, labels specimens, or carries out other curatorial chores, those costs are also included. Costs may be much higher or lower for some collections due to unusual conditions such as tightly packed specimens that require much handling when data are recorded, or the presence of an extremely accurate and well-organized card index that greatly speeds up the data-entry process. Every effort is made to match the work procedures to the characteristics of the collection to cut costs.

Inventory: a major reason for automating collection management

Automation of the museum's collections and collection management processes received a considerable boost in 1978, when the Smithsonian Institution implemented a policy requiring that comprehensive inventories of all collections be completed by June 1983. That policy grew primarily out of a concern for the security of the collections, which had never been completely inventoried, and were often not documented well enough to provide satisfactory security and collection control. The United States Congress provided additional funds, and as a result the museum's ADP effort more than doubled in a six-month period.

The inventory has consolidated and strengthened the collection information system: collections that were not yet using ADP were brought into the system; data entry terminals were installed in all key areas; more people were trained to conduct ADP activities; and considerable attention has been given to strengthening the collection documentation procedures, which must produce the inventory and keep it up-to-date. An especially important result is that the inventory has helped overcome the reluctance of many staff members to use ADP systems, because it has provided the staff and resources needed to complete collections quickly so that curators could obtain useful reports and indexes. Support for the effort has also been bolstered by the top management of the Smithsonian, which has continued to give the inventory top priority when making funding decisions.

The inventory policy requires each museum to document the contents of its entire collection in a manner appropriate to the kind of specimens held, and to verify the inventory records with existing catalogues and accession records. NMNH decided that it would not be possible or practical to document each of its 60 million items in the five years allotted to the inventory. Instead, the museum gave priority to compiling specific records for all specimens of high intrinsic value, all type specimens, specimens to be moved to the new Museum Support Center and certain other especially important specimens. Ten to fifteen items of data are recorded for each specimen or lot, such as name, catalogue number, location where the specimen was collected, and number of specimens. Inventory records generally contain fewer items of data than records produced during cataloguing.

The remaining specimens are being inventoried *en bloc*, by collection. This effort is referred to as the 'Inventory of Collections' (as against the inventory of specimens). A collection, for the purpose of this inventory, consists of a set of related specimens stored in one place. Typical examples are: Rotifer non-type slides; water beetle larvae; non-type specimens of fossil crinoids; unsorted locality suites of Mississippian fossils; Vaughn collection; and meteorites. A SELGEM record is created for each collection, containing information such as its name and description, where it is located in the museum, how many specimens or lots it contains and how much and what kind of storage space it occupies. All specimens in the museum are to be included in the Inventory of Collections, which will contain over 2000 records. Standard reports developed so far include a collection location index, an alphabetical list of collections with descriptions, a master list and a computer plotted chart showing the hierarchical organization of the collections together with a histogram of selected data, such as number of specimens.

Although it will not provide an accounting of individual specimens or lots, the Inventory of Collections will provide a systematic, uniform and comprehensive picture of what the museum contains, and it will provide a base line for planning and organizing further specimen-level inventories. With the addition of other data such as curatorial information and notes on documentation, the collection information data base can be a useful tool for collection management. For example, the collection information data base could provide storage volume for wet and dry collections, and could be used to plan new storage facilities. It could also be helpful in assessing where staff assignments need to be changed to provide better curatorial oversight of collections. One of its most important uses will come when the museum reports to higher administrative officials and to Congress. For the first time we will be able to describe the status of the collections and support requests for more collection management funds, using objective data, standardized across the museum and summarized to present a concise picture.

The specimen-level inventory is 85% complete: over 1.8 million inventory records have been compiled out of the 2.2 million required. The data bases also contain an additional 600 000 records for specimens that do not belong to the high priority inventory groups. Table 6.1 summarizes the status of the computer files for inventory and cataloguing.

Both the cataloguing files and inventory files are used regularly by scientists and collection management personnel. SELGEM provides several ways to query and report data from files and extensive use is also made of some non-SELGEM query/report programs, including one that allows online interaction with a file. The great majority of the questions asked of the data bases by scientists are answered by standard indexes and lists printed for each data base and readily accessible in the departments. Requests from outsiders are often answered simply by sending copies of the appropriate pages of some standard report. If the data base must be queried to answer a request, the data manager of the associated project formulates the question and submits the request to the ADP Office for processing. Answers are generally provided to outsiders at no cost, except when the cost is high. Cost estimates are provided in advance.

Future plans

Data processing has proven itself to be a useful and valuable addition to museum operations at NMNH. The quality of collection documentation has improved, and information can be retrieved much more rapidly and in a much wider and more useful variety of formats. The process of installing automated techniques has required revision of related collection

Department	Current coverage	Upcoming processing	Computer records
Anthropology	Archeology,Ethnology, Physical Anthropology, Natl. Anth. Archives (part)	Natl. Anth. Archives (part)	500,000
Botany	Types, Marine Algae, unprocesses plants, diatoms	Wood samples	150,000
Entomology	Types,ticks,certain carabid beetles, Malaphaga,Anopleura miscellaneous	Valuable specimens, MSC specimens	310,000
Invertebrate zoology	Types,valuable mollusks, pectens,Bureau of Land management samples from US coastal areas, miscellaneous	MSC specimens	230,000
Mineral sciences	Minerals,gems,rocks	Meteorites	220,000
Paleobiology	Types,Burgess Shale,fish, selected vertebrates, selected locality suites, sediments	Remaining valuable specimens and MSC specimens	330,000
Vertebrate zoology	Eggs and nests,endangered birds,MSC birds,sea birds, MSC fishes,all mammals except the majority of rodents,US reptiles and amphibians,MSC reptiles and amphibians,types, miscellaneous	N.American freshwater fishes,remaining reptiles and amphibians	745,000

Table 6.1 Summary of the state of computerization of collections records, December 1982 (Record counts refer to sizes of current databases and include inventory records and cataloging records. 'MSC' refers to specimens to be moved to the new Museum Support Center.)

management policies and procedures, which has resulted in better collection management programmes overall. The fact that the museum had a functional system in place made the inventory feasible: to inventory a collection of similar size without information processing aids and experience would be much more difficult.

Much more development and improvement are needed, however, to make the system more efficient, more complete and more useful. SELGEM is a highly reliable and capable system, but it does not provide the online processing many in the museum feel we should have in this day and age. An automated registration system should be developed to control loans and accessions, and we need better means of managing our large data bases. Planning for meeting these challenges is underway. A major step forward will be the design and development of the system for the new Museum Support Center, which is under construction a few miles away. A substantial portion of the MSC will be devoted to collection storage, under the best storage conditions that can be created, and an equally modern information system will be installed to control the MSC collections. Several other events are scheduled for the near future which will also support advancements in systems development.

The Smithsonian recently appointed an Information Resource Manager, Richard H. Lytle, to consolidate planning and management of information resources. This event is a significant indication of the importance given to information systems of all kinds by the highest echelons of the Institution, and sets the stage for major new developments in collection information systems.

Chapter 7

Documentation and control of collections at the Metropolitan Museum of Art

John Buchanan

Introduction

The Metropolitan Museum of Art was founded in 1870. It is a not-for-profit corporation operating under a charter issued by the State of New York. The Museum occupies a building owned by the City on land in Central Park. The Cloisters, a branch museum of European medieval art, is situated on the northwestern tip of Manhattan in a building owned by the Corporation. The private/public status of the Metropolitan Museum is not uncommon in the United States: a quasi-public institution, funded largely by private money and its own resources and to an extent by public funds from New York City, with privately-owned collections housed for the most part in a public building.

The museum's collections number about two and a half million objects, organized into 18 curatorial departments. The collections are encyclopaedic, representing most of the world's cultures. The collection continues to grow at a steady rate.

Office of the Registrar

The Office of the Registrar is in charge of receiving and documenting objects acquired by the Museum. Staff members involved in documentation of the collections include curators, administrators, art handlers, photographers, and secretaries, but Accession Numbers are assigned and Accession Cards completed by an Administrative Assistant in the Office of the Registrar. The background of people who have filled this job has varied, but the basic qualifications are secondary education, good typing and clerical skills, the type of mind that understands the necessity for and strives to maintain good organization and the constant maintenance of a system of documentation and control, and a passion for accuracy. If I were forced to choose one of these qualifications as the most important, I would opt for the latter.

The costs of documentation and control are very difficult to estimate.

Costs of equipment, paper, and cards are minimal. The major cost is staff time of various people in many departments. Our best estimate for 1982 is $5500 for equipment and materials, and $100 000 for staff time, with perhaps half of the latter sum attributable to curatorial costs.

Documentation procedures

Objects are acquired by gift, bequest, or purchase, as authorized by the Board of Trustees or one of its committees. The process is called accessioning, and an object for which an Accession Number has been assigned is an accessioned object or, simply, an accession. It is general Museum policy that no object is ever accessioned until authorization is given, in writing, by the proper executive authority and the object is actually in the Museum. The accessioning process can be divided into pre-accessioning and accessioning.

Pre-accessioning documentation is performed by the curatorial departments. It must be thorough enough that, should the object be acquired, the information provided will allow the Registrar to complete the accessioning process. This information is provided in either an *Offer of Gift or Bequest form* (Figure 7.1) or a *Recommended Purchase Blank* (Figure 7.2). The latter is supported by a detailed seven page curator's report. A copy of the relevant form is sent to the Registrar, alerting him to a potential accession. Once the appropriate executive authority has approved the acquisition of an object, the Secretary notifies the Registrar by forwarding the official authorization papers of the meeting of the Board of Trustees or one of its committees.

In the accessioning process the first step is the most important: the assignment of an Accession Number to an object. It is the only fixed point of reference in the system. As research goes on during the life of an object, details of the artist, title, date or provenance may change. The Accession Number, however, never changes. This rule may only be broken if it is necessary to correct an error, and such a change can only be authorized by the Registrar.

The importance of the Accession Number to the Museum's system of object documentation and control is such that it is appropriate to explain this numbering system in some detail (Table 7.1).

The Accession Number records the acquisition of an object in chronological order. The first two figures (four after 1969) indicate the year of acquisition. The second number, or group of numbers, after a decimal point indicates the transaction in its proper sequence during the year the object was accessioned. The third number, after a second decimal point, identifies the particular item in that transaction. Lower case letters, a, b, c, etc., following the number indicate the separable parts of an object. When only one object is acquired in a transaction, only the first two groups of numbers are used.

Since the Museum was founded in 1870, and the first accessions occurred in that year, after 1969 it was necessary to make a slight change in the system and use all four digits for the year of acquisition; thus, the first accession of 1970 was numbered 1970.1. With that exception, there have been no major changes to the system since it was established in 1906, and

THE METROPOLITAN MUSEUM OF ART

OFFER OF GIFT OR BEQUEST

(See reverse side for Report)

Department: _____

Donor: _____

Address: _____

_____

Offer received by: _____

Acknowledged: _____

Object received on consignment by Registrar: _____

Artist, dates, nationality or school, period:

Title or descriptive title:

Material:

Dimensions in inches and centimeters:

Recommended Loan Class: _____

Curator's Valuation for
Membership Credit: _____

Submitted by: _____

Curator of: _____

Date: _____

Recommendation of:

Accept: _____
or
Decline: _____   Date: _____

Director

Curator's recommendation received: _____

Acquisitions Committee _____
Action of: Board of Trustees _____
Executive Committee _____

Notification of action sent to donor: _____

Accession number: _____

Figure 7.1(a) Offer of Gift or Bequest form (front)

there is no reason to change it, for it has the two primary virtues of a numbering system: simplicity and capacity for expansion.

When the Accession Number is assigned, it is given to the curatorial department that is in charge of the object. The curatorial department then completes a *Location Card*, which is filed in that department by Accession Number. Thereafter, it is a rigid rule of the Museum that whenever the object is moved — to another gallery in the Museum, to a storeroom, out of the Museum on loan, back to the Museum from loan, to Conservation, to the Photo Studio — no matter for what length of time, the movement and the date of movement must be recorded on the Location Card. The accuracy of these cards is subject to spot checks by the Registrar. The format for this

OFFER OF GIFT OR BEQUEST—CURATOR'S REPORT

I.   Full description of the object, including the description of all parts. Transcribe any inscriptions, describe marks and mention any added attachments or missing parts, etc.

II. Describe the condition of the object, indicating any repairs and attempting a prognosis for future condition.

III. List all published references.

IV. State the importance of the object in relation to the existing collections.

V.   Give a resume of your reasons for recommending the object for acceptance, being candid as to its strengths and weaknesses, its rarity of quality, technique, type, etc.

VI. Other comments.

Figure 7.1(b) Offer of Gift or Bequest form (reverse)

card is left up to the curatorial departments, but for each department minimum information must include the Accession Number and either typed or handwritten notations concerning each movement.

After an Accession Number has been assigned, the number is painted on the object in oil paint with a sable hair brush by a member of the Registrar's staff. This person must be an experienced art handler and possess patience as well as the manual dexterity necessary to paint numbers legibly on surfaces ranging from monumental sculpture to the edge of a thin coin. Numbers are placed in inconspicuous locations that are at the same time reasonably accessible when undertaking inventories. In addition to oil paints, other methods are also used to affix Accession Numbers, depending on the nature

THE METROPOLITAN MUSEUM OF ART

RECOMMENDED PURCHASE BLANK

TO THE DIRECTOR AND THE ACQUISITIONS COMMITTEE:

I recommend the purchase of the object(s) fully described in the attached report and briefly captioned
below.

Classification _____

Artist, title, date:

Vendor: Recommended loan class:

Price:

Additional expenses: Transportation $ _____   Insurance $ _____
                        Sender to pay   Sender to pay
                        M.M.A. to pay   M.M.A. to pay
                        Installation $ _____   Restoration $ _____
                        Photography $ _____   Other $ _____

Recommendation approved: Submitted by:

_____
Director   _____
                                                Curator of _____

                                                Date _____

FOR USE OF SECRETARY'S OFFICE ONLY

ACTION BY ACQUISITIONS COMMITTEE
                                                To be charged against the
Purchase (authorized)   _____
         (not authorized)

Reported to Board _____   _____
                                                Gift and/or Fund
         Executive Committee _____
                                                Authorized at $ _____
         Acquisitions Committee _____
                                                Secured for $ _____
Accession number _____
                                                Purchase authorization no. _____

3/82

Figure 7.2 Recommended Purchase Blank form

of the material: for example, cloth labels for textiles and metal tags for arms
and armour.

One master copy and two flimsy copies of a 3×5 inch *Accession Card* are
now made out (Figures 7.3). Two designs are used: for either gift or bequest,
with space for the donor's name; or purchase with space for the vendor's
name. The Accession Card itself is forwarded to the Photo Studio, and the
curatorial department concerned sends to the Photo Studio an order for
record photography. One flimsy copy is filed permanently in the
Donor-Vendor file, alphabetically by name. The second flimsy copy is filed
in the Accession Card File by Accession Number. This is a temporary card

```
(1) 61.7.11ab is the Accession Number for a silver dish with cover and
signifies:

    61 - the year of acquisition was 1961;
    7 - the 7th transaction of that year;
    11 - the 11th object in that transaction;
    a - the dish (the major part of the object);
    b - the cover (the separable part of the object).

(2) 61.8 - the next transaction in 1961 concerned only one object, an ivory
diptych.

(3) Separate Accession Numbers are assigned to objects which are complete
entities in themselves, even though they are described as pairs. For
example:

    14.63.1,2 - shoes (pair);
    50.211.19,20 - cup and saucer;
    50.211.32,33 - vases (pair).
```

Table 7.1 The form of the accession number

to indicate that the permanent Accession Card is in the Photo Studio and to identify the object bearing that number.

The Accession Card is eventually returned to the Registrar from the Photo Studio, with the negative numbers and negative sizes appropriately entered. The flimsy copy is pulled from the Accession Card File and replaced with the permanent Accession Card. The flimsy copy is destroyed. Sometime after the Accession Card has been returned, the Photo Studio will send to the Central Catalogue four copies of the *Photograph Record Card* (Figure 7.4), a 3×5 inch card containing the record photograph in reduced size, the Accession Number, the negative number(s), and the size(s) of print available. (On occasion, when there are overlapping curatorial interests, more than four copies will be sent.) One Photograph Record Card is given to the Registrar to be filed behind the Accession Card; the second copy remains in Central Catalogue; the third copy is sent to the curatorial department concerned; and the fourth copy is sent to the Photo Sales Department.

That final step, the distribution of the Photograph Record Cards, completes the basic system for documenting and controlling the Museum's collections. As noted above, the Museum also maintains for reference and research a *Central Catalogue*, which is a scholarly compilation of data on its collections. The Central Catalogue is a subject file organized in general by civilization, followed by material, followed by country or century, with further breakdowns as necessary. The Central Catalogue data on an object will contain most of the information found on the Accession Card (except prices paid and names of anonymous donors), together with information of scholarly interest (such as detailed description, provenance, bibliography, ex-collections, etc.). Information in the Central Catalogue is noted on blank 3×5 inch cards. (Figure 7.5 illustrates the first of a series of cards for object 65.182.2.) This file is open to qualified researchers. It is not part of a national system.

The Accession Card File is the official record of the Museum's holdings and, in conjunction with the Location Record File maintained by the curatorial departments, is the core of the Museum's system of documenting

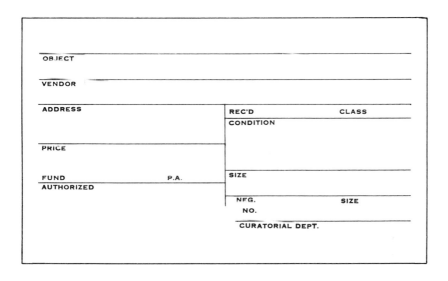

Figure 7.3 Accession cards for donor and vendor

and controlling its collections. The Accession Card File is open only to the Museum's staff, since it contains confidential information such as prices paid and the names of anonymous donors. It is used constantly by the staff to check the accuracy of other records, to service requests for information from the public, and to check credit lines. It also is not part of a national system.

62

```
1979.19(.2.
21&02
(3x4) (8x10)
```

Figure 7.4 Photograph record card

```
65.182.2                              Class I
    CHIMNEY PIECE OF THE ELIZABETHAN ROOM FROM GREAT
YARMOUTH, NORFOLK: carved stone; arched opening; (see
attached card)

Carved stone               H. 63-1/2, W. 97 in.
Purchase, 1965       Parke-Bernet Galleries
    Edward Pearce Casey Fund
Ex coll.: (see attached card)

Prov.: Star Hotel, Great Yarmouth, Norfolk
Sculpture-Architectural    XVI century    English
                           (ca. 1600)
```

Figure 7.5 Central Catalogue entry

Loans and special exhibitions

The Registrar also maintains official records on outgoing loans (by the Museum), incoming loans (to the Museum) and special exhibitions. Loan requests are processed by the Loans Office, working closely with the curatorial departments and the Registrar. The latter only takes action to record, pack, insure and ship an outgoing loan when the Loans Office informs him, in writing, that the appropriate executive authority has approved the loan. The outgoing loan records are kept in vertical files and are classified permanent.

The Registrar either receives or collects incoming loans upon receipt of written notices from the curatorial departments (Figure 7.6). There are two key permanent records: a 3×5 inch card, filed by loan number, with format similar to the Accession Card, which is stamped 'Returned' with the date when the loan is sent back to the owner; and the final receipt signed by the lender. The Registrar also maintains an alphabetical file of lenders.

THE METROPOLITAN MUSEUM OF ART

TO THE REGISTRAR — DATE

Expect □ / Collect □ — From: Name — DELIVERY DATE:
Deliver To □ — Complete Address — COLLECTION DATE:

The following objects
Valuation $

For	Gift □	Loan □	Purchase □	Examination □	Special Exhibition □	
Via	Express □ Parcel Post □	Messenger	(Theirs □ (Ours □	Truck □ Station Wagon □	(Theirs □ (Ours □	Foreign Shipment □
Charges	Collect □	Prepaid □				

Insurance and Transportation

Transit insurance to be placed } by M.M.A. □ Sender □ — Premium to be paid } by M.M.A. □ Sender □

If purchased, transportation and insurance to be deducted from Purchase Price □
If returned, M.M.A. to insure and pay □ Ship collect □ or Ship prepaid □
" " " and bill □

Department ______________ Signed ______________

Figure 7.6 Notice of incoming loan

This department organizes insurance, packing, logistics, and security in transit for special exhibitions, on which three people spend at least half of their time.

Future developments

In 1972, the Museum ended a four year pilot programme on computerization of the Registrar's records, with primary emphasis on the accession records. During that time, the GRIPHOS system was used. The decision not to proceed was made because of lack of money, and it was the feeling of the present writer as well as officers of the Museum that, given the severe shortage of funds, computerization would have to wait for better times. Computerization of accession and other records will come, as it should. In the meantime, we will continue to use the procedure which has been most effective for over three-quarters of a century.

Conclusion

Museums do many things, and it is in their public role of exhibiting permanent collections, putting on special exhibitions, and providing education programmes that they gain public attention and either accolades or brickbats. Behind the scenes, however, the vital function of documenting and controlling the collections is more important to the long-term health of a museum than yesterday's lecture or tomorrow's special exhibition.

Chapter 8

The Museum of Modern Art

Eloise Ricciardelli

Introduction

The Museum of Modern Art, founded in 1929, was granted a charter by the Regents of the University of the State of New York for 'establishing and maintaining in the city of New York, a museum of modern art, encouraging and developing the study of modern arts and the application of such arts to manufacture and practical life, and furnishing popular instruction' (Hellman, 1964). It became the first museum devoted to modern art in the United States.

In 1929, the Museum acquired just nine works, all prints and drawings; in 1930 18 works, consisting of paintings, sculpture, watercolours, and photographs. From this beginning the collection has grown to approximately 100 000 works.

The Museum of Modern Art is unique in being the only multi-departmental museum in the modern field, representing the arts of industrial and graphic design, architecture, photography and film as well as printmaking, drawing, painting and sculpture. The Department of Painting and Sculpture now has a collection of 3400 works. The Department of Architecture and Design, established in 1932, has a collection of 3000 architectural drawings, design objects, architectural models, and another 2500 pieces of graphic design (including posters), plus 30 000 architectural drawings in the Mies van der Rohe Archive. In 1935 the Museum continued to expand with the Film Library, later changed to the Department of Film, whose collection of approximately 8000 motion pictures dates back to 1894 and covers fiction, documentary animation, and the avant-garde, plus archival material of posters, film scores, and over three million film stills. The Museum had presented numerous photography exhibitions in the 1930s before the Department of Photography was established in 1940. Today there are over 20 000 photographic prints plus a collection of rare books, letters, and other archival material. A print room opened in 1949 with a collection of 3000 prints dating from about 1880, and expanded in 1966 to include the museum's collection of drawings. Today the Department of Prints and

Illustrated Books has a collection of approximately 40 000 works. The Department of Drawings, which became a separate department in 1971 now has a collection of more than 5000 drawings.

The Museum painting, sculpture, drawing, print and architectural works have shown a continued growth of approximately 790 new acquisitions a year over the past ten years while films have added 150 new prints each year.

Department of Registration

The Museum's first registrar came to the museum as assistant secretary in 1929, and served as registrar from 1932 to 1936. Dorothy H. Dudley then joined the staff and held that position until her retirement in 1969. We are indebted to Dorothy H. Dudley and Irma Bezold Wilkinson, former registrar at The Metropolitan Museum of Art, New York, for their very useful and informative publication, *Museum Registration Methods*, which has helped establish museum standards for the handling and record keeping of material (Dudley and Wilkinson, 1979).

The Department of Registration works with all six curatorial departments: Painting and Sculpture, Drawings, Prints and Illustrated Books, Architecture and Design, Photography, and on a limited basis, Film. The responsibility of the registrar varies in accordance with the structure and needs of each department. Overall, the registrar's responsibility lies in the transportation, packing, and handling of all objects brought into the museum for all exhibitions, works lent to other institutions, pending acquisitions, and the recording and documenting of acquisitions and exhibition loans.

An average of 500 loans from the museum collections are made yearly to other institutions. During the year the registrar also processes over 2000 works of art for approximately 20 exhibitions directed and prepared by curators for installation in the Museum. In some cases these exhibitions travel abroad under the jurisdiction of the International Program and within the country under the auspices of the National Program of Circulating Exhibitions.

The Department has a staff of 15 people: a traffic coordinator, six art handlers, a secretary, and various collection, loans, and exhibitions assistants. The assistants are responsible for outgoing loans from all curatorial departments subsequent to curatorial written approval, for bringing works into the Museum for acquisitions meetings, and for coordinating all loans to Museum exhibitions, whether in the Museum galleries or for travel in the United States or abroad. The secretary and assistants are all college graduates, and some also have graduate degrees. Knowledge of another language is helpful, and most of the staff are fluent in one or more languages. Prior to joining the Department all the assistants worked in other major museums in positions with varied duties, such as classifying and numbering acquisitions, handling exhibitions, assisting in laboratories, curatorial research, and administration. The traffic coordinator is responsible for all works received for exhibitions and all painting and sculpture storage.

Daily reports are issued showing the movement of all works for the collection and for exhibitions as they are received, released, and moved within the building. Location cards are used for collection work storage.

Documentation procedures

When a work comes into the Museum a number of forms are used to record its entry. If a work is brought in for viewing by a curatorial department and is to be collected within the week, a departmental receipt, which does not have a museum number, is issued. The registrar receives a copy at the time of entry, and when the work has been collected the signed notice of disposition is sent to the registrar for filing. Works entering for a variety of reasons, such as curatorial consideration or restoration, need a receipt to document their deposit, and for this the Museum uses a *temporary receipt form* (TR) with a sequential identifying number (Figure 8.1). As with all forms, one copy is retained by the registrar and additional copies are sent to others as required.

For new acquisitions in any of the curatorial departments, except film, the

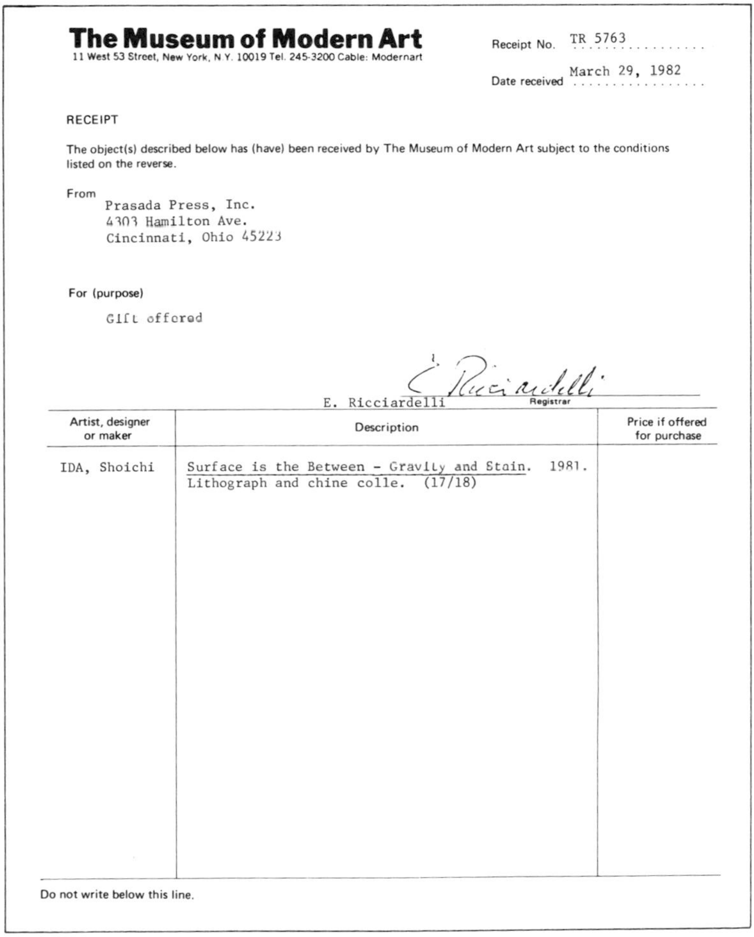

The Museum of Modern Art
11 West 53 Street, New York, N.Y. 10019 Tel. 245-3200 Cable: Modernart

Receipt No. TR 5763

Date received March 29, 1982

RECEIPT

The object(s) described below has (have) been received by The Museum of Modern Art subject to the conditions listed on the reverse.

From
Prasada Press, Inc.
4303 Hamilton Ave.
Cincinnati, Ohio 45223

For (purpose)
Gift offered

E. Ricciardelli
Registrar

Artist, designer or maker	Description	Price if offered for purchase
IDA, Shoichi	Surface is the Between - Gravity and Stain. 1981. Lithograph and chine colle. (17/18)	

Do not write below this line.

Figure 8.1(a) Temporary Receipt (TR) form (front)

registrar is responsible for assigning the accession numbers after committee approval. This number is composed of two parts, the year in which the work is accepted into the collection and a sequential number within that year.

Newly acquired paintings, sculptures, and drawings are catalogued by a registration assistant, whose *collection worksheet* is then sent to a curator for approval before the data are entered into the computer (Figure 8.2). The departments of Prints and Illustrated Books, Architecture and Design, and Photography catalogue their own acquisitions but send the completed worksheets to the registrar for entry into the computer.

For each entry, for which there may be as many as 38 categories, the following 10 categories are used consistently: artist, artist's nationality, title, date, medium, measurements, credit, photography sources, classification by administrative department, and accession number. Since 1969 the Museum has maintained its art catalogue in machine readable form in addition to

Conditions Governing the Receipt of Objects Deposited with the Museum of Modern Art Under This Receipt

This receipt supersedes any temporary receipt issued by curators or other staff members who received the objects listed overleaf.

1. The Museum of Modern Art (hereinafter referred to as the 'Museum'), shall not be responsible for the protection and safekeeping of objects belonging to others beyond the exercise of such precautions as are taken for the protection and safekeeping of comparable property of its own. The absence of condition notes on this receipt does not imply that the material listed was received in good condition.

2. Unless special arrangements are agreed to in writing, the Museum will not carry insurance on objects deposited with it. In no case shall any object be insured for more than market value.

3. Attributions, dates and other information shown on the face of this receipt are as given by the depositor. Any valuations or prices shown are those stated by the depositor and not to be construed as appraisals by the Museum.

4. Unless the Museum is notified in writing to the contrary, objects listed on the face of this receipt may be photographed and reproduced for its private purposes.

5. Property covered by this receipt may be removed from the Museum by the depositor or his duly authorized agent after reasonable notice upon surrender of this receipt or the delivery of the depositor's written order.

6. The Museum may request removal of property deposited with it by written notice directed to the depositor at the address shown on the face of this receipt. Failure of the depositor to remove property within 30 days after the mailing of such notice will permit the Museum to return such property to the depositor by express collect or to deliver it to any warehouse company to be stored for the depositor's account.

7. Unless special arrangements are agreed to in writing, the Museum will not provide transportation for objects deposited with it.

Special Conditions Governing Objects Offered For Sale Or Gift

A. If the property covered by this receipt has been offered to the Museum for sale or as a gift, the vendor or donor will be notified in writing of the approval or acceptance thereof and this receipt shall thereupon become null and void as respects the whole or part to be acquired by the Museum. If such property is declined by the Museum, the vendor or donor agrees to take delivery of the whole or part declined within 30 days after written notification has been mailed to him at the address appearing on the face of this receipt. (See Paragraphs 5, 6 and 7 above for conditions regarding removal).

B. Copyrights. In the event that any property offered for sale or as a gift is the subject of copyright, the depositor agrees if he has knowledge of such copyright to inform the Museum thereof and to furnish the Museum with an assignment of all rights thereunder in such form as the Museum may reasonably request.

C. Warranties. In the event that any property listed on the face of this receipt is offered for sale, the depositor agrees to furnish the Museum with a warranty of title in such form as the Museum may reasonably request prior to payment by the Museum of any part of the purchase price. Should the depositor fail to furnish such warranty, the Museum may cancel its acceptance of the depositor's offer.

D. In the event that any property listed on the face of this receipt is offered as a gift, it is understood that unless the Museum has been notified in writing to the contrary, the gift is outright and unconditional.

Figure 8.1(b) Temporary Receipt (TR) form (reverse)

Master Card PAINTING & SCULPTURE COLLECTION WORKSHEET

66. Museum no: 940.65 a-c

70. Artist: MIRÓ, Joan

106. TR no:

Leica no: 3833c; 6064d

61. Neg. nos: Sunami 1674;

30. Title: OBJECT

Mathews 4680; Mathews 4681

10. Study coll:

Sale or exch:

Date accepted: 12-7-65

9. Price paid:

Date confirmed if accepted by letter:

Ins. Val:

3. Source & method of purchase:

P.O. no:

36. Category: Sculpture

Fractions or restrictions of gift:

76. Nationality: Spain

Dates: Born 1893

83. Date of work: (1936)

47. Medium: Assemblage: stuffed parrot on wood perch, stuffed silk stocking with velvet

garter and doll's paper shoe suspended in a hollow wood frame, derby hat, SEE OVER

Size: 31 7/8 h. x 11 7/8 w. x 10 1/4" d. (81.0 x 30.1 x 26.0 cm.) (overall)

51. a) 31 7/8 h. x 9 1/8 w. x 5 3/4" d. (81.0 x 22.9 x 14.6 cm.)

b) 4 5/8 h. x 11 7/8 l. x 10 1/4" d. (11.6 x 30.1 x 26.0 cm.)

Weight of sculpture: 6 lbs.

55. Primary inscriptions (Sig. & date): Signed bottom of parrot's stand in black ink "miró".

Not dated.

5. Credit: Gift of Mr. and Mrs. Pierre Matisse.

112. Anonymous donor:

114. Anonymous vendor:

33. Alternate titles: Objet poétique. Poetic Object.

99. Related works:

35. Remarks about the object: a. Post and attached elements. b. Hat and fish. c. Parrot

Received without map which forms part of composition (original disintegrated). SEE OVER

Cross references:

91. Ex-Collections: Mrs. Kenneth F. Simpson, New York; Mr & Mrs. Pierre Matisse, New York;

Pierre Matisse Gallery, New York.

Figure 8.2(a) Painting and sculpture collection worksheet (front)

traditional card-file form, the cards being generated by the computer (Figure 8.3). Cards are used in two files in the registrar's office (artist and accession files) and others are used within the curatorial departments, filed either by artist, subject, date, or accession number.

The Department of Film handles its own computerized catalogue system. Their main catalogue file is by original title of the film at the first public showing. A name file is also maintained and covers the individuals that participate in the production of the film: director, producer and other key personnel such as actors, screenplay writer and cinematographer. As films have many individuals participating, not one artist, they can use up to a possible 100 categories with an average of 30 entries per document.

```
Card Two          PTG. & SC. WORKSHEET — Page 2      66. Museum no:      940.65 a-c

Mounting unit (on acq.):

Mounting unit (permanent):

Former MoMA nos:   36.2041 a-e; 59.167; 61.3400.
57. Secondary inscriptions:

        No inscriptions.

        Medium continued:  hanging cork ball, cellulois fish, and engraved map.

        Remarks about object continued: Celluloid fish is not the one shown in
        Sunami photograph 1674.  Cord which connects stocking with log is not the
        one shown in Sunami photograph 1674.


        History:
        Exh. 55-#444* (Exh'd as Object).(36.2041 a-e).
        Exh. 641-#64 (Exh'd as Objet poétique). (59.167).
        Exh. 695-#153*p.63 (Exh'd as Objet poétique). (61.3400).


        Remarks and References:
        James Thrall Soby, Joan Miro, New York, the MOMA, 1959, *p.77.
```

```
Condition Card        Date of condition photo: 12-13-65        Date examined:  12-27-65

Condition on acquisition:  a.Parrot: generally dusty; break at back of neck; head forced
downward; slight loss in feathers around L eye; Perch: slight checking; several cracks
in bark; several scratches & chips on base around screw; several ships at edges of
base; Post: white foreign matter & several curved scrapes on top; heavy checking on side
opposite parrot; scattered light checking; several small checks & holes filled with
white substance; 2 dark horiz. rubs near bottom; Stocking: several small runs near top;
Shoe: not secured to foot; surface worn & ravelling,esp. at toe; interior torn; heel
loose. b. Hat: crack at back of crown; silk trim worn & coming off esp. at edge of
brim; sweatband cracked & crumbling; Fish: 2 cracks at bottom.
```

```
Cataloged by:  EBR                                  Date sent to curator: 12-28-65

Approved by:                                        Date approved:
```

Figure 8.2(b) Painting and sculpture worksheet (reverse)

The GRIPHOS system used by the Registrar and Film Department for cataloguing the collections is totally unrestricted in size and any record can be described in words and numbers without limit (see Chapter 5). This gives tremendous flexibility in updating records.

The Museum has been using an IBM System 3-Model 12 and is in the process of converting to an IBM System 38. The need for interactive online data processing, primarily by the Membership Department, was a factor in the selection of the System 38. The existing temporary configuration will support 12 terminals and can be upgraded to support up to 80 terminals. Of

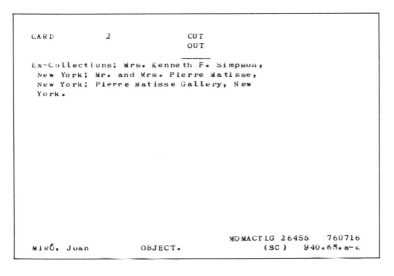

```
MIRÓ, Joan          Sculpture - Spain          940.65.a-c

OBJECT. (1936).
Assemblage: stuffed parrot on wood perch,
  stuffed silk stocking with velvet garter
  and doll's paper shoe suspended in a
  hollow wood frame, derby hat, hanging
  cork ball, celluloid fish and engraved
  map.
31 7/8 x 11 7/8 x 10 1/4" d. (81.0 x 30.1
  x 26.0 cm.) (overall)                 Leica 3833c.
a) 31 7/8 h. x 9 1/8 w. x 5 3/4" d.      Leica 6064d.
  (81.0 x 22.9 x 14.6 cm.).              Sunami 1674.
b) 4 5/8 h. x 11 7/8 l. x 10 1/4" d.     Mathews 4680
  (11.6 x 30.1 x 26.0 cm.).              Mathews 4681.
Wt. 6 lbs.
Gift of Mr. and Mrs. Pierre Matisse.
Accepted 12-7-65.
Signed bottom of parrot's stand in black ink "miró".
Not dated.
a. Post and attached elements. b. Hat and fish.
                             MOMACTLG 26456    760716
MIRÓ, Joan          OBJECT.          (SC)   940.65.a-c
```

```
CARD          2          CUT
                         OUT
                         ____

Ex-Collections; Mrs. Kenneth F. Simpson,
  New York; Mr. and Mrs. Pierre Matisse,
  New York; Pierre Matisse Gallery, New
  York.




                             MOMACTLG 26455    760716
MIRÓ, Joan          OBJECT.          (SC)   940.65.a-c
```

Figure 8.3 Computer-generated catalogue record (2 cards)

the three installed terminals, one is for the use of the registrar and film departments.

A *history card* for collection works is maintained showing each time a work is exhibited in the Museum galleries, either as part of the permanent collection on view or a special exhibition, and in other institutions (Figure 8.4). If a catalogue is published in conjunction with an exhibition in which a Museum work appears these data are also added to the entry.

Registration for exhibitions is basically the same as that of cataloguing new acquisitions. *Loan receipts* are issued when works are received, showing

```
History
Exh. 55-#444* (Exhibited as Object). (36.2041).
Exh. 641-#64 (Exhibited as Objet poétique). (59.167).
Exh. 695-#153*p.63 (Exhibited as Objet poétique). (61.3400).
Exh. 855, "Dada, Surrealism, and Their Heritage"-#243*
     Los Angeles County Museum of Art, July 15 - September 8, 1968.
     Art Institute of Chicago, October 19 - December 8, 1968.
Exh. 974.
Exh. 1002, III. Removed September 27, 1973.
Exh. 1044-*p.71 (color).
Exh. 1002, III, January 29 - April 30, 1974.
Galeries Nationales du Grand Palais, Paris, exh. "Joan Miro",May 18-
     October 13, 1974.
Exh. 1002, III, 3 (vitrine), January 8, 1975 - March 17, 1980.
Exh. 1293, III-3, (vitrine), October 23, 1980 - January 3, 1982.
Exh. 1330, mezz. gal.(vitrine), March 8, 1982 -




MIRO, Joan                    Object                    940.65.a-c
```

Figure 8.4 Exhibition history record

the arrival date, the purpose for which the loan was brought into the Museum, the loan number issued by the registrar, description, and insurance value (Figure 8.5). At the end of a loan period, a receipt of delivery (a part of the loan record form) is sent to lenders to sign and return on receipt of their work. To distinguish accession and loan numbers, the year preceeds the sequential digit in loans and follows in acquisitions.

The *loan record sheet* used to catalogue exhibition works is more complex than the collection worksheet, as additional information is needed such as the carrier used for shipping, description of case used for packing, case size, wrapping material, special return instructions and frame record (Figure 8.6). A registration assistant has to be well informed about packing techniques for evaluating cases as they are received and in preparing the packing of exhibitions that are consolidated at the Museum for travel in the United States and abroad.

A condition photograph is often made on arrival of a particularly fragile or high-value work. After the work is recorded for inscriptions, signature, date, medium and size a condition report is made. If there are any doubts regarding the condition or medium of the loan a Museum restorer is consulted. The Museum has three restoration departments (Painting, Sculpture, and Paper) and the staff is always available for consultation.

Additional information added to the loan record sheet is the title, photograph number, lender number, former Museum loan number if the work had been borrowed previously, and the current loan number. A copy of these forms is given to the director of the exhibition, and the original is filed with the loan agreements in the registrar archival file. From the information on these sheets loan and lenders cards are made. If the work had been previously borrowed the current exhibition and loan number are added to the

LOAN RECEIPT
The Museum of Modern Art, 11 West 53 Street, New York, N.Y. 10019 (212) 956-6100
Cable: MODERNART NEW YORK Telex: Western Union International 62370

Date received .. August 11, 1976 ....

The object(s) described below has (have) been received by The Museum of Modern Art as loan(s) under the conditions
noted on the back of this receipt.
from

    Cooper Hewitt Museum of Design
    9 East 90th Street
    New York, New York 10028
for

    The Natural Paradise: Painting in America 1800-1950
    exhibition.

                               E. Ricciardelli
                     Registrar   E. Ricciardelli

Museum Number	Description	Insurance Value
76.621	Frederic Edwin Church, ICEBERG (1859), Pencil, oil on cardboard	

Figure 8.5(a) Loan Receipt form (front)

original card. In some cases the work may have changed ownership since its previous loan to the Museum and the current owner's name is added to the original loan card, a system that records the provenance of these works.

Conclusions

There are a number of ways in which our documentation of works of art is a major source of information both within and without the Museum. The documents in the department archives are available to Museum staff,

CONDITIONS GOVERNING LOANS

1. The Museum of Modern Art will exercise the same care with respect to loans as it does in the safekeeping of comparable property of its own.

2. Loans shall remain in the possession of The Museum of Modern Art and/or other museums participating in the exhibition in question for the time specified on the face of this receipt, but may be withdrawn from exhibition at any time by the director or trustees of any such museum.

Unless the Museum is notified in writing to the contrary, loans will be returned only to the owner at the address stated on the face of this receipt. If the legal ownership of the work should change during the period of this loan, whether by reason of death, sale, insolvency, gift or otherwise, the owner will, prior to its return, be required to establish his legal right to receive the work by proof satisfactory to the Museum. If the address of the new owner should be of much greater distance than the locality from which the loan was borrowed, the new owner will be required to pay any difference in the charges for the delivery of the work.

3. Unless the lender expressly elects to maintain his own insurance coverage, The Museum of Modern Art will insure this loan wall-to-wall under its fine-arts policy for the amount indicated on the face of this loan agreement against all risks of physical loss or damage from any external cause while in transit and on location during the period of the loan. The policy referred to contains the usual exclusions of loss or damage due to such causes as wear and tear, gradual deterioration, moths, vermin, inherent vice, war, hostilities, insurrection, nuclear reaction or radiation, and for damage resulting from any authorized repairing, restoration or retouching process.

If a work which has been industrially fabricated is damaged, and it can be repaired or replaced to the artist's specifications, the Museum's liability shall be limited to the cost of such replacement.

The lender agrees to U.S. Government Indemnity, if applicable to this loan, at U.S. dollar value as of the date of this loan agreement.

If the lender elects to maintain his own insurance, the Museum must be supplied with a certificate of insurance naming The Museum of Modern Art and each of the participating museums as an additional assured or waiving subrogation against the Museum and each of the participating museums. Otherwise, the loan agreement shall constitute a release of the Museum and each of the participating museums from any liability in connection with loaned property. The Museum can accept no responsibility for any error or deficiency in information furnished to the lender's insurers or for lapses in coverage.

4. If the loan listed on the face of this receipt is for sale, it is understood that the selling price shall include a Museum handling charge as follows:

On sales up to $10,000.	10%
On the next $15,000.	7½%
On everything over $25,000.	5%

The Museum waives its standard handling charge on sales of the work of living artists when the artist himself or his gallery is the seller.

MF 715a

Figure 8.5(b) Loan Receipt form (reverse)

research staff of other museums and private collections, art historians, gallery personnel, auction houses, and graduate students. These include exhibition correspondence and records, collection worksheet files to which are attached curatorial memoranda documenting new information, outgoing loan files, collection, loan and lender card file and printouts.

The Department also touches many areas of the Museum with the computer-produced printout of its holdings: a printout of just donors and their gifts to the Museum is used by the Department of Membership and Development in the promotion of fund raising; the Library finds a printout of

```
THE MUSEUM OF MODERN ART—LOAN RECORD SHEET        LENDER  New York              MUS. NO. 76,621
        THE NATURAL PARADISE: PAINTING IN                (Cooper-Hewitt)
EXHIBITION    AMERICA 1800-1950                                                OLD NO. _____

ARTIST  Frederic Edwin Church                    EXH. No.  1148        LENDER NO. _____

TITLE  Iceberg                                   CAT. NO. _____   PHOTO NO. Lender

MEDIUM  Pencil and oil on cardboard
                                     SIGNATURE
DATE  Not dated (1854)               AND DATE  Not signed - if signed verso, Not visible due
INSCRIPTIONS                                          to mat and backing


SIZE
                                              Sight                        Sight
     Painting, drawing or print: Height  11 3/8" (22.7 cm)       Width: 19" (47.8 cm)

     _____ Height: _____        Width: _____

     Sculpture: _____

     _____  Weight: _____


SHIPPING:
     Received: 7/11/76 via  Hahn _____

     Box size:    Height  24"    Width  30"     Depth  8"     Weight _____
     Flat pack   Wood, plywood top and bottom        Waterproof paper      Box may ride flat
     Slide box   Plywood        Screws              Packed face up         Directional markings _____
     Tray box    Wood           Nails              Packed face down        Special marking _____
     Internal braces _____ Wrapping glassine  Padding etha/foam      Filling _____

     Special return instructions _____

     Returned: 12/8/76 via  Hahn

FRAME RECORD:

     Height  17 3/4"         Width  23 3/4"          Depth  1 8"

     Description & Condition: _____

     _____  _____  _____

     Reframing record: _____
     Frame       Inner Fr.       Passepartout    Mat        Mount       Plexiglas    Glass
     Stretcher   Strainer        Crossbars ____  Keys _____ Hangers     Screweyes    Wire
     Backing     Plates _____  Label           Other: ____
     corrugated cardboard

REGISTRATION:
     Loan Form      Loan Rec.        Custodian Bk.      Lender Cd.   Insur.      Insur. Cancelled
     Release 8257   Rec. of Del.     Conservation       Lender Cd. Completed     Rec. Bk.
     Old Obj. Cd.   Obj. Cd.         Obj. Cd. Completed Cond. Photo

REMARKS _____  CAT. BY  TH      DATE: 8/11/76
```

Figure 8.6 Loan Record sheet

the entire collection indexed alphabetically by artist, architect, designer, and photographer useful for scholars using its facility; the Department of Public Information is able to answer many queries from journalists with its copy; Rights and Reproductions finds its list useful, especially as all photographer numbers from both museum and outside sources are listed (Figure 8.7). Printouts are also used by the curatorial departments for listing their own holdings, and the International Program has been able to request printouts by artist's nationality in the planning of future exhibitions.

There is tremendous satisfaction working with original works of art and, by doing the documentation, developing a greater awareness of both the art and artist. The updating of new information constantly increases one's

```
THE MUSEUM OF MODERN ART                                    PAGE 840

   Museum.  Leica 3042a. Sunami 16,253.  Drawing  721.59
MIRO, Joan                                                  MOMACTLG 16335
   LEIRIS: BAGATELLES VEGETALES.  (1956).  Illustrated      NUMBER 15,340
   with six color woodcuts,  Gift of Mr. and Mrs. Armand P.
   Bartos.  Illus. Book  50.58.1-6
MIRO, Joan                                                  MOMACTL2  8873
   LE LEZARD AUX PLUMES D'OR.  (1971).  Fifteen lithographs NUMBER 15,341
   with title page and colophon,  Gift of James Thrall Soby
   (by exchange).  Illus. Book  16.72.1-15
MIRO, Joan                                                  MOMACTL2 15784
   MAGDALENIANS.  (1958).  Etching, printed in black,       NUMBER 15,342
   moderate blue, vivid yellow, deep red orange, strong
   purple red and deep blue green.  Plate 4 1/2 x 5 1/2"
   (11.5 x 14.0 cm.).  Sheet 10 7/8 x 13 5/8" (27.7 x 34.7
   cm.).  Bequest of Eve Clendenin.  Print  15.75
MIRO, Joan                                                  MOMACTLG 23632
   MAKEMONO.  (1950).  Lithograph,  Gift of Mr. and Mrs.    NUMBER 15,343
   Maxime L. Bermanos (the donors retaining a life interest).
    Print  644.64
MIRO, Joan                                                  MOMACTLG 26720
   MIRO: CARTONS.  (1965).  Poster,  Don Page Fund.  Leica  NUMBER 15,344
   3926d.  Poster  329.66
MIRO, Joan                                                  MOMACTLG 26721
   MIRO: OEUVRES GRAPHIQUES.  (1965).  Poster,  Don Page    NUMBER 15,345
   Fund.  Leica 3926e.  Poster  330.66
MIRO, Joan                                                  MOMACTLG  1704
   MONGOOSE.  (1938).  Wool,  62 x 80".  Abby Aldrich       NUMBER 15,346
   Rockefeller Fund.  Leica 1699d. Sunami 8896.  Painting
   308.38
MIRO, Joan                                                  MOMACTL2  6901
   MOONBIRD.  (1966).  Bronze,  90 1/8 h. x 81 1/4 w. x 59  NUMBER 15,347
   1/8" d. (228.8 x 206.4 x 150.1 cm.). Weight: c. 1378
   lbs.  Acquired through the Lillie P. Bliss Bequest.  Leica
   6057b. Mathews 4567. Mathews 4568.  Mathews 4569.
   Sculpture  515.70
MIRO, Joan                                                  MOMACTLG 23162
   MURAL PAINTING.  (1950-51).  Oil on canvas.  6' 2 3/4" x NUMBER 15,348
   19' 5 3/4" (188.8 x 593.8 cm.).  Mrs. Simon Guggenheim
   Fund.  Leica 3655c. Pollitzer 2631.  Painting  592.63
MIRO, Joan                                                  MOMACTL2  7120
   OBJECT.  1931.  Assemblage: painted wood, steel, string, NUMBER 15,349
   bone, and a bead,  15 3/4" h. (40.0 cm.) incl. wooden base
   1 7/8 h. x 8 1/4 w. x 4 3/4" d (4.6 x 21.0 x 12.0
   cm.). Wt. 5 lbs. incl. base.  Gift of Mr. and Mrs.
   Harold X. Weinstein.  Leica 3063b.  Sculpture  7.61
MIRO, Joan                                                  MOMACTLG 26456
   OBJECT.  (1936).  Assemblage: stuffed parrot on wood     NUMBER 15,350
   perch, stuffed silk stocking with velvet garter and doll's
   paper shoe suspended in a hollow wood frame, derby hat,
   hanging cork ball, celluloid fish and engraved map.  31
   7/8 x 11 7/8 x 10 1/4" d. (81.0 x 30.1 x 26.0 cm.)
   (overall)  a) 31 7/8 h. x 9 1/8 w. x 5 3/4" d. (81.0 x
   22.9 x 14.6 cm.). b) 4 5/8 h. x 11 7/8 l. x 10 1/4" d.
   (11.6 x 30.1 x 26.0 cm.). Wt. 6 lbs.  Gift of Mr. and
   Mrs. Pierre Matisse.  Leica 3833c. Leica 6064d. Sunami
   1674. Mathews 4680 Mathews 4681.  Sculpture
   940.65.a-c
MIRO, Joan                                                  MOMACTLG 24162
   OPERA SINGER.  (1934).  Pastel,  Gift of William H.      NUMBER 15,351
   Weintraub (the donor retaining a life interest).  Leica
   6321a. Leica 3655e. Mathews 5793.  509.64
MIRO, Joan                                                  MOMACTLG 18304
   L' ORIGINE DE LA BETE HUMAINE.  (1933).  Charcoal,       NUMBER 15,352
   collage of decalcomania, wash,  Sheet 25 1/4 x 17 1/8"
   (64.0 x 43.3 cm.).  Gift of Nelson A. Rockefeller.  Leica
   2511d. Sunami 14,250.  Drawing  184.56
MIRO, Joan                                                  MOMACTLG  1375
   PAINTING.  June 13, 1933.  Oil on canvas,  68 1/2 x 77   NUMBER 15,353
   1/4".  Gift of the Advisory Committee (by exchange).
   Leica 196b. Sunami 1300. Color 1-337-0031. Color
   1-337-0125.  Painting  229.37
MIRO, Joan                                                  MOMACTL2 10259
   Study for PAINTING.  February 11, 1933.  Cut and pasted  NUMBER 15,354
   photomechanical reproductions and graphite pencil,  Sheet
   18 1/2 x 24 7/8" (46.8 x 63.0 cm.).  Gift of the artist.
   Keller 66.  Drawing  131.73
```

Figure 8.7 Artist printout

knowledge of the subject. The result of this documentation is an invaluable source of information as indicated by the number of staff and outside researchers who use the facilities. Our effectiveness will also increase as our ability to compile more information through the computer continues to grow.

Chapter 9

The Detroit Art Registration Information System (DARIS)

Judith L. Schulman

History

In 1883 a group of interested art patrons mounted a major exhibition of 5000 works of art loaned by Detroit collectors and Eastern art galleries. The loans, many for sale, were housed in a facility funded and built specifically for the exhibition known as the Detroit Art Loan. It was in this year, 1883, that the first works which would become part of the modern Detroit Institute of Arts collection were acquired and catalogued (Figures 9.1 and 9.2). By 1885 the Art Loan had been incorporated as the Detroit Museum of Art (DMA) and built a museum in central Detroit. The DMA became the Detroit Institute of Arts (DIA) in 1919 and by 1927 had moved to what was then the edge of the City, now known as the Cultural Center. Also in 1919, the Founders Society, the philanthropic body of the museum, was organized. In 1985, the Detroit Institute of Arts will celebrate its Centennial. The modern DIA contains 101 galleries displaying a fine and decorative arts collection of catholic scope, rich in European, American, Ancient, Asian and Ethnographic Art.

Through the century of collecting, the record keeping style has remained consistent, one indication of the desire to carefully record information on art objects. Although over the decades works have been reattributed, the main format and required information has remained the same. Five registrars have recorded the collection of the DIA on cards. Interestingly, just by noting the variation in editing style and typewriter font, one is able to discern the cataloguing styles of the past three Registrars.

The obligation of the keeper of the central records was to produce three original manual 4×6 inch cards of archival quality for each work of art. One card was for a chronological file, following our accession scheme (year and chronological accession, such as 83.1). A second card was for a category file (Painting, Italian, seventeenth century) and a third was for the Art Curator's file.

As in all manual systems, expertise of the collection was required to find a specific work of art. For example, in order to find Artemisia Gentileschi, it

83.1	Painting	
American		neg 5439
		14159
Millet, Francis Davis		16819
1846-1912		slide 1627
		neg 16820-
Reading the Story of Oenone		gallery vw.)
Canvas. Four young women seated on classical couch; right figure, semi-reclining, faces reader of scroll. Two women at left face central figure. All women dressed in classic style. Pastel tones of mauve, beige and golds. Signed at left: F.D.Millet		
H 30" W 57 7/8" (76.2 x 147.0 cm.)		
Purchased from proceeds of the Art Loan and popular subscription funds, 1883		$1,000
Form C of D—3-AC (4-62)		

Figure 9.1 First purchase for the Detroit Museum of Art Collection

was necessary to know that she was an Italian, a painter and worked in the seventeenth century. This did not discourage collection research as a Registrar was available to respond to all scholars and public inquiries. However, as the duties of the Registrar's Office increased to include the inventory of galleries and storage, documentation of the collection through photographs and slides, organization of loan and exhibition shipments and upgrading of existing object records, the interpreter of the manual records became more burdened. Still the practice continued and rich information was housed in a central area at the DIA.

It is possible that the DIA would still have a manual system today had it not been recognized that there was a need for an inventory control process that was more efficient than the cumbersome, year-long process based upon manual location cards and augmented by the assistance of volunteers. Also, the mid-1970s were a period in which registration methods in general were being examined by museologists and federal funds were being made available for studying registrarial responsibilities and functions as recorders of cultural history.

Description of systems

In 1978, the Founders Society Detroit Institute of Arts (FSDIA) applied for and received a generous grant from the National Endowment for the Arts (NEA), a federal agency in Washington, D.C. The decision was then made to place our inventory on the computer that was already in use for the

```
 83.2                        Painting

         Italian School (North)                    neg 6782
         c. 1700

         The Spiritual Betrothal of St. Catherine of
         Alexandria with the Infant Jesus

         Canvas

         H   36"   W   51"

         Gift of His Holiness Pope Leo XIII

         Minutes D.M.A. 1883                        $1,000
         Exh.: Detroit Art Loan, Catalogue of Art Works
             Exhibited 1883:  82,  nr 910


         Form C of D—3-AC (4-62)
```

Figure 9.2 First gift to the Detroit Museum of Art Collection

FSDIA membership and mailing labels (including library exchange). This application was known as Detroit Art Locator Information System (DALIS). It produced a hard copy object location printout. Before this printout of location practice was abandoned, we were producing two 12 inch-high volumes, generated monthly and distributed around the building. Though unwieldy, these lists were more timely than the manual card or someone's memory and at the same time offered security of inventory. With this nucleus of information (object accession number, curatorial department and some locations) entered into the computer we arrived at the next logical step, that is, determining that we should have a terminal access to information and that full online cataloguing should be pursued. The FSDIA approached the Burroughs Corporation, as our current computer was of their manufacture and proposed an automated art collections management and research application. Burroughs generously upgraded our system by giving us a mid-sized mainframe computer with terminal access to data and affording us facilities for gathering and querying object location.

A design phase lasting one year was begun in 1978. During this time, staff worked with outside consultants/programmers and solicited cataloguing input from our Art Curators, Service Departments and Administration. From this activity, the Detroit Art Registration Information System (DARIS) was developed and for the next three years we had the luxury of entering information on collections in parallel to program design (Schulman, in press). This was accomplished by a series of programming stages called releases. There were five releases of data entry and retrieval design. With each release we were able to enter certain data, building on the basic record, examining new inputs and redesigning the character or appearance of the system outputs. During the design phase we did not receive a great deal of input from our curatorial staff, but this was not surprising as we had no measuring stick to offer them. Further, because the DIA collection is universal, both globally and historically, an overall system that would meet the needs of ten fairly discrete curatorial departments was not easily achieved (Figures 9.3 to 9.7). Rather, accommodation of the diversity of the objects came with actual data entry. As the real data became available to Curators, they were able to offer more concrete input into design and needs. The current data base is, to a large extent, the result of cooperation with DIA staff from several orientations: curatorial, educational, registrarial and administrative.

The artist authority list was created over an 11-month period using a Burroughs word processing package. The authority list was comprised of all artist names associated with works in the DIA collection. Standards for the list were achieved by consulting source materials such as Thieme-Becker and Benezit and by consulting current published research. The authority list was then keyed into the data base and through formatted screens was attached to the appropriate accession number. From the beginning of online data entry, we adhered to a minimal standard record to prevent information being entered that could not be retrieved or understood. As we were a pilot project and did not know if funding would be continued, we wanted an articulate and logical data base even if time only allowed us to enter information on 10 or 12 fields per object for the entire collection. By the end of the second release we had title, accession number, department, location and records of artist, dealer and donor with appropriate attributes.

Decisions on vocabulary access fields were difficult to make and once decided upon were changed as new and different types of objects were accessioned and catalogued. Standard vocabulary should never be construed as a limited vocabulary. It requires thoughtful control and application of language. It cannot be emphasized enough that vocabulary control is the only guarantee for retrieval of like works. Information retrieval, like other aspects of automation, is fluid and requires constant attention and upgrading. In Detroit, vocabulary lists are generated as Standard Reports. They are used as a tool for control and upgrading and allow for flexibility of vocabulary within the various disciplines within a museum of great breadth.

From its inception DARIS software has produced a random selection of 200 objects per month or 20 objects per curatorial department. Each department is then charged with the responsibility of locating its objects, reviewing existing and ordering new photography, reviewing and updating insurance, editing the online cataloguing and submitting the information to the Inventory Control group for data base updating.

What we have learnt

A major spin-off of automation in Detroit has been the upgrading of manual forms for all aspects of the collection. For example, the inventory control procedure necessitated an art movement control form, without which a Preparator will no longer move art. Other standardization of forms as a

```
52.253                                    Painting

        Italian                                        neg 9288
                                                       slides
        Gentileschi, Artemisia                         1106
        1597-after 1651                                1107
                                                       1108
Cat 1066  Judith and Maidservant                       4751
          with the Head of Holofernes                  4752
                                                       4753
        Canvas.  Because of its closeness in style to  4754
        paintings by the artist in the Uffizi and Pitti 4755
        Galleries this canvas is thought to have been  4756
        painted in the early 1620's.                   neg 21510

        H  72-1/2"   W  55-3/4"                         $9,000

        Gift of Leslie H. Green                         (over)

        Minutes  AC 2/12/53
```

```
52.253

Ex-Collections:  Prince Brancaccio, Rome

Ref.: Fredericksen & Zeri 1972: 80

References:  E.P.Richardson, "A Masterpiece of
             Baroque Drama" Bulletin DIA, vol XXXII,
             no 4, p 81;

             Id, Art Quarterly, vol 16, no 2, Summer
             1953, p 91-92 (illus);
DIA, Art in Italy, 1600-1700, April 6 - May 9, 1965, cat. no. 8, pp
     29, 30 (Illus.);
The Themes and Writers Series: Perception, Themes in Literature, (Publ.
     Webster Division, McGraw-Hill Book Division, 1969).  color repr. p.
     145,
R.E.Spear, Caravaggio and his Followers, Cleveland (1971), pp.96-97
B.S.Myers (ed.), Encyclopedia of Painting, N.Y., Crown (1970),
     illus. p.194 (col.pl.77)
Monthly Art Magazine Bijutsu    Techo (in Japanese) 28 (May 1976)
     (##407), illus. (n.p.)
```

Figure 9.3 Manual cataloguing of 52.253

result of automation occurred in the areas of loans and both new and duplicate photography.

The most difficult form to change was the accession sheet. A one-page form was expanded to three pages that follow the formats and information requirements of the data entry screens, requiring more information from the curators at the time of accessioning.

We borrowed from 20th century design aesthetics, 'form follows function'. The new forms designed as a result of developing the automated system have increased the amount of information that we are able to gather about the collection. Today, with 86 data elements searchable in '*n*' combinations, DARIS is ready for the researcher of the future.

82

```
               category: Painting
                 52.253: Judith and Maidservant with the Head of Holofernes
            object date: c.1625
           object place: Europe, Southern Europe, Italy, Rome
                   name: Gentileschi, Artemisia (3452)
                  lived: 1593-1652/53
            citizenship: Italian
             birthplace: Europe, Southern Europe, Italy, Rome
                 period: Baroque
               function: religion
        medium/technique: Oil on canvas
        medium/technique: canvas
                          paint, oil
           measurements: 184.15cm X 141.61cm (6ft 1/2in X 55 3/4in) [E]
            description: Judith wearing a gold-colored dress over a white blouse,
                          leans forward, her right arm crossed over her body,
                          holding a sword. Her left arm is raised; her hand shields
                          the light of a candle from her eyes. Her maidservant
                          crouches at lower right, pulling a sack over the severed
                          head of Holofernes. Red drape in the background.
       object accessory: frame
             references: DIA BULLETIN, vol 32, no 4, 1953, p 81.
                          DIA, ART QUARTERLY, vol 6, no 2, 1953, pp 91-92 (ill).
                          DIA, ART IN ITALY, 1600-1700, April 6-May 9, 1965, no 8,
                            pp 29, 30, (ill).
                          Spear, R. E., CARAVAGGIO AND HIS FOLLOWERS, Cleveland:
                            R. E. Spear, 1971, pp 96-97 (ill).
                          Myers, B. S., ed, ENCYCLOPEDIA OF PAINTING, New York:
                            Crown, 1970, p 194, color pl 77.
                          Fredericksen and Zeri, 1972, p 80.
                          Harris, A. S. and L. Nochlin, WOMEN ARTISTS, Los Angeles
                            County Museum, Dec 23-March 13, 1976, p 122, no 13,
                            color pl 70.
                          Nagle, J., THE RESPONSIVE ARTS, Sherman Oaks, CA: Alfred
                            Publishing, 1980, p 124, fig 12-4.
                          Broude, N. and Garrard, M. eds., FEMINISM AND ART HISTORY,
                            QUESTIONING THE LITANY, New York: Harper and Row,
                            Pub., 1982, no.17 (ill).
        add'l info with: Curator, Conservation
         accession data: gift $9,000 Arts Commission minutes 1953/02/12
            credit line: Gift of Mr. Leslie H. Green
             provenance: Formerly in the collection of:
                          Prince Brancaccio, Rome
             department: European Painting
                  slide: 1107, 1961, Detail, Judith
                  slide: 1108, 1961, Detail of servant
                  slide: 4753, 1970, Detail, hand with sword
                  slide: 4754, 1970, Detail, maidservant's head
                  slide: 4755, 1970, Detail, maidservant's arm
                  slide: 4756, 1970, Full view
               negative: 9288
               negative: 21510
         inventory data: moved from W174 moved to N003 on 1984/10/23
            search data: Found on 1979/07/27
        insurance value: $500,000 evaluated on 1979/05/14
```

Figure 9.4 DARIS cataloguing of 52.253

Through a three-year dialogue with three programmers, we discovered that software designers will learn more about art history and museology than museum staff will learn about computer programming. This is advantageous, since knowing the constraints of programming would probably limit museum staff requests and demands for the system. We were often told by our programmers that our requirements could not be converted into design, but eventually, through museum staff tenacity, they were.

The DARIS system is constantly being upgraded through new programming requests. As users become more familiar with the system, they

DARIS(R) DETROIT ART REGISTRATION AND INFORMATION SYSTEM - PHOTO LABEL   0/24/03

Judith and Maidservant with the Head of Holofernes   c.1625
Oil on canvas
184.15cm X 141.61cm (6ft 1/2in X 55 3/4in) [E]

Gentileschi, Artemisia
Italian   lived 1593-c.1651

Gift of Mr. Leslie H. Green
52.253

Copyright (c) 1983 Founders Society Detroit Institute of Arts
European Painting   negative 21510

Figure 9.5 Artemisia Gentileschi, Italian, 1593-1652/53. Judith and Maidservant with the Head of Holofernes. Oil on canvas. Detroit Institute of Arts, Gift of Leslie H. Green 52.253

make more demands upon it. Primary and integral to enhancements are the quality and standards of the data. Early in the software development we were advised by our consultants that the system design was secondary. The integrity of the information, control of vocabulary and standards imposed on the entered data were paramount to the success of automation. The time and energy spent on standards has allowed for enhancements of the DARIS system through software changes. Software and hardware are never static, and upgrading of both is mandatory for system growth.

Parallel to the growth of systems and machines is the growth of staff. It should never be assumed that a computer will replace staff. In fact, it becomes a vehicle for creating new and more structured functions for staff. In Detroit we now have a professional staff of Cataloguers where once we had only a Registrar. In addition, we also have an Inventory Control team to monitor galleries and supervise secured storage areas where previously only Curators were responsible for their specific collections. Computerization has

```
            DARIS(R)DETROIT ART REGISTRATION AND INFORMATION SYSTEM 10/25/84 14:16 PAGE    1
82.52
                              category: Sculpture
                                 82.52: Funerary Figure
                        title variation: Tau-Tau
                            object date: n.d.a.
                           object place: Asia, Southeasy Asia, Indonesia, Celebes
                                 people: Toraja (10770)
                            citizenship: Indonesian
                                 region: Asia, Southeast Asia, Indonesia, Celebes
                        format/typology: statue
                               function: funerary
                       medium/technique: Polychromed wood
                       medium/technique: wood, carved, polychromed
                                         paint
                           measurements: height x width at hips 100.33cm X 21.59cm (39 1/2in X 8
                                         1/2in) [E]
                                         width at shoulders 20.96cm (8 1/4in) [E]
                            description: Standing female figure with a flattened and elongated
                                         torso.  The head is flattened in profile view, and the
                                         the features are somewhat small in proportion to the
                                         size of the head.  There are wooden dowels at intervals
                                         where there normally would have been hair.
                                remarks: Condition at accession:  wood weathered to gray; traces of
                                         white pigment; wood weathered away at ankles, feet
                                         missing; arms missing.
                                         Probably very early example of this type of figure, which
                                         has been used for about thirteen generations.
                                         Such figures were dressed in the deceased's finest clothes
                                         and placed where the ancestor-spirit could keep a vigil
                                         on the living.
                      add'l info with: Curator
                        accession data: gift $20,000 Founders Society minutes 1982/11/16:L82.97
                            credit line: Gift of Mr. Solomon Maizel
                             provenance: Formerly in the collection of:
                                         Anthony Plowright
                             department: African, Oceanic & New World Cultures
                                  slide: 7532, 1982/08/09, front
                                  slide: 7533, 1982/08/09, back
                                  slide: 7534, 1982/08/09, side
                               negative: 26915, 1982/08/09, front
                               negative: 26916, 1982/08/09, side
                               negative: 26917, 1982/08/09, back
                         inventory data: moved from N365 moved to W073 on 1983/01/07
                                      :
                                  donor: Maizel, Solomon (5053)
                                address: Wayne, New Jersey




                              Copyright (c) 1984: Founders Society Detroit Institute of Arts
```

Figure 9.6 DARIS cataloguing of 82.52

resulted in greater access to and familiarity with the entire museum collection and has precipitated an increase in photo-documentation, which has in turn required an increase in the Photography Department as well as the Rights and Reproductions Department. All additional staff provide more opportunities for more articulate and accurate dissemination of collection information.

As the demand for access to information increases, so too do demands for security levels regarding stored information. It is imperative that thoughtful security codes be built into the design. For example, on the DARIS system,

DARIS(R) DETROIT ART REGISTRATION AND INFORMATION SYSTEM - PHOTO LABEL 10/25/84

Funerary Figure   n.d.a.
statue
Tau-Tau
Polychromed wood
height x width at hips 100.33cm X 21.59cm (39 1/2in X 0
1/2in) [E]
width at shoulders 20.96cm (8 1/4in) [E]

Toraja
Indonesian

Gift of Mr. Solomon Maizel
82.52

Copyright (c) 1984 Founders Society Detroit Institute of Arts
African, Oceanic & New World Cultures   negative 26915, 1982/08/09, front

Figure 9.7 Toraja People, Indonesian, circa 19th century Funerary Figure. Polychromed Wood. Detroit Institute of Arts, Gift of Solomon Maizel 82.52

only one person can create new accession records for incoming objects; another can delete records. Object location within the building is entered by only one person and another person enters works out on loan. This builds security of object location and integrity of cataloguing information into the system.

Scope

Although we aimed for a nucleus of records for each object, the scope of the DARIS cataloguing was ambitious from the onset of the project. We felt that as long as we were designing a cataloguing scheme, it should afford ability to extract data for a variety of needs and a variety of departments within the museum. Flexible and standard reports produce standard gallery label information, standard labels for photographs, slides and negatives to be sent to publishers and researchers, formated lists for museum governing bodies for reporting the accessioning process and, of course, reports to guarantee vocabulary standards in all vocabulary fields (geography, period, style, dynasty, function, format and typology, medium, materials and technique).

The documentation to support all aspects of data entry and retrieval has been a continuous upgrading process. Thorough documentation affords the user the ability to work unassisted or without an interpreter, as is required by so many library cataloguing schemes. And a natural outgrowth of thorough documentation was the ability to share the system with off site users.

Beginning in 1980, the FSDIA offered the software and terminal access to DARIS to all museum collections in the State of Michigan. The resulting network became a cooperative for data sharing as well as a cooperative forum for vocabulary standards. Security, in the form of not sharing purchase value, donor confidentiality and storage location was built into the network cataloguing at the inception. Although none of the Michigan Museum Network/DARIS users has completed cataloguing of their collections, retrievable capabilities on portions of all collections are available.

We communicate with our network users by memoranda, through electronic mail on the terminals and at semi-annual meetings where we discuss the status of the cataloguing, programming enhancements and standards for all data elements. Because our documentation is online, our network users can call up any manuals, guides or lexicons at their local terminals or wait for the frequent hard copy we send as documents change.

The Michigan Museum Network/DARIS is comprised of fine arts collections in museums and colleges, archival materials, history collections and archaeology holdings. When all users are connected by the end of 1985, we will have 15 Michigan collections networked.

The major sets that were identified as cataloguing areas for an object were:

accession and donor data;
subjective description of object;
objective description of object;
insurance and inventory data;
artist, dealer, lender and donor information;
institution information;
artist data related to object;
loan and exhibition data;
temporary shipping data.

Within these sets there are numerous other elements and subsets that are searchable. For example, subjective description of object is one of the areas with the most focus on vocabulary standards. This includes:

title;
title variation;
title reattribution;
date of execution;
geographical associations (including historical, contemporary and point of discovery);
style, period, dynasty and school;

format, function, typology, medium, materials and technique;
related works, references, provenance.

All data fields can be searched, some through keywords or strings of keywords in any combination and some directly by using appropriate standard vocabulary associated with the particular data element.

A decision was made early on to impose a hierarchy in the retrieval display as a learning tool for the researcher. The words, however, are stored as a pool in the data base and do not need special strings for actual search. Text fields, such as description, inscription, references, reattributions and accessory description, can be brought together through keyword search.

Philosophically, we were not inclined to subject index each object. Rather, we preferred to group like things together using the language of art history and archaeology to extract groups of objects, thus allowing the researcher an array from which to cull. This has proven to be particularly appropriate given the breadth of the collections being catalogued into DARIS.

Facilities

Another natural outgrowth of creating a data base in a museum for research and collections management was management systems for other aspects of the museum. The membership and mailing label systems carried over from our first computer were the basis for developing a more sophisticated Membership and Development package which includes a corporate campaign system, as well as creating an accounts payable, online cheque writing, a museum shop inventory system, a budgeting system and an extremely flexible mailing label system. These operations, known as Detroit Arts Management Information System (DAMIS) are spread throughout our business departments: Founders Membership and Development, the Museum Shop and Founders Accounting. Our public information desks have terminals that offer information on collections, including locations of objects on display, cataloguing and floor plans displaying hourly changes in gallery openings and closings, assisting our volunteers in servicing visitors. Public events and tickets are available at our Theatre Arts offices using remote printers to produce tickets. We have terminals near our storage areas used by our Inventory Control Staff, several terminals in our Registrar/Cataloguing group, several for curatorial use and for the staff of the Registrar's Office for Loans and Exhibitions.

The FSDIA currently uses a medium sized mainframe driven by a processor with 1 million bytes of memory and 540 million bytes of storage, being accessed inhouse and around the state by 59 addresses. As with software (which can never be too abundant), our hardware is frequently being examined for upgrading.

The NEA grant of 1978 and for four subsequent years mandated us to produce a system that was fully documented, would have application in more than one museum and could be networked. We have done this with the Detroit project and the FSDIA is now marketing its software.

Because we took the position of thoughtful complete entry of information on objects, as opposed to quickly getting data online, we are able to offer a most substantial data base to the researcher. Currently we are ahead of research trends, but the computer awareness developing in our culture will bring that particularly interesting research question to us soon and we are anxiously awaiting the opportunity to share the information.

Chapter 10

A system for analysing museum documentation

Lenore Sarasan

Introduction

The documentation systems of many museums provide as little ease of access to information as overcrowded storerooms provide to specimens. Object records may be incomplete, they may be incorrect, they may even be non existent. Data in the accession ledger may be quite different from that recorded in the main card catalogue which in turn may vary from that contained in the cross reference files. Physically locating any particular object may take hours and trying to extract all the pertinent information contained in the various files about a specific item may take days.

The reasons for this situation are not difficult to fathom. In many museums, there has been less emphasis placed on documenting objects than on amassing and preserving them. It is not unusual for a collection to double or triple in size while the number of staff responsible for maintaining the objects and their associated records remains constant. No common approaches to recording information about objects or specimens have been established by the American museum community and few cataloguing guidelines or procedures have been published. The basic organization of a museum's filing system, card formats, categories of data recorded, absence or presence of cross-reference files, numbering conventions, etc., depends largely on the discretion and preference of whomever sets up the initial system.

As collections grow, a museum's original documentation system may not accommodate the increased number of records or the research needs of users. Some of the features of the basic structure are abandoned while new ones are added. These added features usually reflect the personal research interests and tastes of the curators in charge of the collection rather than attempts to design a consistent, cohesive system of documentation.

As time goes by, more files and cross references are typically added to meet unanticipated needs and the number of components in the system grows. It is not unusual for even a small museum to have over 25 separate files and ledger books comprising its manual system. So much time and manpower are needed to keep all these files current that many may not be updated regularly. Peter Homulos, Director of CHIN, estimates that the Royal Ontario Museum in Toronto, with a catalogued collection of approximately 350 000 artefacts, experiences about 5000 data changes and additions per week. These include corrections and additions to existing catalogue data, changes in object locations, and the creation of new records. Homulos estimates that to handle this volume efficiently in a manual system, seven full-time clerks would be needed (Anon., 1982). Few museums can afford this level of staffing. It is not surprising, then, that rather than functioning as coherent, interrelated systems of information, many museums' collection documentation has devolved into a series of disjointed, poorly integrated files and ledgers.

In the last few years many museums have turned to computers as a potential solution to their documentation problems. And, indeed, computers do offer one of the few viable solutions to the documentation dilemma. However, though the use of computers for purposes related to collection management has increased dramatically in the last five years (there are over 500 individual projects in operation in North American museums alone), most projects encounter serious obstacles and few are fully operational today (Sarasan, 1981). A recent survey of the use of computers in collection documentation applications (Sarasan and Neuner, 1983) suggests that a major contributing factor to the low success rate of museum projects is lack of understanding of the principles of documentation.

Though the trend to automation in United States museums has focused attention on record keeping, it has not given rise to much discussion of the theory of documentation, documentation systems, or the closely related topics of data entry and information retrieval. A comprehension of documentation concepts — what constitutes a good manual system, what information should be recorded, in what form it should be recorded, what roles different kinds of information perform in a system, and how the various ledger books and index card files should interact and be integrated — is essential to a well-designed computer project. But it is the rare institution that after decades of existence can adequately explain the plethora of separate card files it keeps, why certain ones were created, or how they were originally designed to function. It may not be necessary to know these things in order to maintain a usable manual system. However, the structure and function of each component of a manual system must be thoroughly understood before an automated system may be successfully implemented to replace or supplement a manual system. If not, serious problems may occur. Certain key procedures may be omitted, important reports may not be included which then have to be manually prepared in spite of having an automated system, or data fields which are essential for generating forms may be inadvertently excluded.

Systems analysis at the Dallas Museum of Fine Arts

In an effort to avoid these kinds of problems, we have developed a series of exercises which comprise a Do-It-Yourself Mini-Systems Analysis (DIYSA) of a museum's existing manual documentation system. These exercises provide an opportunity to review the manual system and analyse it in depth without the involvement and expense of a data processing expert. The products of these exercises are useful whether or not a museum decides to automate. If the decision is made to computerize, the exercises provide a foundation on which to design and develop an automated system. If the decision is made not to automate, the products provide a valuable overview of the manual system and the basis of a registrar's manual.

The exercises centre around the completion of a set of formatted worksheets which allows the project director to systematically record information about each component of the manual system — data fields, files, reports, and procedures. We have used this system with considerable success in conjunction with several collections including the anthropological and archaeological collections of the Field Museum of Natural History in Chicago, the collections of the National Museum in Riyadh, Saudi Arabia, and the fine art and ethnological collections of the Dallas Museum of Fine Arts in Dallas, Texas (Sunderland and Geyer, 1982). We will describe the system in the context of its application to the Dallas Museum of Fine Arts (DMFA).

The DMFA currently houses a collection of about 10 000 objects representing traditional fine arts materials (paintings, sculpture, prints, etc.) as well as ethnological materials (primarily Pre-Columbian). In late-1983 the DMFA will move to a newly constructed building in downtown Dallas which will more than triple its current space. The size of the collection is expected to double in the two years following the move.

DMFA began seriously investigating computerization in late 1980 under the supervision of Ms Ginger Henry Geyer who continues as the project's director. Initial research consisted of reviewing the available literature and visiting a number of projects within the United States. Most systems which have been implemented in museums may be classified as 'searchable data file' projects. The main goal of these projects is to build a computer file containing data about each object in the collection which can then be searched and sorted to provide information to staff members and researchers. Although searchable data file projects are usually seen as a way of streamlining an existing manual system, in practice their existence usually adds considerable overhead to the operation. A data file of a museum's holdings does not usually affect the day-to-day activities of collection management. Most searchable data files do not help in the preparation of loan forms or reports or the accessioning of materials. Rather, these manual forms must be filled out as they always have been and then, in addition to the manual work, some of the information must be entered into the automated system. Changes to the manual system must be redundantly reflected in the computerized file.

DMFA wanted something more than a searchable data file. The staff wished to have the computer perform collection management activities such as preparing loan agreements, automatically assigning accession numbers to new objects, tracking overdue loans, and keeping tabs on objects not completely catalogued. This application, which we call an automated collection management system, has been tried in only a handful of American museums. The criteria for implementing a collection management system are quite distinct from those required to build a searchable data file. In the latter, emphasis is on (or should be on) the definition of data fields and syntax and vocabulary controls for entering these fields in a way which makes retrieval accurate and efficient. In a collection management system, not only will a searchable data file be built, but at least some of the processes of the manual system are to be performed by the computer. Therefore, it is essential that the structure and components of the manual system are thoroughly understood.

By the summer of 1981, DMFA had decided to pursue computerization. In part this decision was based on the need to tightly control the collections during the move to the new building. The impending increase in the size of the collection was another critical factor in the decision. It became apparent that to replace the manual processing system with an automated one, a thorough review of the existing documentation system was necessary. Rather than incur the expense of an analysis performed by a systems expert, DMFA opted to use a prototype of the DIYSA system. We estimate that DMFA saved approximately $12 000 by performing the analysis themselves, rather than hiring an outside consultant. DMFA pursued this approach with three goals in mind: to become acquainted with the concepts of documentation theory and to familiarize the project director with the existing manual documentation system; to provide a written overview of the existing manual system; and to identify the kinds of information which were available in the manual system and the sources of this information.

The DIYSA approach centres on filling out a series of formatted worksheets. These worksheets systematize information about the kinds of data contained in a museum's documentation system; its form, its location, and its good and bad points. Approximately three man-weeks are needed to complete the analysis. Collection size does not affect this time-frame, although older museums, which tend to have a greater number of documentation components, may need an additional week.

Five separate kinds of worksheet are used: Data Field Worksheets, File Worksheets, Input/Output Worksheets, Procedures Worksheets, and Counting Grids. Each is described below.

Exercise 1: Data Field Worksheets

A data field is the smallest unit of information that can be defined. The information recorded on most catalogue cards is *not* separated into discrete data fields but rather appears as grouped data under larger category headings. For example, under the heading 'Description' on the DMFA's manual catalogue card, several kinds of data are recorded — object name, technique, colour, material(s) of composition, use, shape, size — although they are not labelled as such.

The purpose of Exercise 1 is to introduce the concept of a data field as a precise unit of information as opposed to the less precise catch-all categories which are found in most museum documentation. The computer demands considerably more rigour in the format and control of data fields than does a manual system where a human being serves as retriever and interpreter. Unless these category headings are broken down into their component data fields and are then treated as separate units in the computer, data retrieval will usually be difficult and inaccurate. For example, if a country's name appears on different manual catalogue cards in three different ways —

United States, U.S.A., and America — it may not make too much difference to a user who will readily see that the three forms mean the same thing. In an automated system, however, searching for one of these terms will not retrieve the others and will therefore result in an incomplete and inaccurate response.

A Data Field Worksheet (Figure 10.1) is prepared for each field on the list. As the worksheets are completed, special attention should be paid to syntax and vocabulary control. Questions that should be asked include: Does it matter in what format the data are recorded? Would it make any difference to alphabetizing or retrieving? Should the values of the data field be limited to a short list of terms or can any term be entered into the field? Is this the smallest unit of this information or can it be further divided? Should this field be included in the computer data file?

DIYSA DATA FIELD WORKSHEET

INSTRUCTIONS:

Fill out one Worksheet for each data field identified. 'Alphanumeric' refers to data comprised of either alphabetical characters or both alphabetical characters and numerals. Definitions should be kept brief and concise. 'Format' refers to syntax controls such as 'last name first' or 'zero fill' while 'Controls' refers to terminology controls on the field such as an authority list or encoding scheme.

FIELD NAME: ____________

FORM: ___ Alphanumeric ___ Numeric

DEFINITION: ____________

USES: ____________

FORMAT: ____________

CONTROLS: ____________

EXAMPLES: ____________

LENGTH: ____________

COMMENTS: ____________

NAME: ____________ DATE: ____________

Figure 10.1 Data field worksheet

The concept of a data field is not yet well-established in the American museum community. As a result, the Data Field Worksheets filled out in this exercise may need to be reworked several times.

Exercise 2: File Worksheets

A file may be defined as any collection of records and may appear in the form of a notebook, a ledger or a set of index cards. The purpose of the File Worksheet (Figure 10.2) is to identify *all* of the individual documentation sources within the manual system. It may seem that most manual systems consist of a master file which is cross referenced through a few auxiliary files. However, there are usually a great many more files around than most people suspect. Files have a tendency to proliferate. For example, curators may maintain their own indices to portions of the collection; interns may begin projects that, while not completed, are not discarded; the registrar may maintain a diary or logbook separate from the main files. Prior to analysis, the DMFA staff estimated that there were less than a dozen separate files, ledgers, etc. After completing the analysis, they found that there were actually several dozen.

DIYSA FILE WORKSHEET

INSTRUCTIONS:

Fill out one Worksheet for each source identified. Divide the contents of each category heading into data fields. Include files which are not currently maintained.

FILE NAME:
FORMAT: __ Book   __ Card File   __ Other: _____
DESCRIPTION:

LOCATION:
MAINTAINER:
ARRANGEMENT:

ENTRIES:
USERS:
CATEGORIES: FIELDS CONTAINED:

COMMENTS:

NAME: DATE:

© 1983 by Willoughby Associates, Limited.

Figure 10.2 File worksheet

To gain a complete overview of the manual system, even those files not currently up-to-date should be included in this exercise. Each file is listed on a separate worksheet. Its number of entries, arrangement, physical description, and location are recorded. If the file is in the form of a ledger or logbook, the category headings which appear on each page are recorded. Each category heading is broken down into the data fields it contains. Since the concept of a data field will become clearer during the exercises, this portion of the File Worksheet may need to be reworked later.

Exercise 3: Input/Output Worksheets

The term 'input/output' applies to all forms such as catalogue cards and loan forms as well as to reports which are prepared on a regular basis such as a yearly accession list or a monthly list of new acquisitions. The Input/Output Worksheet (Figure 10.3) will contain details on the purpose and use of each form, its distribution and frequency of generation, and the category headings it contains. As with the File Worksheet, space is provided to break the category headings into data fields.

```
┌─────────────────────────────────────────────────────────┐
│  DIYSA INPUT/OUTPUT WORKSHEET                             │
│                                                          │
│  INSTRUCTIONS:                                           │
│  Fill out one Worksheet for each form or report          │
│  generated.  Divide the contents of each category        │
│  heading into data fields.  Attach a copy of the         │
│  form to this Worksheet.                                  │
│                                                          │
│  FORM NAME: _____                       │
│  FORM TYPE: ___ Input Form ___ Output Form ___ Report    │
│  FUNCTION: _____                       │
│  DESCRIPTION: _____                       │
│                                                          │
│  ORIGINATOR: _____                       │
│  USERS: _____                       │
│  # COPIES: _____                       │
│  WHERE FILED: _____                       │
│                                                          │
│  CATEGORIES:          FIELDS CONTAINED:                  │
│                                                          │
│  COMMENTS: _____                       │
│                                                          │
│  NAME: _____      DATE: _____                  │
└─────────────────────────────────────────────────────────┘
```

Figure 10.3 Input/output worksheet

The major purpose of the Input/Output Worksheet is to gain an overview of the variety of forms used in the same system. Many times redundant forms or reports are produced. Some of these may be effectively consolidated into one or may be eliminated altogether.

DMFA staff members anticipated about 20 separate reports; over 70 separate forms and reports were identified. Interestingly, as the Input/Output Worksheets were filled out, it was discovered that during the first year following the acquisition of an object, the *same* information was recorded on 32 separate forms and reports.

Exercise 4: Procedures Worksheet

A Procedures Worksheet (Figure 10.4) should be completed for each of the main collection management functions — accessioning, cataloguing, and loan processing — as well as subsets of these functions. For example, loan processing may be divided into incoming and outgoing loans as well as short-term and long-term loans. The information recorded should include: who is responsible for each step in the procedure; what, if any, files are created or updated during the step, and what forms are used as input to the step or are generated as output from the step.

DIYSA PROCEDURE WORKSHEET

INSTRUCTIONS:

Fill out one Worksheet for each collection management activity. List the individual steps of the activity in the order in which they are performed. List who performs each step and what, if any, outputs are generated during the step. Also list what files, if any, are created or updated during the step. Use additional Worksheets as needed.

ACTIVITY:
PROCESSING:

WHO	PROCESS	OUTPUT

COMMENTS:

NAME: DATE:

© 1983 by Willoughby Associates, Limited.

Figure 10.4 Procedure worksheet

This exercise is the most difficult because most museums do not have written descriptions of everyday procedures such as registering objects, processing loans, or cataloguing objects. It can be quite challenging to describe activities step-by-step which are performed on a routine basis. One insight which usually emerges during this exercise is that, in general, no one knows what anyone else does with a form or report once it leaves his or her hands. In many cases, work or research which has already been completed is redone. In other instances, two people maintain essentially identical files without realizing it.

Exercise 5: Counting Grid

The Counting Grid (Figure 10.5) is used to determine a realistic figure for the amount of data that are to be converted to computer records. The data fields identified during Exercise 1 should be entered on to the Counting Grid and then used to sample records in the manual documentation. At least 200 records should be sampled regardless of the size of the collection. These should be evenly distributed throughout the manual records. The number of characters in each defined data field of a selected record should be counted and entered on to the Counting Grid. As many grids as necessary should be used. When counting is completed, the average record length should be calculated and multiplied by the total number of records in the collection to

DIYSA COUNTING GRID

INSTRUCTIONS:

Select sample cards or entries from the manual documentation system. Select approximately 200 samples and use as many Counting Grids as needed. Enter the Accession Number or Catalogue Number of each sample across the top of the Counting Grid form. Count the characters that comprise each data field on the sample and record the number in the appropriate place on the Counting Grid. Calculate Totals and Averages.

FIELD NAME												TOTAL OCCURRENCES	TOTAL # OF CHARACTERS	AVERAGE # PER FIELD
TOTALS														

Figure 10.5 counting grid

find the approximate total number of characters that need to be entered. To determine how many hours of data entry this represents, the total number of characters is divided by 6000 keystrokes per hour. While 12 000 keystrokes per hour is the average in business, the complexity and changeable formats of museum catalogue records make halving this rate advisable. The actual time needed to perform data entry will also depend on the sophistication of the data entry programs used. Additional time will be needed for proofreading and editing.

Since the Counting Grid breaks a record into its component data fields, decisions relating to which fields should be entered may be made based on the time and money needed for data entry. This provides the project director with accurate comparisons of the time and money required to enter different combinations of the data fields. The grids also provide information on the frequency with which any particular field appears. These statistics may be used in a variety of ways such as estimating the amount of time needed to research and complete incomplete records or, determining whether different types of objects utilize different data fields.

This exercise will also establish a figure for the size of the computer file that will be built. This will directly influence the type of hardware required to accommodate the file. For instance, a decision may be made to initially enter 20 fields of information for each of 20 000 records. If the 20 fields average a total of 350 characters per record, the resulting computer file will contain over seven million characters. It would probably not be advisable to do this project on a floppy-disc based computer system because of constraints placed on the file size by the capacity of the discs.

Results

At the completion of the DIYSA exercises, several tangible products should exist including: a solid written foundation for a procedures manual outlining each step in the day-to-day collection management activities; a 'data elements dictionary' (Data Field Worksheets) defining the information contained in the system and setting standards for its recording; and a written overview of the components that comprise the manual system. The latter is extremely valuable when making decisions regarding modifications to the system. It provides curators and users with a better understand of the extent of the documentation and its structure.

One of the most important results of this analysis is the wealth of accurate information that can be provided to systems designers and programmers if a decision is made to automate. Many museums simply call in a consultant or programmer and say, "We think we have some problems and we want to computerize. Tell us what to do." This places the institution at a distinct disadvantage and frequently results in an automated system that costs more than anyone would have guessed and which still may not do what was expected. Undertaking a preliminary analysis beforehand allows a museum to ask more meaningful questions of computer professionals and to understand the answers, rather than becoming lost in a sea of jargon. This results in decisions which are based on hard facts rather than on guesswork.

In the case of DMFA, a comprehensive collection management system called MILAM has been developed. MILAM is a set of programs designed to automatically perform many of the day-to-day activities involved in managing a museum collection. These include pre-acquisition activities, accessioning, cataloguing, loan processing, shipping, and inventorying. In addition to providing online access to collection data and automatic form- and report-generation, MILAM also provides a means of logging and keeping track of changes in an object's location, value, and condition, as well as maintaining a history of loans and exhibitions in which the object has been involved.

The results of DIYSA contributed to the design and development of MILAM in several significant ways. The products of the exercises provided the system designers with *written* specifications on which to base the design of each module; ambiguities about the contents of reports and files and the steps followed in producing these materials were reduced; much of the on-going confusion surrounding an automated project of this type was eliminated. The results of the Counting Grid exercise helped eliminate costly errors in defining and entering data fields. In fact, data for one phase of the project — an initial physical inventory which involved entering approximately 10-15 data fields for each of 8000 records — were entered in only six man-days with 99.9% accuracy. During the Data Field exercise it was discovered that eight separate numbering formats had been used during the museum's history rather than the three which had been expected. This discovery alone saved hundreds of dollars in programming modifications which would have been necessary if this detail had not come to light until well after the project had started. Finally, because the staff was intimately involved in the analysis, they were familiar with the details and eccentricities of the system; problems and questions which arose during the design and implementation of MILAM were able to be resolved quickly rather than requiring extensive research and consultation.

The exercise described above helps provide an institution with the information that is needed to make an intelligent decision regarding computerization. Ginger Geyer, now Assistant Curator/Special Projects at the DMFA states: "We thought we had a thorough knowledge of our manual system before we did the analysis but we were wrong. We had no idea that certain numbering schemes existed, that so many odd files had been created, or that the way the data were recorded varied so widely in quality and consistency. Especially startling was discovering the degree of duplication of effort which existed in preparing documentation materials and reports. The detailed knowledge of the system that this analysis imparts is absolutely essential when designing a computerized system." By having to examine the existing manual system in detail in order to perform the exercises, problems that might otherwise undermine a project's success may be anticipated and eliminated.

III MEXICO

Chapter 11

The National Museum of Anthropology, Mexico

Noemi Castillo-Tejero

Introduction

The National Museum of Anthropology is charged with conserving, researching, exhibiting and controlling all the archaeological materials obtained from the archaeological excavations made by national or foreign institutions. It is the most important museum in the country, not only because of the nature of its exhibition materials, but also because of the size of its collections. Those in the archaeological field have more than one hundred thousand items, and the ethnographical collection contains more than 15 000 specimens, with a constant increase in both areas.

The Museum has a history stretching back over one hundred and fifty years. It originated as the Conservatory of Humanities, founded in 1826 by the new government of the Mexican Republic. Later this was transformed into the National Museum of Archaeology and Ethnology, with the purpose of giving a legal framework to the protection of the antiquities of the nation, before and after the Spanish conquest.

The Ministry of Public Instruction and Fine Arts was founded in 1907 with the purpose of protecting the cultural heritage. With the triumph of the Mexican revolution in 1921, the government transferred the old institution to the Secretary of Public Education and named the old Museum as the National Museum of History, Archaeology and Colonial Art. Later on it was separated, based on its collections, into two institutions: The National Museum of History and The National Museum of Anthropology.

The need to protect the cultural heritage and prepare the specialists who would form the group of researchers in this field, led to the establishment in 1938 of the National Institute of Anthropology and History (INAH) and The National Institute of Fine Arts (INBA). INAH is charged to take care of, protect and direct research in the anthropological field, and preserve the cultural property from the moment that man arrived in Mexican territory to the beginning of the Mexican Revolution in 1910. INBA takes care of cultural property in the field of fine arts from 1910 to the present.

Mexican governments through time have been worried about the protection of these items and for this reason many laws have been issued. At present the federal law which rules this matter is one of the most advanced in this field in the whole world. To protect the cultural heritage from illicit traffic of archaeological and historical property, Mexico has several international treaties with different countries, including the United States of America.

The 1972 Federal Law on Archaeological, Historical and Artistic Monuments and Zones declared that all remains of the prehispanic civilizations are national property. Since 1972 private collections cannot be added to and the responsibility of controlling these materials belongs to the INAH.

There are some private museums but the most important in the field of archaeology and history belong to the government. Their administrative organization and research policies are fixed by INAH to which belong the National Museum of Anthropology, National Museum of Viceroyalty (Colonial Period), National Museum of History (Independence Period), and regional museums, local museums, archaeological or historical site museums, etc.

When INAH creates regional museums many of the archaeological materials deposited in the National Museum of Anthropology are transferred to them; and they must follow the same cataloguing system established by the National Museum for the control of cultural materials.

Electronic Machines Section

In order to control these materials while the new building of the Museum was being constructed in 1961, the authorities of INAH and the Museum itself decided on the necessity of a modern system of data retrieval. Thus in 1962 a new office was created with the name 'Sección de Máquinas Electrónicas', to work on the control of all the archaeological materials that existed in the Museum (Castillo-Tejero, 1978). This section should establish a system of cataloguing with standards to allow retrieval of information for administrative purposes and research work based on the data bank. The staff of the Electronic Machines Section comprises eight archaeologists, one historian, one musicologist, one programmer and the administrative staff.

The objectives of this department were planned for both the short- and the long-term. In the short-term they were to review the information contained in the old catalogues in order to understand the system used in the past, with the purpose of standardizing the information and making possible the use of mechanized systems for the retrieval of data. Two years later it was decided to review all information available in order to standardize descriptions of the items, on the basis of the words used in old catalogues. They classified the information and created vocabularies to be used in cataloguing to avoid personal interpretation and to get more systematic information.

The first years were quite hard, not because of the work itself, but due to the cataloguing staff of the museum refusing to accept the new system. This situation changed when young people started to work with us. In order to get systematic information for cataloguing we produced our first vocabularies in 1964 (Litvak, Castillo-Tejero and Thomas, 1964; Olive and López Rivas, 1964) as well as a new catalogue card, even though the archaeologist that worked on this job criticised this new format. For this reason, the research staff of the Department of Electronic Machines revised the former vocabulary, producing a new one (Castillo-Tejero, Garza and Piña Chán, 1972).

This is easy to use, because it is an open dictionary that contains the words for the description of archaeological items. To facilitate its use, each word is preceded by the key code employed in our mechanized system (Figure 11.1). This uses an alphanumerical combination of three digits, which gives a large number of possibilities, which was in accordance with the systems that we had. For example if an object is a *vessel* the key code for computer processing is ACH. This work is carried out by cataloguing staff in a single operation, resulting in a saving of time.

```
4.7.-*Materia Prima.-
    AAK   Algodón
    KCT   Amatista
    JYE   Ambar
    BCU   Andesita
    AA3   Arcilla, barro
    J7S   Asta
    KDQ   Azabache
    B77   Basalto
    DÑA   Caliza   (para lo que comunmente se llama
                    alabastro, tecali, mármol, etc.
                    hasta obtener su análisis petro-
                    gráfico)
    A8W   Calabaza   (jícara, bule, etc.)
    A2H   Carrizo
    BNM   Cinabrio
    AKU   Cobre
    AC8   Concha
    B8V   Copal
    APY   Coral
    JYF   Corteza
    AÑY   Cristal de roca, cuarzo
    A8C   Cuero
    AYO   Espinas vegetales (no de pescado)
    JYG   Estano
```

Figure 11.1 The Dictionary listing, showing the codes for materials

This information was filed on punched cards to add to our data bank. At the same time, we prepared a new catalogue card, because we were in the process of changing from the traditional system of cataloguing to a computerized one. In order to relate the two systems together, we designed and printed three basic layouts. The front of each is exactly the same, and contains the general information for administrative purposes: catalogue number, acquisition details, location in the museum, inventory number, type of object, material, culture, region, site and chronology. The differences on the back of the cards are related to the type of object to be described. Thus one of these layouts is mainly used for vessels, seals, etc. (Figure 11.2), another is used in sculpture and figurines, and the third for ornaments.

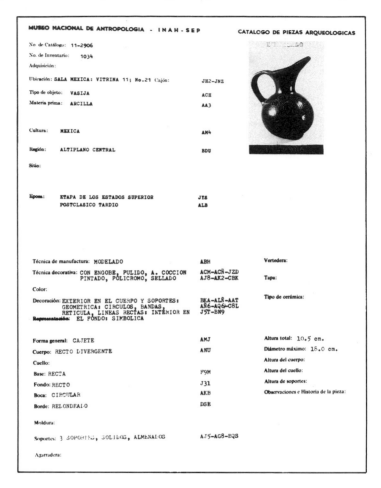

Figure 11.2 An example of the basic record media, used mainly for vessels

Each category of information is preceded by a code for the computer. There is a photograph of the object on the right side. The information contained on the back of the catalogue card is as technical as possible, and for this reason should be prepared by an archaeologist.

Working system

When new material arrives it is received in the reception room, located at the entrance of the store room. Here it receives an accession number, formed by the last two digits of the year and a running number: for example, 82/30 means that it is the 30th item that was entered in 1982. The information written in the accession book is: accession number, type of object, material, culture, chronology if possible, donor, catalogue number and inventory number. By Federal decree we must use two control numbers for our material: an inventory number which is given by a federal office, which controls all national property; and a catalogue number that the museum gives for its own control.

The description of the item is typed on a printed catalogue card, in duplicate. One of these cards is kept in the store room, the other in the central office of the Department of Archaeology, from where the information is passed to the Department of Electronic Machines to be processed for the data bank. Originally data were entered on punched cards; now they are entered on to disk.

The new acquisition of archaeological objects is governed by the Federal Law of 1972 which says that all archaeological items are national property. Thus we obtain new material if it is the product of any archaeological excavations carried out by INAH, or any other institutions with permission to do so. Alternatively a private person may return an item to the nation, or the police may forward an item, after prosecution of the illicit traffic in this material. We do not purchase archaeological objects, although we can purchase ethnographical ones.

By the same law all private collections of archaeological items should be registered at the office of the Public Register of Monuments and Archaeological Zones. Similarly, all archaeological items in Mexican Museums should be registered with the same office. The Department of Electronic Machines of the National Museum of Anthropology, in order to keep this information up to date, has prepared another card and a new edition of the dictionary (Castillo-Tejero and Flores García, 1975). This is a basic card, designed to be used by the Departments which deal with the control of cultural property, such as the Department of Inventory and the Department of the Public Registrar of Monuments and Archaeological Zones. It is specially designed for small museums whose staff are not research people (Figure 11.3).

The dictionaries are used to ensure that the cards, which are generally prepared by middle-level record and inventory staff, are properly filled in, and that the information they contain continues to be as systematic as that of the Museum of Anthropology catalogue. The cards are used not only for archaeological materials but also for historical objects. For the latter we have prepared a dictionary for historical objects in different museums (Goméz de Mendez, 1975).

The equipment

When we started the job of mechanizing the information on the catalogue cards of the museum in 1964, we saw the necessity to create vocabularies to keep the information easy to code. It was also necessary to establish a new type of catalogue card, that was capable of containing systematic information in order to facilitate codifying and transcribing it on to punch cards. At the beginning we did not have a computer, but peripheral equipment, that consisted of a punched card machine, and a tabulator used as a printer, all from the Bull Company.

The 'classificator machine type D.3D' had an special device that allowed

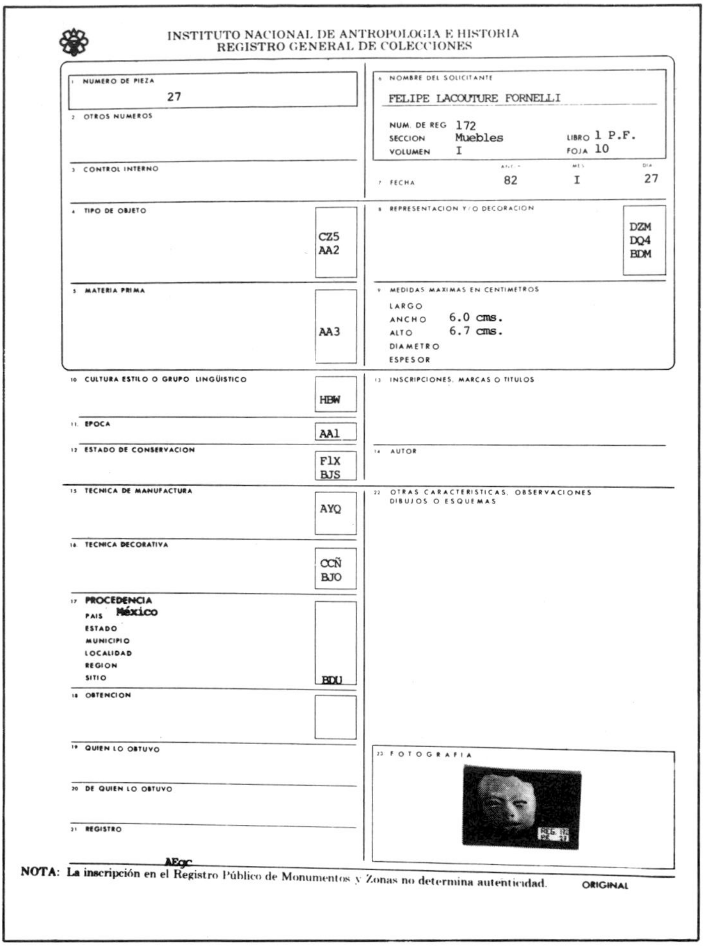

INSTITUTO NACIONAL DE ANTROPOLOGIA E HISTORIA
REGISTRO GENERAL DE COLECCIONES

1 NUMERO DE PIEZA 27

2 OTROS NUMEROS

3 CONTROL INTERNO

4 TIPO DE OBJETO CZ5 AA2

5 MATERIA PRIMA AA3

6 NOMBRE DEL SOLICITANTE FELIPE LACOUTURE FORNELLI

NUM. DE REG 172
SECCION Muebles
VOLUMEN I
LIBRO 1 P.F.
FOJA 10

7 FECHA 82 I 27

8 REPRESENTACION Y/O DECORACION DZM DQ4 BDM

9 MEDIDAS MAXIMAS EN CENTIMETROS
LARGO
ANCHO 6.0 cms.
ALTO 6.7 cms.
DIAMETRO
ESPESOR

10 CULTURA ESTILO O GRUPO LINGÜISTICO HBW

11 EPOCA AA1

12 ESTADO DE CONSERVACION FlX BJS

13 INSCRIPCIONES, MARCAS O TITULOS

14 AUTOR

15 TECNICA DE MANUFACTURA AYQ

16 TECNICA DECORATIVA CCÑ BJO

17 PROCEDENCIA
PAIS México
ESTADO
MUNICIPIO
LOCALIDAD
REGION
SITIO BDU

18 OBTENCION

19 QUIEN LO OBTUVO

20 DE QUIEN LO OBTUVO

21 REGISTRO AEgc

22 OTRAS CARACTERISTICAS, OBSERVACIONES DIBUJOS O ESQUEMAS

23 FOTOGRAFIA

NOTA: La inscripción en el Registro Público de Monumentos y Zonas no determina autenticidad. ORIGINAL

Figure 11.3 An example of the inventory card, used by small museums

information in any part of the punched cards to be retrieved using a key code of three digits. This permitted us to solve many problems in the selection of information. For each standard catalogue card we used two punched cards. As a result, our set of punched cards increased so much from 1964 to 1978 that it was necessary to transform our system and equipment by getting a computer.

For administrative reasons this acquisition could not be as soon as we hoped, and our work was stopped for some time. However in 1981 the 'Friends of the National Museum Association' gave us a minicomputer, a Honeywell Level 6 GCOS Mod. 33, that can operate on a stand-alone basis or as a multi-functional intelligent terminal in a communications network. It has a megabus to which all the elements of the unit are connected: central processor, memory controller, multi-line communications processor, multiple device controller, and disk controller. All these components transfer data through the megabus, which, being an asynchronous device, allows the elements to operate efficiently at different speeds. We have 128K words of memory, a printer, video screens, a reader for punched cards, and a card punch.

This system supports several programming languages. We selected for our purpose, which is mainly research, FORTRAN and BASIC II. The cost of our system can only be given in terms of our annual payment to Honeywell Co., for maintenance and rental of the software, which is $20 400 U.S. The rest of the expenses, from the moment that a new item arrives in the museum to the moment when all the information is included in the data bank, are included in the general expenses of the museum.

We expect to be working full time with this system by 1984, and hope next year to be able to give an initial service to archaeology researchers.

Conclusions

I think it is important to comment that even though many people participate in this process (administrative staff, photographers, researchers, and so on) this is just a small part of their job in the museum.

Up to now we have produced more than 25 research papers on archaeology using our data bank and some books. For the time being we are planning to continue in this direction, especially with our series named *Antropologia Matematica*.

We are proud of our work, which has gone as we planned in the beginning. Now we are moving towards our second goal, which is to store our data bank on computer disc and establish a network for the archaeologist, as well as providing administrative control of the archaeological material considered as national property.

IV   UNITED KINGDOM

Chapter 12

The cooperative development of documentation in United Kingdom museums

D. Andrew Roberts and Richard B. Light

Introduction

There has been a dramatic change in recent years in the attitude of United Kingdom museums to the importance of the documentation of their collections. This chapter describes some of the main historical influences that have led to this change and the resulting development of documentation facilities on a cooperative basis and within individual museums. To place these events in context, it begins with an outline of relevant aspects of the museum community.

The museum community

Estimates of the number of museums in the United Kingdom range up to 2000. The *Museums Yearbook* (Museums Association, 1982) includes details of 1325 separate museums, administered by approximately 750 institutions. Many of these museums can trace their history back 100 years or more, during which they have accumulated large collections.

The national museums are funded by various central government departments in England, Wales, Scotland and Northern Ireland. Most are now administered by boards of trustees, as a result of which they have a considerable degree of independence from their funding agencies.

Non-national museums are supported by local councils (either regional, county or district councils), academic or private organizations, according to local initiatives and requirements. The majority may be categorised as local authority, university, regimental or private institutions. During a reorganization of the structure of local government in 1974 there was a tendency to draw together previously independent local authority museums into new institutions with a single management structure.

An important factor influencing the recent development of the non-national museums has been the formation of the Area Museum Councils

(AMCs). The nine Councils (seven in England, one in Wales and one in Scotland) receive central government grants which are used to provide assistance to their member museums, such as conservation and design facilities, travelling exhibitions and financial aid for new projects.

Support for the seven English Councils is channelled through the Museums and Galleries Commission. The functions of this independent body — established in 1930 as the Standing Commission on Museums and Galleries — include advising the government on the most effective development of museums and promoting cooperation between museums. The Commission is funded by the Office of Arts and Libraries (OAL), the English government department with primary national responsibility for museums. The OAL, although now independent, was formerly a branch of the Department of Education and Science (DES).

The work of these cooperative and advisory bodies is complemented by that of the main professional organization, the Museums Association (Museums Association, 1982). During the last decade, there has also been a growth of specialist curatorial groups, such as the Geological Curators' Group and the Museum Ethnographers' Group.

Documentation developments prior to the 1960s

In the years after their foundation, most of these museums introduced some form of documentation system. The typical approach prior to the 1960s was to maintain a bound register, within which were noted basic details of each acquired group of objects. The records initiated during these years are often still the primary source of information about a collection.

Some of the problems which have been inherited by present-day museums are illustrated by the British Museum, which began to compile records of its acquisitions in 1756 (see Chapter 13). From that date, details of donations were inscribed in bound ledgers known as *The Book of Presents*. Although these early records provide some information, there is often insufficient evidence to link them to specific items in the collections. In 1836, the Department of Antiquities began to complete bound Acquisition Registers (including details of both donations and purchases) of a type still in use today. In addition to these registers, which form the basic inventory of the collections, other sources exist. The most significant of these are scholarly catalogues which have been compiled for specific parts of the collections. Standard practice is for a departmental copy of these catalogues to be annotated to reflect subsequent changes of information (Great Britain. Parliament. House of Commons. Committee of Public Accounts, 1981).

The importance of inventory records in the control and stocktaking of collections in national museums was formalized as early as 1888, when the Treasury issued a Minute concerning the need for a regular 'store audit'. Although of independent trustee status, national museums have to demonstrate accountability for their collections to government and parliamentary authorities. The basic requirements include the maintenance of a formal inventory and a regular programme to check the location of items. The implementation of these procedures is monitored by the Comptroller and Auditor General (the C & AG) who undertakes a periodic audit, after which a report is presented to Parliament, the implications of which are considered by the Public Accounts Committee (PAC).

During the last 70 years, the C & AG and the PAC have undertaken a series of investigations of national museum inventory control and stocktaking procedures. As a result of the first investigations (1912-1915), a committee proposed a new system of inventory records and stocktaking procedures and consideration was given to arrangements for compiling and checking a catalogue of the nation's possessions. Unfortunately, with the outbreak of war much of the impetus was lost. Although a subsequent investigation in 1952-1954 again examined inventory control problems, the plan for a catalogue of collections in the national museums was never implemented.

The idea of a cooperative catalogue of collections in non-national museums was foremost in the minds of the instigators of the Museums Association (Platnauer and Howarth, 1890). Papers circulated in 1888 referred to its primary aims as including the preparation of 'a compendious index of the contents of all provincial Museums and Collections'. The minutes of the meeting in 1889 at which the Association was established, noted the 'indexing of the general contents of Museums' as one of its primary interests.

In subsequent decades, the reports and journal of the Association included a series of papers concerning national catalogues and proposals for documentation systems (such as Hoyle, 1891; Lowe, 1903; Williams, 1919; Codrington, 1931; Hiley and Wallis, 1936; Grassl, 1936; Atkinson, 1955). In one of the last important contributions before the impact of semi-mechanized and mechanized systems, D.E. Owen stressed the role of both initial registration for collections control purposes and subsequent cataloguing for curatorial purposes (Allan, Owen and Wallis, 1960).

Documentation developments: 1960-1976

By the early 1960s, a number of museums were becoming increasingly concerned about the need to gain access to the information held in numerically-ordered registers and catalogues. This concern was focused by a paper about indexing methods (Lewis, 1965) and individual experiments with semi-mechanized and mechanized systems in major museums (such as Brailsford, 1967; Chaldecott, 1967; Forbes, Harland and Cutbill, 1971; Hislop, 1967; Roads, 1968).

Most initial interest came from curators of natural science collections. After a meeting held at the University of Leicester in May 1966, it was agreed to set up an informal committee (the 'Leicester Group') to press for the establishment of a national data processing centre for systematics collections. In parallel with this, Sheffield City Museum and the Museums Association convened a colloquium in April 1967, to discuss the problems involved in information retrieval from museum collections (Lewis, 1967). As a result of the Sheffield colloquium, the Museums Association agreed to establish a steering committee and two working parties to examine topics such as the preparation of data standards, problems of terminology and classification and the interdisciplinary nature of museum records. The Leicester Group was subsequently disbanded, after its members expressed a willingness to work within the Museums Association framework. The resulting committee became known as the Information Retrieval Group of the Museums Association (IRGMA) (Museums Association. Information Retrieval Group. Standards Subcommittee, 1977; Roberts, in press (b); Roberts and Light, 1980).

Although the aim of a national index was a primary influence at the Sheffield meeting, there was a clear appreciation that the first concern of IRGMA should be to develop viable documentation systems for individual museums. It was decided to design a comprehensive range of record cards, based on a set of common principles. The group initiated a project to examine the form and content of a museum record, identifying the different data categories that made up a record, and the way in which these categories were logically related (Museums Association. Information Retrieval Group, 1969; Cutbill, Hallan and Lewis, 1971; Lewis, 1971). This theoretical work on data standards provided the background for subsequent developments of manual- and computer-based systems.

The effort of the voluntary group and its working parties was complemented by a number of research projects. One grant from the DES enabled the group to undertake a survey of United Kingdom museums, based on a proposal drawn up in 1974 (Roberts, 1974; 1975). Although never published, the survey did highlight the poor state of documentation, the willingness of many museums to improve this state and a significant interest in the adoption of new systems. A grant from the Office for Scientific and Technical Information (OSTI) enabled IRGMA to undertake an early test of its theoretical proposals by arranging for the preparation of detailed records about electrostatic instruments in museums, using recording sheets based on the data standards (Hackmann, 1973). A series of grants from OSTI and its successor, the British Library Research and Development Department, supported a major system development team, based at the Sedgwick Museum Cambridge (Cutbill, 1971b; Porter, Light and Roberts, 1976).

With the help of the research team at the Sedgwick Museum, the early experiments were followed by the design of a range of draft record cards. These drafts were distributed to 100 museums for practical evaluation, with completed examples being returned to Cambridge for computerization. Eight finalized cards and associated instructions were published by the Museums Association in January 1976 (Roberts, 1976). (All eight designs are still widely used by museums, as illustrated in Figures 19.1, 20.4 and 21.1.) By the end of that year, approximately 300 000 cards had been purchased by 80 museums and a national programme of seminars and training courses had been undertaken to coordinate their use.

One of the factors encouraging the adoption of the new system by non-national museums was the support of the AMCs. In addition to helping arrange the training programme, the Councils provided financial assistance to museums to purchase the record cards and instruction books. From the outset, the directors of the Councils were active in promoting the use of the system, particularly in museums with only rudimentary documentation procedures.

Another important factor was the local authority reorganization of 1974 which had resulted in the establishment of a number of new museum authorities. At the time of reorganization, comments in an influential report

— the Wright Report — and a DES circular advising on the role of museums, drew the attention of the new institutions to the importance of documentation (Great Britain. Department of Education and Science, 1973a; 1973b). New authorities such as Tyne and Wear County Museum Service (Chapter 20) began to show an active concern for the implementation of a common documentation system for the museums in their care.

Both the Wright Report and the DES circular stressed the potential role of computers for documentation purposes. The report referred to the work of IRGMA in this area, and recommended that funds be made available to continue with the Cambridge research project. The subsequent grant to the Sedgwick Museum included support for the completion of a prototype computer package, termed the Cambridge Geological Data System (CGDS), and its application during the processing of the records concerning the 440 000 specimens in the Museum and the tests of the draft IRGMA record cards. Although the prototype was acquired and used by the British Museum (Natural History) (Brunton, 1979; 1980), it was not felt to be appropriate for general distribution. The research grant also included provision for the preparation of a specification of a successor package which would be suitable for widespread use.

As the research work would take some years to complete, some museums decided to take immediate independent action to gain access to appropriate computer systems. For example, during this period the Imperial War Museum began to develop the APPARAT system (Chapter 14), while in Brighton the council's computer centre produced a local system for use by the city Art Gallery and Museum (Chapter 16).

In museums such as Brighton, Bristol (Chapter 17), Leicester (Chapter 18) and St Albans (Chapter 19) a reason for improving the standard of documentation and considering the adoption of a computer-based system was the urgent need to undertake proper care of the collections. With their increasing size, staffing and public responsibility, non-national museums were becoming more aware of the need to have efficient internal collections management procedures and to be able to demonstrate accountability to outside auditors.

The long-established accountability pressure on national museums was reinforced in 1968 when the C & AG investigated the adequacy of arrangements at the British Museum and the Victoria and Albert Museum. As a result of these investigations, a DES management services team reviewed the position in a number of national museums. It recommended the introduction of major stockchecking programmes based on departmental and central inventories. As the proposals were not acceptable, the DES decided to depart from a simple approach common to all national museums and to instead establish a series of more flexible management objectives: routines for the registration and location of every significant item in a museum; the adoption of a practicable routine for stock checking the presence of items; a long-term programme for the scholarly description and cataloguing of collections; periodic reviews to ensure that collections were effectively organized.

The Museum Documentation Association

By 1977, the cooperative research work on the analysis of museum records and computer system design had reached a critical stage. The AMCs and a number of the national museums agreed to form a new organization, the Museum Documentation Association (MDA), to ensure the continuity of the work (Museum Documentation Association. Development Committee, 1982; Porter, 1978; Roberts, in press (b); Roberts, Light and Stewart, 1980; Stewart, 1983). The Association established an advisory unit, based at Duxford Airfield, near Cambridge, and initially staffed by three research officers and a secretary from the Sedgwick Museum team.

The active involvement of the founding members has continued since 1977, with the Association now being supported by the nine AMCs and 19 national museums. The constituent museums of the AMCs are also considered to be associate members of the MDA, as a result of which the majority of United Kingdom museums can turn to the Association for assistance.

The Association is now funded from three sources which together provide an annual income of approximately £150 000: the members and the Museums and Galleries Commission contribute individual subscriptions, certain specialized projects are supported by specific research grants and charges are made for detailed advice, publications, computer systems and work by a computer bureau. Staff now include eight full-time and a number of part-time employees.

The primary system development programme of the Association has been the production of an integrated Museum Documentation System (the MDS) and a computer package (GOS), both of which are extensions of the IRGMA and Sedgwick Museum work (Light, 1979; Museum Documentation Association, 1980; 1981a; 1981b; 1981c; Neufeld, 1981; Porter, 1981; 1982).

The initial emphasis of these systems was on the curatorial aspects of documentation, particularly the preparation of item records as a basis for manual or computer-based catalogues and indexes. Attention has now been directed to the support of the existing systems and the development of control documentation facilities, with an emphasis on the exploitation of microcomputers (Light, 1982; Museum Documentation Association. Development Committee, 1982; Roberts, 1982).

The MDS facilities include a formal data standard, various recording forms, cards and registers (with associated instructions), computer applications and procedural manuals. These systems are used in departments in over 300 museums throughout the United Kingdom and overseas (see, for example Bamberry, 1982; Dawes, 1982; Hall, 1983; Locke and Pellatt, 1983; Seaborne and Neufeld, 1982; Stradling, 1983). (Practical applications of some of these facilities are illustrated in Chapters 14 and 19-21.)

The data standard incorporates a definition of the data categories that make up a museum record (Light and Roberts, 1981; Museum Documentation Association, 1980). The record can include various general divisions and groups of information, each of which can be omitted or repeated as necessary (Table 12.1). The groups are themselves made up of individual categories such as person, place, date and event. The standard has been used as the basis of both record cards and computer storage formats. In addition to the MDS products, it has also been used by individual institutions when designing local record cards and computer systems (Chapters 17, 18, 21 and 25).

The recording forms, cards and registers are designed to be used according to the requirements of individual museums. Although suitable for manual use, they are also compatible with the automated facilities provided by the system. The three-part *entry form* can be used to record basic information about each group of items deposited in the museum (Figure 12.1). If the group is subsequently acquired, a formal description of the change of ownership can be noted on a *transfer of title* form (Figure 12.2), and formal inventory details can be incorporated within a bound *register*. If any of the items within the group are sent out of the museum, the movement can be logged using an *exit form*. Detailed information about each of the component items in the group can be noted on a range of A5 and A4 *record cards and sheets* (Figure 12.3). These can then be used manually to form a catalogue of the collection which can be supported by one or more indexes, or as the basis for a computer file from which automated catalogues and indexes can be generated or selective retrieval requests fulfilled (Figures 12.4 and 12.5). Instruction books provide basic guidance on the use of these various record cards and forms.

A major use of GOS has been to support the computer systems developed as part of the MDS. These include facilities for inputting information from the full range of MDS cards and routines for producing checking documents, catalogues and indexes (see Chapters 14, 17, 19-21 and 25). GOS has also formed the nucleus of independent applications within individual museums (Chapters 13 and 15). In contrast to many online systems, the package is designed to maintain complex records as a basis for comprehensive printed outputs. It has now been implemented at a number of centres in the United Kingdom and West Germany, including university computing services, county councils, individual museums and the MDA itself. These implementations have been on various types of mainframe, mini- and microcomputers for use by museums and similar organizations.

One of the main users of GOS is the Association's computing bureau. This offers a data entry, processing and management facility which has now been used as part of the computerization plans of over 30 museums in the United Kingdom, West Germany, the Netherlands, and Zimbabwe (Chapters 14, 15, 17, 19-21 and 25). One approach is for the bureau to undertake data entry from sources such as MDS record cards and conventional registers. Alternatively, the museum may prefer to carry out its own data entry, then transfer records to the bureau in machine-readable form for processing and long-term maintenance. The latter approach is now being adopted by the majority of its users.

The advisory work of the Association includes the provision of training in the use of the MDS, seminars on aspects of documentation (such as computer applications and terminology control) and more general assistance to help museums assess the effectiveness of their documentation procedures. Staff from the MDA travel to museums throughout the United Kingdom as part of a regular programme of seminars and visits, many of which are

IDENTITY DIVISION

record managing institution
identity number

PART DIVISION

part name

identification group
  simple name
  full/classified name
    name
    nomenclature system
    type of name
    currency of name
    status of name
  title

pre-production history group
  cross-reference
  type of antecedent
  antecenent identity
  simple name
  full/classified name

production process group
  production statement
    part name
    production method
    person/corporate body
    date
    place
    coordinates
    state
    technical data
    result

field collection group
  locality statement
    cross-reference
    locality identity
    site
    place
    coordinates
    relative position
    vice-county
    habitat
    stratigraphy
    context
    locality type
  collection act statement
    find identity
    method of collection
    person/corporate body
    date

association history group
  association category/nature
  part name
  concept
  person/corporate body
  service
  date
  related item
    cross-reference
    object identity
    simple name
    full name
  document
  event
    cross-reference
    event identity
    simple name
    full name
  place
  coordinates

ownership history group
  type of ownership
  ownership identity
  method of transfer

transfer step
  person
  date
  place
  coordinates
  price
  grant-aid
  conditions

identity number history group
  institution
  identity number
  date

valuation history group
  value
  date

copyright history group
  type of rights
  person/corporate body
  date

storage history group
  location
  date

display history group
  type of display
  purpose of display
  corporate body
  title
  date
  catalogue identity
  conditions

form description group
  form statement
    part name
    aspect
      type of aspect
      description
      date
    conservation
      treatment
      material used
      date
    dimension
      measurement
      result
    inscription or mark
      type
      method
      position
      description
      transcription
      transliteration

interest description group
  simple category
  full/classified category
  interest summary
    part name
    summary
    interest identity
  interest analysis
    part name
    concept
      type of concept
      description
    person/corporate body
    date or period
    object
      cross-reference
      object identity
      simple name
      full/classified name
    document
    activity
    event
      cross-reference
      event identity

  simple name
  full name
locality identity
site
place
coordinates
locality type

process group
  type of process
  process identity
  process statement
    part name
    date received
    reason
      requested treatment
      person/corporate body
      date required
    method
    person/corporate body
    date started
    place
    state
    technical data
    result
      result identity
      simple name
      full name
    date completed
    recommendations
      further treatment
      recall date
      priority
      recommendations

part division

authority
  person/corporate body
  date
documentation

RECORD MANAGEMENT DIVISION

record production statement
  type of record
  method of data collection

record copying statement
  person/corporate body
  date

supplementary file statement
  file identity

computer record statement
  computer record identity

NOTES DIVISION

notes

AUTHORITY DIVISION
authority statement
  cross-reference
  authority identity
  person/corporate body
  date

DOCUMENTATION DIVISION
documentation statement
  cross-reference
  document identity
  reference
    historical reference
    class
    person/corporate body
    date
    title
    journal or publisher
    volume
    reference

Table 12.1 Outline of the MDS data standard

Sheet	Wickamstead Museum,	Institution: group number
of	The School House,	4
	Wickhampstead Green,	Director : F.M. Evans, AMA
	Northampton	
	0998 8512370	

OWNERSHIP

depositor: Mr. H. Middle   phone number: 4210

address: 24 Bridge Street, Kxning, Sussex

owner: as above   phone number: —

address: —

copyright holder: phone number:

address:

GROUP

summary description, identification and history of group

one commemoration mug of wedding of Prince Charles and Lady Diana Spencer; white china glazed with fleur-de-lys, portraits and lettering; bought by Mr Middle, summer of 1981 from W.H. Smith, Highgate, London; unused.

Mug stamped on base with 'Mile End Potteries, London'

ENTRY

method or reason	price	insurance valuation	return required?	agreed return date
gift	—	—	no	

note:

depositor: I agree that the information given on this form is correct and accept the conditions overleaf: signed: J. S. Middle   date: 24|10|1981

museum recipient: I acknowledge receipt of the group described above, on behalf of the museum: signed: J. L. C. Smith   date: 24 Oct 1981

ACTION

group passed to:	curator	temporary store	signed	date
	TRT(DA)	DA.2	P. R. Type	24|10|1981

note:

retained group:	accession number	store	signed	date
	1981.218	DA.2 : 4.3	J. Mackay Smith	1 Nov 1981

returned group. I acknowledge the return of the group described above, in satisfactory condition: signed: date:

ENTRY   © Museum Documentation Association 1981   September 1981   MDA 017
Published by the MDA, Duxford Airfield, Duxford, Cambridgeshire, U.K.

Figure 12.1(a) Completed entry form (front)

arranged in association with the AMCs. Seminars are also given during postgraduate training courses at centres such as the University of Leicester.

A number of the publications prepared by the Association concentrate on giving practical advice, particularly a detailed procedural manual (Museum Documentation Association, 1981b) and a widely-distributed quarterly newsletter, *MDA Information.* Staff also monitor new developments in

ENTRY FORM

For any group of items entering the museum, other than that previously temporarily removed from the permanent collection.

CONDITIONS OF ACCEPTANCE

General

Except in the case of negligence on the part of itself or its officers, the museum does not accept liability for loss of, or damage to, or deterioration in, the item(s) described overleaf. The same care and precautions will be taken for the safe custody of this deposit as for the safe custody of items within the museum's permanent collection.

It is the depositor's responsibility to collect the item(s) described overleaf by the agreed return date. In the event of the item(s) not being collected by the depositor, the museum reserves the right to dispose of the item(s) after they have been in its possession for not less than three months.

The top part of this form will be given to the depositor as a receipt for the item(s). This part must be presented to the museum when the collector comes to retrieve the item(s). Both this part and a museum part of the form will then be signed by the collector in recognition of their having received the item(s) back in satisfactory condition. The collector and the museum will then retain the respective parts of the form.

Enquiries

Neither the museum nor its officers can accept any responsibility for an opinion that may be expressed on items submitted for examination. Opinions may be given only to the owner of an item or to the representative of the owner.

An officer of the museum is not authorised to give valuations, to assist in the disposal of private property or to express opinions regarding the merits of business firms.

Acquisitions

In the case of an acquisition by the museum, the owner (or a depositor acting on behalf of the owner) transfers absolute ownership of the group specified overleaf to the museum, without conditions.

Loans

In the case of loans to the museum, it may be agreed that the museum will undertake to return the object by the return date. In this circumstance, a museum part of the form will be sent with the object. Both parts should be signed by the depositor: the first part to be retained by the depositor and the second part to be returned to the museum.

Special conditions

MDA 017

Figure 12.1(b) Completed entry form (reverse)

museums, libraries, information technology and computing systems. Significant publications are incorporated within a library, which now contains approximately 5000 items. References to this collection are being computerized as the basis for a bibliography of museum documentation, in association with specialists working in related areas (for example, Sharpe, 1983).

Sheet of	Wichamstead Museum, The School House, Wickhampstead Green, Northampton 0998 8512370		Institution: transfer of title number 97 Director : F.M. Evans, AMA	
ACQUISITION	The museum gratefully acknowledges the acquisition into the collection of the items described below, from:			
	Mrs R.S. Meadows, Hazelldell, Walton-at-Stone, Ware, Hertfordshire			
	These items have been acquired by: _gift_		date 3 Feb 1982	
GROUP	group number	accession number		
	31	1982.11	contents of chemist's shop	
	identity number	brief description		
	1982.11.1=13	apothecary jars [with original labels]		
	1982.11.14	mortar		
	1982.11.15	pestle		
	1982.11.16	work bench		
	1981.11.17=20	ledger account books		
	1982.11.21	patent pill making machine		
	1982.11.22=30	pill boxes		
	1982.11.31	box of assorted labels		
TRANSFER	In order to complete the transfer of title from you to the museum, we would be grateful if you could read the relevant notes overleaf and then sign this form. Please retain the first part of the form for your files and return the second part to the museum.			
	Museum officer: _Richard T. Ford_		date: _3 Feb 1982_	
	Depositor: _Mrs R.S. Meadows_		date: _3/3/1982_	
	We recommend that you keep the first part of this form in a secure place. It would help the museum if it could be produced in the event of any query concerning the acquisition or the items.			
	TRANSFER OF TITLE	© Museum Documentation Association 1981 September 1981 MDA 019 Published by the MDA, Duxford Airfield, Duxford, Cambridgeshire, U.K.		

Figure 12.2(a) Completed transfer of title form (front)

Museum developments since 1976

Interest in the use of automated systems grew during the late 1970s as appropriate facilities became more generally available. By the end of 1982, there were approximately 40 United Kingdom museums using computers for

TRANSFER OF TITLE

For items being acquired by the museum.

NOTES

The owner (or a depositor acting on behalf of the owner) transfers ownership of the item(s) specified overleaf to the museum, without conditions.

If the item(s) have been *donated*, the depositor confirms that they are given to the museum as an absolute and perpetual gift.

If the item(s) have been *purchased*, the depositor confirms that he or she was the absolute owner of the item(s) or had full power to sell the item(s), prior to the purchase.

If the item(s) are a *bequest*, the depositor confirms that their acquisition by the museum was at the wish of the deceased, and encloses a copy or extract of the relevant will and probate act.

MDA 019

Figure 12.2(b) Completed transfer of title form (reverse)

documentation purposes, either independently or through the MDA (Roberts, in press (a)).

Some of the major computer users are university and local authority museums with access to large computing centres supported by their parent organization (Chapters 16, 18 and 22) (Davis and Hebron, 1982; Etchells-Butler, 1982; Kirk, 1979; Pettitt, 1981a; Porter, 1982; Turner and

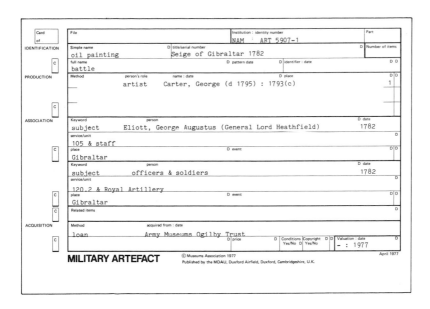

Figure 12.3 Completed manual record card (a) front (b) reverse

Robson, 1979). A number of national and local authority museums have also acquired in-house mini- or microcomputer-based systems (Chapters 13-15, 17, 18, 20 and 21) (Abell Seddon, 1982; Brunton, 1979; 1980; Fraser, 1982; Mollo, 1982; Smither, 1979; Will, 1982).

There is considerable interest in the use of microcomputers for documentation work (Light, 1982; 1983; Light and Roberts, 1984). One

```
** NAM: ART 5907-1

oil painting, "Seige of Gibraltar 1782", battle.

production: artist: Carter, George (d 1795), 1793 (c). ref: 1.

materials: oil on canvas; frame: gilt wood.

dimensions: canvas           151 x 258 cm
            frame            171 x 278 cm

bottom LH (description of scene).

association: subject, Eliott, George Augustus (General Lord
    Heathfield), 1782. Service: 105 - staff, Gibraltar.
association: subject, officers - soldiers, 1782. Service:
    120.2 - Royal Artillery, Gibraltar.
association: campaign, 1779-1783. 468.2 - Gibraltar. Event:
    Siege of Gibraltar.

acquisition: loan from Army Museums Ogilby Trust.

valuation: ...., 1977.

store: ...., 1978.

reproduction: photo (7686-7688).

recorder: BM - JS, 1978.

documentation: (1) Benezit.
```

Figure 12.4 Computer-generated catalogue entry

aspect of this interest is the application of microcomputers for the local data entry of control and catalogue records, with the accumulated information then being transferred to a larger machine (either within the museum or at an outside agency such as the MDA) for subsequent processing. The MDA is involved in a research programme to develop data entry systems compatible with the current range of record cards.

A second aspect is the use of larger microcomputers for the processing work. Most of the processing requirements of the MDA are now fulfilled by an in-house microcomputer, using GOS and the MDS applications packages. The Association also intends to develop these facilities to the state where both control documentation and cataloguing systems are available for independent use in museums.

The introduction of automated facilities has often been part of a major retrospective inventorying or recataloguing programme. The scale of these programmes, particularly in some university and local authority museums, has had a marked impact on the standard of documentation and the resulting ability of the museums concerned to utilize their collections (Chapters 13

```
CROIX, G. F. DE LA (born in Paris, died 1779)
Santa Maria Maggiore, Rome
   architecture, landscape, Rome,
      Santa Maria Maggiore        PD.38-1964   black and white
                                               chalk

DALOU, AIME JULES (1838-1902)
Studies for 'The Reading Lesson'
   reading Lesson                 PD.13-1979 pencil

Study for 'La Boulonnaise'        PD.14-1979   pencil and brown
                                               ink

D'ANVILLE, HUBERT FRANCOIS BOURGNIGNON,
   CALLED GRAVELOP (Paris 1699-1773)
Group of figures
   figures, female (six), male
      (three), dog, cow           PD.15-1970   pen and brown
                                               ink

DAUBIGNY, CHARLES-FRANCOIS (Paris 1817-1878)
View of Subiaco
   landscape, Subiaco (walled hill-town)
                                  PD.20-1978   pencil

DAUMIER, HONORE (Marseille 1808-1879 Valmondois)
Le Rieur
   figure, male (half length, laughing)
                                  PD.16-1951   grey wash

DAVID, JACQUES LOUIS (Paris 1748-1825 Brussels)
An Academy Study of a Male nude
   nude, male                     PD.970-1963 black chalk

DEGAS, HILAIRE-GERMAIN-EDGAR (1834-1917)
Danseuses aux jupes violettes, bras leves
   dancers                        PD.2-1979    pastels
```

Figure 12.5 Computer-generated index entry

and 15-21) (Burnett and Wright, 1982; MacKie, 1980; Orna and Pettitt, 1980; Pettitt, 1981a; Pole, 1983; Roberts, in press (a); Smith, 1983; Thornton, 1983).

Many of the projects in non-national museums have depended upon allocations of resources from government-funded job creation schemes administered by the Manpower Services Commission (Chapters 17, 18, 20 and 21). These have resulted in a major influx of temporary documentation staff — usually school-leavers or university graduates — to assist overstretched permanent curators.

The initiative for the reprocessing work has sometimes come from an external audit report, the effect of which can be a decisive factor in persuading a museum committee to invest resources in documentation. In the case of the national museums, the C & AG and the PAC again investigated the standard of inventory control in 1981, as a result of which they reiterated their views on the importance of inventory records and stocktaking programmes.

As museums involved in reprocessing work have come to appreciate the magnitude of the problems which they face, there has been a perceptible change of emphasis away from comprehensive recataloguing projects towards rapid retrospective inventorying and longer-term selective recataloguing. The key importance of effective control over collections is being recognized by a growing number of institutions.

More awareness is also being shown of the need for careful planning of changes to documentation systems (Museum Documentation Association, 1981b; Orna, 1982; Orna and Pettitt, 1980; Roberts, in press (a)). In recognition of this, a number of museums have recently appointed documentation officers who undertake work such as system development, maintenance of data standards, adoption of terminology control standards, training, introduction and support of automated systems and liaison with advisors in their parent bodies and outside authorities. (The varying roles of some of these officers are illustrated in subsequent chapters.) In most cases, the appointment of professional documentation staff has been a new development.

One common function of these staff is the preparation of procedural manuals defining the conventions to be adopted when recording information about the collections. The MDS instruction books referred to earlier often act as a starting point, the proposals within which are then extended to fulfil the requirements of the particular museum. One of the most significant recent developments has been the preparation of a classification scheme for social history collections, practical use of which has begun in a number of museums (Group for Regional Studies in Museums, 1983; Holm, 1982; Seaborne and Neufeld, 1982).

Reference was made earlier to the magnitude of the physical collections in United Kingdom museums. One problem in documenting these collections is their great diversity. They include many different types of object and also other areas such as bibliographic, archive and audio-visual material. In recent years, documentation staff have been active in developing procedures to process the full range of material they hold (see, for example, Chapters 14 and 15).

In the case of natural science material, curators throughout the country have united to prepare cooperative catalogues of collections in both museums and private hands (Pettitt and Hancock, 1981) and are planning to produce a national register of type specimens (Chapter 22). The grandiose ideas of all-embracing national catalogues have been replaced by viable schemes for specific publications which are genuinely needed by the museum community.

Natural scientists and archaeologists in museums have been active in developing regional locality record centres, with details of sites of scientific interest within a specific geographical area (Cooper et al, 1980; Flood and Perring, 1978; Stewart, 1980a; 1980b). The MDA development programme has included the preparation of locality record cards and a computer applications package, as part of the overall MDS (Figure 12.6).

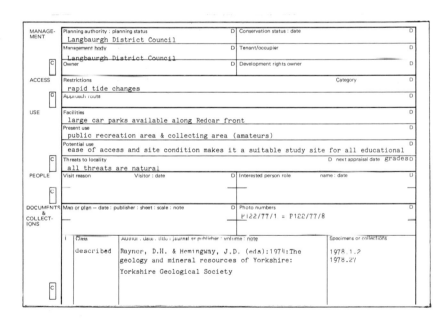

Card of	File			Institution	
	Cleveland/Langbaurgh/Redcar Rocks			ABCDE	
	Filing number			Locality number 62/122	Part

IDENTIFI-CATION

Locality name D
Redcar Rocks

Parish	district	county	region	D
Redcar	Langbaurgh	Cleveland		

Other geopolitical division — D | Status : date — D | Vice-county D

NGR NZ 614253 — accuracy centred — D | Map number — D | Altitude D

Field recorder : date — D | Field recorder : date — D
Lapsley, J.B.:19.8.1977

C Museum recorder : date — D | Record type : method — D
Picottini, L.:1.2.1978 — primary:fieldwork

DESCRIP-TION

Type of locality — D | Condition of locality : date — D
foreshore rock platform (below HWM) — variable with tides:19.8.1977

| Shape | length 1100m | width 550m | height — | depth — | area — | D |

General description of locality
Near continuous exposure of S. angulata & A. bucklandii zones of the Lower Lias.
Sequence of grey calcereous mudstones & shales with some thin impure limestones. D

Part : interest : description of interest — cross-reference D
C :palaeontology:type:ammonites & gastropods & bivalves & bryozoans
:mineralogy:calcite (veining) & rugs (calcite filled) & fossils (pyritised)
:stratigraphic:Jurassic, Lower & Lias, Lower & angulatum zone & bucklandii zone

PRODUCT-ION Method — person's role — name : date — D

LOCALITY
A5 MUSEUM SUMMARY

© Museums Association, 1977 — First edition, June 1977
Published by the MDAU, Duxford Airfield, Duxford, Cambridgeshire, U.K.

MANAGE-MENT

Planning authority : planning status — D | Conservation status : date — D
Langbaurgh District Council

Management body — D | Tenant/occupier — D
Langbaurgh District Council
C Owner — D | Development rights owner — D

ACCESS Restrictions — Category — D
rapid tide changes
C Approach route — D

USE Facilities — D
large car parks available along Redcar front

Present use — D
public recreation area & collecting area (amateurs)

Potential use — D
ease of access and site condition makes it a suitable study site for all educational

C Threats to locality — D next appraisal date grades D
all threats are natural

PEOPLE Visit reason — Visitor : date — D | Interested person role — name : date — D
C

DOCUMENTS & COLLECT-IONS Map or plan — date : publisher : sheet : scale : note — D | Photo numbers — D
P122/77/1 = P122/77/8

	Class	Author : date : title : journal or publisher : volume : note	Specimens or collections
	described	Rayner, D.H. & Hemingway, J.D. (eds):1974:The geology and mineral resources of Yorkshire: Yorkshire Geological Society	1978.1.2 1978.27

Figure 12.6 Completed locality record card

Museums are also curious about themselves. Relatively little information is available about all museums in a region or the whole country, despite the value of such information for planning purposes. Proposals for the establishment of a data base about museums may receive detailed consideration in future years (Norgate, 1982).

Future developments

Despite recent developments, many museums are only now beginning to recognize the magnitude of the documentation problems which they face (Museum Documentation Association. Development Committee, 1982; Roberts, in press (a)). The majority of museum collections are still inadequately documented, often having superficial control procedures and cursory and inconsistent item records, with catalogues and indexes of dubious coverage and accuracy.

As a result of a research project funded by the OAL, a recent report has offered guidance on preferred documentation procedures; methods of assessing a museum's current documentation practice and future requirements; the potential role of automation as an aid to documentation; the principles to follow when planning the revision of a system and the impact such a revision may have on the resources for documentation (Roberts, in press (a)). In stressing the importance of the detailed planning of system change, the report reflects the growing attitude that an effective documentation system is fundamental to the successful management of a museum.

The report proposes the establishment of a government fund to provide substantial assistance with retrospective documentation projects. It recommends that the MDA and other agencies extend their advisory role to provide more extensive support in areas such as data standards, terminology control, the security and preservation of documents, control documentation, retrospective documentation, documentation assessment programmes and automation assessment. It also proposes that the MDA monitors the production of new automated systems and is itself involved in developing specific applications such as data entry systems, processing facilities and data interchange procedures.

Chapter 13

The British Museum

David McCutcheon

Introduction

The British Museum opened in 1759 with the 80 000 objects collected by Sir Hans Sloane and the large Cotton and Harley libraries. Although in the 1880s the natural history collections and in 1973 the British Library were established as separate organizations, the collections have steadily grown to the present level of over six million items. To administer the immense range of the collections the Museum is now divided into nine antiquities departments: Coins and Medals, Egyptian, Ethnography (the Museum of Mankind), Greek and Roman, Medieval and Later, Oriental, Prehistoric and Romano-British, Prints and Drawings, and Western Asiatic.

Throughout its history, the Museum has recognized the importance of comprehensive documentation of its collections. Various documentation systems have come and gone, but a perennial lack of resources had inevitably placed the emphasis on the registration of acquisitions and similar fundamental tasks, to the detriment of the development of systems for the organization, classification and retrieval of information. Moreover, the operational responsibility for the documentation of the collections has always rested with the departments. The consequent disparate documentation procedures, particularly for indexing and inventory control, have in turn produced wide variations in the accessibility of information throughout the Museum.

The comparatively recent development of practical computerized information retrieval systems offered a possible solution to these persistent problems. In 1978 it was decided to assess the feasibility of the design and implementation of a computer-based documentation system in one of the departments. The project started in the Department of Ethnography which was considered to be one of the departments most seriously afflicted with documentation problems. Also, because of the diversity of its collections, it is probably the most representative of the departments, with problems common to all.

This chapter outlines the documentation problems, feasibility study and subsequent computer scheme (or to be exact, the first stage of the scheme) in the Ethnography Department. Other schemes are underway, but the one described here may be regarded as typical of the type of system that has been, and continues to be, implemented for the other departments.

Documentation in the Ethnography Department

The Department of Ethnography of the British Museum is housed separately in the Museum of Mankind. There are approximately 250 000 artefacts in the reserve collections arranged primarily by continent (Africa, America, Asia, Europe and Oceania). For curatorial purposes they are further divided into subcontinents, each with either the Keeper, the Deputy Keeper, or one of the six Assistant Keepers in charge. Within each curatorial area the objects are stored as far as possible in geographical order of country, region and tribe. Very few objects are on permanent display; the limited gallery space is normally used to house temporary exhibitions drawn from the reserve collections.

Once the purchase or donation of an artefact or collection has been approved (either by the Keeper, Director or Trustees, depending on the cost) it is registered by the appropriate curator. Typically, each curator spends at most one to two days a week on the registration process which includes the handwritten documentation of each acquisition in a bound ledger. The details recorded are loosely structured and include registration number, description, materials, measurements, colour, decoration, acquisition details, provenance, observations, often a sketch and, if relevant, the file number of any associated ethnographical documents. At present the registration number consists of the continental abbreviation (AF for Africa, etc.), year of accession, collection and object numbers, and a part number if applicable. Collection and object numbers are allocated in order of accession.

The Department's own registers go back to 1903. For earlier acquisitions, information is available from extracts in the main Museum registers, held either in bound volumes or on 30-40 000 filed slips of paper. There are also various registers which were acquired with some of the large collections. Some of the registers contain rudimentary indexes; there are a few card indexes, mostly incomplete or out of date; and some boxes of slips have been sorted into approximate regional order. But there are no comprehensive indexes to the entire collections.

Over 60 different registration numbering systems have been used. The main series which has applied since 1939 has already been described; its predecessor is similar but has no continental abbreviation and uses the month and day of accession as the collection number. The other series were developed for particular collections and seldom have a continental abbreviation or collection number. Some are simple numerical series but most have some type of prefix (which may be a symbol, or an abbreviation of the name of the collector, cataloguer or country of origin) followed by a sequential number.

The feasibility study

The feasibility study confirmed that there was an evident need by both staff and public for more easily accessible information, whether for answering enquiries, research work or inventory purposes. Tracking down information about the objects is often difficult, certainly time-consuming and sometimes so impracticable as to be considered impossible. The main barriers to obtaining information easily are the size of the collections, the two hundred year old practice of registering objects only in accession order, incomplete and indecipherable register entries, and the relative lack of dependable indexes and cross-references.

The collection of 250 000 items has a relatively slow growth rate of about a thousand acquisitions a year, so any practical solution had to concentrate first on the computerization of the huge backlog of information. Furthermore, the solution had to be determined by the need to minimize costs, consistent with acceptable results. It also was clear that preferential consideration had to be given to the possibility of using the Museum's own computer (a Hewlett-Packard 1000 minicomputer), until then employed mainly on scientific work in the Research Laboratory.

Given such constraints, it was decided that neither the introduction of a sophisticated online retrieval system nor the accumulation of a file of comprehensive records on the computer was justifiable. To convert *all* information on the collections into a form suitable for effective computer use would involve experienced senior staff in an examination of both the objects and the information sources. Completion of such a task was estimated to take at least fifty man-years and was out of the question. It was also unnecessary, as more than eighty percent of everyday enquiries about the collections could be dealt with by the provision of some comprehensive indexes to the registers.

In the circumstances a phased solution to the problem was considered to be more viable, designing and implementing a system in stages:

Stage one. This consists of the extraction from the registers of a limited number of information categories for each object (name, origin, etc.) These are subsequently submitted to the computer to build a master file of basic ethnography records. When these records are complete, typological, geographical and other indexes to the registers will be produced by the computer, and a simple system introduced to retrieve information from the files upon request.

Intermediate stages. Broadly, this involves building up the basic computer records on the master file by adding information from other discrete sources. Typical examples are storage location codes and photograph numbers. Also, the computer itself will be used to add more information to the basic records by, for example, feeding in geographical lexicons and thesauri so that it can automatically extend the hierarchy of place names and insert synonyms.

Final stage. The ultimate aim is to build up a master file of comprehensive records from the original basic records, thus making possible the introduction of a sophisticated information retrieval system. The notification of all details for new acquisitions can be done at the time of registration when the information is at hand. Supplying such detail for the backlog is much more of a problem, and it is intended to notify the information piecemeal as and when the objects or registers are being studied for some particular purpose (such as a by-product of research projects, exhibition planning and similar tasks).

There are definite advantages in a phased approach:

the early stages can be carried out by inexperienced graduates expressly hired for this purpose, monitored by senior Departmental staff;
there is no need to approve an entire costly scheme in advance, but only the initial stage;
the decision to continue with each stage can be made rationally in the context of the success or otherwise of previous stages;
usable information is produced by the computer within a comparatively short time, and at frequent intervals thereafter;
if a decision were made to call a halt at any time after the completion of the first stage it does not mean that the resources used were wasted: the indexes alone are a worthwhile end;
the avoidance of a long-term committment to one particular system would give the freedom to respond to rapidly developing computer technology.

The feasibility study recommended the appointment of a team of five graduates for a two-year period, to work on the first stage of a computerized system under the guidance of senior staff. The task involves the transcription of the selected information categories from the registers on to computer input forms; the transmission of the data through a VDU connected to the Museum's minicomputer by dedicated lines; and checking and correction of the computer-printed output.

It was proposed that the MDA program package (GOS) be used to process the data on the Museum's computer. The package was selected because (unlike most) it could be implemented on the minicomputer, it was flexible enough to accommodate comfortably the complexities of the data, and it appeared to be the one most likely to be used by the majority of British museums.

Savings to the Department resulting from the use of the indexes and information retrieval facility provided by stage one of the scheme were estimated at one and a half man-years per annum. Thus the cost of implementation plus annual running costs are likely to be recovered less than six years after the scheme went into operation. Such savings were, to a certain extent, theoretical: in practice it was likely that because of improved access to information, more use than before would be made of the facilities. The benefit was less a saving in cost than an increase in efficiency, and, as for many other benefits from the scheme, such an improvement in staff productivity was unquantifiable.

The recommendations were accepted by the Trustees of the Museum, and the first stage of the scheme commenced in July 1980.

Stage 1 procedures

It is not practical for the information in the registers to be typed directly into the computer. The register entries are almost unstructured, styles vary, earlier entries are sometimes illegible and geographical names and boundaries have changed over the years (Figure 13.1). The information selected from a register entry must first be written down in a more structured format.

The five members of the data preparation team transcribe selected information from the registers on to computer input form E03 (Notification of Basic Details) (Figure 13.2). This is made up of 16 fields, the roles of which are described below. Each form is designed to hold the details of up to 15 objects, which means that common information does not have to be transcribed repeatedly. This is a valuable saving in time and effort as there is a good deal of repetition in the collections, prime examples of which are acquisition and geographical details. Four fields which change infrequently (recorder, date, year and series) are noted once only at the top of the form. These are common to each subsequent entry.

Recorder and date. The recorder's initials, together with the date of entry, are stored in the computer record when it is created or altered, to provide an 'audit trail' from the record back to the original form.
Year. The year of accession, derived from the registration number.
Series. This is a single letter code introduced to differentiate the various registration numbering systems. The computer master file records are held in registration number order but most of the older numbers are unsuitable for this purpose. The series code, often in conjunction with a newly allocated collection number, overcomes the problem by providing each record with a unique computer-compatible number with minimal adaptation of the original registration number. The computerized registration number now consists of continent code, year of accession, series code, collection number, object number and, if relevant, part number. For example, in two of the many registration numbering systems used for the Christy collections, one used a simple range of object numbers from 1 to 10 000 and the other a range from +1 to +10 000. They now have continent codes, year of accession of the collections, series code 'c' (in common with all other Christy collections), collection code 1 or 2 and the original object number. The '+' prefix has been dropped but each object still has a unique registration number.
Object number. Normally this is a simple number but it is possible to notify an inclusive range of object numbers provided that all of the details entered on the line apply to every object in the range. The computer record created for a range of objects is automatically split whenever corrections or additions are made which do not apply to the entire range.
Part number. Part numbers (or letters) are used for two reasons:

(a) If a registration number has been allocated to more than one object or part object; usually quite separate pieces which are related in some manner (e.g. a knife, sheath and belt). Each part is given a letter, and, like object numbers, a range of parts may be notified.

(b) If a registration number has been allocated to a composite object (e.g. a necklace) or to a set of specific parts (e.g. a tea-set) these may be considered to form a hierarchy. To retain this relationship the part numbers may be arranged within each other to a maximum of three

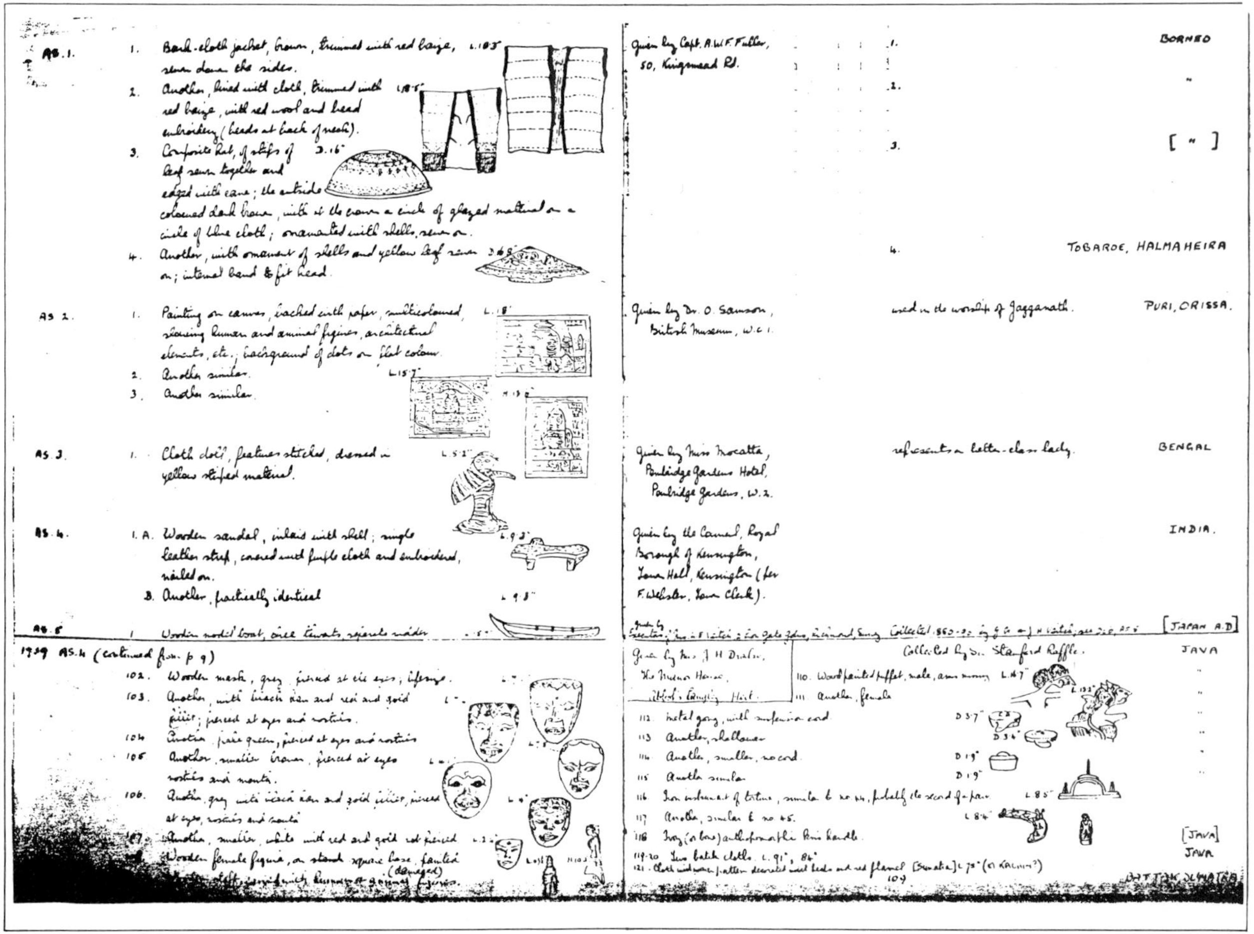
AS.1. 1. Bark-cloth jacket, brown, trimmed with red baize, sewn down the sides. L.10.5" — Given by Capt. A.W.F. Fuller, 50, Kingsmead Rd. — 1. — BORNEO
2. Another, lined with cloth, trimmed with red baize, with red wool and bead embroidery (beads at back of neck). L.18.5" — 2. — "
3. Composite hat, of strips of leaf sewn together and edged with cane; the outside coloured dark brown, with at the crown a circle of glazed material on a circle of blue cloth; ornamented with shells, sewn on. D.16" — 3. — ["]
4. Another, with ornament of shells and yellow leaf sewn on; internal band & fit head. D.6.8" — 4. — TOBAROE, HALMAHEIRA

AS.2. 1. Painting on canvas, backed with paper, multicoloured, showing human and animal figures, architectural elements, etc., background of dots on flat colour. L.18" — Given by Dr. O. Samson, British Museum, W.C.1. — used in the worship of Jagganath. — PURI, ORISSA.
2. Another similar. L.15.7"
3. Another similar.

AS.3. 1. Cloth doll, features stitched, dressed in yellow striped material. L.5.2" — Given by Miss Mocatta, Pembridge Gardens Hotel, Pembridge Gardens, W.2. — represents a better-class lady. — BENGAL

AS.4. 1.A. Wooden sandal, inlaid with shell; single leather strap, covered with purple cloth and embroidered, nailed on. L.9.3" — Given by the Council, Royal Borough of Kensington, Town Hall, Kensington (per F. Webster, Town Clerk). — INDIA.
B. Another, practically identical. L.9.8"

AS.5 1 Wooden model boat ... — [JAPAN A.D]

1939 AS.4 (continued from p 9)
102. Wooden mask, grey, pierced at the eyes, lifesize. — Given by Mrs. J.H. Drake, The Manor House, ... — Collected by Sir Stamford Raffles. — JAVA
103. Another, with black hair and red and gold paint; pierced at eyes and nostrils.
104. Another, pale green, pierced at eyes and nostrils.
105. Another, smaller, brown, pierced at eyes, nostrils and mouth.
106. Another, grey with black hair and gold paint, pierced at eyes, nostrils and mouth.
107. Another, smaller, white with red and gold, not pierced.
Wooden female figure, on stand, square base, painted (damaged) ... figures.
110. Wood painted puppet, male, arms moving. L.47"
111. Another, female.
112. Metal gong, with suspension cord. D.5.7"
113. Another, shallower. D.3.4"
114. Another, smaller, no cord. D.1.9"
115. Another similar. D.1.9"
116. Iron instrument of torture, similar to no. 44, probably the second of a pair. L.8.5"
117. Another, similar to no. 45. L.8.4"
118. Ivory (or bone) anthropomorphic knife handle. — [JAVA]
119-20. Two batik cloths L.91", 84" — JAVA
121. Cloth ... decorated with beads and red flannel [Sumatra] L.7.5" — BATTAK, SUMATRA

Figure 13.1 Sample original register page

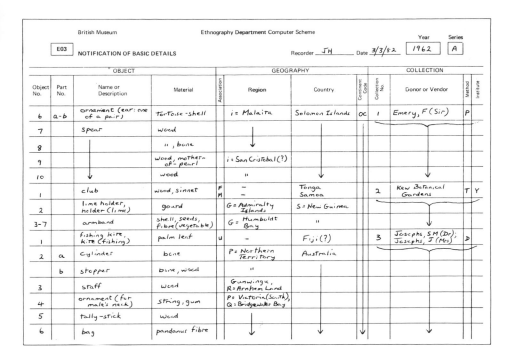

Object No.	Part No.	Name or Description	Material	Association	Region	Country	Continent Code	Collection No	Donor or Vendor	Method	Institute
6	a-b	ornament (ear: one of a pair)	Tortoise-shell		i = Malaita	Solomon Islands	OC	1	Emery, F (Sir)	P	
7		spear	wood								
8			", bone								
9			wood, mother-of-pearl		i = San Cristobal (?)							
10			wood		"							
1		club	wood, sinnet	F M	–	Tonga Samoa		2	Kew Botanical Gardens	T	Y
2		lime holder, holder (lime)	gourd		G = Admiralty Islands	S = New Guinea					
3-7		armband	shell, seeds, fibre (vegetable)		G = Humboldt Bay	"					
1		fishing kite, kite (fishing)	palm leaf	u	–	Fiji (?)		3	Josephs, SM (Dr); Josephs, J (Mrs)	D	
2	a	cylinder	bone		P = Northern Territory	Australia					
	b	stopper	bone, wood		"						
3		staff	wood		Gunwingu, R = Arnhem Land						
4		ornament (for male's neck)	string, gum		P = Victoria (South), Q = Bridgewater Bay						
5		tally-stick	wood								
6		bag	pandanus fibre								

British Museum · Ethnography Department Computer Scheme

E03 NOTIFICATION OF BASIC DETAILS · Recorder JH · Date 3/3/82 · Year 1962 · Series A

Figure 13.2 An E03 input form, with information from the Oceania register for 1962

levels (e.g. a tea-set may have part 'a' for the teapot, 'b' for a sugar bowl, 'c' for a milk jug ... and also, at the next level, part 'a:a' for the pot and 'a:b' for the lid).

Name or description. The name or description is notified as a number of keywords, separated by commas, which are used for classification and retrieval. If necessary, qualifying detail may be added (in brackets) to provide further information without destroying the generality of the keyword.

Material. The same keyword-and-detail system is used to record the materials of which the object is made.

Association. Usually an object is considered to belong to a particular section of the collection according to the place from which it came. But there are also two possible secondary geographical associations — place made and place used — which may differ from the primary association. The association code allows such distinctions to be made. It is usually left blank for the primary, and normally only, association.

Region. The keyword-and-detail system is used to record the region, here defined as any geographical subdivision of a country, be it state, town, village, tribe, site, etc. Each type of region — except tribe, which is the most common — has been allocated a code (e.g. i=island, v=village, p=province or state) to enable the computer to extend the geographical hierarchy in each state) to enable the computer to extend the geographical hierarchy in each record at some future stage. This substantially reduces the amount of geographical information that has to be notified.

Country. A similar system is used for any continental subdivision down to country level. Type codes are notified (e.g. S=subcontinent, W=archaeological country) for levels other than country.

Continent code. This is the continental abbreviation — AF, AM, AS, EU or OC. If it is the primary continent code it forms part of the registration number.

Collection number. This is either the original collection number which is part of a registration number in the main series, or a dummy number allocated to differentiate the subdivisions in some of the other series.

Donor or vendor. The surname of the donor or vendor of the collection is separated from the initials or Christian names by a comma. Title is recorded as detail in brackets except for a default of 'Mr'. A semicolon is used as the separator if there is more than one name. The name of the collector may be included by enclosing it in square brackets.

Method. A single letter code is used to denote the method of acquisition (e.g. P for purchase, D for donation, T for transfer).

Institute. A simple indicator to distinguish a private donor from an institution.

Several times a week, each team member types the data from a batch of completed forms through the VDU into the computer. At the start of each session on the terminal the team member indicates the type of form to be processed (i.e. whether the basic details or one of the correction forms), and a format representing one line of the requested form is displayed on the terminal screen.

Figure 13.3 shows an example of the EO3 format on the terminal screen into which the information from the first line of the sample EO3 form (Figure 13.2) has been typed. The data fields on the screen are large enough to contain most entries; exceptionally large information fields can be added to the record using one of the correction forms.

Once more, full advantage is taken of the considerable savings to be made by avoiding the need to type and transmit common data: the computer is programmed to duplicate each information field through subsequent records on the file until something different is actually entered. The format is designed so that, as far as possible, the information fields least likely to be changed are towards the end of the screen, to reduce both the amount of tabbing between fields and the data transmission time. Thus, to create the next record from the EO3 form in Figure 13.2, only the object number, part number, name and material fields need to be retyped and transmitted. The information in all other fields will be carried forward automatically by the computer.

The data entry process is interactive: the computer checks the information as it is entered and displays an appropriate message on the terminal screen whenever a possible error or inconsistency is discovered. Typical examples are: the object number is not the next in sequence, or it is not the first for a new collection, or the donor's name has not been changed for a new collection. The terminal operator then has the option of amending and

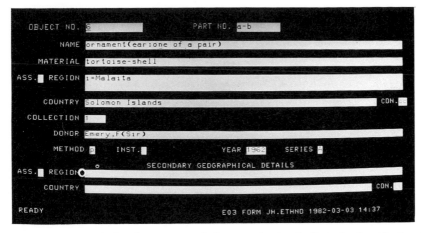

Figure 13.3 The equivalent form on a terminal screen, showing the first entry from the form in Figure 13.2

re-transmitting the field in question or confirming that it is correct as entered.

The interactive data entry system is provided by a program module called VETINPUT which was designed and written in the Museum to interface with GOS. It enables the user to specify input and output formats, screen design, vetting procedures and terminal messages using simple GOS-style instructions.

Once accepted by the computer the input records are stored in a transactions file awaiting the weekly updating processes. At the end of each input session the total number of records accepted by the computer is displayed on the terminal screen for the operators to check against their own set of totals.

An accumulative master file of basic ethnography records arranged in order of registration number is held on magnetic disc. The record contains the information fields notified on the EO3 form. Provision has also been made for the inclusion of object location details — location code, availability of the object, loan details, etc. — during the next stage of the scheme.

Each week there is a batch processing run during which the computer updates the master file. Master records are created and amended using the information held in the input records accumulated on the transactions file during the previous week. The computer also produces a report of any input records that have had to be rejected (e.g. if a new record quotes a registration number already used on the master file), a list of records deleted from file, and a set of control totals. In addition, it prepares the following three lists:

Record printouts (Figure 13.4). Each team member gets a complete set of prints of the master records created from or corrected by the information input by that person during the week, showing all the information held in each record. These are checked against the original input forms and any necessary corrections made on the amendment forms, ready to be typed through the VDU for the next week's update run.

```
RECORD:   As 1880 C 8 62          REASON: E03   19-3-1982 ELJ
NAME:     bowl(food)
MATERIAL: shell(*:coconut)
FROM:     Tribe : Kayan, Town : Longwai, State/Province : Kalimantan(*),
          Indonesia(*)
DONOR:    Purchased from Christy Fund;[Bock, Carl A] [I]
RECORDER: ELJ on 19-3-1982


RECORD:   As 1880 C 8 63          REASON: E03   19-3-1982 ELJ
NAME:     cup(?),bowl(?:food)
MATERIAL: shell(*:coconut)
FROM:     Tribe : Dyak, Tribe : Dayak(*), Tribe : Kayan
          Borneo[S]
DONOR:    Purchased from Christy Fund;[Bock, Carl A] [I]
RECORDER: ELJ on 19-3-1982


RECORD:   As 1880 C 8 64          REASON: E03   19-3-1982 ELJ
NAME:     bottle(storing rice),vessel(*)
MATERIAL: rattan
FROM:     Tribe : 'Dyak', Tribe : Dayak(*)
          Borneo[S]
DONOR:    Purchased from Christy Fund;[Bock, Carl A] [I]
RECORDER: ELJ on 19-3-1982


RECORD:   As 1880 C 8 65          REASON: E03   19-3-1982 ELJ
NAME:     basket
MATERIAL: rattan
FROM:     Tribe : Kenyah, Town : Longwai, State/Province : Kalimantan(*)
          Indonesia(*)
DONOR:    Purchased from Christy Fund;[Bock, Carl A] [I]
RECORDER: ELJ on 19-3-1982


RECORD:   As 1880 C 8 66          REASON: E03   19-3-1982 ELJ
NAME:     cover(rain),mat(sleeping)
MATERIAL: leaves(palm)
FROM:     Tribe : Punan
          Borneo[S]
DONOR:    Purchased from Christy Fund;[Bock, Carl A] [I]
RECORDER: ELJ on 19-3-1982


RECORD:   As 1880 C 8 67          REASON: E03   19-3-1982 ELJ
NAME:     mat(sleeping)
MATERIAL: rattan
FROM:     Town : Bandjermasin, Town : Bandjarmasin(*), Sub district : Little
          Kapuas River, Sub district : Kapuas River(*), State/Province :
          Kalimantan(*)
          Indonesia(*)
DONOR:    Purchased from Christy Fund;[Bock, Carl A] [I]
RECORDER: ELJ on 19-3-1982
```

Figure 13.4 Sample page of the weekly record printout

Geographical index (Figure 13.5). An index, in geographical order, of the additions and corrections to the master file made during the week is produced for the curator in charge of each area. These indexes are designed to be easily checked, and they enable the curators to control and monitor the information being fed into the system.

Typological index. Similar indexes in object name order are also produced for each curator's area.

There are several internal conventions used to indicate the source of the information. In Figures 13.4 and 13.5 for example, information enclosed by single quotation marks was supplied by the donor; that marked by an

```
BRITISH MUSEUM                    DEPARTMENT OF ETHNOGRAPHY              PAGE 12
                                       AFRICA - BJM
GEOGRAPHICAL INDEX                                                       25-3-1982

Sudan(*) also Zaire(*), Central African Republic(*)

     Neam Nam [tribe] also Azande(*) [tribe]
          knife(woman's) of iron                             Af 1867 C 1 4641
          shield of reeds, rattan(?), bamboo, leather, bamboo(?:rind), wood   Af 1868 C 1 4637

Tanzania(*)

          bag of string                                      Af 1910 C 3 404
          hat(?*), food cover(?*), cover(?*:food?*) of basketry   Af 1910 C 3 370
          hat(?*), food cover(?*), cover(?*:food?*) of string    Af 1910 C 3 371
                                                             Af 1910 C 3 373
          ladle of wood                                      Af 1910 C 3 429
          ladle(+ elephant figure) of wood                   Af 1910 C 3 427-428

     Uhha [district/area]
          ring, pot-stand(*) of basketry                     Af 1910 C 3 403

     Ujiji [sub district]
          ornament(neck) of iron, string                     Af 1910 C 3 393

Tanzania(*) also South Africa(?*)

     Ujiji [sub district]
          pincers(nose) of cane, string                      Af 1910 C 3 520

Uganda

          drum of wood(*), skin(lizard)                      Af 1893 C 2 6198

West Central Africa[S]

     Thihu [tribe] also Shihu(?*) [tribe]
          arrow(poisoned) of reed, gut, iron, poison(seeds)  Af 1866 C 1 2915    Part a-s
                                                             Af 1866 C 1 2916    Part a-d
                                                             Af 1866 C 1 2917    Part a-b
                                                             Af 1866 C 1 2918    Part a-d
          bow of wood, bamboo(?), leather                    Af 1866 C 1 2913
          cover, lid(*) of leather                           Af 1866 C 1 2914    Part b
          quiver of leather, iron, cord(leather)             Af 1866 C 1 2914    Part a

West Tropical Africa[S]

          basket of fibre                                    Af 1866 C 1 2802
                                                             Af 1866 C 1 2803

Zaire also Belgian Congo

     East [general region] also Uvira [town]
          armlet, arm-guard(archer's) of wood                Af 1910 C 3 434

Zaire also Congo State

     Luba(*) [tribe] also Lubaland [district/area], Urua [sub district]
          staff(chief's) of wood, copper, iron               Af 1910 C 3 438
```

Figure 13.5 Sample page of the weekly geographical index

asterisk was added by the recorder and awaits confirmation by the curator upon examination of the weekly indexes.

Conclusions

The emphasis placed on the importance of a fast, simple, relatively cheap method of data capture for large museum collections has so far been justified. Eighteen months after the start of the scheme, over 150 000 records are on file and the completion date for stage one is on schedule. There was the expected slow rate of data entry during the initial months, mainly due to staff training and the inevitable teething troubles, but the five members of the team soon reached the average 600 records each a week originally estimated.

The staff employed were not professional typists: the typing rate was seldom over 6000 characters an hour. But the *effective* typing rate was almost 23 000 characters an hour because of the ability to enter a range of objects as one record, only changes in information having to be typed, and there being no field names to be typed. Furthermore, the interactive vetting of data allowed most mistakes to be corrected immediately, considerably reducing the high typing overheads involved in the resubmission of data.

It was never the intention to propose this scheme as a generalized system for the computerization of museum records; on the contrary, it was specifically designed to resolve some particular problems in the Ethnography Department. Nevertheless, the data entry method has proved to be so successful that a similar technique has since been used in the recently started computerized inventory scheme in the Department of Coins and Medals, and is likely to be used in future for other departmental schemes.

Chapter 14

The Imperial War Museum

Roger B.N. Smither

Introduction

The Imperial War Museum, founded in 1917 and formally established by Parliament in 1920, exists to collect, preserve and display material relating to military operations since the outbreak of the First World War in which members of the British Commonwealth have been involved. Since 1936, the Museum's main building has been located in south east London, occupying the surviving central portion of what was formerly the Bethlem Royal Hospital (or Bedlam). The Museum has also established outstations at Duxford Airfield, a former Royal Air Force fighter station south of Cambridge, and HMS Belfast, a Royal Navy cruiser moored in the River Thames.

One of the indications of the size and range of the Museum's collections is the variety of ways used by the seven Departments that administer those collections to quantify their holdings. The Department of Art has 12 000 paintings, drawings and pieces of sculpture and 50 000 posters, as well as other sub-collections ranging from prints and medallions to flag-day tokens and other ephemera. The Department of Documents administers collections of British and foreign papers occupying more than 9000 document boxes and 5000 reels of microfilm. The Department of Exhibits and Firearms, with responsibility for the Museum's collection of three-dimensional artefacts, has well over a quarter of a million items in its care, ranging in size from buttons to a Vulcan bomber, and including, to take one sub-collection as an example, 1.5 tons of badges and insignia. The Department of Film holds 65 million feet of film, the Department of Photographs some five million images. The Department of Printed Books, the Museum's library, has over 100 000 books as well as maps, pamphlets and periodicals, and an annual growth rate of 4000 periodical issues and 5000 other items. The Museum's newest collection, that of the Department of Sound Records, comprises 6000 hours of recordings.

Documentation framework

Documentation of the Museum's collections is, like acquisition, conservation and other aspects of the Museum's curatorial function, divided among the seven collecting Departments. The documentation role is also shared by the non-collecting Department of Information Retrieval, whose area of involvement potentially covers all relevant activities in the collecting Departments. Its functions are, however, those of advice and assistance; it does not have the sort of direct responsibility exercised, for example, by the registrar of a typical museum in the United States

The staff resources devoted to documentation in the Museum are difficult to quantify, since most Departments do not rely solely on 'pure' cataloguing staff. The common attitude is that documentation is a function in which most of the staff ought to participate. This attitude may, with some validity, be interpreted in both a positive and a negative light. Positively, it can be seen to reflect a realization of the central role of documentation in curatorial activities, and a recognition of the wastefulness of developing parallel expertise in both specialized documentation and other staff. More negatively, it may be seen as a reflection of the fact that in most Departments documentation is in competition for scant staff resources with other curatorial functions, and will not receive special treatment.

In 1979, an internal survey identified 20 members of staff who were considered to spend 30% or more of their time on cataloguing and indexing. Allowing for some staffing changes and a broader definition of documentation, that figure could be increased to 26, equivalent to some 18 full posts. This compares to a total main building curatorial staff (i.e. not including directorial, administrative and security staff or staff at the outstations) of about 135. It therefore represents a staff committment of between ten and fifteen percent.

Among those working on documentation, the Museum numbers several people with qualifications in museum studies, archives and librarianship, but none with qualifications in computer or information science. This is not to say that such qualifications would not be welcomed: rather, that the nature of work as currently defined does not make them the primary criterion for recruitment. Typically, a major requirement for staff is knowledge of a topic appropriate to the Museum's specialist terms of reference. It is found easier to introduce subject experts to correct documentation procedures than to induce subject expertise in a professional trainee. Individuals combining both backgrounds are welcome but rarely found. Supervision and training in documentation procedures are carried out partly by the collecting Departments and partly by the Department of Information Retrieval.

Documentation procedures

Documentation relating to the basic management of collections — the registration of accessions, the monitoring of inward and outward loans, the maintenance of inventories, etc. — is the responsibility of the collecting Department. Methods used show all the signs of independent evolution over the sixty or more years of the Museum's life. All Departments maintain accession registers, although there is no Museum-wide standardization of procedures — some, for example, use a loose-leaf format rather than the traditional bound register, the registration being 'fixed' only annually, when that year's records are microfilmed. There is a comparable diversity of procedures for recording conditions and restrictions relating to the movement of items through the Museum's hands. The various strands come together only in the provision for occasional central inspection of collections or for reference to the Director's office of questions of loan management or disposal. The resulting systems are adequate but are not necessarily the most efficient that could be realized.

The collecting Departments also initiate programmes of more detailed documentation work, and it is in these that the involvement of the Department of Information Retrieval is generally sought. Such programmes are responses either to specific stimuli, such as a special exhibition or conference, or to a Departmental policy of improving documentation. The basic documentation of registers and inventories is frequently all a Department has, and the record so provided can be both lacking in detail and physically incomplete. At other times, a Department's documentation may have been compiled by an outside agency and acquired by transfer with the material. When a Department administers several sub-collections of this type (as is the case with film and photographs) the result can be several sets of mutually inconsistent documentation.

The Department of Information Retrieval helps such efforts at improvement in three ways — personnel, procedures and systems. It was noted earlier that in most collecting Departments, documentation is in more or less direct competition for staff resources with other curatorial functions. Information Retrieval — with a staff of a Keeper, four cataloguers and a part time assistant — offers a small reservoir of manpower to boost a documentation project. Normal preference is to encourage, partly by example, the undertaking of documentation work in the collecting Departments themselves. Thus Information Retrieval staff are normally used in the opening stages of a project to accelerate the attainment of a point where progress can be assessed and benefits demonstrated. However, more long-term assistance has also been attempted. For example much of the traditional workload of Information Retrieval staff has been the cataloguing of the film collection, maintaining the momentum of documentation at a higher level than staff of the Department of Film itself would be able to manage.

Information Retrieval staff also help in the formulation of procedures, both within the work of individual departments and in maintaining — as far as possible — consistency of practice and vocabulary between Departments. Sometimes the involvement is in a still broader context: Information Retrieval and other Museum staff participated in the design committees working on several of the cards now produced by the MDA. Similarly a set of film cataloguing rules published in 1976 was in part a reflection of work in the cataloguing commission of the International Federation of Film Archives and has in turn formed the basis for further involvement with the commission (Fédération Internationale des Archives du Film. Cataloguing Commission, 1979a; 1979b; Smither with Penn, 1976).

Current efforts are directed towards the compilation of a cataloguing manual, consisting of three general chapters applicable to all collections followed by chapters prescribing specific procedures for individual collections or sub-collections. The first general chapter contains rules for the treatment of dates and proper names, especially in those parts of the catalogue record from which indexes will be generated, but also in those areas where information is transcribed from the item catalogued. The second chapter specifies procedures for aspects of documentation common to all collections, including the citing of references, description of conservation and other 'processes', and administrative information — acquisition history, storage location and the like. The last general chapter contains instructions on the usage of the cataloguing system, with instructions on the restrictions imposed by the computer system on punctuation and the procedures required for the inclusion of accents, as well as general guidance on house style.

Documentation of collections composed almost entirely of items relevant to twentieth century history, and mainly to military history at that, may present special problems to the writer of cataloguing rules. The century has seen such extensive changes in the political geography of the world and in the evolution of military technology that accommodating these changes in the documentation record can raise serious difficulties — the more so as some of them have overtones of political controversy that a museum may wish to avoid. Decisions must be taken, for example, between accurately reflecting a series of quite rapid changes of name and providing continuity over an extended period, and these decisions can be required equally in the case of British army regiments and the nation states of formerly colonial regions of Asia and Africa. Again, it may be necessary to determine whether the nationality ascribed to a piece of weaponry or other equipment should reflect the country of design, of manufacture, of first purchase or of last use: in some cases, each criterion might suggest a different answer.

Cataloguing items in the Museum's collections also frequently reflects an apparently indirect approach. Objects of military interest are commonly of value by reason of their associations with particular people or events, rather than for any physical attribute. The significance may be even less direct, as when an object is retained because it is of the same type or pattern as one of interest which is itself not available. Moreover, the Museum's terms of reference dictate that a large proportion of its collections will consist of objects generated by a society geared to mass production. Such objects are commonly only distinguishable or valuable to the extent that they diverge from the standard or normal appearance of such objects. The emphasis in the Museum's new cataloguing handbook will therefore be heavily on associative information, and on the minimizing of descriptive cataloguing. Rather than describing in detail dozens of examples of a simple object, the rules specify the full description only of a single MODEL or CONTROL specimen; in some collections, description even of MODELs is by reference to an authoritative published source. Other specimens are then categorized in a hierarchy of SECONDARY MODEL or VARIANT, SPECIMEN, etc., and are described in terms of their divergence from the MODEL description.

An extract from the chapter on the cataloguing of firearms in the draft handbook, Figure 14.1, shows how such a hierarchy of specimen types is applied to one collection, with the intention of reducing the descriptive content of catalogue records. The next two figures provide examples of documentation produced in accordance with this approach. In Figure 14.2,

FIREARMS

Introductory points and definitions

The Museum's collection comprises smallarms, automatic weapons, flare projectors, infantry anti-tank weapons and mortars (heavier weapons form part of the artillery collection). The firearms collection also includes accessories to weapons in that collection but excludes bayonets (except those permanently attached to a firearm) and holsters (except those designed for a specific model of weapon). (Removable bayonets form part of the weapons collection; general purpose or standard issue holsters form part of the personal equipment collection.) Ammunition is also handled as a separate collection.

In view of the size of the collection, and the well-documented research and descriptive work already carried out by scholars and historians outside the Museum on many of the types of firearm represented in it, the Museum's catalogue does not describe in detail each weapon, or indeed a representative specimen of each weapon, in the collection. Detailed description is left, in appropriate cases, to published sources which are indicated in documentary references in the catalogue record. The catalogue does, however, describe differences between weapons in the collection and those described in the sources: it also describes fully those weapons for which there is, in the Museum's opinion, no adequate published description.

Weapons in the collection are therefore given one of the following designations:

(1) CONTROL

A 'control' weapon is the first normal example of a weapon type encountered in the cataloguing process (in other words, the firearm with the lowest catalogue number). Its catalogue entry is used to provide all standard information for that weapon type - ie statements on production, references to published descriptions or (in the absence of a suitable published description) the Museum's description of the weapon, and appropriate notes. A new 'weapon type' is normally signalled by a change in the first or third element of the 'full name' of weapons catalogued (see paragraph 1f below) - ie a change of manufacturer, or of model name or mark number. Note, however, that a change of the fourth element (calibre) within a sequence of unchanged model name will also signal a new weapon type (and therefore a new 'control') when it involves a major change of structure or scale.

(2) SPECIMEN

A 'specimen' conforms to the standard description provided in the relevant 'control' entry in all functional respects and in addition conforms to any one of the range of options (such as barrel lengths) routinely offered for that weapon type by the manufacturer. It may differ from the standard description in minor details such as finish or inscriptions. 'Specimens' are described primarily by reference to the appropriate 'control', with descriptive statements made solely to record the points of difference.

(3) VARIANT

A 'variant' is a factory-produced weapon which differs from the standard description in a form which was not extensively or routinely offered by the manufacturer (eg a special safety system, or an unusual magazine release). Description is still primarily by reference to the appropriate 'control', with additional descriptive notes as required.

(4) MODIFICATION

A modification is a weapon which has been significantly altered structurally subsequent to manufacture (eg barrel shortened; rechambered; etc) when the modification is not reflected - as will be the case, for example, with several military modifications - in the naming of the weapon. Description is primarily by reference to the appropriate 'control', with additional descriptive entries as required.

(5) EXPERIMENTAL

An 'experimental' weapon is one produced in small numbers by a manufacturer for research and development. It may, obviously, be either a prototype for a production model, or a step in a direction not subsequently pursued for large-scale production. Description will depend on the nature of the weapon - a prototype may be describable largely by reference to the appropriate 'control' while a unique or uncommon development may itself require the level of description normally provided for a 'control' weapon.

(6) ORIGINAL

An 'original' weapon is a "one-off", a weapon not conforming to a precise pattern or standard, and normally not produced by factory procedure (mass production), though nonetheless produced for use, as distinct from the research and development purpose of 'experimental' weapons. The 'original' category therefore encompasses hand-made-to-order shotguns and, at the opposite end of the spectrum, 'home-made' or 'do it yourself' terrorist or resistance weapons. 'Originals' will generally require extensive individual description, although components may be open to description by reference.

The Museum catalogues firearms in the configuration in which they are held - in other words, a 9 mm pistol modified to fire .22 ammunition is catalogued as a pistol in .22 calibre - although the catalogue entry may indicate the original form and apparent history of the weapon. Cataloguing of weapons 'as held' also means that weapons are catalogued together with the accessories associated with them. The procedure adopted, which is explained in detail in the rules below, is to catalogue such items in a composite record (firearm with accessory or accessories) in which the firearm will always constitute Part 1 and each accessory will be catalogued under another Part number:

eg Firearm with accessory (pistol and grip extension)
    Part 1: Firearm   (pistol)
    Part 2: Accessory   (grip extension).

Figure 14.1 Explanation of specimen types for firearms, from the draft cataloguing rules

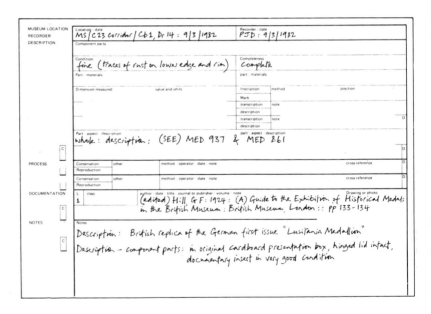

Figure 14.2 Card entry for a British replica of the German *Lusitania* medallion, described as a 'specimen'

the description of a British replica of the German *Lusitania* medallion is conveyed largely by reference to the catalogue entries for the 'model' (MED

```
*id IWM: FIR/6030
*ident *sname submachinegun, retarded blowback *serno S-134114
*fname Savage & Auto-Ordnance & Thompson Submachine Gun Model 1928 & .45 ACP
*prod *meth manufacture *prole manufacturer *name Savage Arms Company
*place USA & Utica, New York
*meth manufacture *prole licenser *name Auto-Ordnance Corporation *place USA &
Bridgeport, Connecticut
*assoc *nature service (inferred) *serv British military services
*nature service *serv Cypriot armed factions & EOKA *event Cyprus Emergency &
1957 (?)
*acq *meth transfer *from Cyprus Police *pin 104/59
*recorder DJP: 9/3/1981
*descg
*compl complete
*insc mark *meth stamped *pos frame (left) *descr "W" in crown (British
Purchasing Commission mark ?)
*insc mark *meth stamped *pos frame (left) *descr "GEG" in circle
*insc inscription *meth scratched *pos butt (right) *transc L410/5/ *descr
(Police evidence number ?)
*descn whole: description: CONTROL *d 1
*docd *doc *l 1 *ref Nelson, T B & Lockhoven, H B: 1963: (The) World's
Submachine Guns: International Small Arms Publishers, Cologne, GFR: Vol 1:
p 62
*notes Identification: the Model 1928 was offered by Auto-Ordnance with a wide
variety of names indicating in some cases the accessories fitted and in other
cases the desire of the Corporation to boost sales by reminding the public of
official US usage. Thus the Model was first named and sometimes marked as "Navy
Model", while Auto-Ordnance Catalogues claimed that US Army weapons were
marked "U.S. MODEL 1928A1". Later models are designated "1928AC" indicating a
weapon fitted with a Cutts compensator or "1928A" indicating one without the
compensator. The Museum's collection includes specimens with markings changed
from one style to another (eg FIR/6190) underlining the essential unity of
this group
*notes Production: manufacture by Savage is indicated by the "S" prefix to the
serial number
#
```

Figure 14.3 Printout of data prepared in-house for the firearms catalogue — a Thompson Model 1928, described as a 'control'

937, a German original) and 'secondary model' (MED 861, a previously catalogued example of the British replica). The cataloguer is able to restrict the description of this item to statements on condition and completeness, and a note on component parts: in other words, to those pieces of information applicable to this specimen only. Figure 14.3 shows the level of detail supplied for a 'control' specimen in the firearms catalogue, the record being produced in accordance with the rules from which Figure 14.1 was extracted. Included here are full production data, bibliographic reference to an authoritative description, and a lengthy note on identification, to all of which reference may be made in future 'specimen' level entries. The 'control' record does, of course, also include those details (associations, tagged '*assoc', completeness, unique inscriptions) which would be provided for 'specimens' as well.

Figures 14.4 and 14.5 provide examples of some forms of output from a Museum cataloguing project: in this case a catalogue and titles index from the medallions project, including references to the record illustrated in Figure 14.2.

```
                              --**--
IWM: MED/1017
medallion, British, (LUSITANIA MEDALLION).
subject, commemorative, British transportation and RMS Lusitania,
(after) 8/1915, First World War, Atlantic, RMS Lusitania, Sinking
of by U20, 7/5/1915, (Eastern) Atlantic Ocean, (South West of)
Ireland, (off the) Old Head of Kinsale.
subject, propaganda, inflammatory, First World War, British
anti-German Propaganda, (after) 8/1915.
MS/C22 corridor/Cbl, Dr 14, 9/5/1983.
whole: description: (SEE) MED/937, MED/861.
fine (slight rusting around edge and rim), complete.
PJD, 9/5/1983.
Description: British replica of the German first issue "Lusitania
Medallion".
Description - component parts: in original cardboard presentation
box, hinged lid intact, documentary insert in very good
condition.


                              --**--


IWM: MED/1018
medallion, German, FELDMARSCHALL VON HINDENBURG.
design, designer, Loewental, A.
subject, portrait, Hindenburg, Paul von (Feldmarschall), German
Army, 1915, First World War, Eastern Front, 1914 - 1915.
deposit, Edward VIII (HM King), 6/1936.
1016.
MS/Art Store security cabinet, 13/6/1983.
whole: description: MODEL, SECONDARY, (SEE) MED/49.
piece: silver, very fine, complete, diameter, 34 mm, inscription:
impressed, rim, DS1 SILBER 990
PJD, 13/6/1983.
Acquisition: see Note to MED/956.
Description - component parts: in specially made fitted
presentation case, see Note to MED/956.
H: (compiled) Schulman, J, 4/1916, La Guerre Europienne
1914-1916. Medailles, Monnaies, Papiers-Monnaie, Catalogue LXV,
(p 65 (ref 697, photograph)).
```

Figure 14.4 Extract from medallion catalogue

Computing systems

The Museum has been concerned to make as cost effective as possible its
investment of staff time in documentation. This has given the Department of
Information Retrieval a continuing interest in mechanization or
computerization. In the late 1960s, the Museum developed an in-house
system based on 80-column punched cards which was used experimentally on
several different collections and applied most effectively to the
administration of the film preservation programme (Roads, 1968). It proved
less successful than had been hoped, however, owing largely to problems in
using as a database packs of fragile, bulky, slow to read and easily muddled

cards. Also the changing economic climate rendered it impractical to provide sufficient staff to keep the system running. In the 1970s, film preservation documentation and the cataloguing of film and sound recordings were transferred to a computer system specially written for the Museum, called APPARAT (Smither, 1979; 1980). In contrast to the card system, APPARAT was designed in all respects — job running, software maintenance, data preparation and output processing — for agency or bureau services. The resulting pattern of operations, which could involve the Museum with up to five other organizations in seeing through a single month's work, proved on occasions very difficult to sustain. These two experiences illustrate the sorts of problems that a single museum can incur in maintaining privately-developed systems, even when there is no realistic alternative to their development. The Museum therefore welcomed the launching of the MDA Computing Service and the straightforward access this offered to the GOS package. Use of the service, combined with a return to some degree of in-house work, most immediately in the sphere of data entry, is seen as the logical direction for Imperial War Museum documentation projects in the 1980s.

The Museum's computerized files currently provide complete technical records on each of the 50 000 cans of film comprising the film collection, catalogue entries for 5000 film titles and 500 sound recordings, and a full catalogue of the Museum's collection of 2000 orders, decorations and medals awarded to British Commonwealth citizens. Work in progress includes continuing input into the film and sound record catalogues, which will rapidly add several hundred new entries, and data entry for a completed cataloguing project on medallions (1100 items). Figures 14.6 and 14.7 illustrate some of the research aids generated by the MDA from the film cataloguing file: a catalogue entry, with a related extract from the subject index, for a film recording tests of a German 'bouncing bomb' during the Second World War. Comparable examples from the medallions project were provided earlier (Figures 14.4 and 14.5). At a preliminary stage are the cataloguing of firearms, ammunition, posters, edged weapons and 'ephemera', but these are all planned as computer files. The average size of record over all these projects is between 400 and 500 characters, although individual records of much greater length are quite common. Investigations into the cataloguing of photographs and into the analysis by computer of the library's classification codes have been initiated.

Financial investment

In financial terms, the Imperial War Museum's main investment in documentation has taken the form of staff costs. This is true of most Museums, although it is a factor easily overlooked. It was noted earlier that the Museum employs 18 staff on its documentation work — this figure translates, using the official Civil Service costing calculations for salary and overheads in central London, into a continuing committment of some £250 000 per year. Investment in the original writing and subsequent enhancement of APPARAT cost the Museum in total £35 000 over seven years. Continuing costs for maintaining APPARAT, running it and using the associated bureaux, and using the MDA Computing Service have also been

```
                              IWM: MED/321

     LUDWIG III KONIG V.BAYERN
                              IWM: MED/737

     LUDWIG III V. BAYERN
                              IWM: MED/902

     LUDWIG III.KOENIG.VON.BAYERN
                              IWM: MED/531

     LUSITANIA MAY.7.1915
                              IWM: MED/841

     [ @ LUSITANIA MEDALLION ]
                              IWM: MED/860 to 871; MED/937 to 940; MED/988; MED/1017;
                                   MEDP/9

     LWOW 22.VI.1915      IWM: MED/222

     [ MACKENSEN ]        IWM: MED/52

     (Maggio MCMXV)       IWM: MED/479

     MAGNA BRITANIA PROTECTRIX
                              IWM: MED/827

     MAGNAE BRITANIAE     IWM: MED/790; MED/915

     MAISTRAUSS.VON.DER.GRUENEN.INSEL.1916.
                              IWM: MED/311

     MAJOR AUGUST V.PARSEVAL
                              IWM: MED/725

     MANFRED V.RICHTHOFEN
                              IWM: MED/595




     IMPERIAL WAR MUSEUM     MEDALLIONS ·     TITLE INDEX     PAGE 35
```

Figure 14.5 Extract from medallion titles index

incurred, but are difficult to quantify. Until April 1982, some part of these costs was absorbed by Government 'allied service' procedures, under which one Government organization would not charge another for work carried out on its behalf. Government policy has now phased out 'allied service', however, and full costs estimated at some £10 000 per year will fall to the Museum. Investment in equipment has been small by comparison: the Museum's total expenditure on machinery related to documentation since 1975 amounts to some £14 000, divided between machines for reading COM and simple microprocessors allowing the Museum some capability for in-house preparation of data for transfer to the MDA Computing Service.

Conclusions

What benefits does the Museum hope to see in return for this investment? It should gain a fuller and more secure knowledge of its own holdings — fuller in that recording what is known about an item can indicate what is not known and stimulate the discovery of the missing information; more secure

```
IMPERIAL WAR MUSEUM FILM CATALOGUE          3/Q2/84                    Page 82

GWY 1496      Access Conditions: LPU    Copy described: D 1/35/N
                                        Previous identity no: MAY 472 (old number)
                                        Previous identity no: TIB REF F.25/15

    ABWURFVERSUCHE MIT DEM GERAT KURI Kugelmodell aus Beton
    [KURT DROPPING TRIALS] (translation)

    (?) 1944          Germany
    CREDITS
    Sponsor:                      Rheinmetall-Borsig

    colour: B + W     sound: mute
    language, sound: None       language, titles: German
    no. of reels: 1     length: 587 ft    running time: 6 mins


    SUMMARY
    Trial drops of the 'Kurt' bouncing bomb.

    The bombs, both with and without attached rocket unit, are released both singly and (in two
    cases) in pairs from a low flying FW 190.  They bounce across the water for some distance
    before sinking and, in the final drop only, exploding.  The drops are filmed from various
    camera positions both in slow motion and at normal speed.  ('Aus Beton' in the title implies
    that all except the last bomb are concrete-filled test weapons.)

    Copyright: Enemy Property Act      Acquisition: Ministry of Aviation
    Catalogued:  DW 8/1979


    NOTES
    Remarks: some good shots - especially of the only trial drop (apparently) using an armed
    bomb.
```

Figure 14.6 Extract from film catalogue

```
        GWY 1460 - [HS 117, ENZIAN AND TAIFUN TRIALS] (after) 1944, Germany
               Trial firings of the Hs 117, Enzian and Taifun missiles.
Wasserfall
  1943
        GWY 1516 - [ROCKETS 2] (?) 1943, Germany
               A series of stills showing missiles before and just after launching with plan
               diagrams and performance graphs.
    1944
        GWY 1464 - [WASSERFALL HOISTING PROCEDURE] (?) 1944, Germany
               Hoisting a Wasserfall ground-to-air missile into a vertical position.
Wasserfall, [R and D]
    1944
        GWY 1458 - [HS 117 AND WASSERFALL TRIALS] (after) 1944, Germany
               Firing trials with the Hs 117 and Wasserfall missiles.
        GWY 1465 - [WASSERFALL HOISTING PROCEDURE] (?) 1944, Germany
               Tests and launchings of Wasserfall, Enzian and other unidentified rockets.
        GWY 1466 - [WASSERFALL AND SMALL ROCKET TRIALS] (?) 1944, Germany
               Firing trials of a small rocket and of the Wasserfall guided missile.

WEAPONS, GERMAN - ROCKET
   8 cm Raketen-Vielfachwerfer, [R and D]
    1943
        GWY 1518 - VERSUCHSSCHIESSEN MIT DEM 8-CM-VIELFACHWERFER (48 SCHUSS) : Entwicklung des
                    SS-Waffenamtes (?) 1943, Germany
               Specifications and trials of a multiple rocket launcher.
   [R and D]
    1943
        GWY 1518 - VERSUCHSSCHIESSEN MIT DEM 8-CM-VIELFACHWERFER (48 SCHUSS) : Entwicklung des
                    SS-Waffenamtes (?) 1943, Germany
               Specifications and trials of a multiple rocket launcher.

WEAPONS, GERMAN AIR - BOMB
   Kurt bouncing bomb, [R and D]
    1944
        GWY 1494 - [KURT BOUNCING BOMB TRIALS 1] 8/1944, Germany
               Trial drops of the 'Kurt' rocket-assisted bouncing bomb at Leba in August 1944.
        GWY 1495 - [KURT BOUNCING BOMB TRIALS 2] (?) 1944, Germany
               Trial drops of the 'Kurt' bouncing bomb.
        GWY 1496 - ABWURFVERSUCHE MIT DEM GERAT KURT Kugelmodell aus Beton (?) 1944, Germany
               Trial drops of the 'Kurt' bouncing bomb.
   Kurt/Walze bouncing bomb, [R and D]
    1944
        GWY 1492 - [WALZE] (? title written on film leader) (?) 1944, Germany
               Tests of a rocket-propelled spherical bomb, projected against obstacles.
        GWY 1493 - [WALZE] (? title written on film leader) (?) 1944, Germany
               Three firing trials with a rocket-assisted bouncing bomb.
```

Figure 14.7 Extract from film subject index

in the sense that, unlike the extensive personal knowledge of many of the Museum staff, knowledge recorded in documentation is not vulnerable to individual absence or departure. It should generate a wider awareness of the Museum and its collections and more informed use of its resources. (Publication of catalogues to at least parts of collections is an ultimate goal of all the Museum's collecting Departments, so far achieved for sound recordings and film.)

Documentation cannot be a substitute for access to Museum materials but it can assist in the accurate matching, at a saving of both time and risk of unnecessary wear and tear, of collection items with user requirements. At its best, moreover, the accuracy of the match need not imply a negative or restricting process: the mere act of cataloguing the Department of Art's collection of medallions reminded the Museum's exhibition planners of the potential value of medallions for inclusion in more than one new exhibition. Those involved in the Museum's documentation effort look forward to more such positive contributions.

Chapter 15

Documentation services at the National Maritime Museum: Project Petrel

Jonathan L. Cutbill

Introduction

The National Maritime Museum is a trustee museum founded in 1934. It incorporates the Royal Naval Museum, the Greenwich Hospital collections, the Admiralty collections, the Sir James Caird collection and many others. Good documentation procedures were established at the start, but the War caused considerable disruption, and in the period of growth that followed disorder and divergence crept in. We are now rectifying this situation, an operation called Project Petrel (after the Stormy Petrel, a bird famous for its ability to fly in very bad weather). This chapter describes our general approach, the achievements so far and some personal thoughts on the future.

Documentation services

Documentation services involve much more than the data on the collections and the indexes and published catalogues relating to them. Documentation is involved in museum activities as diverse as decision-taking on acquisitions, design of galleries and exhibitions and sales to the public of items such as photographs. Efficient documentation procedures are vital to the success of the museum.

In the late 1960s it was decided to renew the public areas of the museum and follow this with a period devoted to conservation and cataloguing. The first Information Retrieval Officer was appointed in 1969. A Central Information Retrieval Index with 250 000 cards relating to ships, places, people, events and general maritime subjects was constructed in the following years. There was also a growing awareness among the staff of the importance of documentation.

More resources were made available for documentation in 1975 when work on the galleries was nearing completion. In early 1976 we surveyed the existing situation and also the enquiries received from the public. We proved to have about 800 000 documentable items (omitting 1 000 000 news cuttings and 400 000 photographic prints which distort any attempt at statistics). Of these, 23 000 are three-dimensional museum objects (medals, models, uniforms, etc). The rest include prints and drawings, historical negatives, books and pamphlets, manuscripts and ships plans. Significantly the total includes about 300 000 information records covering such areas as histories of individual ships, indexes to instrument makers, lists of chronometers and many other topics.

In 1976 we were dealing with 20-25 000 public enquiries a year. Only 4% related directly to our objects. The rest were requests for information. The public see us as a source of maritime data rather than as a repository of maritime objects. This explains why almost 40% of our records are general data indexes.

We also found that 40% of our collections had no proper records. Of those records that did exist few were adequate. Only 4% of the collections were covered by published catalogues and these were largely out of date.

Policy

In November 1976 we agreed on plans to improve the situation. The first steps involved two stages.

In stage 1, all our data — good and bad — would be reorganized so that they could be worked with efficiently. In practice this meant that all data eventually required in catalogues and indexes or for museum management would be entered into a computer system. We could then use computers for the repetitive and labour intensive clerical procedures necessary when working with such data.

In stage 2 the data would be checked and improved until they were good enough to be included in a museum publication. Both the improvement process and the eventual publications would cost less because of the computer. Even so, this second stage would still require much staff time for two reasons. Curators had seldom noted the source or authority for the 'facts' they recorded. Also the data had often been copied from index to index, sometimes seven or eight times and by unqualified people. You know the party game where a message is passed in whispers round a circle? The result here is similar. We do not know the accuracy of any of the data. Each piece must be checked, corrected if necessary, and the authority noted. After that it is easier. Computers may not be very bright but they do copy accurately.

We decided to proceed collection by collection. In each case the existing manual systems would stay in operation until an appropriate point in the changeover. We decided to follow the data standards and formats being created by the MDA, developing them as necessary for our own needs. Common conventions and procedures were to be applied throughout the museum. This means that where departments record the same kinds of data and use them in the same ways, the conventions and procedures used would be the same. Provision would be made for real differences of data and use.

We decided not to control terminology during stage 1. Once the data are in the new system we can use the computer to help us evaluate our use of terms and plan cost effective improvements. The curatorial departments would carry out the work of improvement. Creating documentation is a curatorial function and does not need a separate group of clerical or data processing staff. The Information Retrieval Section was to be strengthened by the addition of a research assistant but its role was to be planning, development, training and monitoring. Curators would work directly with the computer and control their own work. There was not to be a documentation empire separate from the curatorial departments.

The Information Retrieval Section was given one further very important role. It was responsible for estimating for and procurement of all computing resources such as computer programs and hardware, services from bureaux and external data preparation. Decisions as to which data to put in the system and how they should be exploited were to be made jointly by the Information Retrieval Section and the curatorial department. The details of the systems were to be left to the technical experts.

Current situation

We thought it would take three years to get all departments involved and ten to fifteen years to complete stages 1 and 2 throughout the museum. Five years later we have 25% of our records through stage 1 and into stage 2. 4% are through stage 2 — that is of publishable quality. The scale of the archievement and some of the problems that have been encountered in particular departments are noted below.

Library. In 1976 it was decided to recatalogue the library collection according to AACR2 and the UDC classification. Of the 100 000 books and pamphlets in the library, over 20% have now been reprocessed. These are supported by microfiche author/title and classified lists for use by the public and museum staff. Holdings information about the 50 000 periodical volumes has also been processed. A new system is being introduced for library acquisition procedures.

Manuscripts. The manuscript collection occupies approximately 11 000 feet of shelving, and can be considered to consist of 60 000 catalogue items. The published guide to these manuscripts includes a computer-generated index, the production of which resulted in a significant reduction in the staff time and publication cost that would have been required using conventional methods. An inventory of manuscripts in Nelson's handwriting (1200 items) is through both documentation stages and is available on microfiche.

Oil paintings. Records for all 5100 items in the collection have now passed through stage 1 and into stage 2 of processing. Computerized information from the original out-of-date manuscript catalogue was used to produce numerical and location lists. These lists were reconciled with the acquisition records and against the collection itself, as a result of which the information was corrected and upgraded. The corrected file will then be used as a basis for title, artist, subject and negative number lists which will be further checked. The resulting file will be used to produce a new computer typeset concise list and indexes to the collection.

Prints and drawings. A similar project is underway to improve the existing basic documentation for the 70 000 items in the prints and drawings collection.

Historical photographs. 40% of the 100 000 items in the negative collection were supported by existing manual slips, information from which has been automated using the MDA computing bureau. These records are now being checked. Work is also underway to process the large number of previously-undocumented negatives.

Navigation and astronomy. As the 2500 objects in this collection are already well documented, priority has been given to other departments. 2400 charts, however, represent a major outstanding problem area.

Ships plans and technical records. The collection of 480 000 ships plans (corresponding to approximately 60 000 catalogue items) is already supported by manual lists and indexes. These are to be complemented by an automated guide.

Ships equipment and model collections. The collection of 2500 items has an existing card index.

Archaeological Research Centre. Although the nominal size of this collection is only 460 three-dimensional items, a single one of these may be the evidence from the excavation of a boat. They are complemented by 10 000 items such as photographs and plans. Excavated material is to be included within the museum system from the outset, with a microcomputer being used for site recording.

Weapons and antiquities collections. The existing records for the 14 000 items in these collections are being processed by the MDA prior to enhancement by the department staff.

Central Information Retrieval index. 50% of the collection of 250 000 records have now reached stage 2 of processing, including 45 000 ship histories and 3000 event records. An index of shipbuilders and shipping companies is being prepared. The resulting indexes are designed for use by museum staff rather than the public.

Photographic services. The MDA has also automated the records of the negatives of items in the museum collection, which comprise approximately half the 40 000 negatives held by Photographic Services.

Costs

Of 380 staff, 178 regularly work with the curatorial documentation systems. Only 93 of these are in curatorial departments. An estimated 20% of the time of these 178 is spent on activities directly involved with documentation, at a cost of approximately £350 000 per year. Of this total 5% (£15 000-£20 000 per year) is used to buy computing resources — equipment, programs, bureau time and external data preparation — and 7% is used for support staff (2.5 people in the Information Retrieval Section). Thus 12% of the total is being used to make improvements in the systems themselves (as opposed to adding data to or use of the systems). The figure has remained stable since we started project Petrel and the computing element of the costs has been consistently below the estimates made in 1976.

Problems and some lessons

The important word here is skills. At the start we could only plan on the basis of my saying 'do it this way'. We had difficulty finding a Research Assistant for the Information Retrieval Section with the necessary skills, and this section has only been at its full effective strength since 1981. Most of the development work has been done by one rather than the two people originally planned. This has slowed us down.

Progress has been linked to the spread of skills among the staff. Apart from myself there are now three section heads with a good knowledge of what is involved. A further twenty staff have worked with the computer methods. This is 32% of the curatorial staff.

Because of the new skills we have been able to start a Petrel Coordinating Committee. It has representatives from every department including relevant non-curatorial ones such as Design Services. Its members were chosen because they are involved on a day-to-day basis with documentation. The committee meets every three or four weeks, providing a forum where we discuss common problems, and exchange ideas and experience. It has taken on the responsibility for the standardization of conventions and procedures within the museum. It is also responsible for advising the Deputy Director on priorities in allocation of the resources available for development.

In retrospect we should have started this committee earlier. However it does take a lot of effort to keep such a group interested and involved unless its members already have the skills to work on problems without much guidance. For the first time we are planning on the basis of informed dialogue. This is just as important an achievement as the 25% of our records we have got through stage 1 of the improvement process.

Technical considerations

Here I want to say something about our approach to computers and the way we find solutions to our problems. We decide first on our aims, such as what data will be available at the end of a project, what products we are going to derive from these data and in what ways must we be able to use these data. After this it is the job of the Information Retrieval Section to design the cheapest solution. This is purely a technical matter and curatorial staff will only accidentally have skills that can be used. It will already be clear if the staff resources are available for a project and, as indicated above, support costs are usually a small percentage of staff costs.

The computer side of a project involves the supply of computer programs, computers on which to run them, a system which enables curators, programs and machine to combine to produce the end result and curators trained in the use of the system.

Choice of computer programs is one of the most important considerations. Unless the programs are really up to the work there are endless problems. It is all too easy to choose a bad program and find yourself stuck with restrictions such as only being allowed 10 descriptors for an object, or having to truncate people's names to 20 characters, or being unable to sort names starting with Mc, Mk, M', Mac, St, Saint, etc., into sensible order. These restrictions are all quite unnecessary but this has not yet penetrated to most software designers.

We use the GOS package supplied by the MDA (Chapter 12). For most of our work it is ahead of anything else, even though it was designed in the early 1970s. There is nothing absolute about our choice. Part of the job of the Information Retrieval Section is to keep abreast of software development. If anything better turns up we will use it. However GOS is so good that for most purposes there is no need for the curatorial staff to ask whether we can do this or that. If it is logical, we can do it.

The choice of computers depends very much on the state of the art and this changes fast. I expect most of our big projects will begin on one machine, end up on another and have used two others along the way. At the start we opted to use a computer bureau for most of our work (the IBM 370/165 at Cambridge University). We bought cheap simple computers with floppy discs (CommStor machines) for the curatorial staff to enter data. Our capital investment was therefore low and we retained flexibility. We bought our first serious microcomputer in 1981 and our second in 1982. We expect to have transferred all our work from Cambridge to these machines by 1983. Our reasons are mainly economic. Our bill at Cambridge had reached £8000 per year and was rising steadily with each new project. It has now become cheaper to have our own machine. The second reason was to get experience with microcomputers to make sure we are ready for the electronic office revolution which is only four or five years away.

The machine configuration in the Museum includes three Cromemco microcomputers, floppy and magnetic disc units, a magnetic tape drive and printers. Two of these machines are based in the Information Retrieval Section and the third in the Archaeological Research Centre. In the former cases, the initial Z80 processors are to be upgraded to MC68000 processors with 512K memories, after which the machines will each be able to support three or four users at any one time.

The systems to link machines, programs and people are also vitally important. Their design takes up most of the effort of the Information Retrieval Section. The cost of getting a project going often exceed the cost of the computing necessary to complete it. It is this side of documentation systems which is most often not allowed for in costing projects or planning timetables.

We expect our curators to work directly with the computer, entering their own data, submitting their own jobs and so on. We have put a lot of work into making the systems 'user friendly'. When the curator goes to the terminal the machine asks which project they wish to work on and which process they wish to carry out (entering new data, editing existing data, creating indexes and so on). The idea is to cut to a minimum the amount they have to remember and to make it difficult for them to make mistakes. The systems as they now stand are still far from ideal but are evidently usable. We hope to make the systems on the new microcomputers even better.

Staff training is again an important area. None of the procedures are difficult or complex but they are often strange. As we get more and more people involved training gets easier. When the library took on two new cataloguers they were trained entirely by the existing library staff and Information Retrieval Section did not get involved. One of these new staff had previous experience of computer cataloguing systems. But this is still an area that causes us problems.

The future

Turning to the future, I offer my personal view of what could happen. The results we have achieved so far indicate that we could carry on as now and probably come close to our target of having most of our curatorial data under control by the end of the decade. To attempt this unthinkingly is to court disaster.

The museum has come through a period of rapid growth. Our ability to produce more work has been achieved by adding new staff within the existing structure. This structure was designed for an organization one-third our present size. Little major reorganization has been attempted. The museum already has a bureaucratic load which it cannot handle and an acute problem of space. We have few staff with a strong interest in making the museum's systems work efficiently. We are entering what will probably be a long period of little or no growth in real resources. Continued growth in the use of the museum by the public can only come through radical internal reorganization based on reappraisal of our objectives and involving the introduction of information technology. This is a process that must of necessity take five to ten years.

I have no instant solution to these problems but two things are clear. The reorganization of the staff should be around function rather than class of object and the new structure must make it easy to bring staff together on a temporary basis into teams for specific projects.

Of course our problems are not caused by the new computer technology. But almost every museum activity involves data handling of some kind and the arrival of the 'electronic office' provides us with new tools that are most opportune. By the end of the decade it will be possible to handle the entire clerical and documentation work of this museum using computers. The cost of giving every relevant member of staff (200 plus) the necessary terminals at their desks and access through these to all data and information relevant to their work will be under £500 per person. Nobody really knows yet what working in such an environment will be like. But we will not be allowed to stand aside from it any more than we could have stood aside from the typewriter and telephone. The methods we use now will be too costly in comparison. If we are to control the introduction of the technology we must start now. We should look for viable applications of microcomputers to our existing office operations. Possible applications include word processing in the typing services, accounts and financial control, purchase and control of supplies, staff records, planning duty rosters for warding staff and so on. Each successful scheme will extend the skills of the staff and makes us better placed to plan the future.

On the curatorial side we already plan to link our curatorial computers to those used by our Design Services Section for label production. This will enable them to draw directly on curatorial data for inclusion in labels for galleries and give the curatorial side access to their computer typesetting capability for the production of lists and catalogues. We have just started to plan a similar link up of Photographic Services, Photographic Sales and curatorial records.

By extending and integrating in this way we could achieve a steady evolution as more staff get involved. It also means that the planning can involve all our staff. We can avoid having solutions imposed on us from outside by teams of so called experts. We must acquire the skills to find and use for our own purpose people with the appropriate skills.

Looking to 1990 and beyond, I see three areas where there should be a marked improvement in service to the public.

With all our data in order and with the kinds of office system we will then have we should be able to answer enquiries faster and more effectively. We have already made plans for a separate Enquiry Service that would coordinate and facilitate the answering of all curatorial enquiries.

For obvious reasons access to the library, manuscripts, plans, and print collections must be tightly controlled. Similar problems do not arise with computerized data. I expect all our data (except anything that must be confidential) will be available to the public via terminals in public areas and probably at home via teletext systems (such as Prestel in the United Kingdom). This is a completely new departure and I do not think any of us know how this will change the ways the museum is used. As a first step we plan to place our computer produced indexes in a public area as they are completed.

The third development will be in the construction and publication of authoritative compilations of maritime data. I have in mind such things as histories of British naval vessels, indexes to shipbuilders and shipowners, biographical data and so on. In the past, attempts at such projects have been numerous and usually failed because of the limitations of 5×3 index cards and hand copying of data. The quality of the results was not good enough. With the systems we will then have, as well as our data and expert staff resources we will be in a position to produce such high quality research tools at relatively low cost. It would be a natural response to the demands for information already made on us.

Chapter 16

Royal Pavilion, Art Gallery and Museum, Brighton

Charles A.B. Steel

Introduction

The collections and buildings administered by the Royal Pavilion, Art Gallery and Museums Department of Brighton Council have diverse origins. The nucleus of the museum and art gallery collections came from the Royal Brighton Literary and Philosophical Society. When the town purchased the Royal Pavilion estate in 1850 they were housed in the upper rooms. As the collections grew it became necessary to find larger premises and in 1871 the former Royal Stables were converted to a museum and lending library, opened to the public in 1873. These premises were extended in 1894, the new extension being opened in November 1901.

In 1874, Edward Booth resolved to build a museum in Brighton to house his unique collection of British birds. This museum opened in 1876. After his death in 1890, the museum and its collection passed to Brighton Borough Council. Preston Manor, the home of the Stanford family, was willed to Brighton in 1925, subject to a life interest on behalf of Sir Charles Thomas Stanford and his wife. On their deaths in 1932, the museum was opened as a country house museum. The Grange, Rottingdean, was also acquired for use as a library and museum in 1954.

An extraordinary wealth of material is held within these buildings. The principal benefactor, Henry Willet, served on the Borough's Fine Art Committee for many years and it was largely due to his constant drive and support that a properly run museums service was established. Between 1859 and 1901 he gave the museum his collections of pottery, porcelain, Old Masters and chalk fossils.

There are fine collections in all fields, including the Lucas collections of ethnographic and osteological specimens, the Spencer collection of musical instruments, the Pocock and Furner collections of local drawings and the Hall collection of Nymphalid butterflies. One of Brighton's most important collections has been built up over the last 15 years: the internationally recognized twentieth century decorative art and fine art collection.

Every field except science and technology is represented, with the total number of items estimated at over one million (most of which are natural history specimens).

Development of documentation plans

Prior to 1972 the Department was seriously understaffed. As a consequence, little other than rudimentary documentation had been maintained. With the creation of a number of new curatorial posts, a more dynamic approach to curation resulted in an upsurge of public and academic interest in the collections. The department began to service a growing number of enquiries that required information to be extracted from the collections. It soon became obvious that existing documentation was inadequate. Parallel to developments within the department itself, Brighton Borough Council's Finance Department and its insurers became aware that some form of inventory control was needed for the collection.

For some years, Brighton had been watching the development of CGDS and IRGMA with a view of adopting any system that became operational (Chapter 12). By 1974, however, the need for computer assistance in Brighton had become so great that it was decided to proceed with development of a local system to cater for Brighton's specific needs (Kirk, 1979). This was not as much a step into the unknown as it might seem. From 1973 to 1976 Brighton had been running the British Museum (Natural History) version of CGDS on its computer, thus the computer section was familiar with the philosophy of using computers for museum accessioning. Also, Brighton had just recruited a Keeper of Geology whose experience in the use of computers in geological work made him an ideal link between the Museum and the computer. These two factors, coupled with a good deal of spare capacity on the Council's computer, persuaded those concerned to take the view that the development of a local system was a realistic goal. It was specified that any system developed in Brighton had to meet the following criteria:

it had to be able to store information about all Brighton's current collections and any new ones built up in the future;
the output from the system had to meet the needs of the curator, the researcher, the insurer/accountant and — ultimately — the public;
the preparation of data for inputting to the system had to be simple, enabling the cataloguer to record as much as required when and as it could be done.

To meet the criteria, any system design had to be flexible, open ended, and from the operational point of view, capable of manipulating what would eventually become a very large database.

The development of the system took about fifteen months from conception to routine operation. During this period advice was sought from a variety of sources. It was decided that, as far as possible, the data standards adopted would be the same as those of IRGMA. It was also decided that the computing system had to be capable of being operated by people who had no knowledge or even interest in what it was meant to achieve. The philosophy behind this decision was simply that operators in local authority computer bureaux tended to work mainly with information which required no interpretation by the operator. To expect them to switch from this to complex text which required interpretation would not only slow them down, but would also make the work unpopular and eventually disrupt the system. A major advantage of this approach was that input for Brighton's system could be handed to any punch operator familiar with the use of 80-column coding sheets and the data could then be entered without any prior training.

The corollary was that it required a good deal of discipline and some training on the part of those generating the data. This was not in itself a bad thing since it made the curator/cataloguer think about the process and approach the task in a more professional way. If the output is rubbish then, failing a major computer fault, the finger of suspicion points at the originator of the input.

Once initial trials had been carried out it became possible to make some assessment of how long it was likely to take to complete the job. It was thought that a ten-year programme would be required to accession all the collections apart from entomology, which was to take twenty years. (Present evidence suggests that the ten-year target for collections other than entomology was realistic, but that the target for entomology was over-optimistic.)

All curatorial staff are involved in documentation and much use has been made of volunteers, temporary staff and students. It had been found that with very little training such categories of assistant can considerably speed up the rate of accessioning. The assistant does all the routine recording requiring little or no critical appraisal, leaving the curator to concentrate on the data requiring his expertise and knowledge to interpret or elucidate. It is estimated that the time spent on all aspects of accessioning is the equivalent of having two full-time staff allocated to this task.

Documentation practice

Prior to being catalogued for the computing system all objects are entered in a day book immediately on receipt by the museum, and are at this stage allocated their permanent accession number. The one exception is biological specimens which require preparation, in which case a temporary number is allocated until preparation is complete. Title of objects donated to the museum is established by sending a letter to the donor listing the objects donated and thanking the donor for the gift.

Before commencing accessioning, the curator must learn the conventions used for writing certain characters in order to make them unambiguous, and also which of the 200 or so subject and sub-subject codes (data categories) are appropriate to the material being catalogued. After the first few dozen records these will have been memorized so there will be no need to refer to the documentation manual except when new or obscure categories of information are being recorded. All data are handwritten in capital letters directly on to the data sheets (Figure 16.1).

The structure of information is simple: each line of data on the 80-column coding sheets is prefixed by a series of 12 characters. The first six characters represent the unique accession number of the specimen, the next four the nature of the data or subject and the next two the sub-subject, where it is wished to maintain a link between associated categories of information. The

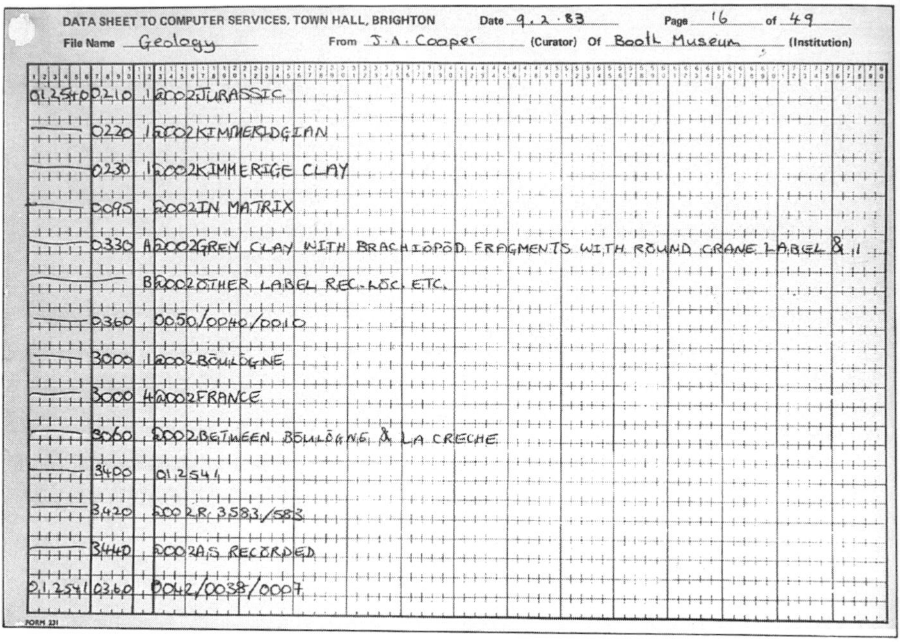

Figure 16.1 Data entry sheet

last two characters are also used to define a continuation line where the information is too long to fit into one line. By thoughtful allocation of sub-subject and continuation codes, quite sophisticated indexing strategies are possible. The remaining 68 columns are occupied by the data themselves.

This structure results in every line of data being 'tagged' with a unique 12-figure sequence of characters which determine their relationship to all other data in the system. Lines of data sharing the same accession number are combined to form records, and records are accumulated to form files, the number of which is only governed by the amount of equipment, time and space Brighton Borough Council is prepared to make available to the system. Nominal sizes are 999 999 records per file, 9999 subjects per record and 1369 lines per subject. By using this type of structure the amount of information that can be recorded about one object is effectively limitless.

Files are normally processed separately, although they can be combined if necessary. Each file generally covers one subject area, such as Fine Art, Antiquities and Geology.

As noted above, the information about any given object is built up from a series of lines. These may be entered in any order; indeed circumstances sometimes dictate that information about an object may be entered over a period of time and certainly may be separated by several pages of intervening information about other objects. These lines of data are sorted into order by the computer. Data can be altered with ease, it being merely necessary to write another line bearing the same 12-character sequence: this will then replace the existing line in the data bank. Lines may be deleted by simply writing down the 12-character code followed by a '-' sign. One device that makes life easier for the cataloguer and speeds things up is the multiple entry facility, by means of which the same piece of information may be incorporated in up to 999 consecutive catalogue entries by writing one line of data. Thus subjects such as Cataloguer, Storage and Collector, where many serially numbered specimens will have the same information are very simply and speedily added to the file and boring repetition avoided.

Having built up a batch of data sheets (up to 50), the curator sends them off to the systems supervisor, a member of the curatorial staff who makes certain checks on the input and records details in a diary. The systems supervisor then passes the batches on to the computer section for punching, accompanied by a batch header which ensures that batches are processed in the correct order and amalgamated with the appropriate file. After punching, a transcript is returned to the curator for checking and correction. Once corrected, the transcript is returned to the computer section for correction and input. This update run produces three reports:

Control Report. This lists all the batches input and any lines rejected because they have more than 80 characters or a non-numeric character in the accession or subject number.
Accession Register Folio. This lists all new data lines in the sequence in which they appear in the Serial Catalogue. These folios are serially numbered to assist the curator when checking the receipt of a report on every update.
Update Report. This lists all lines removed from the data bank with an indication whether they were deleted or substituted. It also lists all lines not accepted because another line with the same characters in column 1 to 12 was input later during the same run.

The new information is also added to the serial catalogue tape on the computer and from this a new serial catalogue may be produced, although working practice is to only do this about twice a year. In the serial catalogue all current information about a specimen appears in the correct order. No information is ever lost from the data bank since all deleted or altered information is stored on a history file tape.

Products of the system

The serial catalogue along with simple and compound indexes provide the principal means of obtaining information from the data bank (Figure 16.2).

For all files the serial catalogue is produced on COM (Computer Output Microform) although some of the smaller files (with conservative curators) use a back-up paper copy as the working document. COM is favoured because it is so much more compact and durable than paper. It is also easily and cheaply duplicated, making it possible to supply individuals and institutions with copies of all or part of the catalogue at minimal effort and cost.

In the accession register and the serial catalogue each subject and sub-subject code generates subject or sub-subject name thus making these documents more readily intelligible to an outside user.

```
ROYAL PAVILION, ART GALLERY AND MUSEUMS, BRIGHTON    SERIAL CATALOGUE          RUN ON  2. 3.1981        PAGE   23
ART GALLERY AND MUSEUMS, BRIGHTON                                          INCLUDES FOLIOS 1 TO      0

600060  0610 L1  MAKER                       BSA
        0610 L6  NATIONALITY OF MAKER        ENGLISH
        3160 AA  MONOCHROME PHOTOS           NEG. FILE NO 98
        3540     DATE OF ACCESSION           1976/12/01
        3570 AA  CATALOGUER                  LEGG G DR
        3580 AA  STORAGE                     STRONG ROOM/MUSEUM CHURCH STREET
        6198  0  CONSERVATION                1980/11/13
        6198 0A  CONSERVATION                WAX-OILED CLEANED

600061  0300 AA  TYPE OF OBJECT              RIFLE
        0302 AA  SYSTEM OF IGNITION          CENTRE FIRE
        0303 AA  CALIBRE OR BORE             11 MM
        0391 AA  LICENCE NO. & DATE          FIREARMS CERTIFICATE NO 006940 GRANTED 1976/09/12 VALID UNTIL
        0391 AB  LICENCE NO. & DATE          1979/09/11
        3160 AA  MONOCHROME PHOTOS           NEG. FILE NO 99
        3540     DATE OF ACCESSION           1976/12/01
        3570 AA  CATALOGUER                  LEGG G DR
        3580 AA  STORAGE                     STRONG ROOM/MUSEUM CHURCH STREET
        6198  0  CONSERVATION                1980/11/13
        6198 0A  CONSERVATION                WAX-OILED CLEANED

600062  0300 AA  TYPE OF OBJECT              PISTOL HOLSTER ONE OF A PAIR
        0302 AA  SYSTEM OF IGNITION          FLINTLOCK
        3580 AA  STORAGE                     STRONG ROOM/MUSEUM CHURCH STREET
        6198  0  CONSERVATION                1980/11/13
        6198 0A  CONSERVATION                WAX-OILED CLEANED

600063  0300 AA  TYPE OF OBJECT              CARBINE FLINT
        0301 AA  SERIAL NUMBER               142
        0302 AA  SYSTEM OF IGNITION          FLINT LOCK
        0303 AA  CALIBRE OR BORE             16 BORE
        0304 AA  LOCK(S) OR ACTION           CARBINE FLINT BY  STAUDENMAYER
        0304 AB  LOCK(S) OR ACTION           ENGLISH
        0304 AC  LOCK(S) OR ACTION           MARKINGS:  LOCK OUTSIDE STAUDENMAYER
        0304 AD  LOCK(S) OR ACTION           LOCK: JAW SCREW OF HAMMER SNAPPED, WATERPROOF PAN, ROLLER FRIZZEN
        0304 AE  LOCK(S) OR ACTION           SPRING, SUN/RAYS ENGRAVED BEHIND PAN, TUMBLER FITTED WITH DETENT
        0304 AF  LOCK(S) OR ACTION           TRIGGER:  TRIGGER GUARD & TRIGGER PLATE OF BRASS
        0305 AA  BARREL(S)                   MARKINGS:  UNDERNEATH 142 & PROOF MARKS: TOP STAUDENMAYER LONDON.
        0305 AB  BARREL(S)                   SIGHTS: FORE BLADE & REAR DOUBLE LEAF
        0306 AA  BARREL LENGTH               0760 MM
        0307 AA  BARREL FORM                 CIRCULAR TAPERING SLIGHTLY
        0308 AA  BARREL CHOKE OR RIFLING     7 GROOVE
        0308 AB  BARREL CHOKE OR RIFLING     DEXTRAL
        0308 AC  BARREL CHOKE OR RIFLING     .75 TWIST/BORE LENGTH
        0309 AA  STOCK                       WOOD: WALNUT FULL STOCK
        0309 AB  STOCK                       CHEEK PIECE A FITTED WITH BRASS HINGED BUTT TRAP
        0310 AA  MATERIAL OR MEDIUM          STEEL, BRASS & WOOD
        0311 AA  FURNITURE OF FIREARM        BARREL KEYS 3OF STEEL WITH BRASS INLET SURROUNDS, STEEL SLING
        0311 AB  FURNITURE OF FIREARM        FIXINGS PRESENT. FORE END TIP BRASS
        0311 AD  FURNITURE OF FIREARM        RAM ROD GUIDES 2 OF BRASS
        0311 AE  FURNITURE OF FIREARM        RAM ROD STEEL & BRASS TIPPED 0762 MM SWOLLEN TOWARDS FLAT DISTAL
        0311 AF  FURNITURE OF FIREARM        END
        0320 AA  PARTS LIST                  GUN
        0320 AB  PARTS LIST                  RAM ROD
```

Figure 16.2 Catalogue

In addition to the production of the serial catalogue, facilities exist for the generation of indexes to the collection. These are of two types: simple and compound (Figure 16.3).

In the case of the simple index, one subject or sub-subject is indexed at a time, the data entries being sorted in standard character set sequence and each datum printed followed by a block of accession numbers that have the datum in common. Up to 60 simple indexes can be made during one computer run. Simple indexes have proven to be very useful in locating specimens from particular collections, producing storage location lists, answering enquiries about holdings of specimens from particular localities and checking the conformity of the data to the data standards.

The compound index is specified by quoting up to five different sub-subject codes in any order. For each sub-subject an exact required datum may be specified. The five data lines are printed followed by a block of relevant accession numbers. If no data exist for a sub-subject then asterisks are printed. Compound indexing may also be used for indexing a specified block of accession numbers. Compound indexes are useful for indexing particular types of object or named collections.

For complex enquiries a further means of extracting information is available. By using the SPECOL (Special Customer Orientated Language) program, complex relationships between data may be sought and the information output precisely specified. A fairly simple example would be to search for all objects of specified type/s donated between specified dates and stored in specified location/s and then to print out all or part of the

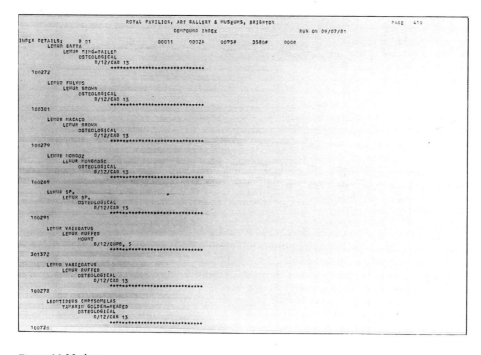

Figure 16.3 Indexes

information available about these specimens (not necessarily including the data upon which the original search was made). In practice this facility is not often required but it is useful, should normal methods prove to be inadequate.

It is unfortunately impossible to give costings for the running of the data processing system in Brighton since all computer costs are included in the central establishment charge paid by the department to cover the costs of legal, estate management, personnel, financial and computer services provided centrally.

In 1981-1982, 156 batches were processed which added 178 481 lines to the data bank. Eighty simple indexes and six compound indexes were produced. In addition, special paper serial catalogues were produced for four files, as well as the annual complete fiche catalogue for all 13 currently maintained files. The total size of the data bank was 1 044 430 lines relating to 79 704 objects. The average size of each record was approximately 15 lines.

Conclusion

Use of the documentation tends to vary from curator to curator. To some extent it depends upon both the quantity of information recorded for each object and also the extent to which a collection is catalogued. The ease of entering information is a positive encouragement to the curator to make full use of the system and by so doing build up a comprehensive entry for each object. Where collections are completely catalogued with extensive information the work of the curator in managing the collections is considerably simplified as is answering enquiries. The output from the system gives advantages over traditional index cards both in terms of speed of access to the information and also the security of the information itself. COM is a surprisingly efficient medium, although subject to widespread initial prejudice.

The time saved by having documentation in this form is considerable: an enquiry that might have taken several hours' searching through card indexes and then through the collection can now be answered in a matter of minutes by the curator. The serious researcher also benefits in that the information is so simply presented and easy to use that it can be extracted from the system quickly and without having to constantly refer back to the curatorial staff for guidance. Without a doubt the ability of the system to provide large numbers of simple indexes is the key to its efficiency.

The decision taken in Brighton to re-document the whole of the collection caused a good deal of misgivings amongst staff. With almost six years' worth of records on file and many collections fully documented, the benefits are tangible and the original decisions vindicated. One unforeseen result is that the curators are probably more familiar with the objects in their care than they would otherwise have been since each object documented has been carefully examined during the documentation process.

Chapter 17

The development of documentation procedures in the City of Bristol Museum and Art Gallery

Charles J.T. Copp

Historical perspective

The City of Bristol Museum and Art Gallery is one of the larger provincial museums in the United Kingdom with collections amounting to an estimated three million items. The precursor of the present Bristol Museum opened in 1823 in the Bristol Institution for the Advancement of Science, Literature and the Arts, which had been formed amongst other objectives for that purpose by members of the Bristol Philosophical and Literary Society (Conybeare, 1836). The museum was originally only open to members of the Society or those introduced by members but this was enough to keep the early curators busy for much of their week, showing visitors round the displays.

The Museum was housed in a building at the bottom of Park Street, Bristol and was one of many being founded around this time by private societies. The immense growth of local museums and private collections in the early nineteenth century and their subsequent demise accounts in great part for the scatter of important collections, particularly of natural history and geological material, across the United Kingdom and for the present sorry state of many of these collections. In many ways the Bristol collections have been among the more fortunate but even so the events of 160 years have left some historically based problems which have coloured our approach to documentation.

Bristol was an important provincial centre of scientific and cultural activity at this time and the Bristol Institution therefore attracted a great deal of active support. The Museum was fortunate from the outset in that it attracted exceptional men as curators (sometimes for atrocious working conditions and no salary at all!) and the City's position in a geologically rich area and as a major port dealing with the African and West Indian trades ensured a constant accumulation of both local and exotic material. The Museum's first curators, J.S. Miller (circa 1779-1830) and Samuel

Stutchbury (1798-1859) both made full use of their contacts with ship owners and captains to obtain new material. Both were geologists and zoologists of sound reputation, in close contact with the greatest scientists of the day, so that the museum came to hold much important material and many newly described species.

The main growth of the collections was in geology and the tradition of appointing a geologist with a strong subsidiary interest in zoology (particularly molluscs) as a curator continued right into this century.

The Institution had a continual history of financial problems. In 1871 it was finally forced to merge with the Bristol Library Society to form the Bristol Museum and Library Association which moved to newly built premises at the top of Park Street, a short way up the hill from the original building. Some important material came with the Library Association including a 'hortus siccus' of Jamaican plants collected by Dr Arthur Broughton (died 1796) which contains type and many cited specimens (Crane, 1981a).

The old institution had most of its specimens listed in various manuscript donor books, annual reports and a few subject catalogues. Further cataloguing was instituted after the move and many of the specimens were re-labelled at this time. The curator E. B. Tawney (1841-1882) made copious annotations in the earlier manuscript catalogues and publications describing the material in the collections.

The Bristol Museum and Library Association was itself ill-fated and the building, together with its collections, passed into the hands of the Bristol Corporation in 1894. The debts of the Society were written off by generous private donation and a new phase of display and expansion of the collections was embarked upon. The museum was now open freely to the public for the first time (Barker, 1906).

A new accessioning and numbering system was introduced at this time. As an example of the work undertaken, most of the zoology collections were completely re-labelled over the next twenty-five years. Unfortunately none of the zoology manuscript labels were kept. The situation was somewhat better in Geology and Archaeology, so that recent curators in these subjects have been able to carry out much valuable work on the historical aspects of their collections.

In 1905 an Art Gallery was built adjacent to the Museum through the generosity of Sir William Henry Wills (Walton, 1980). The ethnographical and archaeological collections with some natural history displays were moved into the new building and the two institutions functioned side by side under somewhat complex administration until 24th November 1940 when the original building was badly damaged by fire during an air raid. The main damage was done to the geological and invertebrate zoology collections. The zoology curator's office containing all the natural history card files and similar documentation were destroyed although the registers and accession books survived in the strong room.

The museum building was very badly damaged and the surviving collections were moved into the Art Gallery building where they are still housed. It was originally hoped to build a new museum at another site in the city, so the old museum building was sold to Bristol University in 1946. By 1972 it was realized that the new museum would never materialize and a major effort was undertaken to restore and revitalize the museum reserve collections which had languished in the Art Gallery basement for thirty-two years. The toll was sad; many natural history specimens had to be destroyed and many more were divorced from their data. The geological collections had, however, been much better cared for and overall the quality of the Museum and Art Gallery's collections is still remarkable. A great mass of documentary information pertaining to them has survived in manuscripts, books, registers, and historical files whilst many new and important collections have been added since the war.

The first phase of the effort to revitalize the collections began in 1972 with the complete refurbishment of the museum stores (Elkin, 1975) and a commitment to continued investment in storage and conservation. This phase of collection care, in providing adequate housing and conditions for the specimens, was absolutely essential and no serious attempt to upgrade the documentation could have taken place without it.

General documentation procedures

The documentation procedures used by the museum today are generally attributed to Herbert Bolton (1863-1936), appointed as curator in 1898 and as the museum's first director in 1911 (Hiley and Wallis, 1936). The differences in procedure between the museum and the art gallery are due to their separate origins (Figure 17.1).

In 1936, Hiley and Willis introduced the use of an accession book to cover all transactions concerning specimens (analogous to the 'day book' still used by many museums). In practice, this book eventually became used only as a means of recording the acquisition of new specimens. Few details are recorded and a single accession number can refer to just one object or a whole collection. The value of the accession number resides solely in linking a collection to its acquisition data and any available documentation until the constituent objects can be individually catalogued by the specialist sections. The indexes produced from the accessions register have historically been poorly ordered and with the exception of the donor index are of relatively little value.

The Museum and Art Gallery has grown substantially since the beginning of the century and is now divided into a number of sections (Geology, Natural History, Archaeology and History (including Ethnography), Technology, Agricultural and Social History, Applied Art, Fine Art and Oriental Art). There are also two service sections (Design and Conservation) and a Schools section. Each section maintains its own registers under curatorial control in which each specimen receives its own unique number. The degree of sorting, registration and cross-indexing of the collections varies enormously between sections. The greatest problems occur in natural sciences and archaeology where the vast numbers of specimens (circa 1.5 million in archaeology, circa 0.5 million in geology and circa 0.4 million in natural history) and the fact that the acquisition of many specimens predates current registration methods means that complete cataloguing and indexing of the collections is a task of prodigious proportions.

Historically, the museum has been concerned with acquiring large numbers of specimens and artefacts whilst the role of cataloguing and

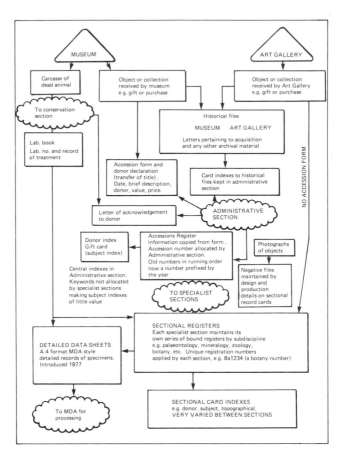

Figure 17.1 Outline of the acquisition documentation system

handling of data has been restricted to factual items related only to the identification and acquisition of these objects. Little has been made of the gradual enrichment of information that tends to build up as any specimen is studied or handled by various users.

Virtually all the specimens in the museum have been handled, classified and stored at some time and may have a variety of numbers inscribed upon them or on associated documents. Much information can exist about the specimens, either directly associated with them or in related historical files and sectional collections of manuscripts. This spread between sources means that data can become divorced from the specimens and occasionally important specimens may be overlooked within the collections. A degree of inadequacy or incompleteness in the documentation of collections must occur in all museums but the problem created unexpected repercussions at Bristol.

Recent developments

In 1977, following a District Auditor's report which suggested that existing documentation and security arrangements did not adequately cater for the protection of specimens, a major review of procedures was ordered by the City Council's Arts and Leisure Committee. One of the problems was the historical situation described above; another was financial, as the monetary value of even the commonest museum objects has escalated out of all proportion to their traditional worth. A Court case following the theft of items from the museum collections showed how inadequate traditional documentation methods can be in proving ownership, recording movements or even providing proper descriptions of museum items.

Members of the staff had been aware of these problems for a number of years. Bristol was one of the museums to participate in the original IRGMA card trials of 1976. Some staff had also been associated with the committee which had originally established IRGMA following the meetings of the Leicester Group in 1966 (Chapter 12). Prior to the instigation of the Arts and Leisure Committee's review in 1977, discussions had already taken place to approach the newly-formed MDA on the subject of an improved data recording sheet for the natural history section of the museum.

The Committee required curators to define the areas within their collections which were either of great value or portable and to prepare an inventory of these items. Virtually all curatorial time was to be spent on inventory recording with the suspension of all but essential unrelated activities. The city's Management Services Department reported back to the committee with advice on the form that recording procedures should take. At the same time the MDA was invited to discuss the existing procedures with curators and advise on any changes which could be made in the light of recent experience.

The principal interest of the controlling body was thus the production of an 'audit checklist' with the minimum of researched curation whilst it was just this upgrading of documentation that was being sought by those curators cooperating with the MDA. This divergence was a potential source of conflict but in practice a valuable compromise was reached.

Following the discussions with curators, each section defined a number of inventory cataloguing tasks in consultation with the museum management team. The data recorded were expected to be simple and a time limit was given for each task. At the same time a major programme of photographing items for security purposes was instigated. To cover the extra cost of the work a new documentation budget was created which also enabled certain sections to undertake the upgraded documentation trials with the MDA.

The work with the MDA was in two parts. The first was to upgrade the way in which information was recorded. A number of new draft record sheets were prepared for all sections (Figure 17.2). These were based on the MDA data standard, like the familiar MDS cards, but of A4 format, colour coded by subject and the boxes arranged in a manner easier for the extraction of 'audit information'. These sheets provide a detailed record of information about an object or a summary of the full information maintained in separate folders. They are filled in according to standard

MDA conventions, providing the facility for later manipulation in computerization projects.

Sheet of

IDENTITY STORE
file: British Bird's Eggs | registration number: BRSMG Ab4734 | part: 1–7
store date: Cabinet 88 : 1979 | accession number: 97/1947
historical file number: 3449M

IDENTIFICATION
common name: British Robin | type of specimen: Eggs
phylum class: Vertebrata : Aves | order: Passeriformes
super family: Muscicapidae | family: Turdinae
genus: Erithacus | species author: rubecula :
status: cited | identifier date: Lewis, Stanley : 1906 1.

SYNONYMY
genus species author: B.O.U. number 325 | previous indentifier date

FIELD COLLECTION
locality name: The Holloway (near) | locality number
place names: Dulcote & Wells (near) & Somerset
NGR: ST 565446 | vice county: 6
altitude: – | depth: –
habitat: Bank & Roadside

ACQUISITION
collection method | collector date: Lewis, Stanley (1870–1949) : May 1906 | collection number: 432
method: Donation | acquired from date: Lewis, Stanley : August 1947
price | conditions

VALUATION
insurance valuation date

DESCRIPTION
number: 7 | sex | age
form: ringed (resembling Red-backed Shrike) 1.2. | phase | variety
condition: good (very) | completeness: Complete (blown)
dimension | dimension | dimension

LOANS & EXHIBITIONS
loans and exhibitions

PHOTOS
method | photographer date | photo number

CONS. RECORDER
method: fumigated (Methyl Bromide)
conservation number date: : 1980 | recorder date: Swansborough S.A. : March 1979

NATURAL HISTORY RECORD SHEET MDAU

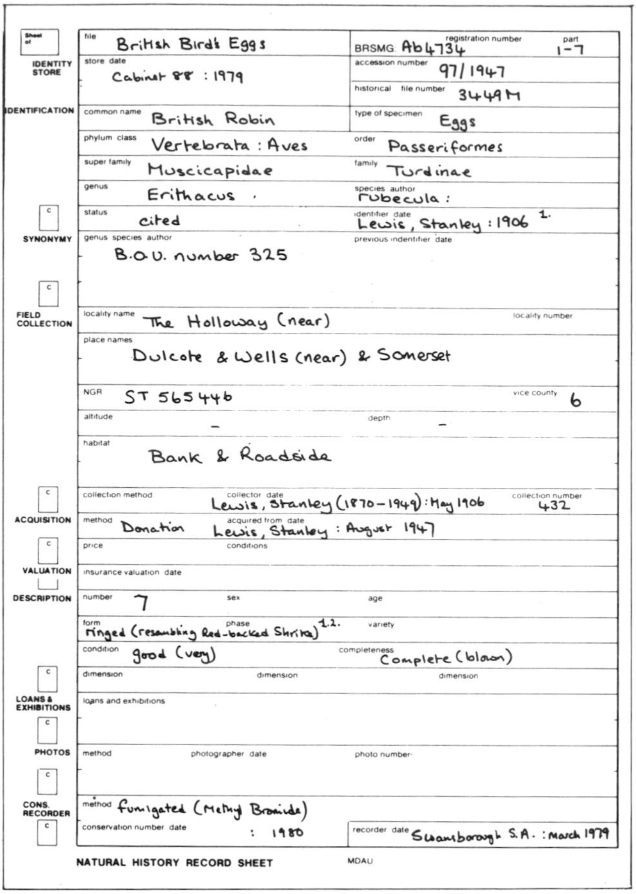

Figure 17.2(a) Completed example of a natural history record sheet (front)

Despite the general support voiced for the MDA work, the response from the different sections varied widely. The Art Gallery did not adopt the forms as they regarded their existing records as reasonably near completion and the number of objects too low to make the change of system worthwhile. Within the Museum only Natural History, which historically had the poorest records, took unreservedly to the new cards whilst some use has since been made of them by Archaeology and History and Agricultural and Social History. The Geology section fully supported the system but introduced specialized forms of its own to cover the research on specimens, collections and bibliographies required to produce the catalogue of type, figured and cited specimens defined as one of its priority documentation tasks, and a task which had long been regarded as important within the section.

The second part of the work with the MDA has been the computerization of the data sheets by the MDA computing bureau. In Natural History, the

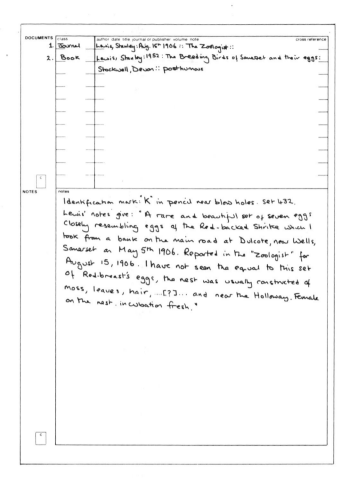

Figure 17.2(b) Completed example of a natural history record sheet (reverse)

herbarium was chosen as the subject for full documentation. This was because the herbarium contains a significant amount of manuscript information, much of it of direct scientific or conservation interest. It had never been adequately catalogued and the sheets themselves can be easily damaged by repeatedly rummaging through them for individual items.

In geology the main use of the MDA facilities was in the compilation of a search list of possible type and figured specimens, gleaned from an extensive but selective literature survey. This list was later compared to indexes and the existing collections to prepare a critical catalogue of specimens known to be, or have been in the collections or thought likely to be in the collections. The full use of the facilities of the upgraded documentation system was required and several practical problems had to be overcome. For instance, it was found necessary to find ways of dealing with so-called 'open nomenclature' and with the various qualifications that had to be made about the status of specimens. Particular attention was paid to the ways in which previous statements and opinions about the specimens were recorded and to noting detailed histories of ownership and acquisition. The first of a projected series of published geological type, figured and cited catalogues based on this work appeared in 1981 (Crane, 1981b).

Since 1978 the documentation project has been grant-aided by the Area Museum Council for the South West. This has provided an annual budget of between £1000 and £2000 for cataloguing purposes with up to £750 for related projects, including the microfiching of information and the purchase of equipment for the environmental records centre.

The outstanding problem of documentation to date has been staffing. The continual cutbacks and recession of the past few years have made it impossible to appoint permanent documentation staff to aid or oversee projects or a registrar to centralize and coordinate the non-specialist aspects of documentation procedures. The lack of such a person has contributed greatly to the unsatisfactory organization of centralized museum records such as the historical files. There is little hope of this position changing in the forseeable future.

On the other hand, since the formation of the Manpower Services Commission and job creation schemes in 1977, several sections of the museum have been able to take advantage of posts under temporary employment schemes. Most of the preparation of data sheets from the herbarium has been done by a member of staff employed in this way. For the 1981/83 projects we had nine staff employed on a Community Enterprise Project in natural sciences and one Area Museum Council supported trainee curator. The 1983/84 project for Natural History employed seventeen extra staff and other sections have also been well supported by temporary personnel. The normal staff complement of these sections is a curator and assistant curator in both geology and natural history, a part-time geologist and a shared museum assistant. There is also a natural history conservator and a geological conservator within the conservation section. The staff and supporting expenses available under these schemes have played a valuable part in the progress of the documentation project within the museum.

Results and future developments

It is now seven years since the inception of the 'Inventory Exercise'. During this time cataloguing has remained the priority of the museum. Most of the high priority tasks are now complete and the longer term, lower priority tasks continue. Curators are once again looking at the possibilities of a new documentation system. One of the problems that remains is the confusion between data standards and data handling. The new data sheets designed in 1977 have only had moderate success, partly because they have been regarded solely as computer input and not as a data store in their own right.

A number of problems arose in the use of the sheets for computerization through the MDA. These included the fact that they were non-standard format requiring special treatment and the sporadic flow of sheets from curators to the MDA caused scheduling difficulties for their preparation. This, coupled with a rather slow turn-around time in the early stages, lead to a loss of interest. It is a tedious job to complete a batch of sheets, copy them for security purposes, post them off for processing, wait for the source listing, return that checked and then wait again for the final printout. The service is now faster and more efficient, but the desire for a more direct interaction with the data entry and handling process is now strongly established and fuelled by the widespread (although usually not understood) promotion of microcomputers in the media.

In an attempt to find a more direct method of data handling which would give scope for a more generalized approach to various management activities (as opposed to primary cataloguing) an approach was made to Bristol University in 1981 to undertake trials on their computer. The University had recently installed a Honeywell computer including an interactive system supported by highly sophisticated software packages.

The museum undertook tests using a relational data base package called LINUS (logical inquiry and update system) which is a moderately 'user-friendly' subset of the Multics Relational Data Store System. LINUS stores data within user-defined fields called 'domains' which are themselves arranged in groups called 'relations'. Items in different relations can be associated by overlapping domains and in this way information which is identical for many specimens need only be entered into the machine once, thus saving much data preparation time. An editor system allows the user to search the data base for any combination of variables or data strings. Complex search statements can be written and saved which allow the user to substitute varied terms for dummy arguments when they are next invoked. In this way a powerful and flexible data base can be readily created and maintained. The curator has direct control over the information for update or retrieval whenever needed and a simple command sequence can produce copies of data in whatever form they might be required.

One drawback of data bases of this type is that the size of domains (data fields) must be defined from the outset which limits the information that can be recorded or demands a strategy of using domains to point to other storage locations where extensive information is kept outside the data base (e.g. other computer files or microfiche files). Other drawbacks are problems of access to the computer and finances.

In March 1982 the museum purchased a 16-bit Sirius 1 microcomputer. Its intended use was to create formatted data files for transfer to the University Computer but we soon realized that it was powerful enough to satisfy many of our documentation requirements on its own.

The presence of the Sirius has generated much new interest in the documentation project and in June 1982 a Computer Users Group was formed to oversee the allocation of resources and to discuss the way in which we should progress. The first major decision was to suspend the work on the University computer until we had fully assessed the capabilities of the micro-system. This was principally an economic decision because the cost of storing data on the mainframe was very high. The group chose the alternative of purchasing a commercially available data base package for the microcomputer. Of the several available we chose 'DMS' because of its 'user-friendly' attributes. This makes it relatively easy for even a novice user to set up and operate new data bases (really a misnomer on microcomputers) whilst there are plenty of prompts, safeguards and checks to avoid disasters. This has proved very popular and now several of the museum's sections are making use of the machine for a range of applications including mailing lists, storage location indexes and the analysis of mummy wrappings. By 1984, our system had grown to three microcomputers with associated printers and plotters, running a much wider range of software including word processing, various data base packages and graphics systems. We now see the current development of sophisticated and powerful microcomputers, especially when networked together to share common resources, as offering the best value and most potential for our museum data management needs in the foreseeable future.

The museum is at present using four computer-based systems for different purposes. Our links with the MDA are maintained for ongoing extensive data projects, including the herbarium documentation project. The Bristol University computer and the in-house microcomputer system can be used for selected data bases requiring rapid update and retrieval of information. Finally information on the contents and whereabouts of natural science collections in south-west England is being entered on forms and sent to the Federation for Natural Science Collections Research (FENSCORE) Unit at Manchester (Chapter 22).

Conclusions

If it seems that after seven years we have not advanced far towards a final system, still trying out various possibilities and considering procedures, this is not surprising, considering how, for instance, the whole field of computers has changed in this time. There has, however, been a distinct evolution of our attitudes to documentation, prompted by the emphasis of the MDA on quality of data recorded and fired by the possibilities of computer-based information systems. To some extent there has been a move away from the original naive thoughts that all our data sources would end up on computer file to a more realistic approach utilizing a composite resource of traditional files, microfiche and computer indexes. However, the future needs of users are very difficult to anticipate and the criteria for selective data-capture are themselves difficult to assess. The versatility of a system which allows for comprehensive recording of information is still very attractive.

We have also become more aware that the implications of remote access to computerized data must be considered. In this context it is essential to attribute and date all statements about the objects recorded and to indicate to what extent such information is the assumption of the present or past recorders. There is a great danger in the compilation of union catalogues and national data bases founded on uncritical data. Such an approach requires 'researched curation' which in Bristol was not part of the original management directive but in the case of the Bristol type, figured and cited catalogue was shown to be the only acceptable way to proceed.

Having experienced the practical problems of the computerization of detailed specimen catalogues it does seem likely that we will be more selective about what groups we record in this way. However, the availability of fast, interactive data base systems suggests that computerized catalogues or indexes are becoming economically feasible and worthwhile for non-national museums. Meanwhile the new micro-based systems lend themselves readily to other aspects of museum documentation such as the maintenance of loans files, day books and audit checklists which are more properly regarded as management functions. In the short term these aspects of automated documentation are likely to be the fastest developing area of our work but hopefully the attitudes to the importance of information will have taken strong root and will become the future backbone of our progress.

Chapter 18

Computerizing records from Leicestershire's museums

Anthony Fletcher

Background

The Museum in Leicester was founded in 1849 around a nucleus of the collections of the Leicester Literary and Philosophical Society which had existed for about one hundred years previously. In 1974 the Leicester City Museum amalgamated with other museums to form a countywide Museums Service offering a very wide range of services and employing about 140 staff. The range of services includes the Leicestershire Record Office, two field Archaeology teams (site recording and excavation), conservation (Arts and Antiquities), Taxidermy, Education and School Loans Services, and 11 branch Museums. The range of disciplines includes Fine and Decorative Arts, Costume, Biology, Earth Sciences, Antiquities, Social History and Technology, with additional subsections of Botany, Entomology, Numismatics, Asian Studies and Archaeology. Various environmental site recording schemes are also in operation. The collections are currently estimated to include about one million items (objects), plus possibly 10 million items housed in the Record Office.

For some years we have been aware that our systems for cataloguing and retrieving information on the museum's collections were not meeting fully the needs of the service. This issue, discussed in the Wright Report of 1973, was highlighted by subsequent investigations by the Public Accounts Committee and District Audit Services in various parts of the country (see Chapter 12). The increased awareness that museums are publicly accountable for their collections has resulted in our placing 'Care and Maintenance of the Collections' at the head of our priorities. Within this priority, documentation has played the major part since 1980.

In May 1978 representatives of the Museums Service and the County Council's Personnel and Management Services and Computing Section formed a working party to examine the existing situation regarding collections documentation and to make appropriate recommendations. The terms of reference included appraisal of the systems for registration and cataloguing of the collections in all parts of the service, and examination of loans systems, insurance procedures, libraries and environmental records, together with specialized applications. Over 20 Museum sections and subsections were identified as accumulating data and having information retrieval needs.

The working party presented its report in December 1979. It gave a detailed analysis of the current operations of the Museum's documentation and information retrieval systems and illustrated their shortcomings. It also proposed detailed specifications for a computerized replacement system. The recommendations of the report were accepted by the County Libraries and Museums Committee.

In the same month a new Museum section was created, entitled Documentation and Information Retrieval, to be headed by a Keeper. This new section was intended to supervize staff in documentation procedures (including loans), to oversee the work of libraries, to initiate and maintain documentation systems and to maintain contacts with outside bodies in the relevant disciplines. The immediate concern of the section has been to implement the recommendations of the working party, the overall priority being the design and installation of a computerized cataloguing system. The main elements of this system are described below.

Computerized museum management

The Museum's needs were described in the working party report as:

a standardized method for describing objects;
secure storage of information and protection from anonymous alteration or falsification;
sufficient index capability to give an adequate range of indexes which are readily accessible;
the integrity of the collections to be maintained while allowing individual objects to be described;
a cheap and efficient method for updating catalogues and indexes;
documentation to be quickly and generally available;
a centralized procedure for loans;
a valuations and insurance asset register;
to avoid duplication of records and reduce handling of primary documents;
the ability to cope with up to one million museum objects and two million Records Office deposits;
to adopt nationally agreed documentation standards.

It was decided that these needs could all be met from a centralized, object-based catalogue. In addition, several apparently more peripheral needs could be assisted or augmented from a well maintained object-based catalogue, particularly as relevant completed records could be automatically generated. In particular, it was felt that the catalogue could be an efficient museum management tool, helping with a wide variety of tasks. The ultimate aim of the project is to create such a museum management system. It will then aid:

answering enquiries;
inward and outward loans processing;
inward and outward loans reminder generation;
valuation lists and their updating;
preparation of specimen labels;
indexes to collections archive material;
research operations such as processing results from archaeological and biological fieldwork and incorporating them into the museum catalogue;
donor acknowledgements and transfer of title records;
insurance schedules;
changes in storage locations;
conservation reports and process reminders;
acquisitions financial records;
exhibitions records;
scientific field recording.

The project is considered to have three phases. After two and a half years' work we are close to the end of phase one which gives us a definition of the cataloguing and index standards needed, methods for data entry by all museum sections, and the production of catalogues and indexes in batch mode. Phase two, to take about one year, will give the facility to read an up-to-date catalogue entry directly from online disc-based storage, an interactive search and request system usable from a terminal by any staff member, and a loans processing system. Phase three will give us all other facilities outlined above and may take several years to complete.

Advantages of a computerized system

The working party appraised various alternative systems in some detail. A continuation of the then current manual system was rejected on the grounds of cost. Maintenance of that system to the desired standard was calculated to need 25 additional clerical staff, together with a large investment in typewriters and storage materials.

Computerized methods, on the other hand, were much more attractive. No extra staff would be needed, other than the Keeper of Information Retrieval. The County Council computer could be used and County Council programming staff could be employed to develop the system. Costs would be minimal and confined to hardware installed on museum premises. An overriding advantage lay in the fact that any computer processing and programming done at County Hall would be effectively free of charge. This is because the Museums Service, in common with all other County Departments, pays an annual fee for computer services, even though they may not be used. Further advantages lie in the considerable amount of computing expertise available within the County computing section, the opportunity to design a system that will exactly suit our own present and future foreseeable needs, the ease of maintenance of in-house written programs and the ready availability of disc-based storage.

While our local government system has these advantages it is necessary to conform to their own particular policies affecting the computing environment and staff structure. For example, the system supports COBOL as the principal programming language. Since no COBOL packages suitable for Museum applications were available elsewhere we were obliged to design a system from first principles, and this is a time consuming process.

The County UNIVAC 1100/60 computer has a large disc storage capacity (with 14 200-300Mb drives, 10 of which support removable disc packs) but multiple access work is poorly supported at present. In addition, the computer is five miles away and the telecommunication interfaces can be slow. Consequently, we were obliged to use screen-handling processors which allow data to be transmitted as 'screenfuls'. Finally, the museum's system programming time has to be fitted into the existing priorities of the County Hall staff.

Equipment

Six museums, soon to be extended to eight, have computer terminals. All are connected to the computer by British Telecom Tariff Y2 circuits. Two types of terminal cluster are in use. At two museum sites 'slave' VDU's (Dacoll M246) are connected to control units (Dacoll M245) which allow up to eight terminals per station. All other sites have 'stand-alone' terminals (Dacoll M248). Three of the sites have 120 character per second dot-matrix printers (Centronics 702). This hardware configuration is well-proven and is used extensively in the Countywide service, supported by long standing maintenance agreements. Racal 26LSI modems with an additional Racal 23C at County Hall complete the network. The capital investment (at 1981 prices) has been over £22 000 with a further £3000 per annum for rental and £3400 per annum for maintenance.

The museum also has a small microcomputer used for word processing, small-scale accounting, etc. The machine, a Digico Prince (64Kbyte memory, CP/M operating system, twin flexible diskette drives) has an Olivetti daisy-wheel printer and software packages (WORDSTAR, DMS, BASIC interpreter). It is intended to interface this machine with the mainframe computer at a later date. The total cost of this configuration was £5550, plus £1000 for an annual maintenance contract.

Personnel

Except for the Keeper of the Documentation and Information Retrieval section the Museum's computerized cataloguing system operates with no permanent increase in staff. Instead, the existing curatorial and clerical staff are trained and encouraged to use the system in favour of the less efficient manual system.

The data are written on to Object Data Forms by curators. Data are entered at the terminals by clerk-typists. Four trained typists are engaged upon data entry for up to 30% of their time. These typists are not especially trained in documentation work and are expected to do no more than copy data on to the screens very quickly and to check each entry before transmission. However, with experience, most have learned the Documentation Standard and can apply corrections to data when needed.

Although the intention is to reduce paperwork, at this transitional stage between a pre-existing manual system and the new computerized system a good deal of filing of paperwork is needed. This forms part of the duties of one clerk.

The Government-sponsored Manpower Services Commission Youth Employment and Work Experience schemes are used to provide supplementary staff when appropriate persons are available. Both school-leavers and graduates have been found to be very useful; school-leavers for filing and clerical assistance and graduates in cataloguing items appropriate to their academic training. It is hoped that in the future staff could be employed on research contracts leading to collections documentation.

Recording

Curatorial staff prepare data to the standards determined by the Keeper of the section. Users are assisted by a manual which explains the meanings of all tagged entries, with examples. Accompanying this manual are keyword and classification lists. Most sections also maintain internal user guides describing local terminology and standards.

All handwritten sources are kept in archives after data entry. This source may be a preprinted form, a tabulated chart or pre-existing documentation.

The accessioning and cataloguing procedure is:

Keeper of the curatorial section allocates an accession number;
Curator prepares the label;
Curator fills out Object Data Form or enters data directly at the terminal;
Keeper checks data;
typist enters data from sources provided by curator;
computer produces update reports and proof-reading lists (overnight);
corrections made at the terminal by typist or curator;
master files now ready for catalogue and index production.

The data categories required by each section are indicated on the Object Data Forms. These forms are split into two sections. The first includes minimum data needed for museum management purposes as defined by administrative and curatorial staff. The second part is defined entirely to suit curatorial indexing needs.

Data entry

The data format follows that described in the MDA instruction booklets. All data fields have been incorporated into a system of 100 tags (00-99) each of which subdivides into 26 subfields (A-Z). This allows a maximum of 2600 subfields, but only about one-quarter of these have been employed so far. Tags are aggregated into a data structure compatible with that used by the MDA.

Tag and subfield codes appear on the Object Data Forms, together with an explanatory heading, so that forms can easily be filled out and as easily used for data entry at the terminal (Figure 18.1). Forms are preprinted in permanent ink on ledger quality paper since, being primary handwritten sources, they should be kept in perpetuity.

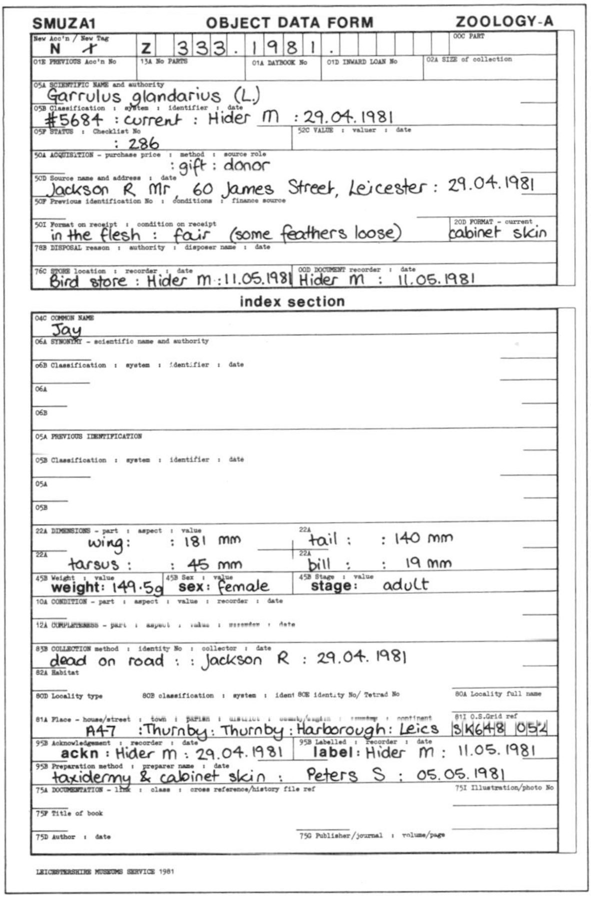
SMUZA1 OBJECT DATA FORM ZOOLOGY-A

New Acc'n / New Tag: N + | Z | 333.1981. | 00C PART

01E PREVIOUS Acc'n No | 13A No PARTS | 01A DAYBOOK No | 01D INWARD LOAN No | 02A SIZE of collection

05A SCIENTIFIC NAME and authority: Garrulus glandarius (L.)

05B Classification : system : identifier : date: #5684 : current : Hider M : 29.04.1981

05F STATUS : Checklist No: : 286 | 52C VALUE : valuer : date

50A ACQUISITION – purchase price : method : source role: : gift : donor

50D Source name and address : date: Jackson R Mr, 60 James Street, Leicester : 29.04.1981

50F Previous identification No : conditions : finance source

50I Format on receipt : condition on receipt: in the flesh : fair (some feathers loose) | 20D FORMAT – current: cabinet skin

78B DISPOSAL reason : authority : disposer name : date

76C STORE location : recorder : date: Bird store : Hider M : 11.05.1981 | 00D DOCUMENT recorder : date: Hider M : 11.05.1981

index section

04C COMMON NAME: Jay

06A SYNONYMY – scientific name and authority

06B Classification : system : identifier : date

06A

06B

05A PREVIOUS IDENTIFICATION

05B Classification : system : identifier : date

05A

05B

22A DIMENSIONS – part : aspect : value: wing : : 181 mm | 22A tail : : 140 mm

22A tarsus : : 45 mm | 22A bill : : 19 mm

45B Weight : value: weight: 149.5g | 45B Sex : value: sex: female | 45B Stage : value: stage: adult

10A CONDITION – part : aspect : value : recorder : date

12A COMPLETENESS – part : aspect : value : recorder : date

83B COLLECTION method : identity No : collector : date: dead on road : : Jackson R : 29.04.1981

82A Habitat

80D Locality type | 80B classification : system : ident 80E identity No/ Tetrad No | 80A Locality full name

81A Place – house/street : town : parish : district : county/region : country : continent: A47 : Thurnby : Thurnby : Harborough : Leics | 81I O.S.Grid ref: SK648 052

95B Acknowledgement : recorder : date: ackn : Hider M : 29.04.1981 | 95B Labelled : recorder : date: label : Hider M : 11.05.1981

95B Preparation method : preparer name : date: taxidermy & cabinet skin : Peters S : 05.05.1981

75A DOCUMENTATION – link : class : cross reference/history file ref | 75I Illustration/photo No

75F Title of book

75D Author : date | 75G Publisher/journal : volume/page

LEICESTERSHIRE MUSEUMS SERVICE 1981

Figure 18.1 Example of obverse of an Object Data Form

The computer system relies on data-capture screen formats which resemble the forms. Only tag and subfield identities are displayed, together with enough space to accommodate an average entry. Automatic generation of successive screens allows the whole form of 37 or more lines to be split across several screens. These screens are followed by an unlimited number of 'other data' screens which allow entry of data too long to be accommodated elsewhere and for tags from the Documentation Standard which, being rarely used, do not appear on the form. Additional screens include one for tabulated data which allows groups of similar items to be entered very rapidly, and an update screen which allows corrections to be made to existing catalogue entries.

Data entry at the terminal is controlled by a transaction program which displays error messages. Most important is its facility for rejecting any screen which fails to meet the minimum data standard. For example, unauthorized users are politely turned away and essential data such as store location, recorder and object classification codes must be filled out. Some protection against mis-tagging is also provided.

This data capture system operates interactively and transactions are accumulated on to disc. Over 100 objects per day per terminal can be achieved. With practice the data entry screens can be used for direct input from existing documentation or from memory. The computer-produced output then becomes a primary source document in its own right.

The screen data are further validated during the overnight batch processing run. Here double-accession numbering and mistakes such as mis-spelled keywords are detected and illegal operations are rejected. The batch system produces a proofreading list which is issued to users together with a control totals and update report which details who used the system, when, and for what reason. Control reports are used for security monitoring and to check on progress. Batch mode data-validation is deliberately employed as an alternative to online updating so that alterations to the catalogue can be accounted for.

The catalogue is stored on disc in index-sequential file format, with magnetic tape backup. Keyword fields are held as codes cross-referring to dictionaries which are maintained and updated automatically by the system. Updates always preserve the original version and deletions from the catalogue entries are disallowed after the entry has been corrected to an acceptable level. From then on, only additions can be made to the entry.

Data retrieval

Information can be retrieved in two ways. The batch mode allows generation of standard indexes and catalogues to provide output satisfying the most common enquiries. This mode is also used for enquiries which would generate too much output to be received at the terminal. Many of these indexes are produced regularly without user prompts in order to satisfy the most frequent uses for management and enquiries. Indexes can be specified for any tag or subfield combination and for any data elements or part of an element, with range scanning, etc.

Online data retrieval, though still undergoing final specification, will follow the same principles. It is intended that interactive interrogation will display the accession numbers of catalogue entries satisfying the search criteria together with a minimum data display, such as full name or storage location, or whatever is required. Typing the accession number of an object will give a direct display of the catalogue entry in its most up-to-date form.

External liaison

It will be seen from this account that the Leicestershire Museums system is purely a local solution to local needs, using local resources. It is not expected that this system will suit other museums' needs or fit into their resources. We hope, however, that some of the ideas contained within it may prove to be useful, just as we have extensively incorporated ideas prevailing in the systems of other museums.

This awareness of the systems in use in other museums, libraries etc., is an important part of the job function of the Keeper of Documentation and Information Retrieval, and a generous allowance is made available for travelling. As we feel that it is especially important to maintain some kind of national, and indeed, international standard for museum documentation, considerable stress has been placed on the adoption of standards recommended by the MDA. If such standards prove to be internationally applicable, then the Leicestershire system will be able to supply data in machine readable form, via magnetic tape, and it is hoped that we will be able to receive such tapes from elsewhere.

Chapter 19

Collection recording at St Albans Museums

Sheila M. Stone

Introduction

The St Albans Museum Service comprises the City Museum (founded in 1898) and the Verulamium Museum (opened in 1939). The collections cover the natural sciences, social history and archaeology and include two research collections of national importance: the Salaman collection of craft tools and an archaeological collection from excavations since 1930 on the site of Verulamium, the third largest city of Roman Britain. The collections are continually being added to, mainly as a result of the active programme of archaeological excavation carried out by the Museum's Field Department on sites scheduled for development in the St Albans District. The Museum service is funded by St Albans District Council and receives central government grants for certain excavations from the Department of the Environment, and for specific museum projects through the Area Museums Service for South Eastern England (AMSSEE).

Documentation background

In 1973 a feasibility study on the development of the museum service in St Albans was produced by St Albans District Council in conjunction with AMSSEE. This report highlighted the inadequacy of collection records for all but the most recently excavated material, a situation of grave concern to museum staff and Council auditors.

The existing documentation system consisted of an inadequate and out-of-date accession register for a small proportion of the City Museum collection, and two incomplete card indexes arranged by object type and site for the Verulamium Museum (produced in the 1930s). Both museums lacked an effective procedure for the registration of incoming material. Enquiries regarding the collection were taking an unnecessary length of time to process, adding to the frustration of staff. Research on the collection was difficult and daunting for any but the most persistent of students. Clearly, the significance of the museum's collection required effective documentation and information retrieval methods if its potential was to be exploited fully, and to achieve this end substantial resources would need to be provided to make up for years of underdevelopment.

In 1978 a temporary research assistant was appointed to set up a documentation scheme, financed by St Albans District Council with assistance from AMSSEE. The main aim during the first twelve months was to examine the various documentation systems available to see if any would be suitable for the particular needs of St Albans, thus saving the considerable amount of time and expertise that designing an in-house system would entail. The MDA system was found to be suitable for the museum's needs and came complete with computer programs 'off the peg', offering information retrieval methods which had the advantage of being neither space nor labour intensive. The MDA system was subsequently chosen for collection recording at the Verulamium and City Museums. The success of the initial project resulted in the appointment of a Keeper of Documentation in 1979 (Stone, 1978; 1979).

In 1980, as part of a restructuring exercise, the post was changed to a Keepership of Archaeology with continuing responsibility as Documentation Officer. Money provided by St Albans District Council for documentation was augmented by central government grants, through AMSSEE, in 1978, 1979 and 1980. By the end of 1981 over 12 000 objects and specimens (approximately ten percent of the total collection, excluding the boxes of sherds, bones, tiles, etc., which form the bulk of the excavation archive) had been catalogued and the documentation system firmly established.

Development of new procedures

When the documentation project commenced in January 1978, the lack of adequate existing documentation proved, ironically, to be a distinct advantage as it provided the opportunity of initiating new numbering and cataloguing procedures. In order to cope with the immense backlog of material to be catalogued, a policy decision was taken to aim for a non-intensive register of the collections in the first instance, allowing for conversion of this to an intensive record within the various curatorial departments as staff time and resources allowed. The primary objective was to assign accession numbers to objects and record as much of the non-intrinsic information about them as possible. This was particularly necessary before old labels became detached from objects or faded beyond legibility. Even information that was actually written on the objects was not always comprehensible. The balance between transcribing original documentation faithfully, and interpreting it in the light of curatorial knowledge for users of the collection, has not always been easy to achieve. The use of a pair of symbols to denote inferred information ('[ ]') has helped to ease this problem.

To allow maximum flexibility of the central museum catalogues, that sacred cow of generations of museum registrars and local government auditors, the bound accession register, was abandoned. At worst, it was felt to be cumbersome to use, a problem to update, impossible to carry from office to store, and allowed totally idiosyncratic recording of data about objects by curators. In addition, the problems of legibility experienced by staff using the old handwritten register of the City Museum (and the appalling handwriting of museum staff) provided further reason for avoiding the bound register, and it was replaced by the use of MDS cards as the recording format at both central and departmental level. A variety of MDS cards are used (Archaeology Object (Figure 19.1), History Artefact, Mineral Specimen, Geology, Museum Object, Pictorial Representation and Natural History) to suit the range of material in the museum's collection.

Card of

File — Institution : identity number SABMS:81.2301 — Part

IDENTIFICATION C
Simple name D bowl — Materials keyword/detail glass — Number
Full name or classified identification pillar moulded bowl & form 3 — System Isings — D Identifier : date Allen, D.: 6.4.1981 D

DATING C
Object period or date roman & 10AD = 80AD (approx)
Dating method typology — Cross reference — Researcher : date Allen, D.: 6.4.1981 D

COLLECTION OR EXCAVATION C
Site name Ver Site B — Site number Insula XIV — Lat Long — NGR — Value & units/accuracy
Place name/detail St. Albans & Hertfordshire & U.K.
Context B I & layers 68 and 70 — Context period or date 60AD = 75AD D
Locality detail
Collection method excavation — Collector or excavator : date Frere, S.S.: 1959 — Find number 1 D

ACQUISITION C
Acquisition method donation — Acquired from : date Verulamium Excavation Committee
D Price — Conditions Yes/No D — Valuation : date D

DESCRIPTION C
Condition keyword/detail fair — Completeness keyword/detail incomplete (base fragment only)

STORE
Store : date Ver & Main Gallery & V3: 6.4.1981 — Recorder : date Stone, S.M. : 6.4.1981

ARCHAEOLOGY ©IRGMA 1975 1/12/75

DESCRIPTION
Dimension measured — value & units/accuracy — Dimension measured — value & units/accuracy
width (of fragment) 5.5 cm
length (of fragment) 5.8 cm
Inscription / Mark — Method — Position
Transcription / Description — Detail D
Part : aspect : description keyword/detail D
whole : colour : blue = green
whole : production method : cast
inner surface : finishing method : rotary ground
inner surface : decoration : horizontal wheel-incised lines above base
outer surface : decoration : ribbed
outer surface : finishing method : fire polished
C

PROCESS C
Conservation / Reproduction / Conservation / Reproduction — Other process — Method/detail : operator : date : detail — Cross-reference D

DOCUMENTATION C
L 1 — Class listed — Author : date : title : journal or publisher : volume : detail Charlesworth, D. IN Frere, S.S. : 1972 : Verulamium Excavations : Oxford University Press : Volume I : page 198, number 11 and 12 — Drawing or photo

NOTES C
Notes

Figure 19.1 Example of completed MDS archaeology object card

After examination and discussion of the benefits and drawbacks of the various accession numbering systems in other museums, we decided to use a simple serial sequence of numbers, date-linked to reflect the year of registration, but otherwise non-significant. To avoid duplication, accession numbers are assigned in blocks by the Documentation Officer and departments with more than one member of staff involved in cataloguing keep a running list of numbers used.

The cataloguing procedure begins with the curator preparing a handwritten record of an object on one or more MDS cards, using a Rotring pen and block capital letters for maximum legibility. A typed copy of this record is produced and proofread by the curator, then stored in accession number order in lockable card index cabinets, forming the central museum catalogue. The handwritten copy is filed by the curator at department level. Duplicating the record in this way provides additional security for the information contained therein and, by producing a clear copy, saves money at the computer input stage (reducing the costs of data preparation by up to 30%), and curatorial time when checking computer output.

When the project was set up in 1978, staff resources devoted to documentation included a full-time research assistant, responsible for recording the archaeological collection, and two members of the curatorial staff responsible for social history and the natural sciences who spent roughly 20% of their time on cataloguing. The restructuring exercise in 1980 concentrated staff resources on archaeological recording. The Keeper of Archaeology and one Deputy Keeper spend approximately 50% of their time on documentation, and a part-time research assistant spends ten hours a week sorting and cataloguing archaeological material.

Progress with collection documentation

In four years, from 1978 to 1981, 8500 archaeological objects have been accessioned out of a collection of 50 000 discrete objects. Very little impact has yet been made on the estimated 600 000 sherds, tiles, bones, samples, etc., which form the bulk of the excavation archive as this material presents special documentation problems and is regarded as low priority as far as collection security is concerned. However, as the old excavation archive is crucial to the understanding of the Roman city of Verulamium and is consulted regularly by researchers, attempts have been made to make it more accessible, and most of the material from the 1930-1940 excavations has been sorted and roughly listed as a preparation for cataloguing.

The social history collection is catalogued by the relevant Keeper with no assistance and currently 2000 objects have been accessioned. A museum assistant spends 50% of her time working on the natural history collection and 1500 specimens have been catalogued so far. The only other member of staff involved with documentation is the Administrative Officer who produces typed copies of completed accession records on a non-regular basis.

Computerization experience

During the first year of the documentation project the possibility of computerizing records was explored with the MDA. A series of pilot projects, each involving 500 records, was undertaken. These provided valuable feedback regarding the structuring and layout of information on the cards and demonstrated the importance of terminology control and consistency. Internal conventions had been established before cataloguing started and these were expanded in the light of experience gained from computerization. The success of the original projects led to a decision to computerize all the archaeological accession records, producing updated indexes and catalogues as necessary. Nine indexes to the archaeological collection were produced initially, and this number has been increased to eleven as we gain more experience from the users of the collection (museum staff, research students, schoolchildren, teachers and the general public). Examples of the indexes include:

a place name index;
a site name index (Figure 19.2);
a storage location index (Figure 19.3);
an excavator index (replacing the conventional donor index which has little relevance to our collection);
an index cross-referencing publication numbers to accession numbers (Figure 19.4);
an index cross-referencing conservation numbers to accession numbers;
a simple name index;
a materials index;
a valuation index;
indexes to object dates and context dates.

Due to the immense backlog of objects to be catalogued, each computer project comprises one year's records. For each year from 1978 to 1980 there is a printout catalogue and set of indexes. These are available as paper copy and COM. The 1981 records are currently in preparation and once these are in the computer it is hoped to produce a set of indexes incorporating all the 1978-1981 records. Updating of records takes place at intervals, and a set of source listings are kept at the museum for marking up corrections, additions, or changes to records such as storage locations, etc., as necessary. Eight thousand archaeological records have been processed to date, the record size averaging 450 characters.

Conclusions

Setting up a documentation project at St Albans has made a fundamental impact on the museum. It has led to a complete reorganization of the stores to facilitate information retrieval, and a comprehensive programme of conservation and record photography for much of the material. The procedure for dealing with enquiries and identifications has been streamlined and formalized to ensure that relevant information passes to museum files. A history file has been created for all accessioned archaeological objects, containing copies of photographs, correspondence, specialist reports, information about loans etc. for each object. More efficient information retrieval and increased familiarity with the collection have served to identify worthwhile areas for research, and provided a more substantial basis on

```
ST. ALBANS MUSEUMS (SABMS)    ARCHAEOLOGY        SITE NAME INDEX    Page 6

(INSULA III)
   (VER BLDG. 1)
    coin                    SABMS: 78.749; 80.1277; 83.470; 83.480;
                                   83.496; 83.501; 83.762; 83.1179; 83.1414
    counter                 SABMS: 79.642
    cup                     SABMS: 82.1672
    dagger                  SABMS: 80.795
    dish                    SABMS: 83.129
    fitting                 SABMS: 82.1
    fragment                SABMS: 81.101
    jar                     SABMS: 82.983
    knob                    SABMS: 78.126
    linch-pin               SABMS: 78.529
    mortarium               SABMS: 82.1464 to 1465
    pin                     SABMS: 78.306; 78.312; 78.320; 78.333; 79.590
    sheet                   SABMS: 82.1549
    sherd                   SABMS: 83.168
    strip                   SABMS: 82.1574
    stud                    SABMS: 80.1713; 80.1722; 80.1831
    terminal                SABMS: 81.3165
    tweezers                SABMS: 78.964
  VER BLDG. 2
    adze-hammer             SABMS: 78.517
    bead                    SABMS: 78.481; 80.720; 80.777; 80.787; 80.789
    bottle                  SABMS: 81.102; 81.104; 81.107 to 109; 81.111;
                                   81.116 to 117; 81.119; 81.126; 81.132;
                                   81.135 to 136; 81.138 to 139; 81.144;
                                   81.147; 81.152; 81.156; 81.159; 81.167;
                                   81.174 to 175; 81.319
    bottle, flask           SABMS: 81.110
    bowl                    SABMS: 81.120; 81.128; 81.140; 81.149;
                                   81.2583; 81.2639; 81.3130
    bracelet                SABMS: 78.463 to 464; 78.1957; 79.341
    brooch                  SABMS: 78.439; 78.443; 78.448; 78.987;
                                   78.2548; 78.2555; 78.2562; 78.2581; 79.101
    buckle                  SABMS: 81.3480
    chopper                 SABMS: 78.588
    coin                    SABMS: 78.746; 80.286; 80.295; 80.1232;
                                   80.1265 to 1266; 83.477; 83.539; 83.545;
                                   83.552; 83.601; 83.671; 83.1226 to 1238;
                                   83.1265; 83.1312 to 1313; 83.1315 to 1325
    cup                     SABMS: 83.86; 83.189
    disc                    SABMS: 80.1604
    dish                    SABMS: 82.1694; 83.99
    fitting                 SABMS: 81.3273
    flask, jug              SABMS: 81.166; 81.172
    fragment                SABMS: 81.100; 81.105; 81.112 to 113; 81.115;
                                   81.118; 81.125; 81.130 to 131; 81.134;
                                   81.143; 81.145 to 146; 81.148; 81.150 to
                                   151; 81.153; 81.155; 81.164 to 165; 81.168;
                                   81.170 to 171; 81.173; 81.446
    gouge                   SABMS: 79.777
    handle                  SABMS: 78.812
    ink pot                 SABMS: 80.1750
    jar                     SABMS: 81.3092; 82.1263; 82.1307
```

Figure 19.2 Example of computerized archaeological sites index

which future collecting policies may be established. The publication of comprehensive catalogues to parts of the collection will soon be possible, aided by computer technology. The most fundamental effect, however, has been to make more efficient use of staff time in dealing with the collection: collections management has replaced the organized chaos of the past.

ST. ALBANS MUSEUMS (SABMS)   ARCHAEOLOGY   STORE INDEX   Page 19

(VER)

(F11)
plate	SABMS: 79.863; 79.904
ring	SABMS: 81.3414; 81.3425
strap-end	SABMS: 81.3481
strip, ?mount	SABMS: 79.924

F12
binding	SABMS: 79.895; 79.897; 81.3401
boss	SABMS: 79.894; 79.896
brow-band	SABMS: 82.1361
buckle	SABMS: 82.193; 82.1099; 82.1106; 82.1108
chape	SABMS: 79.876; 82.1094
cuirass hinge	SABMS: 82.1065
fastener	SABMS: 82.897; 82.1091
ferrule	SABMS: 79.878
fitting	SABMS: 79.852; 79.875; 79.2504; 81.3418; 82.1081; 82.1225
hinge	SABMS: 82.1215
hook	SABMS: 82.1211
mount	SABMS: 79.899; 82.1101 to 1102; 82.1328
pendant	SABMS: 82.1335; 82.1338
plate	SABMS: 79.855

FF
amphora	SABMS: 80.1019
beaker	SABMS: 80.1020 to 1021; 80.1025 to 1027; 80.1031; 80.1029 to 1030; 80.1038; 80.1040 to 1041; 80.1045
bottle	SABMS: 80.1033
cup	SABMS: 80.1035 to 1036; 80.1042
jar	SABMS: 80.1028; 80.1046 to 1047
jug	SABMS: 80.1022 to 1024; 80.1032; 80.1034; 80.1037; 80.1039; 80.1043 to 1044

FF1
hand axe	SABMS: 79.2200 to 2203; 79.2206; 79.2211; 79.2213; 79.2215; 79.2217; 79.2294; 79.2296 to 2297; 80.324; 80.637; 80.1897
?hand axe	SABMS: 79.2209
?implement	SABMS: 80.485
?scraper	SABMS: 79.2204; 79.2222
worked flake	SABMS: 79.2299

FF2
axe	SABMS: 79.2328
flake	SABMS: 80.514
hand axe	SABMS: 79.2223 to 225; 79.2227 to 2229; 79.2231 to 2234; 79.2238 to 2239; 79.2241 to 2242; 79.2327; 80.326; 80.330; 80.1893; 81.2806

FF3
core	SABMS: 79.2243 to 2244; 79.2255; 79.2265
core flake	SABMS: 80.1899

FF4
flake	SABMS: 79.2220; 79.2256 to 2264; 79.2266
hammer stone	SABMS: 79.2270
hand axe	SABMS: 79.2267 to 2269; 79.2272; 79.2287;

Figure 19.3 Example of computerized museum storage locations index

```
ST. ALBANS MUSEUMS (SABMS)     ARCHAEOLOGY        REFERENCES INDEX    Page 10

(FRERE, S.S., 1972, Verulamium Excavations, Oxford University Press, Volume
I)
    (figure 33, number 52)
       pendant              SABMS: 79.849
    figure 33, number 53
       buckle               SABMS: 79.912
    figure 34, number 55
       dress-fastener       SABMS: 78.377
    figure 34, number 57
       junction piece       SABMS: 79.870
    figure 34, number 61
       pin                  SABMS: 78.425
    figure 34, number 62
       buckle               SABMS: 79.858
    figure 34, number 63
       ?fitting             SABMS: 79.913
    figure 34, number 64
       handle               SABMS: 80.1079
    figure 34, number 65
       seal box             SABMS: 78.241
    figure 34, number 66
       seal box             SABMS: 78.239
    figure 34, number 67
       seal box             SABMS: 78.240
    figure 35, number 68
       scoop                SABMS: 79.2178
    figure 35, number 69
       ligula               SABMS: 78.412
    figure 35, number 71
       probe, ?instrument   SABMS: 78.875
    figure 35, number 72
       probe                SABMS: 78.877
    figure 35, number 73
       probe, ?ligula       SABMS: 78.881
    figure 35, number 74
       spoon                SABMS: 78.841
    figure 35, number 76
       amulet               SABMS: 82.7
    figure 36, number 77a
       chain                SABMS: 80.230
    figure 36, number 77b
       staple               SABMS: 82.92
    figure 36, number 79
       chain                SABMS: 80.229
    figure 36, number 80
       chain                SABMS: 82.196
    figure 36, number 81
       split-pin            SABMS: 82.81
    figure 36, number 82
       chain                SABMS: 82.202
    figure 36, number 83
       ring                 SABMS: 79.254
    figure 36, number 84
       ring                 SABMS: 79.2184
    figure 36, number 85
```

Figure 19.4 Example of computerized index of publication numbers cross-referenced to accession numbers

Chapter 20

Tyne and Wear County Museum Service

John C. Baker

Introduction

In the spring of 1975, twelve months after the implementation of local government reorganization in England and Wales, the responsibility of operating local authority museums and art galleries in Newcastle, Gateshead, South Shields and Sunderland was transferred from district level to the new Metropolitan County Council of Tyne and Wear. This amalgamation was carried out in the belief that the rationalization and establishment of centrally-based services such as administration, conservation, design and display would improve standards. It was also hoped that the Service would provide a greater opportunity for museums in Tyne and Wear to interpret the heritage of the area in a manner more attractive and stimulating to the general public.

There are nine museums in the Tyne and Wear Service. The Laing Art Gallery, Newcastle, assumes a regional importance for the fine and decorative arts. The Shipley Art Gallery, Gateshead, has European paintings of the sixteenth to nineteenth centuries, local collections, and a contemporary craft gallery. The John George Joicey Museum, Newcastle and Grindon Museum, Sunderland, cover social history and include period room settings. At South Shields there is the Roman Fort Museum and the Central Museum and Art Gallery with multi-disciplinary collections relating to the town's history. Sunderland Museum has large multi-disciplinary collections with a local emphasis, including maritime history, but in addition has English fine and decorative art collections. Its natural history collections, including important geological items, have a regional significance (Davis, 1978). The Museum of Science and Engineering at Blandford House, Newcastle, houses collections (some of national importance) relating to the scientific, industrial and maritime history of the North-East. Monkwearmouth Station Museum, Sunderland, covers the history of land transport in the region (Sinclair, 1979).

Collections total 250 000 objects, comprising 12 000 fine art, 10 000 applied art, 4000 costume, 57 000 social history, 5000 ethnography, 5000 archaeology, 30 000 science and technology, 9500 maritime history, 7500 land transport, 90 000 natural history and 20 000 geology items, maintained by 14 Keepers and 8 assistants.

Documentation background

The above gives some indication of the diverse nature of museums and their collections administered by Tyne and Wear County Council. At the time of amalgamation the documentation and cataloguing system of each museum was different. In most, record keeping was inadequate.

The Laing Art Gallery had a comprehensive system of record-keeping as regards control procedures — day books, accessions and loans registers, etc. Moreover, it had a manual index of record cards (including cross-referencing) enabling adequate retrieval of information relating to collections. Curatorial procedures at the Sunderland Museums were also adequately recorded but information retrieval regarding specific collections was difficult because the record card index was a chronological one, merely repeating information in the accessions registers. Keepers had established cross-referencing systems for their collections in only a few subject areas. The other museums recorded only the barest of information in registers.

Development of procedures

In order to rectify these deficiencies a standardized system of documentation and cataloguing was established as a priority, designed to deal with the special needs of the County Service. The main problems were created by the physical distance between the various museums and the fact that some curatorial staff had collections not only in the museum in which they were based but in two or three others as well.

Books of control forms for recording reception and movement of items within the County Service and with outside bodies were designed and printed. These comprise Day Books, Accessions Registers, Memorandum of Gift Books, Enquiry Forms, Loans In and Loans Out Books, Object Delivery and Collection Forms. Copies of each are kept at the nine museums with the exception of the Accessions Registers. These are kept by the Keepers for their particular collections, which may be divided between museums.

The *Day Book* forms (Figure 20.1) which deal with the initial reception of an item are in duplicate so that a copy can be forwarded to the Keeper responsible (who has collections in the museum but is not based there) informing him that an object has to be 'processed'. A tick in a particular 'box' indicates to the Keeper whether the object has been deposited as a gift, bequest, purchase, loan or enquiry. Other sections on the form remind the Keeper to take action, and the date on which this was done can be entered. Dates of correspondence and the accessioning and insuring of the object (where appropriate) are also recorded. The *Memorandum of Gift* Book (Figure 20.2) is signed by the donor at the time of the presentation and is intended to overcome problems which arise when demands are made for the return of an item originally given as a gift but now claimed to be a loan.

For standardized cataloguing of collections the Service adopted the system already established by IRGMA which had the advantage of being computer

TYNE AND WEAR COUNTY COUNCIL MUSEUMS   340

Day Book Vol. _TWO_

For Attention of: _S. BARDY_ at _SCIENCE MUSEUM_   Mus/A.G.
ASST KEEPER   _BLANDFORD HOUSE_
MARITIME HISTORY   _NEWCASTLE_

Received at: _SUNDERLAND MUSEUM_   Date _21/7/81_
Mus/A.G.

By: _T. PETTIGREW ASST. KEEPER NAT. HISTORY._

Object(s): _BUILDER'S SHIP MODEL OF M.V "LA CORDILLERA" BUILT BY DOXFORD & SONS LTD, SUNDERLAND IN 1946 FOR BURIES, MARKES, LONDON, LTD._

Owner's Information: _FURTHER TO YOUR RECENT TELEPHONE CONVERSATION/ WITH MR MASON, MODEL HAS BEEN LEFT FOR YOUR INSPECTION_

Condition of Object(s): _GOOD (RIGGING REQUIRES REPLACEMENT)_

Owner Address: _MR. D. MASON QUAYSIDE ANTIQUES THE WHARF SOUTHWARK, LONDON._

I have deposited the above object(s) at the above named museum, as indicated in box below.

Signed _D. Mason_ .... Owner/Representative

Gift	Loan In Bk. No.		Accepted _27_ / _7_ / _81_
	Page		Declined / /
Bequest	Enquiry		Returned _29_ / _7_ / _81_
	Bk. No.		Letter Sent _29_ / _7_ / _81_
Purchase	✓ Page		Acc. No. _F2/64_

Insured:- Long Term For £ _850_
Short Term From / /
Permanent To / /

Figure 20.1 Day book form used to record information during the initial reception of an object

compatible, providing more scope for comprehensive information retrieval than a simple manual system.

The hope that improved standards of consistent documentation, leading to computer processing of records, would be established throughout the country, rested heavily on national and provincial museums accepting and implementing the IRGMA system. As one of the largest provincial museum services in the United Kingdom it was obvious the Tyne and Wear Service should use the new system. Although the record cards would be used initially on a manual basis the system would lead to the retrieval of information by computer — a necessity if maximum use was to be made of the Service's large and diverse collections. Even regarded as a manual record the IRGMA (subsequently MDA) card seemed to have advantages over other systems. Its structured format and the demands it makes on the Keeper in the use of

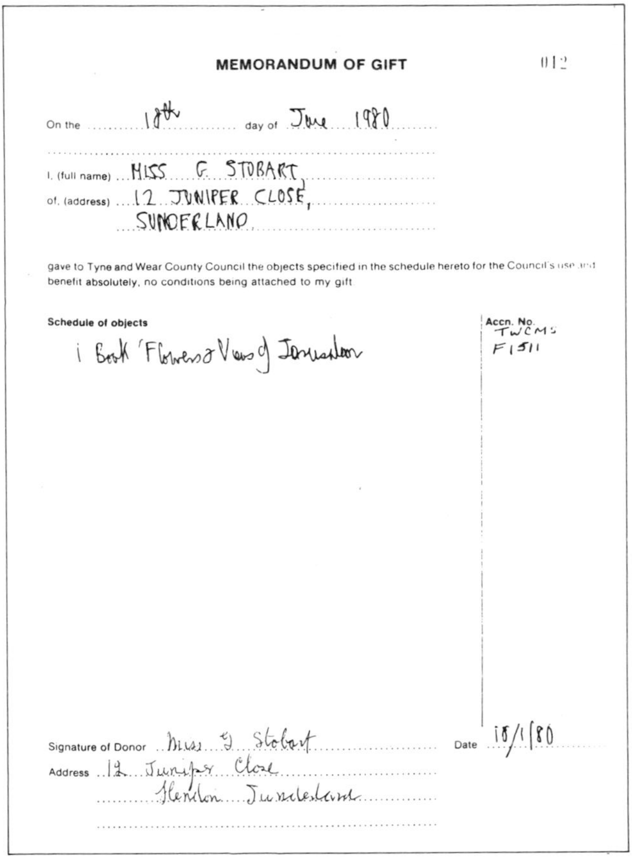
MEMORANDUM OF GIFT 012

On the 18th day of June 1980

I, (full name) MISS G. STOBART,
of, (address) 12 JUNIPER CLOSE,
SUNDERLAND

gave to Tyne and Wear County Council the objects specified in the schedule hereto for the Council's use and benefit absolutely, no conditions being attached to my gift

Schedule of objects

1 Book 'Flowers & Views of Jerusalem'

Accn. No. TWCMS F1511

Signature of Donor Miss G. Stobart Date 18/1/80
Address 12 Juniper Close
Hendon Sunderland

Figure 20.2 Memorandum of gift form

consistent language result in information being recorded in a more thorough and disciplined manner.

The procedure adopted within the Tyne and Wear Service revolved around a newly created post of cataloguer/typist based at Museum Headquarters in Newcastle (Figure 20.3). Keepers record information about a museum item on a 'flimsy': a thin sheet of A4 paper which, on one side, reproduces the front and reverse of an A5 MDA card. The flimsies are printed internally with the permission of the MDA. The hand written flimsy is forwarded to the cataloguer/typist who types the information on two copies of the matching MDA card (Figure 20.4). One copy is forwarded to the appropriate museum and Keeper who files the card according to the particular needs of the discipline. The other copy is kept at headquarters in a file maintained in numerical sequence which acts as a security measure against any loss of records in the museums.

202

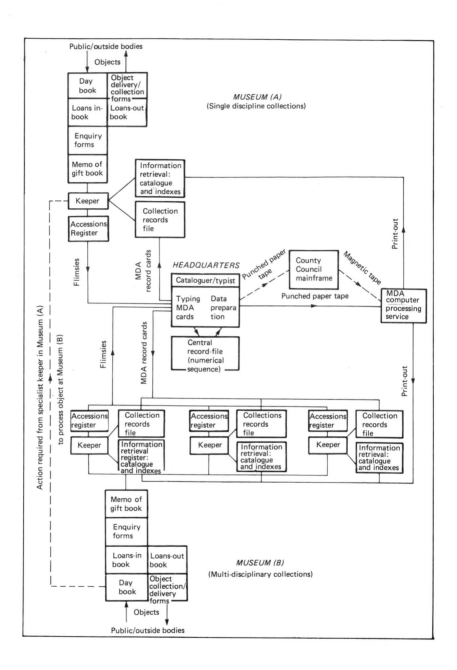

Figure 20.3 Documentation procedures within Tyne and Wear Museum Service

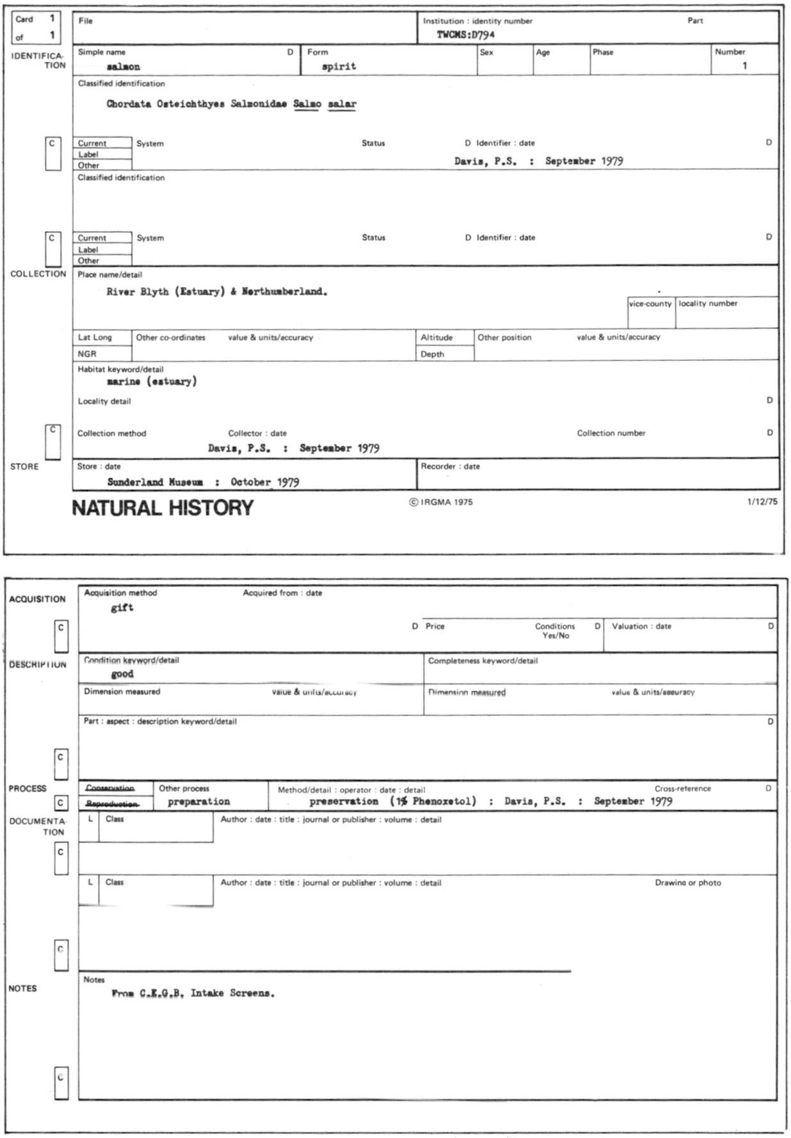
Card 1 of 1 | File | Institution : identity number TWCMS:D794 | Part

IDENTIFICATION | Simple name salmon | D | Form spirit | Sex | Age | Phase | Number 1

Classified identification
Chordata Osteichthyes Salmonidae Salmo salar

C | Current Label Other | System | Status | D Identifier : date Davis, P.S. : September 1979 | D

Classified identification

C | Current Label Other | System | Status | D Identifier : date | D

COLLECTION | Place name/detail
River Blyth (Estuary) & Northumberland.
vice-county | locality number

Lat Long | Other co-ordinates | value & units/accuracy | Altitude | Other position | value & units/accuracy
NGR | Depth

Habitat keyword/detail
marine (estuary)

Locality detail | D

C | Collection method | Collector : date Davis, P.S. : September 1979 | Collection number | D

STORE | Store : date Sunderland Museum : October 1979 | Recorder : date

NATURAL HISTORY | © IRGMA 1975 | 1/12/75

ACQUISITION | Acquisition method gift | Acquired from : date
C | D Price | Conditions Yes/No | D | Valuation : date | D

DESCRIPTION | Condition keyword/detail good | Completeness keyword/detail
Dimension measured | value & units/accuracy | Dimension measured | value & units/accuracy

Part : aspect : description keyword/detail | D
C

PROCESS | ~~Conservation~~ ~~Reproduction~~ | Other process preparation | Method/detail : operator : date : detail preservation (1% Phenoxetol) : Davis, P.S. : September 1979 | Cross-reference | D
C

DOCUMENTATION | L | Class | Author : date : title : journal or publisher : volume : detail
C
L | Class | Author : date : title : journal or publisher : volume : detail | Drawing or photo
C

NOTES | Notes
From C.E.G.B. Intake Screens.
C

Figure 20.4 Completed MDS natural history record card

Progress with collection documentation

With other duties to perform, Keepers could catalogue new acquisitions but had little time to re-accession items. For audit purposes, listings of collections in those museums with inadequate records had to suffice.

In 1976 after a brief familiarization period with the complexities of the

the MDS record card and the syntactic system involved, curatorial staff made good progress in the cataloguing of collections, especially in natural sciences which benefited from having a recognized and fully comprehensive taxonomy. In other subjects staff spent considerable time establishing internal procedures and thesauri of keywords specially related to their discipline. The use of the general record cards (History Artefact and Museum Object) also had drawbacks. This situation has been largely rectified by the MDA introducing cards (for example Decorative Arts and Pictorial Representation) which are tailor-made for the recording of information relating to specific subject areas.

The huge task of re-accessioning the Service's 'total holdings' began in earnest in the spring of 1977 with the help of a documentation and cataloguing scheme sponsored by the Manpower Services Commission. Under this project a team of cataloguers, with graduate qualifications and supervised by the permanent curatorial staff, recorded information about collections on flimsies. These were forwarded to a team of typists at headquarters (supervised by the cataloguer/typist) who produced the necessary duplicate copies of MDS cards. The MSC have renewed the scheme annually, with an average of 15 cataloguers and four typists per year being employed. The MSC cover the wages of the staff involved and operating costs (mainly stationery such as flimsies and MDS cards). It also provides capital for the purchase of equipment such as typewriters and filing cabinets. At the end of the scheme the Museum Service will have the option to return such equipment or buy them from the MSC. At the end of 1982 the finance involved totalled around £460 000, comprising £441 500 in wages, £11 500 in operating costs, and £7000 in capital costs. By that time well over two-thirds of the Service's 250 000 items had been re-accessioned.

Computerization experience

As more and more record cards were typed the need for computerization became imperative. Most Keepers managed to produce simple manual cross-references but this was time consuming to establish and keep up to date. Computerization would make index production and file maintenance far more manageable.

In 1978 the Service had been involved in a MDA pilot computerization project processing 300 fossil fish records. A catalogue and various indexes were produced on printout. In other experiments in 1981 the MDA processed 200 fine art and 120 natural history records (Figure 20.4 and 20.5) and confirmed that computerization was entirely feasible but that costs were high. The level of demand for information retrieval required the Service to computerize records relating to about 100 000 of its items. The average price of £1 to £2 per record charged for 'external' computerization made costs prohibitively high. The only way forward was for the Tyne and Wear Service to undertake its own data preparation, the highest cost factor in computerization.

In 1982 the duties of the cataloguer/typist were extended to cover data preparation. Aided by an MSC sponsored assistant, a programme of work was begun, the target being the preparation of 20 000 records per year. The typists produced punched paper-tape which was sent to the MDA for

```
(Northumberland, River Blyth estuary)

      ling              TWCMS:  D827; E1378; D2904
      mackerel          TWCMS:  E2907
      mullet thick-lipped grey
                        TWCMS:  E1378
      pipefish greater
                        TWCMS:  E2901
      plaice            TWCMS:  D784; E2902
      pogge             TWCMS:  D773; D825; E4893
      ray starry        TWCMS:  D828; E2910-2911
      rockling five-bearded
                        TWCMS:  D822; E2899; E4053
      saith             TWCMS:  D788
      saithe            TWCMS:  E2914; E4696
      salmon            TWCMS:  D794
      sand smelt        TWCMS:  D779
      sandeel           TWCMS:  D762
      sandeel greater
                        TWCMS:  D831; E2898
      scad              TWCMS:  E4675; E4695
      sea scorpion      RWCMS:  D776; D805; E4894
      sea snail Montagu's
                        TWCMS:  F1052
      shanny            TWCMS:  D248
      smooth hound      TWCMS:  E4651
```

Figure 20.5 Computer-generated geographical index

processing on the Cambridge University computer using the GOS program. Subsequently, improvements in the procedure were made by feeding the paper-tape on to the Tyne and Wear County Council's mainframe and transferring it onto magnetic tape. Using a VDU the cataloguer/typist is able to make corrections so that a 'clean' magnetic tape can be forwarded to the MDA for processing.

Until the Service can implement GOS the MDA will be required to process data. It seems unlikely that the Service will use GOS on the County Council's mainframe which is an ICL machine rather different from those on which the package has already been implemented. The Service hopes eventually to do its own in-house processing of records using GOS on a microcomputer.

Conclusions

Few museums have been confronted with the same problems of cataloguing as the Tyne and Wear Museums Service. It would have been impossible to rectify more than one hundred years of documentation neglect without MSC sponsorship. The County Council could not have provided the finance or manpower resources to undertake such a huge programme of re-accessioning. Although the Service benefitted greatly from the MSC scheme, it must be borne in mind that MSC aims have also been fulfilled, in that unemployed people have found renewed purpose whilst in temporary employment. Many of them have found permanent jobs, some in museum services, due to the training they have received.

The museum profession tends to be a conservative one. Most of the curatorial staff within the Service originally showed little enthusiasm for the adoption of the MDA system because its insistence on 'common standards' cut across personal methods of recording evolved over a number of years. There was also a suspicion of anything involved with 'new technology'. Some staff still hold these prejudices but the majority have recognized the advantages of the new system. Indeed, as main users of the system, many Keepers welcomed the opportunity to cooperate with the MDA in the production of a wider range of cards, more suited to particular disciplines.

The importance of establishing and using internal conventions was recognized at an early stage (Pettigrew and Holden, 1978). However, the MSC scheme necessarily involved frequent turnover of cataloguing and typing staff and consequently internal conventions have been difficult to maintain. Despite being both thoroughly supervised by permanent staff and diligent on their own part, cataloguers have had a tendency to introduce their own methods. Many errors, both curatorial and typing, which have been made on the record cards, can be rectified at the data preparation stage.

The adoption of the MDA system has undoubtedly led to improved standards of cataloguing within the Tyne and Wear Service. With the continuing support of MSC, it is anticipated that the programme of re-accessioning all the collections will be completed by 1984/5. By that time there may be scope to broaden the cataloguer/typist post into that of a registrar, responsible for handling information retrieval for the public, outside bodies, and curatorial staff. This would give the latter more time to develop exhibitions, permanent displays and public activities. Such work would benefit from improvements in the interpretation of collections brought about by more efficient records management.

Chapter 21

The Hunterian Museum and Art Gallery, University of Glasgow

Frank Willett

Introduction

The Hunterian Museum and Art Gallery forms a widely scattered department of the University of Glasgow. Its collections include items acquired by the University since soon after its foundation in 1451. It takes its name from William Hunter, the eighteenth century anatomist, physician and teacher who was one of the outstanding collectors of his time. On his death in 1783 his collections were left in trust to his partners, who used the anatomical and pathological collections, and probably his books, in their teaching in London. A purpose-built museum to house them was opened in 1807 at the College of Glasgow. The University moved to its present site in 1870 and subsequently, as the University grew, many of the collections were placed in the teaching departments when they moved into new buildings. Thus the teaching departments of Anatomy, Pathology, Zoology and the University Library now house the appropriate parts of Hunter's collections together with later acquisitions. The departments of Botany, Chemistry, Music and Natural Philosophy (Physics) have collections of post-Hunterian material (the latter principally associated with Lord Kelvin and J.P. Joule). The Museum proper now houses the geological, archaeological, ethnographic and coin collections, whilst the art collections are housed in the new Hunterian Art Gallery which opened in 1980.

The collections serve for teaching and research, as well as being displayed in exhibitions which are open to the public. They vary greatly in size and scientific importance.

Documentation background

Comprehensive catalogues have already been published of the anatomical and pathological collections and of the Greek, Roman Imperial and Anglo-Saxon coinage and of the type specimens of fossils — this last on microfiche, with the text stored on magnetic tape (Rolfe *et al.*, 1981) so there is no urgency for these to be recatalogued. The rest of the collections, however, are recorded mainly in handwritten acquisitions books, sometimes supplemented by 5×3 inch index cards. Unfortunately no catalogue was prepared of Hunter's ethnographic holdings and the entire ethnographic collection was recatalogued during the twentieth century. This means that there is considerable uncertainty about the accuracy of the information recorded.

The development of new systems by IRGMA and the MDA encouraged the staff to consider the desirability of cataloguing the collections so as to have better retrieval facilities. However, with only ten curatorial staff members, there seemed to be little hope of undertaking this enormous task. University museums in Britain are able to command very limited resources with no special allowance being made for them in the Government grant to Universities. In such circumstances, the establishment of Manpower Services Commission schemes to help the unemployed was a great opportunity. The use of newly qualified and inexperienced graduates for up to one year makes them less efficient than using the curatorial staff, and close supervision is needed. Nevertheless, substantial progress has been made with their help, and in return many of them have found employment in the museum profession (one such is an editor of this volume) so the training they receive from us is being disseminated throughout museums in Britain.

Development of new procedures

In the early stages the cataloguers tended to develop their individual terminology, but the importance of uniformity in areas such as artefact classification soon became clear. Internal conventions have been drawn up (McInnes, 1978; MacKie, 1978 and 1980). These documents are under constant revision in an attempt to conform with nationally accepted rules (Figure 21.1).

One simple procedure was soon adopted: the completion of A4 paper copies showing both sides of the A5 MDA card before the cards themselves were filled in. This allowed a clean card to be typed but also permitted the compilation of an index of draft sheets which allows quick checking of what has been done. It also provided the added security of a duplicate record.

We found that the availability of cataloguers and the needs of the collections varied, so we set up four levels of cataloguing:

Research: completing as much as possible of the card including extensive searches of the literature (e.g. identifying the cutting and layer from which an artefact was excavated). Such an approach is possible only with small collections but it does increase their value enormously. For the reason indicated above, this approach has been especially rewarding with our ethnographic collection (Glaister, 1981). The Senior Curator responsible for this collection is now preparing for publication a catalogue of our eighteenth century and early nineteenth century material.
Intermediate level: cataloguing with less detail.
Basic: only outline information (e.g. taxon, locality, collector), done by a qualified cataloguer who checks this data.
Superficial: used only when no qualified staff could be recruited, simply to

```
4(c)  Production :

This is a new section suitable for historically recorded material and
describes where the object was manufactured;  it may of course be a
locality far distant from the place of collection.

Part refers to what part of the object is being described.  If the whole
object was made in one place then the Full Name is repeated here, otherwise
the name of the part concerned.

Method:  a variety of terms can be used here although this element should
be filled in only if there is certainty about it.  Relevant terms include

              carved            sown
              cast              woven
              engraved          embossed
              turned            embroidered
              painted           tie-dyed
              ground            flaked
              forged

If more than one method was used these can be given as a set of keywords,
e.g.

         Part                      Method

         decoration                painted * stamped

Name, group:  The aim of the compilers of the Ethnography card was that
it should be possible to identify the makers of the object in as much
detail as was available, starting with something equivalent to a tribal
or national name and progressing downwards to a named person where that
was possible.  However, because of the complexity of the terms used in
Anthropology to identify social groups it was decided not to specify a
uniform hierarchical sequence of identification - from broad to narrow
but simply to construct an hierarchy afresh each time using whatever
terms were appropriate for the case concerned.  Each keyword of course,
is the name of the people, tribe or individual concerned but each must
be qualified by the identifying term, with an / between them.  It is as
if the place name hierarchy had to be written each time as:

Place / Dun Mor Vaul * parish / Tiree * county / Argyllshire * country /
Scotland

instead of

Dun Mor Vaul * Tiree * Argyllshire * Scotland

In the Ethnography card the qualifying terms, or qualifiers, can refer
to social organizations, individuals and to impersonal material culture
they can include:-

         Anthropological    Material culture    Personal

         group              culture             name
         tribe              industry            rank
         clan people                            role
                                                        /........
         sub-tribe                              sex
         class

These should be listed as keywords in descending order of importance, e.g.

people / Maya * tribe / Lacandon * role / woodcarver * name / Eduardo Cocom
```

Figure 21.1 Example of Museum documentation manual

transfer the data from the existing record without checking. These entries
need to be reconsidered at a later date by a qualified cataloguer.

When we started, no MDS cards were available in certain fields. Although
we subsequently assisted in the development of them, we use our own
double-sided A4 size cards for the art collections (modified from one used by
the Fitzwilliam Museum, Cambridge) and our own A5 card for the coin
collection.

Progress with collection documentation

The different museum collections present particular problems that have caused us to adopt a variety of approaches.

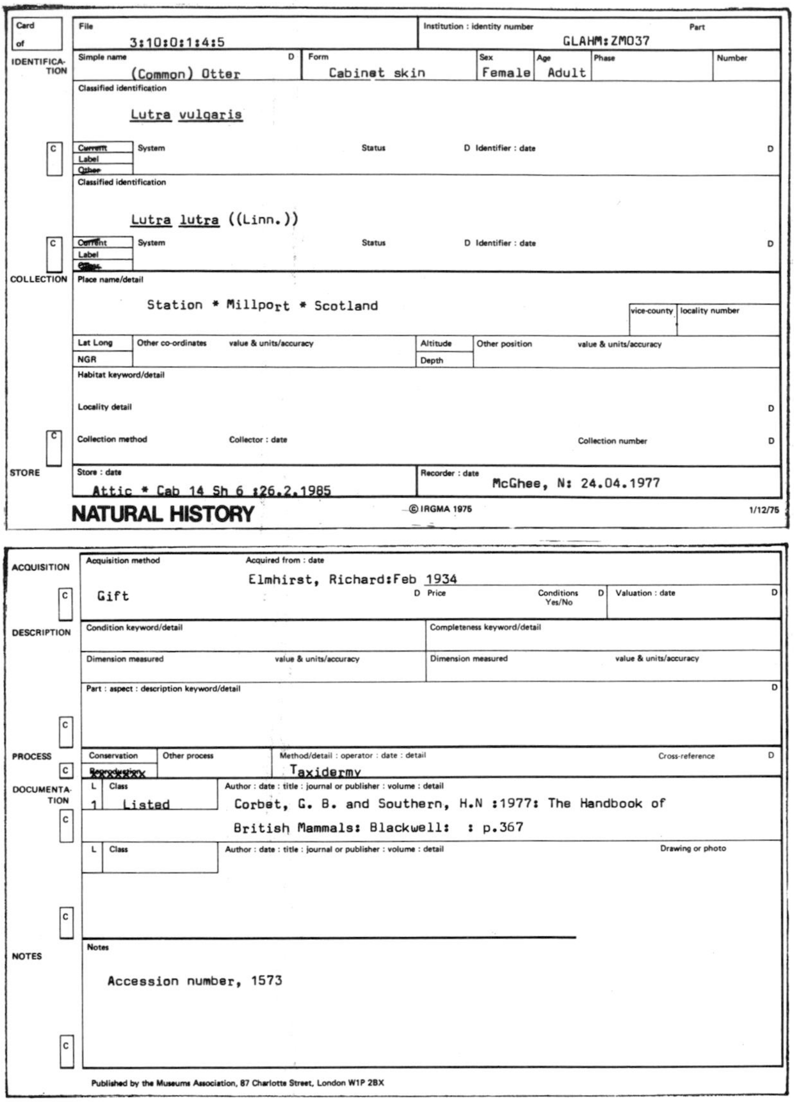

Card | of | File: 3:10:0:1:4:5 | Institution : identity number: GLAHM:ZM037 | Part

IDENTIFICATION
Simple name: (Common) Otter | D | Form: Cabinet skin | Sex: Female | Age: Adult | Phase | Number
Classified identification: Lutra vulgaris
C | Current / Label / Other | System | Status | D | Identifier : date | D
Classified identification: Lutra lutra ((Linn.))
C | Current / Label / Other | System | Status | D | Identifier : date | D

COLLECTION
Place name/detail: Station * Millport * Scotland | vice-county | locality number
Lat Long | NGR | Other co-ordinates | value & units/accuracy | Altitude | Depth | Other position | value & units/accuracy
Habitat keyword/detail
Locality detail | D
C | Collection method | Collector : date | Collection number | D

STORE
Store : date: Attic * Cab 14 Sh 6 :26.2.1985 | Recorder : date: McGhee, N: 24.04.1977

NATURAL HISTORY | © IRGMA 1975 | 1/12/75

ACQUISITION
Acquisition method: Gift | Acquired from : date: Elmhirst, Richard:Feb 1934 | D | Price | Conditions Yes/No | D | Valuation : date | D
C

DESCRIPTION
Condition keyword/detail | Completeness keyword/detail
Dimension measured | value & units/accuracy | Dimension measured | value & units/accuracy
Part : aspect : description keyword/detail | D
C

PROCESS
C | Conservation / Reproduction | Other process | Method/detail : operator : date : detail: Taxidermy | Cross-reference | D

DOCUMENTATION
C | L: 1 | Class: Listed | Author : date : title : journal or publisher : volume : detail: Corbet, G. B. and Southern, H.N :1977: The Handbook of British Mammals: Blackwell: : p.367
C | L | Class | Author : date : title : journal or publisher : volume : detail | Drawing or photo

NOTES
Notes: Accession number, 1573
C

Published by the Museums Association, 87 Charlotte Street, London W1P 2BX

Figure 21.2 Completed MDS natural history record card

The *zoological collections* include an extensive range of material accumulated over the years, primarily as demonstration specimens used in teaching systematic zoology. Documentation of these pieces is poor or absent, so this material has been excluded from the MDS cataloguing project. The rest of the collections have been developed for reference and research use, and include important collections of insects, coelenterates, molluscs, horns and antlers, and bird skins and eggs. These are mostly well-documented so MDS cataloguing has concentrated on these. The bird and mammal material (Figure 21.2) has been completed, as has a large part of the molluscs; about 11 000 cards altogether.

In contrast, the *geological collections* form the largest part of the museum, numbering around half a million specimens, mainly fossils. Temporary staff have either recatalogued the mineral collections on to MDS cards, or catalogued, for the first time, important old rock collections, or recently acquired research collections in palaeontology and petrology. By the end of 1986, we expect to have all 30 000 minerals on MDS cards at a basic level of cataloguing. To complete MDS cataloguing according to the full specification could take up to twenty years, and is not felt to be justified at present.

An index of the important rock collections should be prepared by late 1984, although the MDS geology card is not being used for this task. It may be possible to produce a computerized catalogue of our 25 000 rock thin-sections directly from the existing book-catalogues, without intermediate MDS cards. At the outset (McInnes, 1978), the petrological code developed by the Institute of Geological Sciences for computer use was adopted for cataloguing our 55 000 rock specimens (Harrison and Sabine, 1970). However, the advantages of this system for sorting data are outweighed by the extra time required to assign codes, and we have abandoned this approach. The problem has been exacerbated by the (in other respects fortunate) recent lack of unemployed graduate geologists. However, it has been possible to train non-geologists (ranging from a radio-repair man to a post-graduate research economic historian) to undertake some of this work.

Almost 20 000 of the rock and mineral specimens have been MDS catalogued. These are largely recently acquired research collections. With accessions averaging 8000 specimens a year, it is difficult, with the fluctuating manpower available for this work, to see an end to this task. Priorities are therefore being assigned for cataloguing collections. Low priority items are accessioned and stored, occasionally to be catalogued in our old book catalogues. The variation in the rate of accessions bedevils any attempt at long-term planning. In the year 1979/80, for example, potential accessions of 33 000 specimens passed through the hands of geology section staff. This included two collections of 18 000 and 12 000 specimens respectively. This is comparable with the 30 000 specimens received annually by the Geological Departments of the British Museum (Natural History), with their one hundred staff in contrast to our four. Some of these specimens have been forwarded to more appropriate repositories (e.g. National Museum of Wales and Trinity College, Dublin), but even so, 23 000 specimens require to be catalogued for the Hunterian Museum: about eight man-years' curating time with our present numbers of temporary staff.

The relatively small size of our *ethnographical collections*, together with the potential historical importance of the older material, meant that it was possible and useful to devote a considerable research effort to the material while recataloguing it in the maximum detail (Figure 21.3). This has resulted in the recovery, over the last four years, of a mass of information

212

about the earlier items which had been mixed up or mislaid during the nineteenth century. It can now be seen that the collection includes a much higher proportion than previously believed of historically valuable material including much from near the time of the first contact with Europeans.

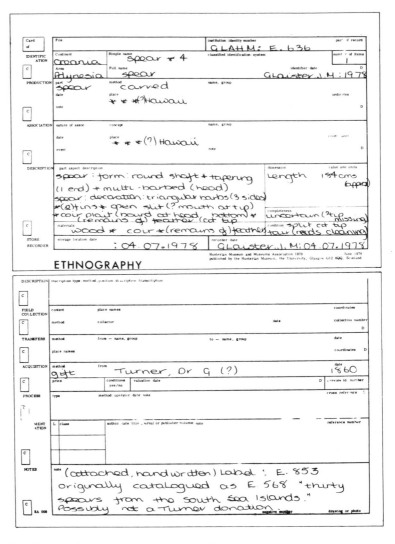

Figure 21.3 Completed museum-designed ethnography record card

By contrast with the ethnographical material very little prehistoric *archaeological material* was obtained by William Hunter and relatively few items were presented to the Museum during the nineteenth century. Most of it was given by private collectors, or obtained on excavations, in the twentieth century. Scottish and English prehistory is well represented, as is the Palaeolithic period in France. As with the other collections the quality of the information available about the prehistoric material has been greatly increased as the objects have been recatalogued on MDS cards.

The *Roman collection* is one of our chief glories and began to be formed by the University long before the Hunterian Museum itself was established. The Museum has had the advantage of a specialist member of staff in this field from the 1930s onwards so the collection is already well catalogued and much is already available in the form of published excavation reports. The transfer of these records on to MDS cards has therefore been accorded a somewhat lower priority; nevertheless recataloguing is now about 80% complete. About 50 000 specimens in ethnography and archaeology have been catalogued.

The Museum possesses a considerable collection of material from Egypt, the Near East, Greece and Etruria. The greater part of this has now been catalogued through the efforts of temporary staff who were specialist graduates in the relevant fields.

Historical material, partly relating to the University since its foundation in 1451 and partly miscellaneous items deriving from random gifts over the last two hundred years, has almost all been catalogued on MDS cards.

Cataloguing of the *art collections* has had to proceed intermittently as the preparation of a new building has occupied the time of the three curatorial staff members. The drawings and water colour collections have been partially catalogued (793 items) and a start has been made on the print collection of over 15 000 items, over 10 000 of which have been catalogued (Figure 21.4).

Computerization experience

At an early stage we held discussions with the MDA, the Council for Museums and Galleries in Scotland (now the Scottish Museums Council), and the University of Glasgow Computing Service to establish how best computerized cataloguing could be arranged for Scotland. It was decided that the cheapest procedure would be to have all the data preparation carried out by the MDA at Duxford and have it fed into the Cambridge University computer which could generate any indexes or lists we might require. We adopted this procedure, but are now finding that it has disadvantages.

The cataloguer writes out the details on a draft A4 sheet which is then typed. (To minimize errors, where a large group of material is being catalogued with features in common (such as locality or stratigraphy), this information is typed on a master card from which the necessary number of cards is printed. The typist then needs to add only the variable items of data.) The cards then have to be checked by the cataloguer, and corrected if necessary. The typed cards are sent to the MDA who retype the data into machine readable form, returning a printout to us which again has to be corrected, returned to the MDA and then returned to us again for final checking. This repeated proofreading is very time-consuming for the permanent staff.

We are therefore now moving to a simpler method (Figure 21.5). Three microcomputers have been purchased on which the cataloguers are able to enter the data from their own cards and make all necessary corrections

CARD OF	PAINTINGS, PRINTS & DRAWINGS		Inventory No: GLAHA 6556	
Identification & Production	Artist: dates _Tempesta, Antonio : 1555 = 1630_		School _Italian_	
	Title: date _I deal Woman , after Michelangelo : 1613_			
	Simple name _print_	Dimensions _215 x 151 mm_		Mount/frame
	Medium _in R_		Support _paper_	
	Production detail _etching_		Artist detail	
Description	Content			
	Condition _light staining * surface dirt * platemark with thin margin_			
Process	Conservation/reproduction			
File	Watermark			
	Signature _l r corner of margin . Ant T inc 1613_			
	Inscription _bottom margin : Michaelangelus Bonarotus inuen_			
	Acquisition _bequeathed by Professor W R Scott 1940_	Valuation: date		
	Provenance _P Mariette 1648 , see Lugt 1787 -1790_			

Figure 21.4(a) Completed museum-designed fine art record card (front)

before obtaining a printout for record purposes. The data can then be transferred from disc to tape and sent to the MDA. Our first efforts however have revealed that the curatorial staff still wish to retain typed MDS cards which they find useful. We hope that eventually the data will be stored on the University of Glasgow computer affording us direct access. This facility already exists for the coin collection which has been dealt with entirely on our own campus. In this case no printout is necessary at all, except as a

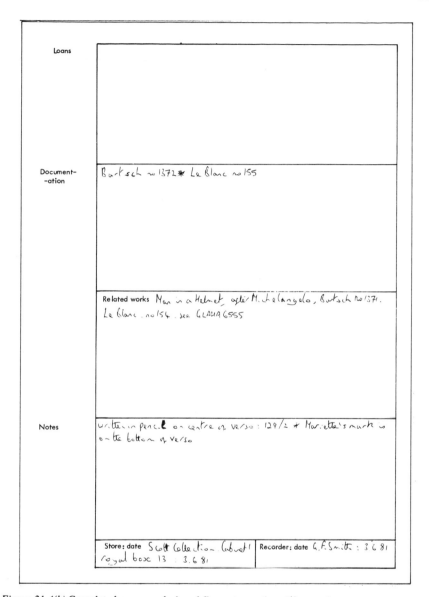

Loans	
Document--ation	Bartsch no 1372 ✱ Le Blanc no 155
	Related works Man in a Helmet, after M. Helangelo, Bartsch no 1371. Le Blanc no 154. see GLAHA 6555
Notes	written in pencil on centre of verso: 129/2 ✱ Mariette's mark is on the bottom of verso
	Store: date Scott Collection Cabinet / royal box 13 : 3.6.81 — Recorder: date G.F.Smith : 3.6.81

Figure 21.4(b) Completed museum-designed fine art record card (reverse)

permanent record of a search for information. Unfortunately GOS is written in BCPL and the difficulties of running this program with a compiler in Glasgow are formidable. Until then we shall have to continue to use bulky printouts, limited to the types of index for which we have asked (e.g. donor, location, material and class of object), rather than have the facility of direct interaction with the data (Figures 21.6-21.9). Ultimately we hope to be able to ask narrower questions cutting across several of these fields and to obtain

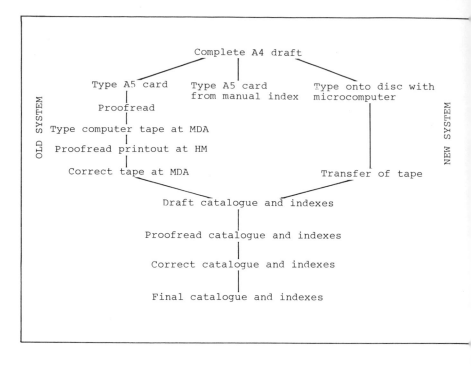

Figure 21.5 Computerization procedures

instant answers. These questions can of course be asked of the MDA service but involve delay. We intend also to transfer the full printout on to microfiche for easier storage and access.

Ideally we should like to see a national computer network dedicated to museum collections, or at least a central data store, so that one could, for example, discover which museums hold material from a classic archaeological site or geological exposure, or search ethnographical collections for the name of all recorded crew members of Captain Cook's voyages. In the meantime we have prepared data on our holdings in cooperation with the Natural History Collections Research Unit set up by the Scottish Museums Council (see Chapter 22). We see the improvement of our own cataloguing not simply as benefitting our own work but as helping to make knowledge of our collections more widely available to anyone who may be interested.

```
Dunlop, Dr. J.C.
    gift
        quiver, dart  GLAHM: E.1981.7

Durant, Dr. G.
    gift
        adze          GLAHM: E.1977.7

Dyer, H.
    gift
        gun           GLAHM: E.293

Easton, Dr.
    gift
        idol          GLAHM: E.560

Eck Collection
    gift
        animal figure GLAHM: E.147; E.295/2
        bowl          GLAHM: E.305
        branch ornament
                      GLAHM: E.296
        drinking tube GLAHM: E.143
        fan           GLAHM: E.281
        figure        GLAHM: E.219; E.295/1
        handle ornament
                      GLAHM: E.282
        human figure  GLAHM: E.144
        lamp          GLAHM: E.134
        maté pot      GLAHM: E.142
        Pandaeau pipes
                      GLAHM: E.239
        pipe          GLAHM: E.299
        pot           GLAHM: E.148-152; E.158-165; E.167
        pot, animal figure
                      GLAHM: E.153; E.166
        pot, figure   GLAHM: E.155-156
        slipper, pair of
                      GLAHM: E.302
        statuette     GLAHM: E.145; E.280
        tray, cup     GLAHM: E.136/1
        tusk          GLAHM: E.99
        vase          GLAHM: E.303-304
        work basket   GLAHM: E.283

Ewing, Dr.
    gift
        book of Ruth, synagogue roll
                      GLAHM: E.1931.8

Findlay, Mrs.
    gift
        Buddha tablet GLAHM: E.253/1

Fisher, P.
    gift
        tree          GLAHM: E.1902.3
```

Figure 21.6 Computer-generated ethnography donor index

```
36/8
   macehead         GLAHM: E.1927.5
   pipe             GLAHM: E.1925.28; E.1925.40
   pipe bowl        GLAHM: E.1925.39
   quern            GLAHM: E.1936.2

36/9
   cloth            GLAHM: E.631
   hairpin          GLAHM: E.1925.36/2
   mortar, pigment bowl
                    GLAHM: E.1925.27
   necklace         GLAHM: E.1925.33-34
   pomade pot       GLAHM: E.1925.36/1
   powder puff container
                    GLAHM: E.1925.35
   sherd            GLAHM: E.1925.32

36/10
   armlet           GLAHM: E.1925.42; E.1925.42/1;
                       E.1925.43-44; E.1925.47-48;
                       E.1925.48/1; E.1925.49-50
   ear ornament     GLAHM: E.1936.57
   girdle, necklet  GLAHM: E.1925.41
   gold dust box    GLAHM: E.1932.2
   medicine         GLAHM: E.1925.51/1-6
   necklace         GLAHM: E.1925.54
   sherd base       GLAHM: E.1925.52/1
   sherd, base      GLAHM: E.1925.52/3
   sherd, rim wall  GLAHM: E.1925.52; E.1925.52/2

36/11
   anklet           GLAHM: E.13/1; E.23
   basket           GLAHM: E.21
   brooch           GLAHM: E.65
   button           GLAHM: E.1979.2
   castanet         GLAHM: E.1979.1
   fire stick       GLAHM: E.11
   flyswitch        GLAHM: E.22
   girdle           GLAHM: E.24
   knife            GLAHM: E.1936.64
   medicine charm   GLAHM: E.12; E.13/1-5; E.13/7-8;
                       E.14/1-4; E.15-16; E.18
   medicine container
                    GLAHM: E.10
   necklace         GLAHM: E.13/4; E.13/7; E.25; E.57;
                       E.66-67; E.1925.55-56
   pipe             GLAHM: E.8-9; E.9/1
   quiver           GLAHM: E.19
   sandpaper        GLAHM: E.20
   shellfish        GLAHM: E.6

36/12
   armlet           GLAHM: E.46/1; E.47; E.47/1; E.48;
                       E.49/1-7; E.50-51; E.51/1; E.53/1-2;
                       E.62; E.62/1; E.64
   bag              GLAHM: E.63
   ear ornament     GLAHM: E.1925.45; E.1925.45/1;
                       E.1925.46; E.1925.46/1-2
   knife            GLAHM: E.55
```

Figure 21.7 Computer-generated ethnography object location index

```
(coir)
   (girdle)           GLAHM: E.496/1; E.516/1; E.533
   headdress          GLAHM: E.524; E.1910.15
   hook               GLAHM: E.466/1; E.659-660
   idol               GLAHM: E.560
   legging            GLAHM: E.462/1
   lei                GLAHM: E.427
   lime gourd         GLAHM: E.558/2
   mask               GLAHM: E.1910.13
   oar                GLAHM: E.401
   pendant            GLAHM: E.496; E.521
   skirt              GLAHM: E.1928.93/2
   sling              GLAHM: E.423
   spear              GLAHM: E.405/2-4; E.405/6-9; E.568/1-2;
                         E.632-633; E.636; E.648
   sword              GLAHM: E.350-351; E.506/1-2

conch shell
   axehead            GLAHM: E.1955.1; E.1955.3
   hoe                GLAHM: E.1955.2
   implement          GLAHM: E.1955.5
   scraper            GLAHM: E.1955.4

copper
   animal figure      GLAHM: E.1935.3
   armlet             GLAHM: E.49/2-5; E.50; E.51/1;
                         E.1925.42/1; E.1936.45-46;
                         E.1936.47/1; E.1936.51
   bag                GLAHM: E.112
   ear ornament       GLAHM: E.1925.45; E.1936.49; E.1936.55;
                         E.1936.57
   girdle             GLAHM: E.1936.54
   gold dust box      GLAHM: E.1932.3-4
   human figure       GLAHM: E.1935.3
   knife              GLAHM: E.3/2; E.1978.15-17; E.1978.19
   money              GLAHM: E.1980.6
   necklet            GLAHM: E.1936.52-53; E.1936.56
   spear              GLAHM: E.2/7
   stool              GLAHM: E.1936.19

copper alloy
   scabbard           GLAHM: E.1914/1; E.1928.14

coral
   branch ornament    GLAHM: E.296

cord
   bow                GLAHM: E.1902.1
   breast, gorget     GLAHM: E.375
   fishhook           GLAHM: E.418
   spear thrower      GLAHM: E.1979.6

cork
   fork               GLAHM: E.558/2
   lime gourd         GLAHM: E.558/2

cotton
   bag                GLAHM: E.1966.36
   basket             GLAHM: E.532/5-6
```

Figure 21.8 Computer-generated ethnography object materials index

```
bag, 5
    bag            GLAHM: E.1935.7; E.1936.34; E.1949.2

basket, 5
    basket         GLAHM: E.183/1; E.1936.29; E.1936.29/1;
                       E.1936.30

battle axe, 4
    battle axe     GLAHM: E.1928.89/1

battleaxe, 4
    battleaxe      GLAHM: E.551; E.1920.26-31; E.1928.89;
                       E.1960.28
    macehead       GLAHM: E.1925.22/1-2; E.1927.5

bedding, 7
    hammock        GLAHM: E.95

biface, 19
    handaxe        GLAHM: E.1925.18/2

blade, 1
    flint blade    GLAHM: E.71/20

blowpipe, 4
    basket         GLAHM: E.532/5-6
    quiver         GLAHM: E.185; E.1981.7
    quiver, dart   GLAHM: E.185; E.532; E.532/2-3; E.1981.7
    quiver, dart, basket
                   GLAHM: E.532/4
    quiver, sharpener, darts
                   GLAHM: E.532/1

boat, 8
    canoe          GLAHM: E.253/2; E.553/1-3
    kayak          GLAHM: E.102; E.584-585
    model, canoe   GLAHM: E.406
    oar.           GLAHM: E.401
    paddle         GLAHM: E.101; E.101/1-2; E.337/1-8;
                       E.338; E.346; E.346/1-3; E.368;
                       E.368/1-6; E.404; E.440; E.527/1-2;
                       E.529/1; E.530; E.565/1; E.566; E.619;
                       E.1928.83
    paddle ceremonial
                   GLAHM: E.529
    paddle ceremonial
                   GLAHM: E.337/9-12

bolas, 4
    bolas          GLAHM: E.175

borer, 1
    awl            GLAHM: E.71/31
    drill          GLAHM: E.435; E.1910.5; E.1939.15

box, 5
    box            GLAHM: E.1977.5/2
    gold dust box  GLAHM: E.1931.1; E.1932.2; E.1932.4;
                       E.1977.5/1
```

Figure 21.9 Computer-generated ethnography object classification index

Chapter 22

Collections research in the United Kingdom

Charles W. Pettitt

Introduction

Despite the tremendous value it would have to all natural historians, a comprehensive, nationwide list of natural science collections does not exist for any country. In the United Kingdom several individuals have produced useful publications which have solved part of the problem (Chalmers-Hunt, 1976; Cleevely, 1982; Sherborne, 1940). The compilation of a national Register of Collections started in 1979 in an attempt to extend these sources. It is expected that most of the available information on collections will have been gathered by 1986. It was the combination of available computer resources at Manchester Museum coupled with the growing spirit of cooperation among natural science curators in the United Kingdom, as witnessed by the recent formation of the Biology and the Geological Curators Groups, that provided the right conditions for the project to start. The scheme soon became known as 'collections research' (Pettitt and Hancock, 1981).

Aim and content of the Register

The aim of the Register is to give curators and other scholars signposts to the location of *assemblages* of material of interest. In particular, it is designed to aid the location of material in the collection of, or associated with, a given named 'collector' or of a given taxonomic group or from a specific part of the world.

In the natural sciences, assemblages or aggregations of specimens are traditionally called by the name of the person responsible for their formation (the 'collector'), and so it is the name of the collector that is used in the Register to identify the records of these assemblages.

The assemblage is the smallest unit referred to in the Register, with little or no information being included about individual specimens within the assemblage. It is the explicit intention of the compilers of the Register that once researchers have shortlisted the material of interest they should contact the relevant institutions holding the material and pursue their detailed researches in the normal way.

The Register is held as a serial data base on the University of Manchester computer. This permits the updating and correction of the compiled records, allows the records to be sorted and indexed easily, and makes the selective retrieval of information possible.

The work has been organized so that it can be achieved mainly by the cooperative efforts of curators, using facilities and resources already available to them. From the outset, the compilers took the realistic view that government funding would not be forthcoming to mount an independent centralized project. Instead, interested curators in the six regions of England, and in Scotland, Wales and Northern Ireland, are collaborating in informal Collection Research Units (CRUs). They have made themselves responsible for recording information on collections within their own institutions and for taking part in tracking down, visiting and recording collections held elsewhere within their area that are not in the charge of a natural science curator.

Schools, colleges, stately homes, university departments, government research institutes, local natural history societies, etc., are included in the survey. Latterly the scope of the data base has been widened to include details of significant collections still in private hands. Living collections, such as culture collections of algae, zoological gardens, rare-breed herds or arboreta have been excluded, as such collections are already well documented.

In some regions more wide-scattered collection-holding sites have been identified than could be coped with, given the available resources. However, as the feasibility and the value of the project have become apparent, CRUs have been able to obtain money from various funding bodies to help with specific regional tasks. In two instances such aid has included the appointment of peripatetic curators on short-term contracts expressly to gather this less accessible information.

Data categories

The categories of information to be noted, and the format in which they are recorded, form the basis for the collection research work. The categories created initially by the pioneer North West England Collection Research Unit were refined in use and developed into the current set used by all the CRUs. There are 18 groupings of information that may be included in the data base:

COLL The name of the 'Collector' or 'Assembler'. This is the primary key upon which the collection records are arranged. If the collection is unattributed it is recorded under the name of the holding institution until further information becomes available.

SUBJ The subject of the collection, briefly described in free text; for palaeontological material, stratigraphic information is included.

GEOG The geographic region(s) from which the majority of the material originates, stated as comprehensively as possible.

PERI The period over which the collection was assembled.

NUMB The size of the collection, estimated in any convenient way, such as number of specimens, or number of drawers, cabinets, storeboxes, etc.

ASSN Any assemblage of natural science material is likely to contain various admixtures of specimens that are themselves associated with other 'collectors', and a list of the names of any such associated individuals, expeditions, ships or institutions is included in the record. The widespread practice of exchanging botanical material, coupled with the tendency for museum herbaria to be stored in a single series, means this list may be very long for some botanical collection records.

LOCN The storage location of the collection, if this is unusual (e.g. not 'in general museum store'). Whether the collection is stored separately or as part of a larger assemblage is also noted.

ACQN How the holding institution acquired the collection, and the acquisition date.

MSSM Details of any unpublished documentation about the collection (e.g. manuscript notebooks, photographs, ephemera, etc).

LREF Citations to any publications dealing with the collection. If these are numerous only a reference to a reasonably complete bibliography is included.

BIOG Any biographical information about the primary collector, and/or a reference to a published obituary.

MUSE The name of the holding institution.

NMCO The name of the curator recording the collection, and the date the record was prepared. If type or figured material is known or thought to be included in the collection, this is noted.

ACTN If the recording curator considers the collection in urgent need of conservation, this is noted.

ADDN Any relevant additional information that does not come into the previous categories.

CLAS The taxonomic codes (see text).

GCOD The geographic codes (see text).

IDEN An arbitrary, unique reference number, assigned to each record to assist computer checking procedures.

CRU members compile the information which is readily available about collections on to these uniform input sheets (Figure 22.1). The sheets are then sent to Manchester Museum direct or via a vetting committee, depending on the regional organization within the CRUs.

Midlands Collection Research Unit (Natural Sciences)	Update Entry	
Data coding form (E)	Lit.ref.only	

	1 4	6	80
1	COLL	Ludlow Museum Collection	
2	SUBJ	Carboniferous fossils; Anthozoa (5 boxes); Brachiopoda (5 boxes); Pisces (2 trays); Mollusca ; Plantae (60 boxes + 3 trays); Trilobita (1 box).	
3	GEOG	Anglesey: Derbyshire : Shropshire : West Midlands : Yorkshire .	
4	PERI	1930's- 1970's	
5	NUMB	ca 70 boxes (ca 15X9"x3") and ca 4 trays (26"x"24")	
6	ASSN	Boynton, Helen; De Courcy, Peele (Miss) (Plantae, Shrewsbsbury coalfields); Phillips, N.M. (Miss)(Fish, Pook Hill, Walsall); Smith, R.; Watkins, Stephen,(Brachiopoda, Anglesey); ? Norton, W.J. ;	
7	LOCN	Geology room, Dept.Natural Sciences, Ludlow Museum, Old St., Ludlow, Shropshire.	70
	ACQN	Donation to Ludlow Museum	
9	MSSM		
10	LREF		
11	BIOG		
12	MUSE	Ludlow Museum Shropshire County Museum Services	
13	NMCO	Green, M. * date 1984, Aug	50
14	ACTN		
15	ADDN		
16	CLAS	GF A17 ZO4 + GF A17 Z13B + GF A17 Z16 + GF A17 BG + GF A17 ZO8 Trilobita	
17	GCOD	XWANG + XNDER + XNSHR + XNYOR + XNWMD	
18	IDEN		

Important consult instructions before completing this form
Use extra sheets if any box is too small; indicate in the box that the entry is continued

Figure 22.1 Completed collection research coding form

Computerization procedure

From 1979 to 1982, the information was input to the computer by the data preparation section of the University of Manchester Computer Science department. It is now input via PET 8032 microcomputers housed in the computer cataloguing unit of the Manchester Museum. Using the interactive input programs on these microcomputers it has proved possible to improve the quality of the records on the data base and reduce significantly the amount of post-input editing required. Data entry is mainly done by temporary staff funded by a governmental job creation scheme, as part of a much larger scheme to catalogue Manchester Museum's own collections (Pettitt, 1981a). Once the data base has been substantially built it will be maintained by Manchester Museum staff.

Immediately after input, two listings of each batch of data are sent to the originating curator, together with the source input sheets. Each curator is responsible for the preliminary checking of the computer record. Any corrections are marked on one listing and returned to Manchester; the second listing is retained by the curator for reference.

Data

Once the records have been transmitted to the University computer they are merged into the data base file. The FAMULUS processing package is used to manipulate the data, and the data base file is kept in the special internal format of the package.

Manchester Museum periodically provides each CRU with indexed listings of the data they have submitted, and such listings are also given to major holding institutions for internal use. The purpose of these listings is to stimulate revision and updating.

Curators are allowed to use free text when completing almost all the sections of the data-input sheet; the writer considers there are several reasons for not using controlled vocabularies in this project. With more than one hundred widely scattered curators completing input sheets over a period of several years, supervising the use of a controlled vocabulary and/or totally stylised format would have been very difficult with the resources available, and the task of editing the inevitable inconsistencies would have added greatly to the work of the Manchester Unit. More important, the use of controlled vocabularies can inhibit the scope of a curator's response, with the concomitant danger that unusual but important information might be omitted. Finally, curators are more prepared to assist if data capture is uncomplicated.

However, an unordered mass of free text information is not very useful, nor can indexes be prepared directly from the data as provided by the curators. Therefore all the records are scanned at Manchester before being input, and a series of sort/search codes is added to each. Thus, records describing collections in diverse ways such as 'marine molluscs', 'shells', 'gastropods and bivalves', 'Cephalopoda in spirit' would all receive the unique code for 'mollusca'. Not only does this permit all the molluscan records to be retrieved with ease, but also the set of codes is designed to allow the records to be sorted readily into the phylogenetic sequence a natural historian would expect (Figure 22.2).

Other code series are used to concord the information on the geographic origins of the collection (Figure 22.3) and for the geological era (where relevant). Adding a few three- to five-character codes to each record takes very little time, but permits wide-ranging use to be made of the data base without submitting the information provided by the curator to laborious editing. It also allows the user to see clearly what information came from the original curator, and what has been added during processing.

It would not, however, be sensible to use the 'coding' approach for the all-important name of the primary collector and the equally vital associated names section, and therefore these are rigorously edited. The only other primary editing done is to correct gross mistakes or typographical errors that cause ambiguity of meaning, or to alter records in response to information received after the record has been input. Any remaining non-critical errors are corrected later as time and manpower resources permit.

Results

The FAMULUS package contains a very efficient and sophisticated SEARCH processor, so that records satisfying complex combinations of criteria can be retrieved easily. While records may be searched for using any term or terms that may be present anywhere in the record, the data base has been structured to facilitate retrieval upon the name of collectors (primary or associated), the major zoological/botanical/geological groupings, geological age or geographic origin.

Manchester Museum offers a selective retrieval service to scholars, covering its own internal data bases as well as the Collections Research data base (Pettitt, 1981b). The service is available free, although the refund of excessive postal charges may be requested. There is no restriction upon who may use the service. In the first six months of 1982, 64 searches were made of the natural science collections data base in response to enquiries. Use of the service is expected to increase considerably when the data base is completed and its existence becomes more widely known.

By prior arrangement with Manchester Museum, users possessing suitable equipment may access the data base remotely by telephone link. Access to the data base is not interactive, although it may be possible to make it so by 1984.

In 1981 the North West England Collection Research Unit, with the aid of the North West Museums and Art Galleries Service, published the information it had supplied to the data base (Hancock and Pettitt, 1981). The published register (available from Manchester Museum) contains details of some 1100 main collections and 1600 associated collectors, together with taxonomic and geographic indexes (Figures 22.2 and 22.3).

The other CRUs also plan to publish registers: the Yorkshire and Humberside CRU in 1985, the Midlands CRU in 1986, and the others hopefully by 1988. All the participants agree, however, that while publication represents an important milestone in the work, it is desirable that the data base should remain in being, both for the selective dissemination of information and for continuing updating.

National coordination: FENSCORE

In February 1981, representatives of all the CRUs and of other interested bodies (such as the National Museums) formed the Federation for Natural Sciences Collection Research (FENSCORE). The primary objective of

```
Warren, Captain W.H. Cawne.          Sylvia, H.M.S.   Foraminifera and
Marine specimens                     Radiolaria.

Wilkins, Capt. A.G.
Insects and other animals.           PROTOZOA RADIOLARIA

Yates.   Biological models.          Sylvia, H.M.S.   Foraminifera and
                                     Radiolaria.
Ziegler, Prof. A.
Embryological models in wax.
                                     PORIFERA

ZOOLOGY GENERAL (GAMEHEADS)          Argo Expedition (1876).   Sponges,
                                     Gorgonids; Mollusca; Crustaea;
Astley, Capt. H. (  -1956).          few Vertebrates & Fossils.
Game heads.   A few cased hawks.
                                     Higgins, Rev. H.H. (1814-1893).
                                     Porifera, Corals, Mollusca, Mosses
ZOOLOGY GENERAL INVERTEBRATES        & Lichens.

Johnstone, J.   Fish Parasites       Manchester Museum.   Demospongia.
and Diseases.
                                     Manchester Museum.   Glass Sponges
Liverpool Biology Committee and      (Hexactinellid).
Lancashire Sea Fisheries.
General Invertebrates.               Manchester Museum.   Sponges:
                                     Keratosa.
Manchester Museum.   Deep-Sea
Benthic Invertebrates.               Mason, Dr. P.B. (1842-1903).
                                     Polyzoa, Sponges & Leafminers.
Manchester Museum.   Invertebrates
other than Crustacea, Mollusca, or   Swainson, George (  -1909).
Echinoderms.                         Microscope slides of mainly marine
                                     animals.

ZOOLOGY GENERAL VERTEBRATES
                                     COELENTERATA
Hignett, James.
Mounted Vertebrates.                 Manchester Museum.   Gorgonids.

                                     Swainson, George (  -1909).
BRYOZOA                              Microscope slides of mainly marine
                                     animals.
Jelly, Miss E.C.   Bryozoa.
                                     Wood, G.W.   Crustacea, Pycnogonida,
Mason, Dr. P.B. (1842-1903).         Coelentrates and Polyzoa.
Polyzoa, Sponges & Leafminers.

Pennington, Arthur Stuart.  Polyzoa  COELENTERATA CORALS
Swainson, George (  -1909).
Microscope slides of mainly marine
animals.                             Argo Expedition (1876).   Sponges,
                                     Gorgonids, Mollusca, Crustacea,
                                     Echinoderms, Bryophytes, Corals, a
Waters, A.W.   Polyzoa.              few Vertebrates & Fossils

Wood, G.W.   Crustacea, Pycnogonida, Higgins, Rev. H.H. (1814-1893).
Coelentrates and Polyzoa.            Porifera, Corals, Mollusca, Mosses
                                     & Lichens.

PROTOZOA FORAMINIFERA                Manchester Museum.   Corals.

Chaffer, Mrs. S.   Foraminifera
(magnified models in plaster).
```

Figure 22.2 Sample page of systematic index (North West England Collection Research Unit)

FENSCORE is to co-ordinate the efforts of the autonomous regional CRUs (Pettitt and Hancock, 1981). Reports of FENSCORE meetings are published in the *Museums Bulletin.*

Future plans: a register of types

Following a pilot study by the North West England CRU, it was decided at the FENSCORE meeting in June 1982 to organize the compilation of a provisional register of type and figured specimens held in the United Kingdom outside the National Museums.

It is intended that records of type specimens would be graded only into 'probably type' or 'possibly type'. Each record would contain:

taxon (original combination, with author and date);
number of specimen(s);
form of specimen(s);

ENGLAND LINCOLNSHIRE

Liassic Ironstone Fossils.
Scunthorpe area.   Westwood, R.E.

Bird Skins.   British, mainly
Lincolnshire and Wales.
Caton-Haigh, G.H.

ENGLAND LONDON

Coleoptera.   Most of Hall's
material is from S. England
(Dover, Deal, and South Gtr.
London area), Later material from
N. England. (See addn. below).
Hall, Christopher George (1842-1890)

Aphids on Microscope Slides.
Britain, mainly London area except
for Haliday's Belfast specimens &
a few others.   Walker, Francis
(1809-1874).

ENGLAND MIDDLESEX

Botany (Flowering Plants and Ferns).
Middlesex.   Marsden, Prosper
(fl.1900-1910)

ENGLAND NORFOLK

Geology (King material from
Norwich).   Pilkington Glass
Museum, St. Helens.

Hymenoptera.   Mainly 'European'
(some in Britain from Norfolk
region).
Hamlyn-Harris, Dr. Ronald
(1874-1953).

Lepidoptera (Macro).   British
Isles, esp. East Anglia.
Robinson, Arthur (1865-1948).

ENGLAND NORTHUMBERLAND

Coleoptera.   British, mainly
Northumberland.
Keswick Museum.

ENGLAND NOTTINGHAMSHIRE

Muscologia Nottinghamiensis.
Nottingham.   Howitt, Godfrey
(1800-1873) (M.D.) + Valentine,
William (fl.1810s-1884) (F.L.S.).

Hymenoptera.   Newark (Notts.)
Hadfield, Rev. James.

Lepidoptera.   Sherwood Forest.
Hardy, John Ray (1844-1921).

ENGLAND OXFORDSHIRE

Botany (Rust Fungi).
Banbury, Oxfordshire.
Liverpool Microscopical Society.

Fossils, Middle and Upper
Jurassic (Vertebrata + Mollusca);
Jurassic and Pleistocene (Mammalia).
British Isles, Oxford.
Manning, Percy.

ENGLAND SCILLY ISLES

Marine Algae.   Jersey, Dartmouth,
Portland, Weymouth, Penzance, Scilly
Isles, Torquay.   Warrington Museum.

ENGLAND SHROPSHIRE

Pleistocene Mollusca.   Gloppa,
nr. Oswestry.   Nicholson, A.

Insect, Coleoptera.   British
(especially Oswestry area).
Hignett, James.

Insects (mainly Trichoptera & minor
orders).   British Isles (mainly
Cheshire & Shropshire). Burrows, H.L.
(1897-1970).

Entomology.   Mainly Cheshire and
Shropshire.   Burrows, H.L.
(1897-1970).

ENGLAND SOMERSET

Jurassic Brachiopods (a few Agate
Pebbles).   England - Wiltshire,
Somerset, Dorset, Gloucestershire.
Brocklehurst, Miss Marianne (-1898)

ENGLAND STAFFORDSHIRE

Fossil Fish (Lower Carboniferous and
Coal Measures).   British Isles
(Staffordshire).   Ward, John
(1837-1906).

Figure 22.3 Sample page of geographic index (North West England Collection Research Unit)

whether extant or not;
name of holding institution;
any unique identity number assigned by holding institution;
name of recorder/date recorded;
classification code, if appropriate.

The idea of the Register is to provide no more than a signpost to the location of putative type material; it will not be in any way a nomenclatural or taxonomic publication.

Conclusions

Possibly the most important point to emerge from the Collections Research movement is the willingness of most curators to contribute time and effort for the common good. One of the most heartening effects following the formation of Collection Research Units is the close regional links forged between scattered curators now working together towards a common objective. There are now few who doubt that the United Kingdom will soon possess a national register containing details of the majority of significant natural science collections. The worth of the completed data base will be much greater than the sum of its parts, and already several important discoveries and cross-correlations of material have been made. The register of collections and the newly started register of types will be two powerful research tools that will be of great service to present and future generations of curators.

One of the hopes of the FENSCORE committee is that the success of the United Kingdom curators in the compilation of the Registers will encourage curators in other countries to start similar movements, and the committee will give all the advice and help within their power to assist any such movement.

V FRANCE

Chapter 23

Documenting French cultural property

Michel Aubert and Dominique Piot

Introduction

The Ministry of Culture is responsible for a number of different initiatives relating to cultural matters. Its purpose is to support both the creative aspects of culture (e.g. music, theatre, artistic endeavours) and also those aspects concerned with conservation and knowledge of the national heritage (e.g. national archives, general inventory, French museums, archaeology, ancient monuments, etc.). We are particularly concerned here with *knowledge* of the national heritage.

For about ten years the Ministry of Culture has worked to establish data bases of French cultural property. The two directorates within the Ministry of Culture which are concerned with this work are the Directorate of French Museums and the Directorate of Cultural Heritage. The Inventaire Général des Richesses Artistiques de la France (the department of the General Inventory of Art Treasures) has undertaken the vast task of recording cultural property on behalf of these directorates. The Directorate of French Museums has taken responsibility for the public collections of about 1000 museums which come under its jurisdiction. The General Inventory has taken responsibility for other collections, be they private or public (churches, ancient monuments or museums belonging to local societies).

This article is essentially concerned with the achievements of the Directorate of French Museums, but, as it proceeds, we will see that a constant collaboration exists between the researchers of the General Inventory and museum curators.

The establishment of data bases

At present, museum documentation data bases cover five areas: graphic art (paintings and drawings), sculpture, Egyptian antiquities, Greco-Roman antiquities and ethnographic collections. Other areas being considered are decorative arts, prints and national monuments.

We have devised a 'descriptive system' for each subject area. This enables us to standardize vocabulary and our method of analysis. These systems are often produced by several ministry departments working in collaboration. In this way, the systems for painting and sculpture were devised by the Inventaire Général and the Directorate of French Museums (France. Ministère de la Culture, 1981a; 1981b). The National Library is at present working in conjunction with both these departments in order to define an analytical framework for prints.

In these descriptive systems, each object is described according to a certain number of categories which contain information of an administrative nature (accession number, location, museum, etc.), technical information (size, medium, method of manufacture) and historical information (maker, date, means of acquisition, collector, etc.) (Table 23.1). Detailed information (method of composition, colours, proportions, etc.) is not included as it relates to a complex, in-depth analysis which might impede the efficient use of the documentation. The recorded information is, nonetheless, specific enough for an index to be set up for the identification of items. This means that researchers do not have to carry out laborious work involving the copying of information, use of index cards or endless examination of documents.

The organization of the descriptive systems is the same for paintings, drawings or sculptures, as well as for prints and decorative arts. Thus, the same type of information is assigned to the same heading (e.g. 1310 is the artist category regardless of subject area, 1450 is the category for technique, and so on). If a user is interested in more than one of these subjects, it is possible to save a search that has been undertaken on one file for subsequent use on another file. In contrast to this uniformity, the specific nature of classical collections has necessitated the creation of a descriptive system relevant to each civilization (Egyptian antiquities, Greco-Roman antiquities, etc.). We are currently considering possible means of transfer between these different systems.

Information is collected in the museum itself by a documentation specialist (a graduate in art history or equivalent) whose skills are placed at the disposal of the curator. His or her task is to produce detailed descriptions of the objects, using the museum's existing documentation (Figure 23.1). The process of collecting information is carried out with the aid of the descriptive systems and is rigorously supervised by the curator.

Once the detailed descriptions have been written out they are sent to the Computer Service to be checked and transferred to a machine-readable form. After various validation procedures, the records are entered on the data base and can be interrogated interactively (Figure 23.2).

The history of an object does not cease at a given moment, however, and the data bases are updated regularly. When changes are needed, the necessary information is sent to the Computer Service. Only there can the content of the data base be altered, at the request of the curator concerned.

The organization of the data bases — documentary research

All the Ministry of Culture's data bases can be interrogated, using the BULL Mistral package. Each Mistral record is divided up into fields of different types:

Number	French description	English translation
1000	References documentation	Documentation references
10	No d'inventaire(s)	Inventory number(s)
12	No de folio ou page pour l'enluminure	Page or folio number for illumination
1010	Denomination	Denomination
1020	Appartenance a un ensemble	Belonging to a set
1030	Appellations	Specific terms
20	Titre(s)	Title, titles
21	Appellation ou titre de l'edicule ou de l'ensemble mobilier portant le decor peint	Name or title of a small construction or a set of furniture bearing a painting
22	Titre de l'ensemble d'une autre technique pour lequel a été exécuté le projet peint ou dessiné	Title of the set in a different technique for which the painted or drawn project was executed
23	Appellation ou titre de l'edicule ou de l'ensemble mobilier auquel a appartenu l'oeuvre	Name or title of the set of furniture to which the work belonged
1070	Représentation	Representation
1080	Precisions concernant le sujet de la représentation	Details or specifications on the subject of the representation
1081	Sources écrites	Written sources
1085	Datation de l'evenement ou dates precises du personnage représenté	Dating of the event or precise dates of the person represented
1130	Localisation	Location
1140	Denomination du musée ou de l'edifice public de conservation	Name of museum or public building
40	Adresse de l'edifice de conservation	Address of building
1144	Precisions sur la localisation	Information about the locality
1145	Oeuvre reemployée	Re-employed painting
45	Emplacement precis dans l'edifice	Exact location in the building
48	Localisation des elements d'un ensemble disperse	Location of the elements of a dispersed set
1310	Auteur(s)	Painter, painters
50	Precisions sur l'auteur, l'ecole ou l'atelier de l'oeuvre analysee	Details of the painter, the school or the workshop of the analysed work
51	Part respective de chaque auteur	Part painted by each painter
1312	Auteur(s) du modele	Painter(s) of the model painting
1320	Nom de l'ecole et/ou de l'atelier de l'auteur de l'oeuvre analysee	Name of the school and/or the workshop of the painter of the analysed work
1321	Justification du nom de l'auteur ou de l'ecole de l'oeuvre analysee	Justification of the name of the painter or school of the analysed work
1322	Nom de l'ecole de l'auteur de l'oeuvre originale	Name of the school of painter of the original work
1323	Justification du nom de l'auteur ou de l'ecole de l'oeuvre originale	Justification of the name of the painter or school of the original work
1330	Lieu d'execution	Place of execution
1340	Nom actuel du lieu d'execution	Present name of the place of execution
55	Precisions sur le lieu d'execution	Details at the place of execution
1350	Lieu de provenance ou de destination	Place of origin or destination
1360	Nom actuel du lieu de provenance	Present name of place it came from
60	Appellation et adresse de l'edifice de provenance	Name and address of the building it came from
61	Nom du commanditaire	Name of person who commissioned it
62	Conditions de la commande et/ou circonstances de l'execution	Conditions of execution of the commission and/or circumstances
63	Date de la commande	Date of the commission
64	Autres conditions	Other conditions
1370	Epoque et datation de l'oeuvre analysee	Period and dating of the analysed work
1371	Datation en date precise de l'oeuvre analysee	Dating with a precise date of the analysed work
1373	Justification de la datation de l'oeuvre analysee	Justification of the dating of the analysed work
70	Commentaires historiques sur les dates	Historical comments on the dates
1373	Datation en siecle de l'oeuvre originale	Dating by century of the original work
1374	Datation en dates precises de l'oeuvre originale	Dating with precise dates of the original work
1375	Justification de la datation de l'oeuvre originale	Justification of the dating of the original work
1300	Stade de la creation	Stage of creation
80	Precisions sur le stade de la creation	Details of stage of creation
81	Designation et localisation de l'oeuvre apparentée	Designation and location of the associated work
1390	Materiau du support	Backing material
83	Identification des filigranes	Identification of filigrees
1450	Technique	Technique
84	Precisions sur la technique	Details of technique
1470	Forme du support et de la surface peinte	Form of the backing and of the painted surface
1480	Encadrement	Framing
1490	Dimensions	Dimensions
1510	Conservation - Restauration	Conservation - Restoration
85	Precisions sur l'etat de conservation, les transformations et la restauration de l'oeuvre	Details of state of preservation, alterations and restoration of the piece
1520	Marques - Inscriptions - Emblematique	Marks - Inscriptions - Emblematics
90	Transcription des dates, des noms d'auteurs, des lieux d'execution et des dedicaces	Transcription of dates, painters' names, places of execution and dedications
91	Identification des blasons et armoiries	Identification of coats of arms and armorial bearings
92	Transcription des inscriptions	Transcription of inscriptions
93	Identification des marques de collection	Identification of collectors' marks
1530	Oeuvres reproduites dans une autre technique	Works reproduced in a different technique
1550	Situation juridique	Legal situation
1560	Oeuvre actuellement en depot	Work in store at present
1600	Dates et modes d'acquisition ayant determiné le statut actuel de la propriété	Dates and means of accessioning which determined the current status of ownership
95	Personne ou organisme ayant participé à l'acquisition	Person or organisation having participated in the accessioning
96	Precisions sur le mode et les dates d'acquisition	Details of means and dates of accessioning
1610	Anciens organismes gestionnaires ou lieux de depot successifs	Previous administrative organisations or successive storage locations
1620	Attribution au musée actuellement responsable	Attribution to the museum responsible at present
1640	Dernière appartenance precedant l'entrée dans le statut juridique actuel	Most recent ownership preceding its present legal status
1650	Appartenances anterieures	Previous ownerships
1651	Emplacements successifs de l'oeuvre avant l'entrée dans le statut juridique actuel	Successive locations of the painting before its present legal status
1660	Ventes publiques successives	Successive public sales
100	Date exacte de la vente et no. de l'oeuvre dans	Exact date of sale and catalogue number
1670	Salons et expositions	Salons and exhibitions
110	Expositions precedant l'entrée dans le statut juridique actuel	Exhibitions preceding the entry into present legal status
1680	Anciennes attributions	Previous attributions
120	Nos d'inventaire des autres elements de l'ensemble	Inventory numbers of other elements of the set
130	References des catalogues internes du musée actuellement responsable	References contained in catalogues of Museum responsible at present
131	Corpus	Bibliographical Corpus
140	Numeros de cliches	Plate numbers
150	Numeros de la microfiche	Microfiche numbers

Table 23.1 List of data categories

```
REF :   PE013316
1000:   004013316
10  :   MV 6924
11  :   MV    6924
1010:   TABLEAU
20  :   CHARLES FERDINAND D'ARTOIS, DUC DE BERRY (1778-1820)
1070:   PORTRAIT-ARTOIS CHARLES FERDINAND D'(BOURBON CHARLES FERDINAND DE,
        BERRY DUC DE, HOMME, A MI-CORPS, DE TROIS-QUARTS)
1085:   1778-1820
1130:   -78- -VERSAILLES
1140:   MUSEE NATIONAL DU CHATEAU DE VERSAILLES ET TRIANON
1310:   DANLOUX HENRI PIERRE
1320:   FRANCE (ECOLE DE)
1321:   IDENTIFICATION PAR SOURCE
1330:   EXECUTE A-IDENTIFICATION PAR SOURCE
1340:   ANGLETERRE
1370:   FIN 4E QUART 18E SIECLE
1371:   1796 VERS
1372:   DATE PAR SOURCE
1390:   BOIS
1450:   PEINTURE A L'HUILE
1470:   SUPPORT ET SURFACE PEINTE (RECTANGULAIRE BARLONG)
1490:   27 H3-22 L3
1530:   REPRODUIT EN GRAVURE
1550:   PROPRIETE DE L'ETAT-VERSAILLES, MUSEE DU CHATEAU
1600:   ACHAT-MUSEES NATIONAUX-VERSAILLES, MUSEE DU CHATEAU-1944 DATE
        D'ACQUISITION
1640:   COLL. CAILLEUX
1650:   COLL. MONTAIGNAC
130 :   CONSTANS 1980, NO 1108
140 :   RMN:73 DN 3214
2000:   6924 MV
2500:   2016-11362
```

Figure 23.1 Source record prior to its incorporation in the computer system (Versailles Museum catalogue)

keyword fields (in which vocabulary may be standardized and hierarchically organized);
free text fields (e.g. the title of a painting, or a commentary on provenance such as 'the lintel of the salon of Venus');
numerical fields (e.g. dimensions);
fields associated with dates (e.g. the date of an event depicted on an object).

The lists of keywords appertaining to the various fields are called lexicons or thesauri and can be of different types:

open lists, in which all the keywords are at the same level, and in which the list grows as the collection does (e.g. a list of collectors' names or a list of authors);
closed lists, in which keywords are part of a predetermined list;
hierarchically organized lists, in which keywords may relate to one another either through inclusion or synonymy.

```
1000-004013316-*
  10-MV 6924-*
1010-TABLEAU-*
  20-CHARLES_FERDINAND D'ARTOIS,DUC DE BERRY (1778_1820)-*
1070-PORTRAIT (ARTOIS CHARLES FERDINAND D',BOURBON CHARLES FERDINAND DE,BERRY
     DUC DE, HOMME,A MI_CORPS,DE TROIS_QUARTS)-*
1085-1778-1820-*
1130- -78- -VERSAILLES-*
1140-MUSEE NATIONAL DU CHATEAU DE VERSAILLES ET TRIANON-*
1310-DANLOUX HENRI PIERRE-*
1320-FRANCE(ECOLE DE)-*
1321-IDENTIFICATION PAR SOURCE-*
1330-EXECUTE A-IDENTIFICATION PAR SOURCE-*
1340-ANGLETERRE-*
1370-FIN 4E QUART 18E SIECLE-*
1371-VERS(1796)-*
1372-DATE PAR SOURCE-*
1390-BOIS-*
1450-PEINTURE A L'HUILE-*
1470-SUPPORT ET SURFACE PEINTE (RECTANGULAIRE BARLONG)-*
1490-H3(27)-L3(22)-*
1530-REPRODUIT EN GRAVURE-*
1550-PROPRIETE DE L'ETAT-VERSAILLES,MUSEE DU CHATEAU-*
1600-ACHAT-MUSEES NATIONAUX-VERSAILLES,MUSEE DU CHATEAU-DATE D'ACQUISITION
     (1944)-*
1640-COLL. CAILLEUX-*
1650-COLL. MONTAIGNAC-*
130-CONSTANS 1980,NO 1108-*
140-RMN:73 DN 3214-*
```

Figure 23.2 Corresponding Mistral record

Interrogating a data base involves the selection of a set of documents on the presence of some of their keywords. These keywords can be combined with the help of the Boolean operators 'and', 'or' and 'except'. The form of interrogation used is called primary if it relates to keywords, and secondary if it relates to words, or strings of characters, used in an entry. Secondary interrogation can only occur after selecting a small set of documents through primary interrogation. This is because secondary interrogation requires a far greater search time.

Access to the data bases

At present the data bases are interrogated by the departments of the Ministry of Culture. They are also used by certain departments of other

Ministries who have made a request to the Director of French Museums, such as CNRS (Centre National de la Recherche Scientifique, the National Centre for Scientific Research). We are considering a better defined and more open policy regarding access to these data bases, with the aim of making this computerized information available to a wider public.

At the moment, members of the public who are specialists in art history, and who are also regular users of the museum documentation centres (for example, individuals associated with the Collection of Drawings) may interrogate the data bases. They do so with the aid of a museum documentation specialist who helps them to translate their questions into the Mistral language.

According to the plan laid down by the Directorate of French Museums, each museum must be equipped with a terminal as soon as it becomes a contributor to the data base. In this way it can gain access to all the documentation which has already been entered. Terminals installed in the provinces are linked to the central Ministry computer (a BULL model DPS 7/80) by means of the Transpac network.

The use of videodisc techniques means that images of the object in question can be simultaneously displayed on a television screen. This technique was used experimentally at the exhibition entitled 'The mysterious life of the masterpieces' and we plan to make this method more generally available.

Computerized files can be useful where publication is concerned, as they enable museums to publish concise catalogues of their collections. This has already been attempted with the catalogue of 6000 paintings belonging to Versailles Museum (Figure 23.3). Using an automated photocomposition procedure, we have produced a catalogue directly from the data base. We are currently studying ways of improving these results, using text processing machines which will enable us to reproduce a variety of typescripts.

The present state of the data bases

To make a record of all museum objects is a long-term undertaking. For example, in the case of the data base of paintings, only one-fifth of the works have been analysed after ten years' work. A development plan for computerization was drawn up in 1980. It envisages that the 100 biggest museums will be computerized over the next ten years. They will constitute about 80 of the complete data base. (For a more detailed account of the current state of the data bases, see Table 23.2.)

The Ministry of Culture plans to create large cultural data bases. In keeping with this plan, the Directorate of Museums has made use of computer science for the purpose of documentary research. It has adopted a strict policy of systematically analysing all the property in public collections. By so doing, it provides the means of gaining a better understanding of the wealth and variety of the cultural heritage. It has also guaranteed that this knowledge will be widely disseminated, given that information can now be distributed by means of terminals installed in museums.

C-D	D

C-D column:

1087— LOUISE-MARIE-CHRISTINE, PRINCESSE DE SAVOIE(1629-1692).
MV 3453, INV 3636, LP 3831. TOILE. H(0, 75), L(0, 68).
COMMANDE PAR LOUIS-PHILIPPE POUR LE MUSEE HISTORIQUE DE VERSAILLES EN 1838.
COPIE. ORIGINAL JADIS DANS LA COLLECTION DE MADEMOISELLE DE MONTPENSIER AU CHATEAU D'EU.
EN DEPOT A NICE, MUSEE MASSENA.

* **1088— LAURE MANCINI, DUCHESSE DE VENDOME(1636-1657).**
MV 3482, INV 3623, LP 3884. TOILE. H(0, 38), L(0, 30).
COMMANDE PAR LOUIS-PHILIPPE POUR LE MUSEE HISTORIQUE DE VERSAILLES EN 1838.
COPIE. ORIGINAL JADIS AU CHATEAU D'EU.

1089— MARIE-CHARLOTTE DE CASTELNAU, DUCHESSE DE GRAMONT(1648-1694).
MV 3526, INV 9881, B 1972. TOILE. H(0, 32), L(0, 38).
COPIE. ORIGINAL AU CHATEAU D'EU. EXECUTE EN 1839. ANCIENNE COLLECTION.

1090— PHILIPPE DE MONTAULT, DUC DE NAVAILLES, MARECHAL DE FRANCE(?-1684).
MV 3536, INV 3613, LP 2820. BOIS. H(0, 37), L(0, 28).
COMMANDE PAR LOUIS-PHILIPPE POUR LE MUSEE HISTORIQUE DE VERSAILLES EN 1837.
COPIE. D'APRES UN PORTRAIT DE FAMILLE.

* **1091— SUZANNE DE BEAUDEAN, DUCHESSE DE NAVAILLES(?-1700).**
MV 3537, INV 3613, LP 2820. BOIS. H(0, 37), L(0, 28).
COMMANDE PAR LOUIS-PHILIPPE POUR LE MUSEE HISTORIQUE DE VERSAILLES EN 1837.
COPIE. D'APRES UN PORTRAIT DE FAMILLE.

1092— MARIE-MARGUERITE DE COSSE, DUCHESSE DE VILLEROY(1648-1708).
MV 3557, INV 3626, LP 3901. TOILE. H(0, 32), L(0, 25).
COMMANDE PAR LOUIS-PHILIPPE POUR LE MUSEE HISTORIQUE DE VERSAILLES EN 1839.
COPIE. ORIGINAL JADIS AU CHATEAU D'EU.

1093— MARIE-THERESE DE BOURBON, PRINCESSE DE CONTI(1666-1732).
MV 3602, INV 3627, LP 3892. TOILE. H(0, 36), L(0, 27).
COMMANDE PAR LOUIS-PHILIPPE POUR LE MUSEE HISTORIQUE DE VERSAILLES EN 1838.
COPIE. ORIGINAL JADIS AU CHATEAU D'EU.

* **1094— GUSTAVE-ADOLPHE, ROI DE SUEDE(1594-1632).**
MV 4228, INV 3612, LP 3490. TOILE. H(0, 24), L(0, 20).
COMMANDE PAR LOUIS-PHILIPPE POUR LE MUSEE HISTORIQUE DE VERSAILLES EN 1838.

* **1095— JEAN BART, CHEF D'ESCADRE(1650-1702).**
MV 4307, INV 3614, LP 3519. TOILE. H(0, 37), L(0, 27).
COMMANDE PAR LOUIS-PHILIPPE POUR LE MUSEE HISTORIQUE DE VERSAILLES EN 1838.
COPIE. D'APRES UN PORTRAIT DU XVII EME SIECLE.

* **1096— JEANNE BECU, COMTESSE DU BARRY(1743-1793).**
MV 4448, INV 4137, LP 3235. TOILE. H(0, 34), L(0, 53).
COMMANDE PAR LOUIS-PHILIPPE POUR LE MUSEE HISTORIQUE DE VERSAILLES EN 1837.
COPIE D'APRES GAUTIER DAGOTY. ANCIENNE ATTRIBUTION: D'APRES DROUAIS FRANCOIS HUBERT(1880).

* **1097— LOUIS-PHILIPPE D'ORLEANS, DUC DE CHARTRES(1773-1850).**
MV 4526, INV 4968, LP 3691. TOILE. H(0, 67), L(0, 56).
COMMANDE PAR LOUIS-PHILIPPE POUR LE MUSEE HISTORIQUE DE VERSAILLES EN 1836.
COPIE. ORIGINAL DE GIROUST JADIS AU PALAIS ROYAL. COLL. LOUIS PHILIPPE.

* **1098— EUGENE ADELAIDE-LOUISE D'ORLEANS, MADAME ADELAIDE(1777-1847).**
MV 5243, INV 3628, LP 3613. TOILE. H(0, 24), L(0, 20).
COMMANDE PAR LOUIS-PHILIPPE POUR LE MUSEE HISTORIQUE DE VERSAILLES EN 1838.

* **1099— LOUIS DE BOURBON, PRINCE DE CONDE, 1ER DU NOM(1530-1569).**
MV 7192, INV 3609, LP 1501. TOILE. H(0, 73), L(0, 57).
COMMANDE PAR LOUIS-PHILIPPE POUR LE MUSEE HISTORIQUE DE VERSAILLES EN 1835.

CWICZEK MATTHIAS (ATTRIBUE)
CONNU DE 1828 A 1849

* **1100— GUSTAVE-ADOLPHE, ROI DE SUEDE(1594-1632).**
MV 4227, INV 2056, LP 5562. CUIVRE. H(0, 32), L(0, 21).
ACHAT EN VENTE PUBLIQUE(1843). COLL. AGUADO.

DABOS LAURENT
TOULOUSE, 1761. PARIS, 1835.

* **1101— JEAN-BAPTISTE DE BELLOY, ARCHEVEQUE DE PARIS(1708-1808).**
MV 4735, INV 3630, LP 1934. TOILE. H(1, 77), L(0, 83).
EXECUTE EN 1806. SALON(1806). ACHAT(1836). COLL. HENRY.

DAGNAN-BOUVERET PASCAL ADOLPHE JEAN
PARIS, 1852. QUINCEY, 1929

* **1102— LEON GEROME(1824-1924).**
MV 6080, RF 2848. TOILE. H(0, 86), L(0, 66).
SIGNE, DATE: PAJ DAGNAN 1902 LEGS(1930). COLL. DAGNAN BOUVERET.

DALTON MME
FRANCE, PREMIERE MOITIE DU XIX EME SIECLE.

* **1103— GIBIER MORT.**
MV 7544, INV 3637, LP 1609. TOILE. H(0, 39), L(0, 52).
SALON(1835). ACHAT(1835); OEUVRE DETRUITE LORS DU BOMBARDEMENT DE L'AMBASSADE DE FRANCE A TOKYO(1945).

DANLOUX HENRI PIERRE
PARIS, 1753. ID. , 1809.

* **1104— JACQUES DELILLE ET SA FEMME.**
MV 4550, INV 3665, LP 5974. TOILE. H(2, 36), L(1, 47).
SALON(1802). ETUDES POUR LES VISAGES AU MUSEE DE CHALON SUR SAONE. ACHAT(1844). COLL. VAUDECHAMP.

* **1105— L'ARCHITECTE NICOLAS LENOIR, DIT LE ROMAIN(1726-1810).**
MV 5687. TOILE. H(0, 76), L(0, 65).
ACHAT(1910). COLL. BRUNNER.

37

D column:

* **1106— CHARLES DE FRANCE, COMTE D'ARTOIS(1757-1836).**
MV 6922. BOIS. H(0, 27), L(0, 22).
EXECUTE VERS 1796. ACHAT(1944). COLL. MONTAIGNAC. COLL. CAILLEUX.

* **1107— LOUIS-ANTOINE D'ARTOIS, DUC D'ANGOULEME(1775-1844).**
MV 6923. BOIS. H(0, 27), L(0, 22).
EXECUTE VERS 1796. ACHAT(1944). COLL. MONTAIGNAC. COLL. CAILLEUX.

1108— CHARLES-FERDINAND D'ARTOIS, DUC DE BERRY(1778-1820).
MV 6924. BOIS. H(0, 27), L(0, 22).
EXECUTE VERS 1796. ACHAT(1944). COLL. MONTAIGNAC. COLL. CAILLEUX.

* **1109— LOUIS XVI AU TEMPLE.**
MV 8084. TOILE. H(1, 55), L(1, 19).
EXECUTE VERS 1795. DON(1956). COLL. VILLEFRANCHE.

1110— JEAN-BAPTISTE CANTHANEY, DIT CLERY, VALET DE CHAMBRE DE LOUIS XVI(1759-1809).
MV 8212. TOILE. H(0, 65), L(0, 54).
SIGNE, DATE: H. P. DANLOUX FAC BAT 1798. ACHAT EN VENTE PUBLIQUE(1963). COLL. BESNIER. COLL. ARGENCE.

DANLOUX HENRI PIERRE (ATTRIBUE)

* **1111— LOUIS, MARQUIS DE FONTANES, GRAND MAITRE DE L'UNIVERSITE(1757-1821).**
MV 9215, LP 3380. TOILE. H(0, 91), L(0, 72).
ACHAT(1838). COLL. LANGEAC.

DANSSE DE ROMILLY MME
CONNUE EN 1831.

* **1112— CHARLOTTE-GODEFRIDE-ELISABETH DE ROHAN, PRINCESSE DE CONDE.**
MV 3916, INV 3668, LP 2552. TOILE. H(0, 22), L(0, 15).
COMMANDE PAR LOUIS-PHILIPPE POUR LE MUSEE HISTORIQUE DE VERSAILLES EN 1837.
COPIE. ORIGINAL JADIS AU CHATEAU DE CHANTILLY.

* **1113— LOUIS-HENRI-JOSEPH DE BOURBON, PRINCE DE CONDE(1756-1830).**
MV 3917, INV 3667, LP 2817. TOILE. H(0, 22), L(0, 15).
COMMANDE PAR LOUIS-PHILIPPE POUR LE MUSEE HISTORIQUE DE VERSAILLES EN 1836.
COPIE. ORIGINAL DE DANLOUX AU MUSEE CONDE A CHANTILLY.

DARJOU ALFRED
PARIS, 1832. ID. , 1874.

* **1114— L'EMPEREUR ACCORDE LA GRACE DES FLITTAS. VOYAGE EN ALGERIE, 21 MAI 1865.**
MV 5008, MI 768. TOILE. H(1, 80), L(2, 50).
SIGNE, DATE: A. DARJOU 1865. SALON(1868). ACHAT(1868).

DASSY JEAN-JOSEPH
MARSEILLE, 1796. ID. , 1865.

* **1115— BATAILLE DE SAUCOURT EN VIMEU. JUILLET 881.**
MV 14, INV 3673, LP 2912. TOILE. H(0, 67), L(1, 05).
COMMANDE PAR LOUIS-PHILIPPE POUR LE MUSEE HISTORIQUE DE VERSAILLES EN 1837. SIGNE, DATE: DASSY 1838. SALON(1838).

* **1116— COMBAT DE ROBERT, DUC DE NORMANDIE, AVEC UN GUERRIER SARRAZIN. 1098.**
MV 354, INV 3474, LP 3855. TOILE. H(0, 71), L(0, 79).
COMMANDE PAR LOUIS-PHILIPPE POUR LE MUSEE HISTORIQUE DE VERSAILLES EN 1838.

* **1117— CARIBERT, ROI DES FRANCS(?-567).**
MV 659, INV 3675, LP 3256. TOILE. H(0, 90), L(0, 72).
COMMANDE PAR LOUIS-PHILIPPE POUR LE MUSEE HISTORIQUE DE VERSAILLES EN 1837. SIGNE, DATE: DASSY 1838. SALON(1838).

* **1118— LOUIS 1ER, DIT LE DEBONNAIRE, ROI DE FRANCE(778-840).**
MV 673, INV 3676, LP 2198. TOILE. H(0, 90), L(0, 72).
COMMANDE PAR LOUIS-PHILIPPE POUR LE MUSEE HISTORIQUE DE VERSAILLES EN 1837.

* **1119— FRANCOIS DE COMMINGES, COMTE DE GUITAUT(1581-1663).**
MV 3474, INV 3679, LP 3551. TOILE. H(1, 90), L(0, 97).
COMMANDE PAR LOUIS-PHILIPPE POUR LE MUSEE HISTORIQUE DE VERSAILLES EN 1838.
COPIE. ORIGINAL JADIS AU CHATEAU D'EPOISSES.

* **1120— FRANCOIS-ALEXANDRE PARIS DE LORRAINE(1589-1614).**
MV 4174, INV 3678, LP 4305. TOILE. H(0, 34), L(0, 24).
COMMANDE PAR LOUIS-PHILIPPE POUR LE MUSEE HISTORIQUE DE VERSAILLES EN 1840.
COPIE. ORIGINAL JADIS DANS LA COLLECTION DE MADEMOISELLE DE MONTPENSIER AU CHATEAU D'EU.

* **1121— CHRISTINE DE LORRAINE, ABBESSE DE REMIREMONT(1573-1648), DITE AUTREFOIS CATHERINE DE LORRAINE.**
MV 4219, INV 3681, LP 4304. TOILE. H(0, 34), L(0, 25).
COMMANDE PAR LOUIS-PHILIPPE POUR LE MUSEE HISTORIQUE DE VERSAILLES EN 1840.
COPIE. ORIGINAL JADIS DANS LA COLLECTION DE MADEMOISELLE DE MONTPENSIER AU CHATEAU D'EU.

1122— LE COMTE DE PRECY, GENERAL VENDEE(1742-1820).
MV 5262, INV 22, MR 314. TOILE. H(2, 25), L(1, 80).
COMMANDE PAR CHARLES X POUR LA GALERIE DU CHATEAU DE SAINT CLOUD EN 1825.
SIGNE, DATE: DASSY 1829.
EN DEPOT A CHOLET, MUSEE.

DASTUGUE MAXIME
NE A CASTELNAU MAGNOAC. CONNU ENTRE 1878 ET 1908.

* **1123— HONORE DE BALZAC(1799-1850).**
MV 6394, RF 476. TOILE. H(0, 71), L(0, 40).
COMMANDE PAR L'ETAT POUR LE MUSEE DE VERSAILLES EN 1886. COPIE. ORIGINAL DE BOULANGER JADIS DANS LA COLLECTION D'ALEXANDRE DUMAS.

38

Figure 23.3 Computer-produced concise catalogue (Versailles Museum)

```
Peintures : environ 23.000 oeuvres
            Musées concernés : Paris        Musée du Louvre, Musée de Cluny
                               Versailles   Musée du Château
                               Chantilly    Musée Condé
                               Le Mans      Musée Tessé
                               Lille        Musée des Beaux Arts
                               Bordeaux     Musée des Beaux Arts
                               Marseille    Musée des Beaux Arts
                                            Musée Cantini
                                            Musée Grobet Labadié
                               Caen         Musée des Beaux Arts
                               Avignon      Musée du Petit Palais
                               Remiremont   Musée Charles Friry
                               Bar le Duc   Musée municipal
                               Rennes       Musée des Beaux Arts
Dessins : environ 16.000
            Musées concernés : Paris        Musée du Louvre
                               Marseille    Musée des Beaux Arts
                               Caen         Musée des Beaux Arts
Sculptures : environ 6.000
            Musées concerné  : Paris        Musée de Cluny, Musée Rodin
                                            Musée du Louvre
                               Versailles   Musée du Château
                               Marseille    Musée des Beaux Arts
Antiquités egyptiennes : environ 31.000
            Musée concerné   : Paris        Musée du Louvre
Antiquités Gréco-Romaines : environ 8.000
            Musées concernés : Paris        Musée du Louvre
                               Compiègne
                               Amiens
                               Rouen
                               Bordeaux
                               Agen
                               Saintes
                               Marseille    Musée Borely
Ethnographie :
            Musée des Arts et Traditions Populaires :
                    - objets domestiques : environ 10.500
                    - impressions populaires : environ 1.200
                    - affiches : 3.000
                    - recettes médicales : . proverbes : 1.000
                                           . recettes : environ 3.000
```

Table 23.2 The state of the databases of the Directorate of French Museums, 1982

VI ITALY

Chapter 24

Documentation of the Italian cultural heritage

Oreste Ferrari

Introduction

At present the particular organization of services that protect the cultural patrimony in Italy is distinguished by the fact that all cultural property — fixed or movable and of whatever type, from prehistory to the present day — is subject to the protection of the State. The state authorities carry out cataloguing, restoration work, archaeological excavation, management of museums, and the legal safeguarding of cultural property.

The cataloguing of Italy's cultural heritage is one of the duties of the Ministero per i Beni Culturali e Ambientali (Ministry of Cultural and Environmental Property), and is carried out by local agencies called *Soprintendenze*. The *Soprintendenze* are in three principal categories:

Soprintendenze for Archaeological Property: responsible for archaeological heritage, excavations, etc.;
Soprintendenze for Architectural and Environmental Property: responsible for monuments, historical sites, and the environment in general;
Soprintendenze for Artistic and Historical Property: responsible for objects of historical and artistic value from the Middle Ages to the present.

There are approximately 60 *Soprintendenze* located in the main cities of Italy. Each one carries out its work in a specific cultural sphere; however, the geographic area under its control varies. For example, in Tuscany there is one *Soprintendenza* for Archaeological Property (based in Florence) responsible for the entire region. Architectural and art historical property, however, is assigned to other *Soprintendenze* located in Arezzo, Florence, Pisa and Siena. Each *Soprintendenza* manages the state museums in its area, carries out restoration work, excavations, exhibitions, etc., and is responsible for the safekeeping of the property in its care.

All Italian cultural property is legally protected, including that which belongs to the state, to religious groups, and to public institutions. In general, privately owned property, whether real estate or objects of archaeological and artistic interest, is legally controlled according to specific constraints based on the importance of the property as regards individual items, groups or collections.

Movable and fixed cultural property belonging to local bodies (especially the property of municipalities or Provinces) is subject to the same state laws. In practice, the care of this property is entrusted to the administration of these local and regional groups.

Cataloguing: aims and methodological problems

Cataloguing applies to the entire existing cultural patrimony. It is a specialized intellectual activity whose purpose is not, however, purely academic. It also aims to improve planning and execution in all other spheres of curatorial activity, be it the legal/administrative side or the more technical side. These aims — and their integration with what can be defined as 'the national policy for cultural property' — determine in a significant way the methods and procedures of cataloguing.

As a general rule the actual work of cataloguing can be defined as:

the detailed collection and verification of historical and philological data drawn from archival sources, from specialized bibliographies, and from new research undertaken by the same scholars who are entrusted with the cataloguing;
ascertaining the situation regarding ownership of cultural property;
determining the state of conservation of the cultural property and, as a result, indicating when conservation work is necessary.

As already noted, cataloguing is carried out in the field by approximately 60 *Soprintendenze*. They avail themselves of the services of more than a thousand specialists (archaeologists, ethnographers, art historians, architectural historians) and of many other technicians (photographers, surveyors, cartographers, draughtsmen, etc.). It was necessary, therefore, to create a coordinating body that would be concerned with methods of working and, in particular, with methodological issues.

With these objectives in mind, the Istituto Centrale per il Catalogo e la Documentazione (Central Institute for Cataloguing and Documentation) (ICCD) was founded in 1969 with its headquarters in Rome. It was reorganized in 1975 to incorporate the former Gabinetto Fotografico Nazionale (National Photographic Collection) and the Aereofototeca (Collection of Aerial Photographs) whose services are now administered by the Institute. The specific responsibilities of the Institute are:

to maintain contact with the various *Soprintendenze* in order to prepare coordinated annual programs of cataloguing in all parts of Italy;
to define general principles regarding cataloguing methods;
to establish a central archive in Rome where all the documentation produced by cataloguing can be collected;
to promote the scientific publication of such documentation.

Clearly, the fundamental issue is to define an appropriate methodology.

The vast quantity (some tens of millions) of cultural items to be catalogued, and their typological and chronological variety, have made it imperative to establish principles to guide the gathering of information. These needed to respect the individual characteristics of the various items and of their related disciplines (archaeology, art history, ethnography, town planning, etc.), while allowing for the correlation of different kinds of data.

It is essential to define methodological criteria that are as uniform as possible, not only to guarantee the quality of the information but above all to ensure that the information gathered on every individual cultural item (a painting, an archaeological find, a monument) can be integrated with the information that pertains to the entire group (typological category, chronological moment, geographic context, etc.), of which that item forms part.

It was necessary to plan an extensive system of record cards conceived as a framework for the organized gathering of information relating to:

individual cultural items in relation to their specific categories (works of art in general, drawings, archaeological finds, ethnographic objects, monuments, archaeological ruins, etc.);
geographical contexts (i.e. places containing a variety of cultural property, archaeological sites, urban centres of historical significance, natural history sites, etc.)

Two kinds of record cards have been designed. Type A cards are analytical and detailed (Figure 24.1). Type B cards form a logical synthesis of many Type A cards and deal in a particular way with correlations (ethnological, functional, typological) among extensive groups of cultural property. Table 24.1 lists the various cards currently in use.

Alongside this general methodological definition it was also necessary to deal with problems of a more specific nature. The most difficult of these was the problem of terminology. As the work of the *Soprintendenze* proceeded, the ICCD discovered the existence of numerous discrepancies and inaccuracies even in the naming of similar objects. Local differences of vocabulary (slang and dialect) were partly responsible for this, as was the absence of an authoritative terminology. To this end the ICCD has recently undertaken the publication of a series of Terminological Dictionaries. Volumes that deal with the archaeology of the late Bronze Age and the early Iron Age have been published, as well as the first volume dealing with Arms and Armour (Italy. Ministero per i Beni Culturali e Ambientali, 1980; 1982) (Figure 24.2).

Another problem concerns the graphic representation of surveys of monuments and of urban areas and, in general, that of specialized cartography. Disparate criteria are used in this field as well and the ICCD is developing a standard that will take into account existing international conventions.

The organization of data

Every record card is compiled according to guidelines in the appropriate information booklet. Two copies are made of each card; one remains at the

246

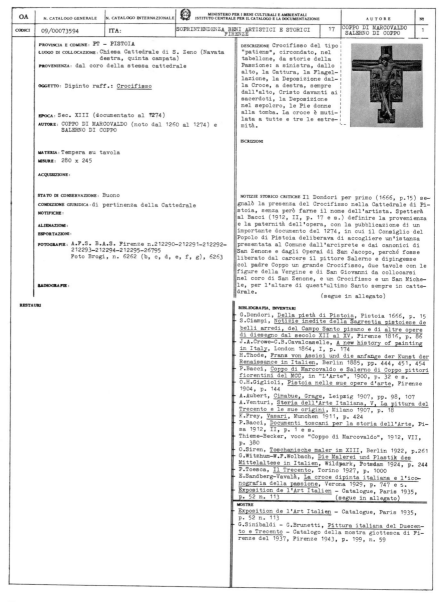

PROVINCIA E COMUNE: PT – PISTOIA

LUOGO DI COLLOCAZIONE: Chiesa Cattedrale di S. Zeno (Navata destra, quinta campata)

PROVENIENZA: dal coro della stessa cattedrale

OGGETTO: Dipinto raff.: Crocifisso

EPOCA: Sec. XIII (documentato al 1274)

AUTORE: COPPO DI MARCOVALDO (noto dal 1260 al 1274) e SALERNO DI COPPO

MATERIA: Tempera su tavola

MISURE: 280 x 245

ACQUISIZIONE:

STATO DI CONSERVAZIONE: Buono

CONDIZIONE GIURIDICA: di pertinenza della Cattedrale

NOTIFICHE:

ALIENAZIONI:

ESPORTAZIONI:

FOTOGRAFIE: A.F.S. B.A.S. Firenze n.212290–212291–212292–212293–212294–212295–26795
Foto Brogi, n. 6262 (b, c, d, e, f, g), 6263

RADIOGRAFIE:

RESTAURI

DESCRIZIONE Crocifisso del tipo "patiens", circondato, nel tabellone, da storie della Passione: a sinistra, dallo alto, la Cattura, la Flagellazione, la Deposizione dalla Croce, a destra, sempre dall'alto, Cristo davanti ai sacerdoti, la Deposizione nel sepolcro, le Pie donne alla tomba. La croce è mutilata a tutte e tre le estremità.

ISCRIZIONI

NOTIZIE STORICO CRITICHE Il Dondori per primo (1666, p.15) segnalò la presenza del Crocifisso nella Cattedrale di Pistoia, senza però farne il nome dell'artista. Spetterà al Bacci (1912, II, p. 17 e s.) definire la provenienza e la paternità dell'opera, con la pubblicazione di un importante documento del 1274, in cui il Consiglio del Popolo di Pistoia deliberava di accogliere un'istanza presentata al Comune dall'arciprete e dai canonici di San Zenone e dagli Operai di San Jacopo, perché fosse liberato dal carcere il pittore Salerno e dipingesse col padre Coppo un grande Crocifisso, due tavole con le figure della Vergine e di San Giovanni da collocarsi nel coro di San Zenone, e un Crocifisso e un San Michele, per l'altare di quest'ultimo Santo sempre in cattedrale.
(segue in allegato)

BIBLIOGRAFIA, INVENTARI
- G.Dondori, Della pietà di Pistoia, Pistoia 1666, p. 15
- S.Ciampi, Notizie inedite della Sagrestia pistoiese di belli arredi, del Campo Santo pisano e di altre opere di disegno dal secolo XII al XV, Firenze 1816, p. 86
- J.A.Crowe–C.B.Cavalcaselle, A new history of painting in Italy, London 1864, I, p. 174
- H.Thode, Franz von Assisi und die anfange der Kunst der Renaissance in Italien, Berlin 1885, pp. 444, 451, 454
- P.Bacci, Coppo di Marcovaldo e Salerno di Coppo pittori fiorentini del MCC, in "L'Arte", 1900, p. 32 e s.
- O.H.Giglioli, Pistoia nelle sue opere d'arte, Firenze 1904, p. 144
- A.Aubert, Cimabue, Grage, Leipzig 1907, pp. 98, 107
- A.Venturi, Storia dell'Arte Italiana, V, La pittura del Trecento e le sue origini, Milano 1907, p. 18
- K.Frey, Vasari, Munchen 1911, p. 424
- P.Bacci, Documenti toscani per la storia dell'Arte, Pisa 1912, II, p. 1 e s.
- Thieme-Becker, voce "Coppo di Marcovaldo", 1912, VII, p. 380
- O.Siren, Toschanische maler im XIII, Berlin 1922, p.261
- G.Witzhum–W.F.Wolbach, Die Malerei und Plastik des Mittelaltese in Italien, Wildpark, Potsdam 1924, p. 244
- P.Toesca, Il Trecento, Torino 1927, p. 1000
- E.Sandberg-Vavalà, La croce dipinta italiana e l'iconografia della passione, Verona 1929, p. 747 e s.
- Exposition de l'Art Italien – Catalogue, Paris 1935, p. 52 n. 113
(segue in allegato)

MOSTRE
- Exposition de l'Art Italien – Catalogue, Paris 1935, p. 52 n. 113
- G.Sinibaldi - G.Brunetti, Pittura italiana del Duecento e Trecento - Catalogo della mostra giottesca di Firenze del 1937, Firenze 1943, p. 199, n. 59

Figure 24.1(a) Completed Type A record card (front)

OA	N. CATALOGO GENERALE	N. CATALOGO INTERNAZIONALE		MINISTERO PER I BENI CULTURALI E AMBIENTALI ISTITUTO CENTRALE PER IL CATALOGO E LA DOCUMENTAZIONE		A U T O R E	N'
CODICI	09/00073594	ITA:		SOPRINTENDENZA BENI ARTISTICI E STORICI FIRENZE	17	COPPO DI MARCOVALDO SALERNO DI COPPO	1

ALLEGATO N. ....1.... OGGETTO Dipinto raff. Crocifisso.............

segue Notizie Sorico Critiche: Il Bacci, pubblicando tale documento, proponeva inoltre di attribuire la figura di Cristo a Salerno di Coppo e le storie del tabellone a Coppo di Marcovaldo. In seguito, fu generalmente ammessa la colla-
borazione dei due pittori (Giglioli, 1904, p. 144; Venturi, 1907, V, p. 18; Frey 1911, p. 424; Toesca, 1927, p. 1000;
Salmi, 1937, p. 349) se si escludono le ipotesi del Witzhum e del Wolbach (1924, p. 244), che ritenevano la Croce dipinta da un pittore locale ritardatario. O.Siren (1922, p. 261) notando una differenza stilistica tra la Madonna di
Siena e di Orvieto, e il Crocifisso di Pistoia, attribisce quest'ultimo a Salerno, trovando consenziente la Sandberg-
Vavalà (1929, p. 747 e s.), che attenua la parte avuta da Coppo nella esecuzione dell'opera, riferendogli soltanto o il
disegno o una eventuale supervisione. La stessa Sandberg-Vavalà ribadisce l'attribuzione a Salerno nel 1940 (p. 48) e
in un articolo del 1946 (p. 233 e s.), ricco di rimandi documentari, bibliografici e iconografici.
Già il Dondori notava nel Crocifisso un realismo quasi brutale ed una tragicità incomposta, definendo Coppo un artista
che direttamente o indirettamente prepara l'arte di Cimabue. Il Thode vi individua invece caratteri schiettamente bi-
zantini, nella figura di Cristo in particolare, l'adesione a uno schema giuntesco. Secondo la Sandberg-Vavalà, il
Crocifisso di Pistoia parteciperebbe sia del tipo giuntesco che di quello cimabuesco, ritenendolo infine influenzato
dallo stesso Cimabue. Reagiscono a questa ipotesi la Sinibaldi e la Brunetti (1943, p. 199), che non giudicano possi-
bile per il Cimabue prima del 1274, la creazione di forme simili a quelle espresse nel Crocifisso di Santa Croce a Firenze; e considerano piuttosto il Cristo di Pistoia molto vicino a quello del Museo Civico di San Gimignano, di Coppo.
Più di recente il Bologna (1962, p.100), accetta e ribadisce l'osservazione di "rara penetrazione" della Vavalà, notando come il Crocifisso di Pistoia mostri "un avanzamento sorprendente che rispecchia un ordine mentale troppo più inten-
so e placatamente grande di quanto possa aspettarsi da un semplice seguace di Coppo".
Segue Bibliografia: L.Coletti, La mostra giottesca, in "Bollettino d'Arte" 1937, p. 54
M.Salmi, La mostra giottesca, in"Emporium", 1937, p. 349
E.Sandberg-Vavalà, Painting by Salerno di Coppo, in "Art in America", 1940, p. 48
G.Sinibaldi-G.Brunetti, Pittura italiana del Duecento e Trecento - Catalogo mostra giottesca di Firenze del 1937, Fi-
renze 1943, p. 199, n. 59
E.Sandberg-Vavalà, A lineal Basis for the Documents relating to Coppo di Marcovaldo and this son Salerno, in "The Art
Bulletin", 1946, p. 47 e s.
F.Bologna, La pittura italiana delle origini, Roma 1962, p. 100
U.Procacci, La pittura romanica pistoiese, in "Il Romanico pistoiese nei suoi rapporti con l'arte romanica dell'Occi-
dente", Pistoia 1964, p. 356 e s.

MODULARIO
P.L.-Belle Arti-82

Mod. 35/3
(Antichità e Belle Arti)

COMPILATORE DELLA SCHEDA Carlo Sissi

DATA 31.12.1973

REVISIONI

ALLEGATI 1

Io sottoscritto mi obbligo alla conservazione dell'oggetto descritto nel presente foglio secondo
le norme della Legge 1 Giugno 1939 n. 1089 e Regolamento approvato con R. Decreto n. 363 del
30 Gennaio 1913; di conseguenza a non rimuoverlo dal posto che occupa, a non apporvarci modifica-
zioni senza conseguire preventiva approvazione del Ministero dell'Istruzione, e a non menomarne in
alcun modo il pubblico godimento.

DATA

VISTO DEL SOPRINTENDENTE   FIRMA

RISCONTRI INVENTARIALI

DATA

VISTO DEL SOPRINTENDENTE   FIRMA

DATA

VISTO DEL SOPRINTENDENTE   FIRMA

DATA

VISTO DEL SOPRINTENDENTE   FIRMA

OSSERVAZIONI

RIFERIMENTO VECCHIE SCHEDE

Figure 24.1(b) Completed Type A record card (reverse)

```
INDICE DELLE SCHEDE E DEGLI INTERCALARI

  RA      reperto archeologico
  MA      monumento archeologico
  CA      complesso archeologico
  SAS     saggio stratigrafico
  SE          intercalare: strato, elemento
          *   intercalari: tabelle dei materiali
  N       numismatica
  OA      opera e oggetto d'arte
  SM          intercalare: strumento musicale
  MS          intercalare: manuscritto
  MM          intercalare: macchina e meccanismo
  D       disegno
* D/A     disegno e progetto di architettura
  S       stampa
  MI      matrice di incisioni
  E       etnologia
  FKO     folklore oggetti
  FKN     folklore narrativa
  FKM     folklore musica
  FKC     folklore cerimonie e riti
  A       architettura
  Aii         intercalare: impianto industriale
  PG      parco, giardino
  PG/B        intercalare: scheda botanica
  TP      settore extra urbano (particelle aggregate per toponimi)
              intercalare: repertorio stato attuale
              intercalare: repertorio indagine storica
  SU      settore urbano
              intercalare: repertorio stato attuale unita edilizie
              intercalare: repertorio indagine storica unita edilizie
* CS      centro storico
  T       territorio (unita base: territorio comunale)
              intercalari: indagini stato attuale
                Tu: urbanistica
              * Tg: geologia
              * Tf: flora e fauna
              intercalari: indagine storica
                Ta: antichita
                Tm: medio evo, eta moderna
```

Table 24.1 List of record cards currently in use

Soprintendenze where the cataloguing was done while the other is sent to the ICCD where it is included in the central archive. If necessary a third copy is given to the person or public body who actually holds the catalogued item.

All copies of the record card are accompanied by photographic documentation and, if necessary, by graphic surveys, drawings, etc., together with other complementary information such as technical reports on restoration. In the central archive located at the ICCD the cards are arranged topographically, reflecting the location of cultural property throughout the country.

Each card is microfilmed using '3M Camera Cards' (Figure 24.3). The essential identifying data about the catalogued item is recorded as well as the general catalogue number. This number consists of 11 digits, the first two of which refer to one of the 20 Italian regions (Lazio, Campania, Tuscany, Piedmont, etc.); the last nine indicate the individual object in the series. The 'Camera Cards' are filed in the central archive according to regional groupings and then in numerical order. As far as access to information gathered in the central archive is concerned, such a system is extremely limited. In practice access is possible only if one has prior knowledge of the exact location of a particular item or the number of the relevant card. Even with some tens of thousands of cards the archive is already quite unmanageable.

At present, more than 1 500 000 cultural items have been catalogued and it is estimated that there are tens of millions of cards still to be completed. It is imperative, therefore, that we initiate a computer system for the

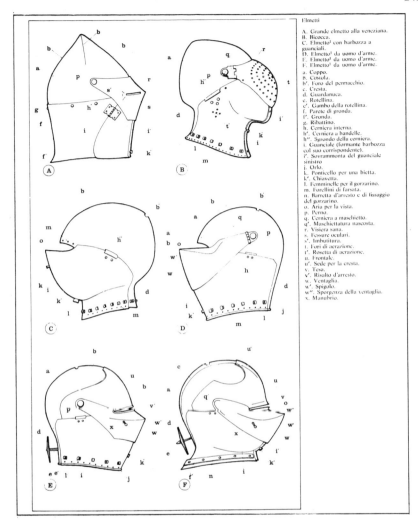

Figure 24.2 Illustration from one of the Terminological Dictionaries

organization and management of the relevant data so that the cataloguing work which has been, and will be, carried out can be utilized for specific purposes.

The requirements of the system

The system for processing catalogued data must be capable of meeting a number of requirements as precisely as possible. First, it must be able to handle the conceptual nature of the data which concern the identification and description of actual objects. However, unlike a bibliographic catalogue where the information already exists in a written form, in this case the

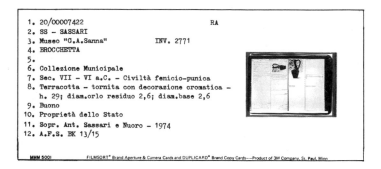

```
1.  20/00007422                                    RA
2.  SS - SASSARI
3.  Museo "G.A.Sanna"           INV. 2771
4.  BROCCHETTA
5.
6.  Collezione Municipale
7.  Sec. VII - VI a.C. - Civiltà fenicio-punica
8.  Terracotta - tornita con decorazione cromatica -
    h. 29; diam.orlo residuo 2,6; diam.base 2,6
9.  Buono
10. Proprietà dello Stato
11. Sopr. Ant. Sassari e Nuoro - 1974
12. A.F.S. BK 13/15
```

MMM 5001   FILMSORT® Brand Aperture & Camera Cards and DUPLICARD® Brand Copy Cards——Product of 3M Company, St. Paul, Minn.

Figure 24.3 Example of a Camera Card

formulation is decided upon by the cataloguer with a certain margin of critical and interpretive subjectivity that is not readily standardized.

The system must also be able to meet the particular needs of those who use it for a variety of purposes. Users may be archaeologists, or art historians who are pursuing philological research. Alternatively they might be town planners considering the development of an urban area or technical experts arranging a programme of restoration or conservation. They might also be curators responsible for the management of a museum's collection, administrators checking the legal situation with regard to cultural property, teachers developing a course or police authorities investigating thefts, sales or exports.

Since those who might use the catalogue belong to a variety of disciplines it is necessary to provide different methods of access to the same data. These methods of access must follow clear, logical guidelines. While some types of requests for information are as a rule predictable, there are always potential requests which are more complex and of a special kind. The system must, therefore, be as flexible as possible at the output stage in order to ensure the maximum communication between the user and the machine.

Finally, the distribution of information must be as broad as possible. This could be achieved by linking a main computer centre with decentralized units (*Soprintendenze* or groups of *Soprintendenze*) and, if necessary, with specialized libraries, universities, local authorities and police headquarters. Once the whole system is fully operative another obvious solution might be to have a network of decentralized minicomputers where the straightforward work could be carried out. Non-routine or more complex work could then be sent to the main computing centre.

Current experiments

Some years ago the ICCD began working in collaboration with CNUCE (Computing Institute of the Italian National Research Council), a specialized institute of the National Research Council, based in Pisa. The aim was to devise a system that could satisfy the above-mentioned requirements and whose structure would be developed in a modular way, thereby allowing for future expansion. There followed an initial phase of informal contact concerning the various problems of the system. In 1980 a relationship was established which has defined more clearly the subject matter and a timetable for the proposed research.

First of all, we sought detailed knowledge of programmes already underway in other national organizations. We found that the one which in many ways bears the closest resemblance to the Italian plan is the procedure developed by the Inventaire Général des Richesses Artistiques de la France (Chapter 23). However, not even this model was thought to fully encompass or match the aims of the ICCD.

On the practical side, an early phase of work entailed an analytical examination of some relatively homogeneous groups of cards. As they were already completed, the data they contained had not been specially prepared for entering on a computer.

As a sample of recording among the various disciplines associated with cultural property we studied the cards relating to threatened buildings ('A' cards), works of art ('OA' cards), and archaeological finds ('RA' cards) from the city of Vigevano in Lombardy (3450 cards). As an example of recording from a single discipline but covering an extensive geographic area we examined cards which deal with works of art ('OA' cards) in all the 33 municipalities in the province of Latina in Lazio (2954 cards). We also studied about 10 000 cards concerning works of art from municipalities in the provinces of Florence and Pistoia as well as one municipality in the province of Siena, about 2000 cards from the 13 municipalities in the province of Parma, and approximately 7000 cards from various municipalities in Calabria.

In order to consider material of typological importance we examined smaller groups of some ceramic collections in both Florence and Rome. As far as cards for drawings ('D' cards), prints ('S' cards), and etching plates ('MI' cards) were concerned, we used the holdings of the National Collection of Prints and the National Calcography Collection (Rome) relating to selected artists of the seventeenth and eighteenth centuries. In the case of archaeological finds ('RA' cards) we examined around 600 cards regarding material recovered from the necropoli in Alfedena (Abruzzi) and Andriolo (Paestum), and 800 cards concerning epigraphic and votive material from the Rome area, and approximately 2000 cards pertaining to a variety of material from the Archaeological Museum in Florence.

As regards architecture, we examined cards relating to some of the historical centres in the province of Verona. We also selected for study a sample group of about 200 cards concerning monuments significantly different from one another either in terms of their typology or their geographic location.

We considered two possible courses of action:

to computerize all the data contained in the cards, making limited editorial changes to the information as it already existed in free-text form;
to computerize only a small group of data relating to a shared fundamental characteristic of the material. Most of these data had already been structured in a formal way.

We decided to opt for the second solution which was in keeping with the general trend of similar experiments abroad (e.g. the standards defined by CIDOC) (Chapter 30). We limited the scope of the computerization to a set of data which were thought to cover the principal aims and more common types of research, in relation both to the task of protecting cultural property and to the initial considerations of historical and philological research.

We hope in the future, however, to carry out a subsequent stage of computerization involving data which are not at present under consideration. Therefore, the first phase (the computerization of basic data) has been devised in a modular way to facilitate the addition of information in the future.

The first compilation of data based on the records described above was run using the STAIRS/VS system on an IBM 370/168 computer belonging to CNUCE. We chose the STAIRS/VS system because of all the available systems it had three major advantages:

it is an interactive system which permits a relatively easy communication between the operator and the machine;
it uses natural language;
it is flexible in that it permits research on a whole text or on parts of a text.

Nevertheless, STAIRS/VS has practical limitations. For example, while it permits simple compilation of data it does not allow for relational indexing of information.

During the course of this experiment which, as indicated, involved the study of existing cards, what emerged very clearly was the problem of standardizing the data. The severity of this problem had been underestimated in the initial stages of organization. In addition, we found that the task of correcting and verifying data *after* they had been entered on the computer entails an enormous waste of energy and is prone to error and inexactitude. It seemed advisable, therefore, to restructure the procedures for data entry by providing guidelines in the form of dictionaries that would allow for the arrangement of information into logically structured categories and subcategories.

We also reached a clearer understanding of the fact that a system's reliability is largely determined by the definition of the logical/conceptual model and its correlation with terminological as well as historical factors (those that are inherent in the various disciplines such as archaeology, art history, etc.). In other words, we realized that the fundamental issue was the compiling of thesauri. This would affect the entire undertaking of processing catalogued data by means of the computer.

The scope of research is thus further extended: while on the one hand the basic structure of the thesauri might be considered intuitive, on the other hand the complexity of related concepts and hierarchies that must be taken into account makes the situation more complicated.

In addition, it is important to bear in mind that the task of compiling thesauri — which have their own specific margins of flexibility — cannot be done completely *a priori*. To a large extent it must follow from work in progress that can be subjected to experimental verification.

Therefore, since the end of 1981 we have been planning to organize a special research group comprised of archaeologists, art historians, and information specialists. They will have the responsibility of devising a preliminary structure for the thesauri based on two or three key groups of record cards relating to specific typological categories in various cultural centres during an historical period of outstanding importance.

VII   THE NETHERLANDS

Chapter 25

The MARDOC Project of Dutch maritime museums

Jan P. van de Voort

Introduction

Since 1970 a number of Dutch maritime museums have cooperated to improve the accessibility of their collections. The five museums involved in this project are the National Museums 'Nederlands Scheepvaartmuseum' in Amsterdam and the 'Zuiderzeemuseum' in Enkhuizen, the Maritime Museum 'Prins Hendrik' in Rotterdam, the Fishery Museum in Vlaardingen and the Navy Museum in Den Helder.

The five maritime museums cooperating in the *Commissie Documentatie Nederlandse Zoutwatervisserij* (Committee on Documentation of Dutch Salt Water Fisheries) first considered bibliographic information retrieval procedures in building an inverted file called 'VISDOC' (Van de Voort, 1974). They expanded their scope in 1975 to include the construction of a data base containing maritime collections in the Netherlands, especially in museums (Van de Voort, 1980). Since then the project has been known as MARDOC. On the 17th December 1981 the newly-formed MARDOC Foundation took over the activities of the former committee.

There are about 660 museums in the Netherlands. Besides the five MARDOC museums there are 26 other Dutch museums with maritime collections, including two regional maritime museums in Sneek and Groningen, and the Rijksmuseum in Amsterdam. At least 21 of them are willing to adopt the MARDOC rules for recording their maritime collections.

Information retrieval methods

At an early stage in the project, an enquiry was held with regard to information retrieval methods suitable for museum collections. On the basis of descriptions of such methods used in the library world, the conclusion was reached that systems using post-coordination were more effective than the pre-coordination systems generally used in museums.

There are at least two reasons for the application of systems using post-coordination in museums. First, in museums, archives and other institutions where historical material is kept, the query pattern usually contains three, four or even more elements: subject/object name, date, geographical indication, and one or more other features such as material, production method, form, etc. Second, the pattern of queries from users of museum documentation is now less predictable than before. The user group is no longer limited to museum staff and researchers, but an increasing number of museum visitors also pose questions. Moreover, the present research work has a multi-disciplinary character, causing further diversification in the query pattern (Van de Voort, 1981).

The combination of these considerations led to the construction of an experimental information retrieval system using post-coordination, in the form of an optical coincidence system. This experiment was intended to give experience with a system of this kind and in working with a controlled vocabulary. As far as contents were concerned, the system was limited to literature documents on Dutch sea fishing history. Besides the so-called entry terms (synonyms, homonyms, related terms, broader and narrower terms), the thesaurus contains 1227 indexing terms, including 690 descriptors. This 'VISDOC' system, which became ready for use in 1973, now contains 3500 documents. The experience gained has largely determined the later approach.

Standardization and recording formats

Following the expansion of plans in 1975, the committee decided to examine a category of objects typical of maritime museums, namely ships' models. A working group of curators was established with the following tasks:

to determine which data on objects in maritime collections should be stored and, on the basis of this determination, to develop record cards;
to standardize the terminology used for the recording of objects.

After a comparison of record cards used in a number of Dutch and foreign museums, the working group chose those of IRGMA in the United Kingdom, afterwards taken over by the MDA (Chapter 12). These record cards were felt to offer the best possibilities and met the MARDOC requirements. The History Artefact card was selected for recording ships' models. For completing most of the boxes on this card, terms should be chosen from prescribed lists of descriptors. The working group published the MARDOC-guide for recording ships' models at the end of 1977 (MARDOC-handleiding, 1977). With the MARDOC-guide as a model, the Dutch Museum Association and its information retrieval section (SIMIN) published the Dutch version of the MDA History Artefact card in 1981 (in consultation with the MDA) (Figure 25.1). In the same year, the MARDOC Foundation published a manual for recording iconographical material (Hogenboom and Van de Voort, 1982). This was followed by a guide in 1982 (Boot, Van de Voort and Wander, 1982).

The next logical step was that of recording (following the MARDOC rules) a number of ships' models representative of maritime collections, and having these records processed by the MDA using the GOS package.

historisch voorwerp		Visserijmuseum, Vlaardingen		

Kaart 1 van 1	Bestand		Instelling: inventarisnummer 432 : 477		Onderdeel a-i

Identificatie	Categorie scheepsmodel		Geïdentificeerd door: datum		Aantal 9
	Specifieke objectaanduiding volmodel & logger	Systeem MARDOC	Geïdentificeerd door: datum		
v	Andere benaming hobbymodel	Type naar doel	Geïdentificeerd door: datum		

Beschrijving	Toestand/bijzonderheid goed,romp & goed,tuigage		Vastgesteld door: datum		
	Compleetheid/bijzonderheid compleet,romp & compleet,tuigage		Vastgesteld door: datum		
	Onderdeel: materiaal/bijzonderheid romp : hout		Onderdeel: materiaal/bijzonderheid		

Afmetingen	waarde	eenheid/nauwkeurigheid	Afmetingen	waarde	eenheid/nauwkeurigheid
lengte	215	cm	hoogte	169	cm
breedte	52,5	cm	schaal	1/10	

Inscriptie — Merk	Methode geschilderd	Positie weerszijden boeg & spiegel & reddingsloep		
Transcriptie Beschrijving	Bijzonderheid VL 179 & Petronella Neeltje Vlaardingen 1904 & VL 179			
Afwijking Toevoeging Wijziging	Bijzonderheid			

Onderdeel: aspect beschrijving : trefwoord : bijzonderheid			
model : voortstuwing : zeilschip			
model : tuigage,alg. : getuigd met zeil			
dek : uitrusting : gedetailleerd			

Vervaardiging	Methode mallemodel	Rol vervaardiger(s) bouwer	Naam Siereveld, G.	Datum vervaardiging 1938(ca.)
v	Plaats vervaardiging Vlaardingen		Bijzonderheid vervaardiging	D 1

Associatie	Associatietrefwoord	Geassocieerde persoon		Geassocieerde datum
	VL 179 & Petronella Neeltje	Burg, Fa. H. van der		1904=1918
v	Geassocieerde plaats Vlaardingen	Gebeurtenis		
	Bijzonderheid associatie tewaterlating bij werf A. de Jong,Vlaardingen,op 23-06-1924			

Verwerving	Wijze van verwerven schenking	Verworven van: datum Comité Vlaggetjesdag,Vlaardingen: 1967-02-02		
v			Prijs	Voorwaarden: Ja-Nee	Verzekeringswaarde: datum 15000 : 1976

Behandeling	Conservering Reproductie	Andere behandeling	Methode : bijzonderheid : uitvoerder : datum : bijzonderheid schoongemaakt:Hardonk,C.:1977-08-22	Kruisverwijzing
v	Conservering Reproductie			

Documentatie	R	Aard referentie	Auteur: datum: titel: tijdschrift of uitgever: volume: bijzonderheid	Tekening of foto
	1	vermelding	:1967-02-22: :brief	

Standplaats	Standplaats: datum BZ : 1978	Beschrijver: datum Voort,J.P. van de: 1979-02-13

Opmerkingen	Opmerkingen a=model;b=houten standaard;c-d=2 lenspompen;e=1 los luik bij voormast;f=anker; g=aantal puntbreels met touw aan elkaar verbonden;h=reddingsloep;i=los deksel op kist naast krcbbe aan SS. Aan de hoofdmast een blauwe scheepswimpel met scheepsnaam. A.w. nr. 376

© mda/nmv

Figure 25.1 Completed MARDOC history artefact record card

In principle, the staff of the **MARDOC** museums record the museum objects, and the staff of the **MARDOC** office (one information retrieval officer and one part-time assistant in 1982) check the record cards for the correct application of **MARDOC** rules and terminology, and to evaluate the results of computer processing. However, most Dutch museums with maritime collections are understaffed. Therefore the **MARDOC** Foundation is trying to get temporary staff for recording museum objects. In 1979, 635 ships' models from 19 different museums were thus recorded. Recording a ship model on a History Artefact card (inclusive of typing) took 62 minutes on average. This long recording time was caused by the poor documentation in most of the museums concerned. The unfamiliarity of the recorder with the situation in the 19 museums he visited also affected the recording time. Recording by the museums' own staff will reduce this figure. Checking of record cards by the MARDOC office took three minutes per item. From these records the MDA has produced a printed catalogue (Figure 25.2) and nine indexes. These include a so-called dictionary index which contains all descriptors in alphabetical order and lists after each the record numbers (identity number) of the objects where these descriptors occur. This index can be used both as a searching tool and as a useful instrument for tracing mistakes and inconsistencies (Figure 25.3). The computer processing of the test file produced data on production costs, procedures and duration of various actions and checks. Checking the first computer printout of the ships' model catalogue took five minutes per record of 1700 characters.

```
** 432: 1031
(Visserijmuseum, Vlaardingen)

Onderdeel: a-b. Standplaats: SZ 1971.

scheepsmodel, volmodel - hektreiler (MARDOC), naar doel:
    reconstructiemodel.

vervaardiging: stapelmodel, bouwer: Buys, A.N., 1969.
    Scheveningen.

toestand: goed, romp; compleetheid: compleet, tuigage.

materiaal: romp: hout.
aftmetingen:
            lengte          102 cm
            breedte          18 cm
            hoogte           46 cm
            schaal         1/50
 geplakt, weerszijde boeg - schoorsteen, (SCH 6 Alida & AZ),
     uitgesneden - geplakt, dekhuis - wimpel, (Alida).
 aantal: 2.
 model: voortstuwing: eenschroefschip - motorschip, diesel.
 model: tuigage, alg.: ongetuigd.
 dek: uitrusting: gedetailleerd.

associatie: SCH 6, Zwan en Zn, NV W. van der, 1967.
    Scheveningen. (bouwjaar 1967).

verwerving: aankoop, von Buys, A.N., 1969-11-13. [zie 1].

verzekeringswaarde: ....., 1976.

(a = model; b = houtenstandaard).
(a.w. nr. 1095).

** Gijsbers, P., 1979-01-08.

[1] vermelding, 1969. brief.
```

Figure 25.2 Computer-produced catalogue entry

```
                    MARDOC  Dictionary  Index

Sneek          (geassoc. pl.)          ** 383 K 50

               (verv. pl.)             ** 229 73

                                       ** 383 K 36

                                       ** 383 K 37

                                       ** 383 K 40

                                       ** 383 K 44

Sneek I        (soort. assoc.)         ** 383 K 50

snijkopzuiger
               (spec. naam)            ** 379 2

snik, binnenschip
               (spec. naam)            ** 429 1572.6

Snoei, G.      (geassoc. pers.)        ** 348 M 1458

Société Annonime d'Armement d'Industrie et de Commerce
               (geassoc. pers.)        ** 038 B 102 (4)

Société nouvelle des forges et des chantiers
               (geassoc. pers.)        ** 348 M 1370

Soerabaja      (soort. assoc.)         ** 348 M 1333

Soerakarta     (soort. assoc.)         ** 348 M 1320

Soetermeer, Cornelis
               (geassoc. pers.)        ** 037 Mar Cat 372

                                       ** 222 1979040 (2)

Sommelsdijk    (geassoc. pl.)          ** 366 2563

               (soort. assoc.)         ** 348 M 1166

somp           (spec. naam)            ** 348 M 78

South Shield
               (geassoc. pl.)          ** 037 Mar Cat 843

spantmodel     (wijze v. verv.)        ** 7039 B 30

                                       ** 037 Mar Cat 31

                                       ** 037 Mar Cat 511
```

Figure 25.3 Computer-produced dictionary index of the MARDOC catalogue of ship models

Survey of maritime collections in Dutch museums

In 1979 MARDOC surveyed 31 museums with maritime collections (Aarts, 1979), using procedures based on the questionnaire in a thesis by D.A. Roberts (Roberts, 1974) (Chapter 12). It provided data on size and range of maritime collections, information storage and retrieval procedures used, the use of documentation and the staffing situation.

The maritime collections in the 31 museums concerned contain at least 200 000 items. This figure is almost certainly an underestimate. For instance, only the maritime collections of the Rijksmuseum have been taken into account, not including the collections of the department of drawings and prints (one million items) and the department of painting (over 5000 items). Beside these 31 museums, there is a large number of other museums and institutions which possess collections (especially pictures) of which an unknown percentage might be qualified as 'maritime'. The annual growth of collections varies, but averages one to two percent per year.

The survey highlighted the great variety of documentation procedures in the 31 museums. Twenty-four of the 31 museums use an accession register, in which is noted the object name (24 times), mode of acquisition (23 times), identity number (16 times) and descriptive data such as measurements (16 times). Twelve museums use inventory books. Twenty-seven museums record loans by drawing up special deeds of transport.

Twenty-two museums use record cards, in 25 different formats. The presence of these record cards does not imply that they are actually filled-in completely or even at all. In only 10 museums do the record cards contain more data than the accession register. Most museums only fill-in the important administrative data. Only nine museums have their complete collection documented, while only four of these have completely filled-in the record cards. Nine museums did not use record cards at all. The recording quality varies. Most museums do not record their photographic collections.

The degree of accessibility of the collections is very low. Only four museums have a systematic catalogue or indexes of their complete collections. Five museums have a storage location index of their complete collections. In some museums there is a systematic catalogue or index for one or a few collections.

As most museums do not gather statistical data on the use of their documentation, the following figures may not be representative. In the 31 museums, 53% of all questions are answered immediately, 35% by telephone and 10% by letter. It is evident that the staff try to answer only 24% of the questions by use of documentation, 5% by referring to the exhibitions and 71% from personal knowledge (without using documentation). The staff succeed in answering an average of 72% of all questions: 17% via documentation, 4% by using the exhibitions in the museum and 51% from personal knowledge. In most museums the accession registers must be used for information retrieval, however unfit for the purpose.

The survey also investigated the activities of staff members with regard to information retrieval. It showed that 51 staff members are engaged in research and identification (18% of their total work load) and 75 in completing record cards (20% of their work). The great proportion of the latter are non-curatorial. The staffing situation in the 31 museums in 1979 can be described as inadequate. The museums are understaffed, especially where skilled staff are concerned. Eight of the 31 museums do not even have permanent staff.

The 1979 survey was not intended to provide financial data. However, the low degree of accessibility and the use of non-curatorial staff for information retrieval meant that museums with maritime collections have not gone to great expenses for information storage and retrieval. There is no reason to suppose that this situation is better in other sectors of the Dutch museum world.

Analysis of the computer project (1980-1982)

It is, however, possible to give some financial data on the MARDOC-project and the MDA offline computer processing. The MARDOC budget for 1981 amounted to approximately dfl. 150 000 of which 80% was spent on salaries. Since MARDOC did not possess the necessary equipment until 1983, there are no hardware costs. In previous years an annual amount of dfl. 6000 had been set aside for outside computer processing. It is not known how much time staff members from the five MARDOC museums spent on MARDOC activities, such as standardization of terminology, recording in accordance with MARDOC guidelines, etc.

Until 1983, trial computerized catalogues and indexes had been produced for two maritime collections. A collection of 635 ships' models from 19 different museums was processed in 1980. The average size of the records was 1400 characters. The costs of data preparation, computer processing and printing of one catalogue and nine indexes amounted to dfl. 3.96 per record in 1980. At the MDA tariffs of March 1982 these costs have increased to dfl. 7.03. The processing of a relatively small collection of 250 paintings in the same manner cost dfl. 25.85 per record in 1981. It should be emphasized that these records were very large (an average of 3800 characters).

Until 1983 the recording activities of MARDOC indicate an annual production of 800-1000 records, of approximately 1700 characters each, provided that the recorder has some knowledge of the subject area. In the case of very large records (e.g. 3800 characters) the annual production would amount to 500-700 records. No doubt the expertise of the recorder and the quality of the present documentation on the collections have an important effect on the production. At the moment MARDOC produces large records in order to collect as many terms as possible for compilation of description lists and the layout of future index formats. In a normal situation the museum staff prefer smaller records and a proportionally larger through-put.

The computer processing costs should be added to the recording costs. In the offline situation prior to 1983, the MARDOC office checked records or sheets filled in by the MARDOC museums for legibility and application of the MARDOC recording rules. The same applies to the check the MARDOC office ran on the first computer printout. Personnel costs have a considerable effect on the total costs of a record, certainly when a small number of records is concerned. Simultaneous recording and data preparation by means of a microcomputer or a terminal on a minicomputer system, filling in the data categories shown on a screen, will reduce the costs.

Conclusion

The MARDOC project has slowly developed since 1970. The experience acquired in the five MARDOC museums has, nevertheless, led to a distinct approach to information retrieval problems in museums. This approach can be summarized in three terms: post-coordination, standardization and cooperation. Because of the low degree of accessibility of maritime collections in the Netherlands and the growing diversification of the query pattern, the museums are forced to increase the output of recording and indexing. However, this is hampered by lack of funds and staff.

Computer processing costs are increasing, especially by the growing labour costs for data preparation. Therefore, MARDOC is now looking at the possibilities of combining the two actions of recording and data preparation into one by means of a microcomputer and a terminal on a minicomputer system. In 1983 and 1984, the MARDOC museums acquired four microcomputers (Philips P2500), a PRIME 2250 minicomputer and the ADLIB software.

VIII SWEDEN

Chapter 26

Nordiska Museet

Göran Bergengren and Heidi Henriksson

Introduction

The Nordiska Museet in Stockholm is a museum with collections dating from 1521 to the present, the period known in Sweden as the New Age. The objects relate to Swedish life and work of this era. The museum is the largest in this field and so has a leading position among the Swedish museums of cultural history. It was founded by Artur Hazelius in 1871 as a private museum but the collections were later given to the Swedish people in the form of a foundation.

This chapter describes how the documentation procedure is working at Nordiska Museet today — a large usable manual system with some disadvantages and a great many advantages.

Form of the documentation system

Artur Hazelius also initiated the documentation system that is still used today. The ledger of Artur Hazelius still plays the main role in the procedure of registration at the Nordiska museet. These old leather-bound volumes are in daily use, together with all the later ones, the most recent of which is completed with new entries every day. The procedure chart (Figure 26.1) shows the current working system.

Formerly the registrar entered details of all acquired museum objects directly into a ledger. Today the registrar does not describe the objects. She is only directing the flow of work in the museum. Acquisition is undertaken by the three different departments: Production and Social Organisation, Family Life, and Textiles. These departments write their lists of acquisitions once a week, which are then sent to the registrar. Here the acquired collections are listed with data about price, number, source of acquisition and a reference to the responsible curator.

The registrar rewrites these lists of acquisitions on a double form for every separate item. This is called the acquisition index. One copy is filed chronologically. The other is filed alphabetically under the name of the

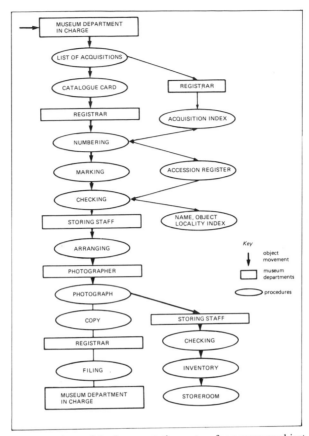

Figure 26.1 Procedure chart of the documentation system for a museum object

donor or seller and forms a name index. In this way the registrar is controlling the flow of acquisitions and has an index of objects already acquired but not entered into the accession catalogue. In this index are all the data from the lists, including the name of the curator-in-charge of every particular acquisition.

Artur Hazelius decided that a continuous sequence of numbers beginning with number 1 was the best for an inventory. Today we are describing objects with numbers around 308 000. Every item that can be described by one word — the object name — is regarded as an object. The separate pieces of an object are all numbered with the same number, with an additional '+' which shows that there is more than one piece belonging to the particular item number.

In the ledger (or accession register) the following entries were and are made:

item number;
object name with description;
date of acquisition;
mode of acquisition;

source of acquisition;
note about further supplementary documents.

Figure 26.2 illustrates the old and new style of ledger used in the museum. Figure 26.2a is the left-hand page from an old ledger, the right-hand page of which (not illustrated) is for supplementary notes. Figure 26.2b is a recent ledger. Today, each item number has six figures. The object name is the first word of the description. Formerly it was underlined; today it is written in capital letters. The object name is followed by a short description including material, colour, technique, marks and stamps and always ended with measurements. Today it consists of five typewritten lines (formerly five handwritten lines). The date of acquisition is recorded and the mode of acquisition (either bought or donated). The seller's price is noted. The source of acquisition is defined as accurately as possible. Receipt papers or other initial documents are filed in a supplementary volume under the same item number. Later on, acquired papers such as conservation protocols are also filed in this way.

A separate supplementary volume is now filled with photographs. All 'new' objects are photographed in 6×6 cm film, with each photograph showing the item number. From these films four copies are made. Three of them are filed in accession number order. The fourth is fixed to the catalogue card. This procedure will slowly be extended to include the objects already in store.

If you compare an old and a new ledger you will find certain differences. First you have the source of acquisition noted with only one name. In this way you are able to browse rapidly to find a collection if you know the donor or seller. This column is identical in both volumes. It is also a protective margin for the following columns with a place for the thumb. A second narrow column is used for a mark which tells that a check has been made that the object, its number and the description all match. The item number is stamped in the ledger by means of a paginating stamp. In the handwritten volume there are five objects entered on each side: today there are thirteen. The broadest column is for the description of the object. Today it consists only of a description. Formerly the date, place, mode of acquisition, price and donor or seller were recorded here. These data are now written separately on the right-hand side, with columns for mode of acquisition, date, source and price. Then there is a column used for special notes about damage, or supplementary information. Further to the right is a broad column where topographical data (place of origin) are recorded separately. This column gives an easy way to browse the ledgers for topographical data.

The old ledger was written with pen and ink. Then it was copied twice with pen and ink and bound in leather. The paper is Swedish hand-made paper of the best quality. The pages have lines and columns prepared beforehand. Two sets are kept, one in the museum as an accession register for daily use and another in the store at Julita. Corrections in the accession register are made only by the registrar. A third series — the draft — is kept in store in Stockholm. Except for the photographic one, there is only a single copy of the supplementary volumes, kept in the museum in Stockholm.

Today the accession register is typewritten by the registrar. The paper is still hand-made and prepared with columns beforehand. The numbering is

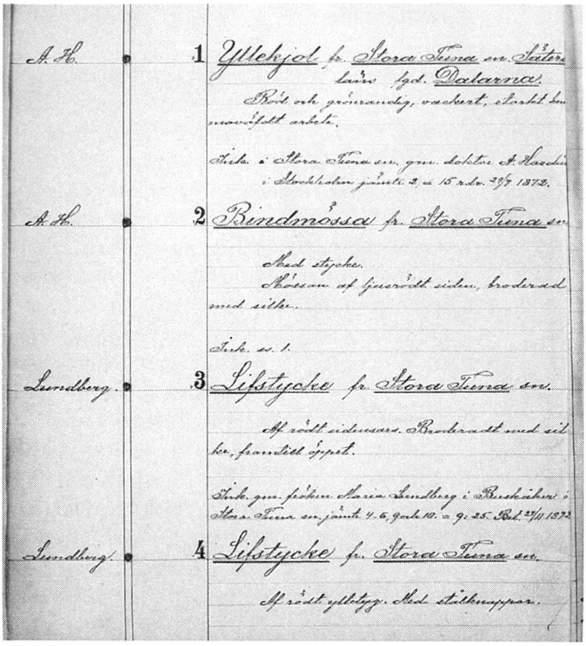

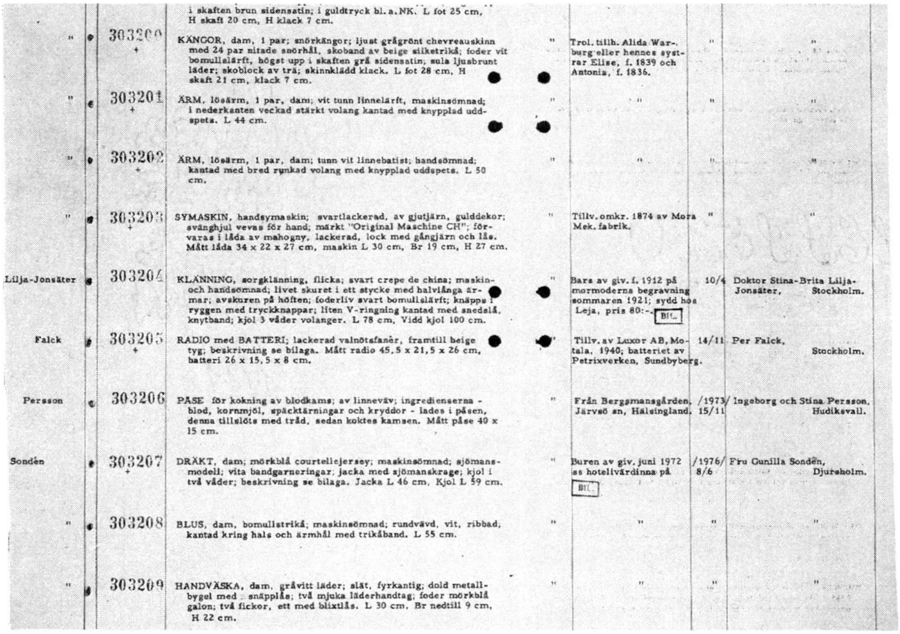

Figure 26.2 Old (top) and new (bottom) design of museum ledgers

done by the registrar herself. The typewriter is an extra broad one and the typing is done over two pages at a time. Formerly the written pages were bound: today they are stored in spring binders with locks.

Fair copies have not been typewritten since 1960. Photocopies have been made of the accessions catalogue to supplement the Julita Ledger. However, the paper used in the copying machine does not last very well.

The accession register is produced by the registrar, whose main task this is. Formerly, the registrar had to do this work, as well as describing every object while entering it in the ledger. Today the registrar has a full-time marking assistant and part-time help from photographers. In Sweden, Nordiska Museet is the only museum with a marking assistant.

The description of the object and the catalogue card are prepared in the departments. As with the accession ledger, the catalogue card is of an old design (Figure 26.3). It is written on hand-made paper, recently with printed headings. Unfortunately, we do not know when the first catalogue cards were produced. Because of this fact it is uncertain how many and which catalogue cards with descriptions of earlier acquisitions are missing. However, the greater part of the collections is described in this way, often with a supplementary drawing or photograph, and the cards are systematically filed by the different departments.

The catalogue card incorporates all the data recorded in the accession register: to the left the item number, object name, material, producer and measurements; to the right the date of origin, if known. The description which follows may be as long as required. The last lines of the card contain data about the acquisition, the name of the recorder, and the date of cataloguing. There is also space for drawings and photographs. You can complete two cards if needed. These cards are sent with the objects to the registrar.

The procedure of accessioning begins with the registrar stamping a piece of paper, a catalogue card and the acquisition index with the number given to the object. The piece of paper is attached to the object, which is then passed to the marking assistant. Existing supplements are also stamped with the same item number. From the catalogue card the registrar takes the data that are needed for the accession register. Mostly the data appear here in a shortened form, always comprising object name, form, material, colour, measurements in five lines. Afterwards the card is put aside to wait for the photocopy.

The marking is done in two different places on every object, if possible at a distance from each other. The same goes for all separate parts of an object. It is done with drawing ink on paper and unpainted wood; with artists' oil colour (black or white) on hard surfaces like painted wood, porcelain, glass, metal; with red lead paint on iron and steel; with electric engraving pen on hard materials suited for this; and with marking-ink on cotton ribbons which are sewn on to textiles.

When an object has been marked with the number it is checked against the text of the ledger. Afterwards the object is photographed and goes into store. The photographs are sent to the registrar, who cuts them, files them and sends one with the catalogue card back to the department in charge. The catalogue cards are kept by the curator in charge of the object group in

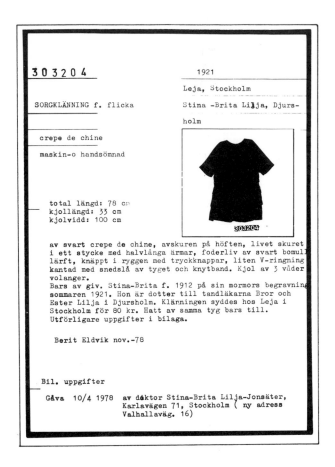

Figure 26.3 Old design catalogue card

question. The classification order depends on the interest of the individual curator.

The tasks of the registrar also include the production of cards for the card indexes. There are three card-indexes: a name-index, an object-index and a topographical index.

The acquisition rate has lately grown so rapidly that the indexes have not been kept up to date because of lack of staff. The object index has a classification that has grown during the years at Nordiska Museet. It consists of broad groups (e.g. hunting, animal husbandry, costume, etc.) with subgroups. It is not indexed in the same order as the catalogue cards in the different departments. It is complete up to 1975. The topographical index and the name index are complete up to 1960. The acquisition index is a supplementary index that can be used for the years after 1960. It does, however, just record names of donors and sellers, not artists. The registrar is responsible for filing of the index cards. The indexes are open to everybody, the public as well as curators.

Recent developments

During the last seventeen years certain modernization has been tried in the area of automation. A form with headings and carbon copies consisting of just one item number has been printed. This form has been used for the re-accessioning of a large collection of the Royal Agricultural Academy (Figure 26.4).

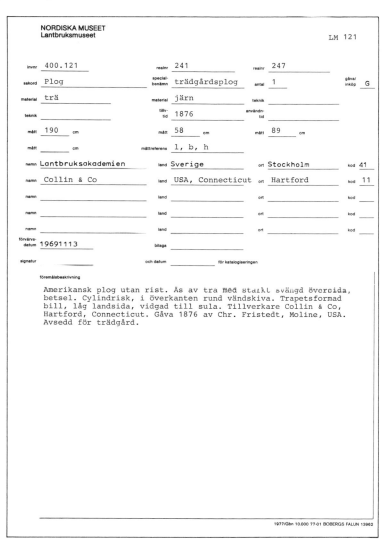

Figure 26.4 New design recording form

As before the registrar receives a catalogue card, which she copies on a form. The headings begin with the item number and the object name, and consist of material, techniques, names linked to locality and a code which tells what link the name has to the object itself (e.g. the name of the owner, the seller, the maker). When the upper part has been completed, the whole description from the catalogue card is rewritten underneath. Afterwards a fair copy is made of the draft on a form with three copies, such that four identical accession entries are produced.

The disadvantage of the system is that no acceptable way of storing these entries has been found. The paper is weak. You cannot bind separate entries. The paper does not stand handling in binders. However this procedure has also produced indexes, which are all the better. The keywords on the upper part of the form, carefully selected, are entered into a computer by means of an online terminal and indexes are made by special programs. The material and measurements have been omitted. The resulting indexes are object index, a name index, and a topographical index. The classification system used is *Outline of Cultural Materials* (Murdock, *et al.*, 1961). This classification is used for information retrieval in small museum collections representing cultural history in general in Sweden. But for a specialized collection like this it has been of no practical use. Most objects — perhaps 80% — belong to the group number 231 (domesticated animals) or 241 (tillage). So the index does not give any help at all in this case. However, the alphabetical indexes with different combinations of years, codes and object names have made very interesting reading.

Through a donation from the Knut and Alice Wallenberg Foundation in 1981 the museum has acquired a minicomputer. Since 1982 the Norrbotten County Employment Board has borne the expenses of an emergency project for transferring the object descriptions in the main catalogue to magnetic disc. At the end of June 1984 we expect the entire main catalogue to have been transferred.

The intention of the data recording is to file the information about the museum objects in a data base management system, for two purposes. One is to produce complete subject, topographical and name indexes in list form on paper. The other is to make data about the objects accessible for direct retrieval via display terminals.

IX HUNGARY

Chapter 27

The history of Hungarian museum documentation, its present application and future aspects

Istvan Éri and Tàmas Bezeczky

Introduction

Efforts to standardize and centralize the coordination of museums in Hungary started in the 1890s. The formulation of the principles and their practical application in all aspects of museums began in the period before the First World War. The problems of documentation, recording and inventory were also discussed. Since the Central Advisory Board of Museums and Libraries was authorized only to give recommendations and to suggest different methods, the results were rather rare. An investigation into documentation and recording methods showed that there were about 28 kinds of inventory and documentation system throughout the country. Most of them were used for the purpose of administration with very little or no technical or scientific information. At the same time, there were about half a million museum objects with no data given about them.

Standard documentation system

The first Hungarian collections containing objects of cultural value were established in the 15th century, during the reign of King Matthias. In later centuries, remarkable collections were gathered by members of the aristocracy and certain scholars, but these were often plundered or destroyed during the frequent wars.

The National Museum was founded by Ferenc Széchenyi in 1802, using his own collections as a basis. In the second half of the century, it included archaeology, ethnography and natural history departments and a library. A coin catalogue was produced in 1808 and the first inventory completed in 1820, both in Latin. From 1846 to 1926, a uniform inventory was used, in which were noted details such as registration number, date and method of acquisition, object name, physical description, collection place, number of items and price (Figure 27.1). In 1926, this style of inventory was replaced

278

by specific inventory volumes for numismatics, archaeology and history. This work within the National Museum formed one of the bases for the more general development of documentation in all Hungarian museums.

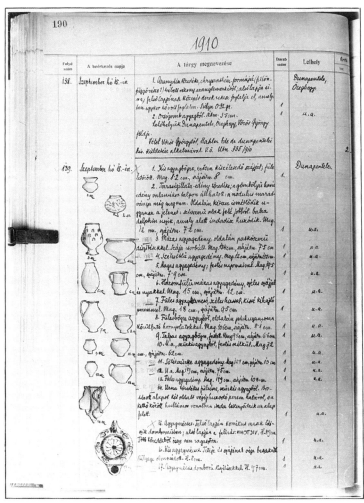

Figure 27.1 A page from the archaeological inventory, National Museum, 1910

The fact that the *Office Internationale des Musées* (OIM) recommended the introduction of a standard museum inventory system in 1927 was very well known among the Hungarian experts (see Chapter 30). Hungarian scientists participated in the discussion over this topic in the journal of the OIM (in issues of *Mouseion* in 1928). E. Petrovics from the Museum of Fine Arts and Gy. Vegh from the Museum of Applied Arts published their mainly sceptical opinions on this subject. More importantly, a young Hungarian ethnographer, J. Honti (1910-1945), took part between 1937-1939 in the Central Office of the OIM in Paris in developing the recommendations in connection with the standard inventory system. In view of the concern with this problem in the Hungarian scientific world, and because the successor of the OIM, ICOM, mentioned this subject in the first general meeting in 1948, scientists in Hungary started in 1949 to introduce a standard Hungarian inventory system, based on the recommendation of ICOM.

The introduction and realization of unified and obligatory rules needed more than the agreement of the members. There had to be binding instructions and an executive body, and the statute 13/1949 concerning the museums and monuments offered the well balanced legal principles for it. The basic aspect of the modern, social oriented law is, that any kind of object of museal value represents a part of the national heritage, regardless of ownership. Their recording is necessary as part of a scientific inventory. A new body, the Central Office for the Museums and Monuments, founded in the same year, was responsible for the compilation and realization of the standardized forms of documentation.

In a relatively short time the new inventory system was worked out and came into force on the 1st of January 1950. From this time on, we can speak about a standard documentation system for Hungarian museums.

The main points of the standard inventory system are:

it refers to every museum in Hungary without consideration of its funding body;

it encompasses every museum object which is under the protection of the cultural policy, as a single object or as a collection. If it is part of a public collection (e.g. church collection or other associations' collection), the inventorying of these subjects is the task of experts from specially designated museums;

the inventory system consists basically of the individual identification of the objects and the recording of their data. For this purpose there is a standardized special inventory book in the form of cards with headings and for recording of more information a so-called 'research description card';

all printed papers in connection with this task were issued centrally and expenses arising from visits to museums without qualified experts were paid from central finances, as well as other administrative issues;

by entering the data from former inventory books with insufficient information, and adding technical definitions, a great part of the country's museum objects were taken gradually into the inventory, and objects not yet taken into the inventory were recorded;

as a future aim, establishing a data bank for the research description cards was discussed in different technical centres (archaeology: Hungarian National Museum; fine arts: Museum for Fine Arts, etc.).

The description of the standard museum documentation system (as an annex to the museum law) is given in the form of an instruction of the Minister of Culture. The current version of the inventory procedure is given as an annex to the updated museum law 9/1963. The system incorporates the use of a diary, inventory and catalogue cards.

The diary of acquisitions is concerned with objects that have not been incorporated into the formal inventory. It can include information about the acquisition and the object and a reference to the provisional inventory number. This information then forms the basis for the inventory entry.

At the beginning, a general inventory book was planned for the purpose of the fundamental inventorying of every kind of museum object. The book had 18 headings and it seemed that it was sufficient to contain all the information regarding the technical-scientific and the proprietory -economical aspects. However, with the exception of museums containing smaller collections (2000-3000 items), this system did not find a widespread usage.

The large national museums (National Museum, Museum for Fine Arts, etc.) with different specialized collections already had inventory and storage systems. They wished to preserve their procedures for recording special technical aspects in the revised inventory system. Therefore, they developed certain differing types of inventory books. So in the large museums several inventories existed simultaneously according to the profile of the collections. Since the curators and experts were responsible for the maintenance of their collections according to those inventory books, they continued their practice without taking into consideration a centralized inventory system. These special inventory books were also used by local museums with heterogeneous collections.

Beside the general inventory book, there are 11 specialized books with 11-16 headings: natural science (for animals, minerals, plants and fossils), anthropology, archaeology, archaeo-zoology, numismatics, ethnography, fine arts, applied arts, historical objects, literature, and industrial history. The headings in these books are illustrated in Figure 27.2.

In addition to the inventory, a catalogue card may be prepared with full details about the object, including a drawing or photograph.

Growth of collections

This practice very much helped the new obligatory inventory tendencies and the taking into inventory of the rapidly growing material of museum collections. In 1950 there were one and a half to two million individually registered objects in Hungarian museums. In 1980 the number was eight million. Each year about 200 000 museum objects are registered. This amount of work pressed very hard on the museum experts as they alone were allowed to make an entry in an inventory, and the drafting of the description cards was their task.

The inundation of the large museums (archaeology in the Hungarian National Museum, ethnography in the Ethnographical Museum, etc.) hampered the processing of the material. The data storage system of the 1950s was, anyway, outdated (the library catalogues were used as models), so the idea of a central data bank could not be realized.

Development of the system

The tardiness of the revised, but still not entirely standardized, museum documentation system hindered the efforts to use it for purposes of scientific research. During the mid 1960s museum experts started to reconsider the

Headings \ Special Inventories	General	Natural Sciences	Anthropology	Archaeology	Archaeological Zoology	Numismatics	Folklore	Fine Arts	Applied Arts	History	Literary History	Technology
1. Registration number	•	•	•	•	•	•	•	•	•	•	•	•
2. Object name and function	•	•	•	•	•		•	•	•	•		•
3. Number of specimens	•	•	•	•	•	•	•		•	•		•
4. Material and technique	•			•		•	•	•	•	•		•
5. Dimensions	•	•		•		•	•	•	•	•	•	•
6. The person or institution involved in the production	•		•		•							
7. Acquisition place, site	•	•	•	•	•	•	•		•	•		
8. Date of production	•	•		•			•	•	•	•		•
9. Condition	•			•	•		•	•		•	•	•
10. Manner of Acquisition	•	•	•	•	•	•	•	•	•	•	•	•
11. Acquired from	•	•	•				•		•	•	•	
12. Date of Acquisition	•	•	•	•	•	•	•		•	•	•	•
13. Price	•	•		•		•	•	•	•	•	•	•
14. Place of storage	•		•	•				•		•		
15. Number of object in documentation department	•							•	•			
16. Name of recorder	•	•	•	•	•	•	•	•	•	•	•	
17. Conservation	•											
18. Notes	•	•	•	•	•	•	•	•	•	•	•	•
19. Number of grave			•		•							
20. Archaeological age			•		•							
21. Description of the object				•		•			•		•	
22. Species					•							
23. Age and sex					•							
24. Place of storage and registration number of other objects belonging to the site			•		•	•						
25. Place of production								•				•
26. Place of use								•				
27. Name of artist								•	•		•	•
28. Date of use								•				

Figure 27.2 Content of general and special inventory books

form of the records. The subjects of their experiments were closed collection units.

The need for improvement of the methods of data storage and processing and of the technical conditions on the one side, and the demand for greater information on the other, made it essential to introduce computer processing of museum records (Bán, 1980; Bezeczky, 1980; Éri, 1971). In order to realize this aim, the Institute for Conservation and Methodology of Museums compiled a long-term plan which allowed its gradual introduction.

A basic concept of this plan was the use of all the advantages of the documentation efforts which were made 30 years ago. A completely new inventory system had to be avoided. The numbering system used in the inventory of the museum objects could serve as a basis for computer processing. This numbering system was made up of year of recording, the number of items each year, additional serial number, and identification number (for differentiation of objects from collection units). The application of pre-numbers was also necessary: comprising the identification numbers of museums and the numbers for the collection in the museums.

We recommended the re-introduction of standard museum inventory books, which are able to collect all the data given for the individual museum objects, within 22 headings. With the help of formal changes the problems of the computerized data processing of the inventory entries and the reproduction of the inventory in the data bank can be solved. The headings in the inventory are:

identification data
   inventory number
   category
   number of the objects
   number of pieces
   dimensions
   name of the recorder
accession data
   method of acquisition
   place of origin
   date of acquisition
   price and number of receipt
   name of collector, vendor or donor
   remarks
scientific parameters
   scientific description
   age or date of origin
   site of production or use
museum procedure data
   state of the object
   method of conservation
   conservation document number
   photo archive number
   archive number
   storage
   control remarks (data)

Parallel with the gradual introduction of the revised inventory system in the museums, the establishment of a central data bank can be started. Potential improvements include:

offering of improved facilities to experts (such as the ability to treat entire collection units);
the introduction of certain terminological rules for free texts;
establishing local data banks of small capacity while ensuring their compatibility.

Priority must be given to large-scale scientific works (edition of collection catalogues, publishing of archaeological and ethnographical topographies).

Last but not least, consideration must be given to a close connection with international practice, assuring the possibility of adaptation and connections to international systems.

The last modification of the Hungarian museum statute — 19/1981 — offers a possibility for the realization of these plans. It contains the changes in the instructions.

X   USSR

Chapter 28

Museum documentation systems and computers: USSR experience

Jacob Sher

Introduction

Computer research and elaboration in the fields of history, history of culture and art criticism have been undertaken in the USSR over a period of more than twenty years. These have made it possible to gain some experience in data standards and research procedures as well as to develop some universal theoretical and methodological principles (Birukov and Heller, 1973; Feinberg, 1981; Gutchin, 1969; Kamenetskii *et al.*, 1975; Kovalchenko, 1977; Mironov and Stepanov, 1975; Nalimov, 1979; Rauschenbach, 1980; Ustinov and Fellinger, 1977; Zaripov, 1971). Special investigations on museum collections computerization were initiated in 1976 at the Hermitage Museum, Leningrad (Aseyev *et al.*, 1980; Chere and Polyakov, 1978; Sher, 1978). Later, other institutions of the Ministry of Culture of the USSR and the Academy of Sciences of the USSR joined in the research into the problem.

A few working models of museum data banks on antique bronzes, drawings by Soviet artists, architectural monuments of Russia and the coins of Sasanian Iran were developed during this time. While working on these models, some common methodological principles on the establishment of a national automated information system for historical and cultural monuments were formulated, and the experience of our foreign colleagues was taken into account. The present state of the museum documentation system and the main problems concerning its computerization are discussed in this chapter.

The present state of the museum documentation system

At present there are more than 50 million museum objects and more than 1300 museums in the Soviet Union. As in other countries, the collections are distributed very unevenly among museums of different towns. In the Hermitage, for example, the collection consists of about three million items; in some museums of small towns the collections are hundreds of times smaller. Therefore, it seems natural to build the automated system in accordance with a modular pattern, beginning with big museums such as the Hermitage, State Pushkin Museum of Fine Art, State Russian Museum, Museum of the Great October Socialist Revolution, etc. Later, the systems of individual museums could be joined by communication lines into a national museum computer network.

Complicated in itself, a problem of the creation of the national system is still more aggravated because most of the museum collections in other countries are privately-owned and the state cannot control their inventory and record-keeping procedures. One of the most important features of the Soviet system of state registration and utilization of historical and cultural property (including museum collections) is that it is based on national legislation (the laws of the USSR and union republics on the preservation and utilization of historical and cultural monuments). As the main part of the museum collections is national property and is stored in state museums, the rules of registration and the form of registration documents are the same for all museums of the country.

The documentation system plays a very important part in the life of a modern museum. The efficiency of collection management and conservation, the quality of restoration, and the quality of research, educational work and exposition in the museum depend on the quality of the documentation system.

The present system was modelled on traditional patterns. It was called upon to solve practical problems and was gradually adapted to the performance of this function. On the whole, such a system had to meet the following requirements and was formed under the following conditions:

providing control over accessioning and storage in order to protect the collection against theft, substitution and damage;
the necessity of scientific description and analysis of museum collections so that they could be studied as monuments of the history of culture and works of art, with due regard for the constant growth of the collections, the development of scientific analysis procedures and the perfection of methods of conservation, restoration and research;
an appreciable growth of interest in the cultural heritage (by both scholars and the general public), that complicated the scientific role and educational activities of museums;
the ever-increasing complexity of collection management problems due to the growing intensification of all kinds of museum activities, and especially of the exchange of museum data at the national and international level.

The museum documentation system has not always remained invariable. As the demands increased and the tasks became more complicated, the system was more than once modified and the appropriate instructions issued (Aseyev *et al.*, 1980).

These changes, however, were more of a limited nature concerning record keeping and filing. They did not affect the problem of scientific description, nor did they eliminate the general contradictions between the constant growth of collection documentation and the limited opportunities offered by the manual filing system. Many examples of problems arising from these contradictions could be listed, but they are well known and described in the literature (Chenhall, 1975; Gardin, 1955; 1975; *Museum*, 1971; 1978). It is impossible to eliminate these contradictions by a simple increase in the number of clerical personnel, because sooner or later the number of such people will surpass the total number of staff.

While the use of a computer does not settle all the problems raised by the information crisis, it does make it possible to adopt intensive methods rather than extensive ones.

The goals of the automated museum documentation system

The main goals of the automated museum documentation system are the improvement of the efficiency and quality of information for scientific research on museum collections (including field and restoration work and also publications of materials and studies) and the improvement of record-keeping procedures and collection management through the availability of accurate information and the reduction of the time and expenditure needed for information retrieval, processing and reproduction. The detailed description of the goals includes such requirements as:

more complete and precise satisfaction of the growing interest of the people in their historical and cultural heritage;
the enhancement of scientific research on museum collections, especially those that are very numerous (drawings, numismatic material, archaeological objects, etc.);
the improvement of collection management through the rational use of museum holdings (new accessions, re-structuring of displays, publication of catalogues etc.);
automation of routine inventory work and control of the preservation of objects;
fuller satisfaction of the enquiries concerning international exchange of information about museum collections, and exchange of exhibitions.

General requirements of the automated system

The main requirement of the automated museum documentation system is that only one document compiled according to a standard pattern should be entered, while a number of documents of rigid and modified pattern can be retrieved as outputs. The observance of this principle gives a scholar some free time for creative work that cannot be formalized.

The system is expected to perform automatically the following functions:

information recognition according to main categories and recording of the information in the appropriate places of computer memory;
multiple-aspect information retrieval according to a given set of attributes;
comparison and adjustment of data according to the given set of programs;
drawing up of statistical summaries, tables and diagrams;
solution of classification tasks;

reproduction on a screen and on sheets of paper of intermediate and final results.

At first, for the performance of these functions it is necessary to separate routine recurrent operations, that lend themselves to algorithmic description and formalization, from the complex mental operations, the execution of which is impossible without an investigator armed with experience and intuition.

The system is being developed as part of the national information system for historical and cultural monuments (AIS 'Pamjatnic'). Besides information on museum collections, the AIS 'Pamjatnic' includes an information system for immovable monuments: secular and religious architectural monuments, archaeological monuments, historical places, historical buildings, etc. The system must also be compatible, at least in certain aspects, with other similar information systems and particularly with foreign systems.

The language of dialogue with the system should be as near to natural language as possible. The system must ensure an online mode for which a user is not obliged to have a special technical education. The necessity of an online mode is determined by a number of reasons that have been considered elsewhere (Aseyev *et al.*, 1980; Sher, 1978).

The system must always allow the addition of data to the system itself and to every input document. It should allow the substitution and editing of data. Some means must be provided for safeguarding confidential information from unauthorized use and for the protection of a scholar's copyright.

Thematic, functional and organizational structure of the automated system

It is expedient to organize the storage of information in the system according to the current classification of museum collections. With such organization of data, the time needed for information retrieval is considerably reduced. The upper level of this classification contains headings such as: painting, drawing, sculpture, applied art, archaeology, numismatics, and historical documents (written and photographic). Under these headings a number of more specific hierarchical structures can be grouped according to a thematic attribute (e.g. tools, utensils, armament, means of conveyance) or according to other attributes (e.g. time, place, material).

The depth of description of every item can be infinite. There are no objective criteria for the determination of the necessary and sufficient level of the depth of description. That is why two types of description have been adopted for the system: general and special.

A regular description includes a standard set of scientific and inventory data empirically obtained. The set of data is limited but at the same time is sufficiently detailed and corresponds to the depth of description which is adopted in short scientific catalogues of different exhibitions. Thus it contains basic information necessary for solving the main record-keeping, scientific, educational, display and management problems.

The general description contains the following data: museum name, department (stock) name, inventory number, author, object name, date, material, technique, dimensions, brief physical description, curator, movement, mode of acquisition, main bibliography and other.

The depth of the general description is not enough for the scientific study of museum collections. That is why a system of detailed description in addition to the regular one is developed for specific research. The detailed description has the same objective attributes as the regular one but it is adapted in its content to the goals of a particular area of research. The description of Sasanian coins made in connection with investigations in the history of Iran of the third century AD is an example of such a description. In addition to the data which are obligatory in the description of any coin there is a special set of attributes which define certain elements of the iconography of the image of a king, a queen, an heir and also iconographic characteristics of the image of the god, the altar, signs on the obverse and the reverse, versions of the legend, etc.

No matter how deep and detailed the description of an item may be, it will never replace the visual perception of it. That is why the possibilities of input, storage, retrieval and processing of graphic information are also envisaged during the work upon systems. Microfiches containing texts as well as pictures of objects can be used as a simplified substitute. Microfiches are stored in special systems providing the possibilities of their automatic retrieval and duplication on paper.

In the system which is being developed, the functions of every subsystem and transitions from one subsystem to another must be precisely determined. In accordance with the order of operations three functional subsystems can be listed:

Labour-intensive manual work is done in the data preparation subsystem. This includes the collection of information, primary description, error control and transfer of data to the usable medium as well as information entry into the system's memory. The blanks of input documents are completed at the time when an object is acquired by a museum (by purchase, transfer from another museum, donation, etc.) or in the field (for archaeological and ethnographical materials). This subsystem can exist separately and independently from the automated information system, and can function as a manual system like a library catalogue.

The data storage, retrieval and processing subsystem is a batch of programs carrying out the main functions of the automated system: distribution of data in files, file updating, data base management and also information retrieval and processing of materials.

The output subsystem consists of programs for the extraction of final and intermediate results of information retrieval and processing. The results are prepared in the form of catalogues, indexes, tables and other documents.

As noted above, most museums in the USSR already use a single standardized documentation system. Thus, if the system were created and tested on the stocks of some big museums then the expansion of the system to all the museums of the country would simply be a matter of organization and method.

The problem of whether a centralized data bank, as in Canada (Homulos, 1978) (Chapter 2), is better than separate banks in different centres connected one with another has not yet been solved. A choice will be made after both variants have been tested on the models.

The software

The system will use a batch of applied programs which has been developed in the Institute of Systems Research of the Academy of Sciences of the USSR (INES) (Arlazarov *et al.*, 1979). This system provides opportunities for solving a wide range of tasks of information storage, retrieval and processing. The INES software consists of a generalized data base management system which does not depend on the specific content of data bases; and a complex of programs for solving different management and other problems. The system allows for a standard or user-specified format. Some data processing is allowed during the output procedure. The structure of an output document is assigned by the user without any special programming. The system contains a vocabulary and a means for data base scanning and correction. INES is an open system which can be operated in an online mode by a number of users at the same time.

Conclusion

In this chapter great consideration has been given to an automated museum documentation system. However, it should be stressed that the demands were formed on the basis of a series of practical experimental elaborations undertaken by the large museums mentioned at the beginning of the chapter. Constant contact between the scholars working at a system and discussion of practical results made it possible to develop a single conception of the whole common national system and to carry on the work to form its separate modules.

XI AUSTRALIA

Chapter 29

A documentation system for Australian art museums

Therese Varveris

Background

Australia has over 100 public art collections, concentrated in New South Wales (with 33 museums), Victoria (with 27, including many of the largest collections), Queensland (with 12), and Western Australia (with 10). The oldest, the National Gallery of Victoria in Melbourne, celebrated its centennial in 1961, but most are much newer. Many are located in isolated country towns. It is estimated they include over 150 000 works.

Some of the major museums have been able to catalogue large parts of their collections. However, in many cases the time and the skilled staff have been hard to find. Much of the cataloguing has been inconsistent in its approach. It is often incomplete or inaccurate, being prepared by staff untrained in registration practices.

This is not due to lack of concern. A widespread and lively interest in the arts increased during the last decade when it became more common to circulate many travelling exhibitions and to originate some excellent ones as well. The difficulty of locating desirable works due to incomplete information or, quite often, the total lack of information, became increasingly troublesome. As expected, of course, the whereabouts of major works was known but the scope of all works available was harder to know.

Australian Gallery Directors' Council scheme

In the mid 1970s it was decided that some decisive national initiative had to be taken. Under the leadership of Ron Appleyard, Deputy Director of the Art Gallery of South Australia, Adelaide, the Catalogue and Information Retrieval Committee of the Australian Gallery Directors' Council was formed to consider the problems (Varveris, 1978; 1983a; 1983b).

The Committee wished to profit from the experience of other museums. The members initiated a programme of visits to museums with well-known registration systems, to study how they were set up, how they worked on a daily basis, and how well they served the staff who needed accurate and complete catalogue information. As it is customary for the professional staff of Australian museums to make periodic visits to European and American galleries in order to be familiar with major institutions and their collections, as well as with special contemporary exhibitions, they were able to do this in an informal way in the course of regular trips abroad.

At that time, relatively few museums had computerized their collections or were planning to do so. However, from the beginning, the use of computers was part of the Australian plan. There were very few computer systems designed for, or suitable for adaptation to, museum catalogues, and none that were completely satisfactory. It was therefore decided to focus attention on the primary task of collecting and recording catalogue information in such a way that it could be used equally well for an interim manual system and later for a partially or completely automated system. It was seen as an opportunity to establish nationwide cataloguing standards. To assure consistent records throughout the country would make computerization easier when it was eventually introduced.

The Committee favoured the procedures developed at The Museum of Modern Art under the direction of Dorothy H. Dudley, Registrar, 1936-69 (Chapter 8). It seemed the most suitable to adapt for their own museums. The manual catalogue was comprehensive, clear and easy to use. Parts of the system had recently been computerized and, although there were problems, the results seemed promising.

Goals of the scheme

The immediate goal of the Committee was to solve the problems of communication and standardization inherent in trying to coordinate organizations spread throughout a large country. It was hoped the Committee's work would lead to uniform cataloguing and a steady progress in recording the nation's diverse art collections.

Although there was no timetable for the overall project, Australia's bicentennial of 1988 was kept in mind. It was decided to concentrate on the cataloguing of Australian painting with the expectation that enough work would be completed by 1988 to make it possible to publish a comprehensive catalogue in time for the celebrations.

The larger, long-term goal was to eventually provide a single, comprehensive, fully computerized, nationwide catalogue of all the public collections. This would be accessible by computer terminal from any of the participating institutions.

The Committee wanted a system that would give museum registrars the ability to use the computer both as a basic tool for inventory control and to print catalogue cards and lists containing extensive information, if they desired to do so. They wished to provide the curatorial staffs with a system they could use for their work in maintaining, researching, exhibiting and writing about the collections, as well as an aid in exchanging information with Australian and foreign scholars.

They hoped museums would be able to produce from the computer records both simple lists and full format catalogues ready for publication. Thus they were looking for a system that could accommodate artists' biographical information, object descriptions, bibliographical references, exhibition history and scholarly comments.

Cataloguing standards

The first stage of the project was devoted to developing and recording cataloguing standards for the various data categories required for Australian paintings. It was decided to use the general data categories developed by David Vance for the Museum Computer Network (Vance, 1975) (Chapter 5). As it seemed probable at the time that future work on standardization would be done through this organization, it was thought desirable for the Australian standards to be compatible with those of the MCN. The cataloguing guidelines were based on the work at The Museum of Modern Art.

It was decided that certain basic classes of information were essential to every catalogue record if it were to serve its purpose of identifying the object. These categories have to be entered as part of the initial record or it might later be difficult, if not impossible, to associate the record with the work it is meant to describe. This is especially true in the case of works such as similar studies on a single subject or series of drawings. They can be very difficult to identify later if minimum information is not recorded at the time of acquisition.

The required classes are accession number, acquisition information, artist, title, date (plus the index classes earliest and latest dates), medium category and medium description (plus media to be indexed), size (sight or approximate measurements if exact size not available at the time of acquisition), cataloguing institution, credit line, country of object (Figure 29.1).

These are only some of the data categories recorded when a work is catalogued immediately upon acquisition. However, as this is not always possible, the minimum information usually can be obtained from Proposed Acquisition forms, Acquisition Lists, correspondence from donors or lenders and catalogues.

Data analysis

The MCN system of separating free text and index classes seemed desirable and was retained. The MCN generally follows the custom of separating data into odd-numbered free text categories in which unlimited amounts of text can be entered and corresponding even-numbered index classes in which relatively controlled index terms to the free text are entered.

The purpose of having the two types of category is to allow complete freedom for recording information in the free text classes. This can be to the detail required without being concerned about the number of characters being used or what keywords the computer would search for retrieval purposes. Then short, keyword, index terms are entered in the index classes. Cataloguers can specify exactly the terms that should be looked at for retrieval and so searches are faster than they would be if the computer had to scan the entire record.

For example, if the free text class is medium and it contains 'collage of

NB *Categories so marked must be completed.
†Categories so marked are index categories.
The following information is generally obtained from acquisition records

Catalogue Worksheet
Australian Gallery Directors Council, 1980

†*1024 Accession no. 1981·29

†* 2 Cataloguing institution (initials)   V BA

† 8 Department

†* 70 Artist WESTWOOD, Bryan

†* 36 Media category Painting

†* 30 Title Still Life

† 132 Secondary category

† 10 Status

† 33 Other title(s)

208 Artist's country Australia/United States

· 3 Acquisition information Accepted 1st December 1981 Purchased from Australian Galleries

213 Birth/death years 1930 —

†* 22 Acquisition date 1981 12

† 212 Year of birth 1930

† 14 Vendor

† 214 Year of death —

† 114 Confidential vendor

Previous nos. —

7 Copyright

61 Photo nos.

† 6 Legal restrictions

11 Self-imposed restrictions

9 Confidential information

The following information is generally obtained from the curator

· 5 Credit line Purchased with the assistance from the Visual Arts Board.

† 12 Donor

† 112 Confidential donor

† 105 Homage

91 Provenance

† 90 Ex-collectors

† 190 Confidential ex-collectors

99 Related works

71 Remarks about attribution

†* 76 Country of object —

† 78 Place of object

79 Remarks about country or place of object

Figure 29.1 Catalogue worksheet

The following information is generally obtained from the physical examination of the object.

*83 Date of work   (n.d.)

†*82 Earliest date   1945   †*84 Latest date   1981

85 Remarks about date

*47 Medium description   Oil on canvas

†*48 Medium

*51 Size (and weight)   121·6 ×121·6 cm (47⅞ × 47⅞"),

*55 Signature and date   Signed ·L·L in ink "W". Not dated.

57 Secondary inscriptions   ———

35 Construction or manufacture

The following information is generally obtained from the physical examination of the object.
The information will not be entered into the computer and should be recorded manually on the catalogue cards

Mounting and framing unit (on acquisition)

Mounting unit (permanent)

Condition on acquisition

Tertiary inscriptions — On reverse, torn label in L.L corner "FOSTER/ WHITE
GA _ _ _ S / Artist BRYAN WESTW _ _
TITLE : DURER'S _ _ _ _ _ _ _ _
3 11½ Occidental S. Seattle , WA _ _ _ 04 '20 _ _ _ ':
— On reverse white chalk mark '22' in a
circle
— " " Label '22'.
— " " Label "Australian Galleries/ dealers
in fine art/ 35-37 DERBY ST COLLINGWOOD/ TELEPHONE
41 4303, 41 4382 / TITLE. PILLOWS/ARTIST, BRYAN

The following information can generally be provided by either the curator or registrar.

† **38** Subject (proper name)

39 Subject (proper name remarks)

† **40** Subject (generic index)

41 Subject (generic remarks)

43 Subject description

The following space is reserved for entering information on 72 Collaborating artists and for continuing information from other data categories.

† **72** Collaborating artists

Continuing Information from other data categories

| **100** Incomplete worksheet

Remarks by cataloguer and curator

Date recorded 17 - 11 - 83   Date approved 23·11·83   8·12·83

Initials KM   EBR cut-and-pasted paper and gouache, mounted on cardboard', the index entries can be limited to 'collage', 'paper' and 'gouache'. An arbitrary decision was made that only the support and the three most important materials and/or techniques would be indexed in order to avoid including trivial materials.

This approach is also useful in indexing the variety of date entries. For example, when the free text entry reads '1890s', a search on the text would retrieve the work only if the year 1890 is requested. But, by entering 1890 in the earliest index date and 1899 in the latest index date, the work will be retrieved by searches based on a date greater than or equal to 1890 and less than or equal to 1899, a more appropriate range.

Thus, retrievals are more accurate and the time needed for the computer to search for criteria is reduced by a small amount for each record. But this minute difference spread over a great many data categories and a large number of records can mean a significant reduction of the resources required.

Some data categories, of course, do not need both a free text and an index entry. For example, one title entry serves both purposes. There are many free text categories which you would never search for retrieval and do not need to be indexed, such as dimensions and inscriptions.

Another reason for deciding to record data this way was that it was not known what computer package would be used. We did not want to limit ourselves to any preconceived notion of its capabilities. The decision whether to computerize the entire text of a record, or only to maintain a computerized index to the collections, or a combination of the two, can be delayed. The recording will be accurate and ready regardless of the choice to be made later.

Cataloguing manual

A cataloguing manual was prepared as a basic guide to curators (Varveris, 1980; 1981). The purpose of this manual was to establish consistent standards for recording information about works of art. Although not intended as a rigid set of instructions, it was expected that many museums would follow it exactly. It was also understood that other institutions would use it as a prototype and go on to adapt the standards as appropriate to their own collections and curatorial needs.

The data categories are arranged in the same order as they appear on the catalogue worksheet. The book is in looseleaf form so cataloguers can insert their own notes in relevant places. A number of authority lists and glossaries are included to make the manual as self-contained as possible.

The material for the manual was developed in constant consultation with the Committee members to clarify the usage they wanted, and with David Vance to ensure adherence to the meaning of the Museum Computer Network data categories. Early versions of the manual were examined by the Committee who gradually refined its contents.

When the draft of the manual was completed, copies were given to a few registrars for reference and criticism. The purpose was to determine if the guidelines were easy to understand and use under working conditions, and to ensure details had been included for all the problems to be met by curators. This process resulted in many suggestions which were incorporated into the manual. The registrars almost completely redesigned the worksheet and card designs to make them larger and to include more data categories with more space for each.

New developments

With the manual published, attention turned to the steps that it is hoped will lead to widespread computerization. The National Gallery of Australia, under the guidance of Daniel Thomas, Curator of Australian Art, a member of the Committee and a contributor to the manual, has redefined its cataloguing procedures to be compatible with the standards described in the manual. It has been entering its records into a computer using programs created for its own needs.

At the Victorian Ministry for the Arts in Melbourne, Eric Rowlinson, a member of the Committee, a contributor to and the editor of the manual, now Assistant Director for Special Projects, has been developing a plan that would be suitable for the different kinds of regional museums throughout the state of Victoria, and thus also appropriate for the diverse museums throughout Australia. The regional gallery collections of approximately 15 000 works are small enough to serve as a pilot project from which costs and working methods can be projected for larger collections, many of which have begun using the standards established in the manual.

Eric Rowlinson has looked at several computer products and has spent some time defining specifications for a museum version of a bibliographic text processing package. Although no decision will be made about the use of a particular package until more records are ready for entry into the computer, some benefit has resulted from working on these specifications. There has been further analysis of what is required of an online system to satisfy the daily needs of a museum staff. The linking of the regional museum into a network, as well as interaction with a central data bank has been considered.

Catalogue cards and lists continue to be thought desirable, as well as special programs to produce typesetting instructions for publishing catalogues under computer direction. However, there is also interest in finding out if satisfying online queries of museum personnel through video screens can make some or all of this printed material unnecessary.

Video screens have been designed, grouping related information together. Lengths have been assigned to the various data classes so they can fit on the screens. All this has been necessary and very useful preparation for the cataloguing and computerization of Victoria's regional public collections.

Now the main emphasis and allocation of the limited resources available is being concentrated on the cataloguing effort. Various steps have been taken to fund this part of the work.

The Ministry provides grants to the Regional Galleries Association of Victoria for centralized staff positions that cannot be justified as full-time positions at each of the sixteen regional galleries. In May 1983, Joseph Pascoe, then Curator of the Geelong Art Gallery, was appointed registrar to oversee the cataloguing of regional gallery collections and eventually to become systems manager of the planned computer network. He surveyed the registration problems of the galleries and recommended appropriate systems.

Assistance was also obtained from the Federal Government under the Wages Pause Scheme. Three cataloguers were approved for a period of nine months, from October 1983 through June 1984. The intention was to help galleries with their backlogs of cataloguing. Once this has been done, each institution will be responsible for keeping its records up-to-date.

Work began with a week's training session which was also attended by students completing the Victoria College Museum Studies Course. It was agreed that at least two of the students would help with the cataloguing during their placement.

Each of the three cataloguers completes a little over forty worksheets per week which they bring to the Ministry for proofreading. The Ministry keeps a copy of the first two pages which will be entered into the computer and returns the originals to the galleries. By the end of 1983 work on the collections of the Benalla Art Gallery, the Horsham Regional Art Gallery, the Latrobe Valley Centre, the McClelland Gallery, the Mornington Peninsula Arts Centre and the Bendigo Art Gallery was under way and in some cases completed.

It is expected that 4500 works will be catalogued by the end of the 37 weeks of the grant. That is about one-third of the 15 000 works in the regional galleries, substantial progress in such a short time although there is still a great deal to be done.

Funds are now being sought to continue the work so that solid plans can be made to proceed with the next step of this ambitious and exciting project.

XII INTERNATIONAL

The development and coordination of museum documentation by international agencies

Paulette Olcina

Introduction

What strikes one, when reading the outlines of the various methods which museums have used to document their collections, is the great variety of systems described.

If museum documentation is as old as museums themselves, it is, nevertheless, a relatively new discipline, and one could be amazed to think that at least a minimum amount of coordination had not been adopted from the start. This would have avoided a great deal of trial and error. Obviously it would always have been impossible to hit upon one universal and ideal system, with standardized procedures accepted by all, but at least a few major systems would have been compatible with each other, and would have provided international research with the possibility of making rapid and logical use of the collections of almost any museum.

This did not happen. There are many reasons why, which can be grouped into three categories:

Urgency. Museums were pressed by the growing mass of information brought to them by the development of documentation systems and which they had to assimilate. This urgency was accentuated by the need of professionals, in particular scientists working in museums, for increasingly detailed and comprehensive information.

Means. It was necessary to build on whatever records were available in each museum, not considering the qualitative or quantitative value of the material inherited from the past decades. Up until the end of the 1950s, the importance of documentation escaped many museum professionals in most countries. Cataloguing and inventories of collections, the basis of all documentation, had been left to the individual curator. The outgrowth of this situation was often two different documentation systems from one museum to the next. Understaffing, an endemic illness in the museum world, further compromised any efforts to improve the situation.

Intrinsic characteristics of each country. It is obvious the problems are different in a country where the tendency is towards centralization from a country where the pragmatic spirit leaves more freedom to individual initiative.

There were certain advantages to the uncoordinated development of documentation. The work of analysts in museum documentation explored paths which might never have been considered and it was possible to assess a variety of practical experiments and to evaluate the results. However, there were also many other, less favourable consequences. International research was among the victims. Much work was delayed by the multiplication of systems and procedures which consumed the time of researchers who had to learn new systems from one museum to the next and to call upon the services of the museum personnel. It was also an added difficulty for students in museum studies. A more serious problem was that habits were formed which are not always easy to change, and which make the necessary coordination and standardization procedures that are essential to computerization even more delicate and arduous.

International agencies

The first international agency to be concerned with museum problems was the International Museums' Office (OIM). This organization, the predecessor of ICOM, existed between 1927 and 1945, and was an organ of the International Institute of Intellectual Cooperation, itself a branch of the League of Nations. The secretariat was in Paris, where it edited and published its museological journal *Mouseion*, and supported a museographical documentation centre.

A survey for a project of unification of museum catalogues was initiated by the OIM's Commission for Arts and Letters in 1927: it concerned only art museums, and was aimed at encouraging cohesion in the publication of catalogues of art collections, point four in the programme of the OIM. This point also recommended the essential elements to be included in scientific catalogues of art collections.

In spite of its restricted field, this survey raised questions that are still raised today concerning the international coordination of documentation procedures; standardized descriptive cards and labels; the international exchange of information held in museum catalogues, whether published or not; coordination of classification systems for iconographical descriptions; and the dangers involved in changing methods and establishing a standard model before an assessment is made of each museum's experience. However, no additional recommendations were made after the enquiry.

The United Nations Educational Scientific and Cultural Organization (UNESCO), the International Council of Museums (ICOM), and its International Committee for Documentation (CIDOC), are the existing organizations which have worked towards coordination and standardization at the international level. Before reporting on their work and the realization of their projects, an introduction to each one is necessary. A brief history will outline the role of each one, defining what links there are between them, specifically in the field of museum documentation.

ICOM and UNESCO

The importance of ICOM is that it is a creation, not of governments, but of the museum profession itself. It was founded in 1946 by a few outstanding museum people who were particularly concerned with defending the most prestigious museums in a post-war world where traditional aesthetic concepts had, apparently, been abandoned. But as the years passed, a more accurate idea evolved of the larger and more beneficial role which the organization could play in the museum world and for museum people.

Organization

ICOM is open to all professionals who wish to join as individual members and all museums who may join as institutional members. The objectives are set by a General Assembly, which meets every three years, immediately after a General Conference where the latest museological problems are debated. The Assembly elects an Executive Council which decides upon the action to be taken to meet ICOM's objectives and which sees that the Secretariat, located in Paris, has effectively taken concrete action on them.

The Secretariat, under the direction of the Secretary General, is composed of an administrative staff and a Documentation Centre. The administrative personnel handle the work on the preparation of ICOM's meetings and the production and distribution of the reports on them; the editing and distribution of ICOM News and various other documents and publications produced by ICOM; the membership service; accounting, and the orders and supplies for other ICOM sponsored publications. The Documentation Centre, under the direction of the Head of the Centre, receives and processes museum information from all over the world. In all, the ICOM staff is composed of fifteen permanent posts, some of which are part-time.

The Committees

The basis on which ICOM's action is founded is the network of two different types of committees, one national and the other international. An ICOM member must work through a National Committee, if one exists, or may join directly if no National Committee has been formed for the country. Members of ICOM may also belong to an International Committee and are encouraged to do so, according to their special interests and professional experience. They must meet certain criteria defined by the committee itself and be approved by the Executive Board of the International Committee in question.

The *National Committees* are multidisciplinary in that they are composed of all the museum professionals who are ICOM members from one country. These committees are the representatives in ICOM of the profession in that country. Their members keep their colleagues on the National Committee informed of new developments at an international level. It is partly through these Committees that information and recommendations on museum documentation from outside their country reach museums.

International committees (25 are presently active) are established by discipline and bring together specialists from different countries. These committees draw up a work programme and their members meet regularly and organize colloquia during which they treat subjects pertaining to their discipline. Each has a Chairman and a Secretary, and according to their size, may have a bulletin or other publications. They work on specific projects, either at their own initiative or at the request of ICOM, towards whom they have an important advisory role. The ICOM International Committee for Documentation (CIDOC), created in 1950, is one of these. The Secretariat of this International Committee is provided by the UNESCO-ICOM Documentation Centre.

The UNESCO-ICOM Documentation Centre

In 1946, UNESCO founded a small documentation service to meet the needs of what was then the Museums Department of UNESCO's Division for Culture. Over a year later, the management was turned over to ICOM. The decision was a vital one, as it meant that this service would be directly under the control of the museum profession itself. The name became the UNESCO-ICOM Documentation Centre. While remaining at the disposal of UNESCO Member States, it was now also opened to the far larger public of all museums and museum professionals in the world.

Museum workers have at their disposal a unique corpus of information which has been compiled for over 38 years in an organization having no other equivalent in the museum world. The information is available either through consultation in the Centre in Paris, or by correspondence. The services provided are the compilation of lists of museums according to the subject which interests the reader, or selective bibliographical lists compiled by the staff of the Centre and based on its holdings, or photocopies of articles published in museological periodicals.

Besides these tasks, the Centre participates in training students in museology and acts as a public service open to all other professions interested in museums: researchers in social sciences, educators, writers, architects, etc.

In addition, under the guidance of Miss Yvonne Oddon who originally built up the Centre, it has always worked towards compatible methods and a standardization of museum records. In fact, in the field of documentation, the links between ICOM, CIDOC and the Documentation Centre are so intermingled and their activities so closely knit, that it is often difficult to say who exactly was behind a certain project or idea. When some doubt arises, as CIDOC and the Centre are both emanations of ICOM, it is ICOM who is credited.

ICOM, non-governmental organization

A year after its foundation, ICOM signed an agreement for cooperation with UNESCO and became what is called, in the language of UNESCO, an NGO (non-governmental organization). This means that, in the field of museology, ICOM is recognized as a professional organization of international character grouping together the most outstanding members of the profession.

UNESCO, therefore, commissions studies, reports and draft projects on which UNESCO services could work; it asks ICOM for its advice on the choice of experts to carry out missions under the UNESCO programme of aid to Member States; it involves ICOM in the organization of meetings of specialists in questions concerning museums. This close cooperation also involves museum documentation.

It is not necessary to introduce UNESCO and to explain its role in the world. But, however, in as far as museums and museum documentation are concerned it would be judicious to recall the direct and indirect help which UNESCO continually provides.

The direct help is provided by the financial support given to the Documentation Centre. Premises and other supporting services are also supplied in the UNESCO building. But, probably the indirect help is the most important, although there is no yardstick by which it can be measured. This is the prestige and the weight which UNESCO carries and which allows it to play the role of a supra-national 'ministry of culture' or of a respected ambassador, even though it may not always be heeded as much as one could hope.

In a sector as specialized as museum documentation, the role of UNESCO could appear to be limited. Its action is nevertheless valuable because of its constancy.

Projects and results

The first UNESCO initiative for museums which marked a turning point in the standardization and compatibility of museum records was the transfer of the management of the Centre to ICOM.

As regards the Centre, the help of UNESCO is particularly notable. In addition to the financial and material help, it contributed a part of its documentation (all of ICOM's holdings being received as courtesy copies). At the present time, through UNESCO's Bureau of Data Processing, the current indexing of the Centre's collections is being computerized.

UNESCO has also created training centres for museum technicians where the problems of museum documentation are an essential part of the curricula. It is due particularly to the experience gained by teaching at the Jos Centre for Museum Technicians (Nigeria) that Yvonne Oddon published *Elements of Museum Documentation*, under the auspices of UNESCO (Oddon, 1967; 1968). This work still does not have any equivalent in the profession.

In October 1976, in collaboration with ICOM, UNESCO organized a conference in Barcelona, on modern methods of inventory for movable cultural property (UNESCO, 1977). The specialists concluded that if computerization cannot solve the problems of the systematic collecting of information about cultural property, it could stock, organize and communicate this information with incomparable speed. The meeting recommended that the UNESCO Member States adopt national policies about the description of the cultural heritage. These policies comprise:

issuing a clear statement of national guidelines for the description of cultural property;

data collecting programmes for the inventory of cultural objects;

programmes aimed at disseminating an awareness of these inventories in order to promote the use of the data by all interested parties.

Following the recommendations formulated at the meeting, a number of states founded national documentation committees for the purpose of coordinating the work on the inventory of cultural property at a national level.

ICOM works primarily through CIDOC. The Committee is composed of experts from 22 countries, divided into three specialized working groups: Terminology, Bibliography and Documentation of Museum Collections. The members of these groups meet for annual colloquia during which they present their experiments, their views on the subjects under study and their suggestions for further work, all of which are submitted for examination by the Committee. The Committee incorporates the suggestions of the groups into a cohesive overall plan and turns it over to the Documentation Centre which writes, produces and distributes the reports and papers, and implements the action where appropriate.

During the 1960s, CIDOC recommended the use of standardized labels for the identification of objects and standardized catalogue cards and inventories. Model cards and registration forms were designed by Yvonne Oddon and incorporated into *Elements of Museum Documentation.*

At the request of CIDOC, the Centre compiled a museological classification scheme which has been used as a model for museum libraries and specialized centres. In response to professional needs, CIDOC edits the *International Museological Bibliography*, an annual publication for which responsibility was jointly entrusted to the Documentation Centre and the Office of Museology in Prague. Since the first volume, appearing in 1968, the Office of Museology has met the costs of printing, which is done in Prague. Since the 1981 issue (volume 15), this publication has been produced by computer.

During the second half of the 1960s, when the museum world became aware not only of the advantages which computerization could provide for museum documentation, but also that it was feasible, new experiments with computer techniques were developed independently in all four corners of the globe. By 1967, CIDOC felt that it was essential to coordinate existing systems on both a national and an international level, if an optimum use were to be made of computer techniques in museums. It formed the Working Group on the Documentation of Collections to study the problems and to meet the objectives set by the Committee.

Because of the difficulty in obtaining information from systems which were scattered throughout the world, years passed before a useful work of synthesis could be accomplished. This situation emphasized even more the absolute priority of establishing a standard data structure for the computerized interchange of information. The complexity of the task was such that, in spite of the efforts of all the working groups who tackled the problems involved, it was not possible to extract normalized procedures which would be satisfactory for the greatest number majority of computerized systems. In the United Kingdom, IRGMA had established a format for this purpose. Even though this format did not, and could not, win the unanimous approval of all the experts, it was chosen as a basis for CIDOC's work (see Chapter 12).

The problems of compatibility were discussed at length during two annual meetings, the first of which was held in Julita, Sweden, in 1978 and the second in Barcelona, Spain, in 1979. It was evident that in the present state of affairs it was impossible to reach the objectives which had been set a few years earlier. CIDOC decided to concentrate on two essential points:

a study of the needs of museums, discipline by discipline, concerning the information required on their collections;
establishing the minimum set of data categories for the description of museum objects essential for the management of collections.

The first point led to the creation of several working groups, based on specific disciplines, working towards the adoption of standardized formats which would meet the professional requirements of each discipline.

In response to the second point, CIDOC adopted the following list of *minimum* data categories for the description of museum objects:

institution (the name of the country and museum);
accession number or registration number;
mode or method of acquisition;
date of acquisition;
source of acquisition;
common object name — in the language of the country;
classification — standard term for the object (in English, French, Latin or free text; or accompanied by subcategories developed by CIDOC following consultation with other ICOM International Committees);
description of the object;
history of the object.

Obviously this list can only meet the minimum requirements of good collection management

Finally, CIDOC is also working on compiling a museological terminology. A *Dictionarium Museologicum*, begun at the initiative of the Institute of Conservation and Methodology of Museums in Budapest, is being developed in a number of languages, including German, English, French and Spanish.

Conclusion

For over thirty years, international organizations (UNESCO at the governmental level and ICOM at the professional level) have worked towards the standardization of museum documentation methods and have coordinated professional efforts towards the adoption of some harmonization in order to improve the dissemination of information among institutions and to facilitate research. These organizations have been assisted in this task by the participation of outstanding experts in the field of museum documentation, united together in the ICOM International Committee for Documentation and by a Documentation Centre which has acquired a certain experience since the diffusion of information to museums is its very reason for existence.

After assessment, the outcome in work actually accomplished may seem unimpressive. But this can only surprise the profane who are not able to accurately measure the three major obstacles:

building a documentation system requires time: using it demands, first of all, a good organization. Therefore, its functioning must be methodical and smooth. Any sudden change or improvization in methods could have results which are felt for years later. Caution in any new undertaking is imperative;
all the members of CIDOC, like all museologists who contribute their time and expertise through National and International Committees, work voluntarily. The result is a slow pace of work, as these are most often the specialists whose professional obligations and responsibilities are the greatest in so far as they are the most renowned. They simply cannot give ICOM, the Committee and the Working Group, all the time they would like;
decisions and their application: professionals can very well approve decisions taken by UNESCO and ICOM/CIDOC, but still not apply them. International organizations can never force anything upon their members — it is up to them alone to turn the recommendations into action.

Familiar working habits die hard. When one thinks that it took nearly two hundred years to see the metric system universally adopted, it would be presumptuous to expect a standardized museum documentation system to be adopted within one generation.

Sources

Procedural guides
  Chenhall, 1975
  Dudley and Wilkinson, 1979
  Fabritius, 1982
  Lewis, 1976
  Museum Documentation Association, 1981b
  Orna and Pettitt, 1980
  Perry, 1980
  Porta, Montserrat and Morral, 1982
  Reibel, 1978
  Roberts, in press (a)
  Sarasan and Neuner, 1983
  Van de Voort, 1981
Data standards
  Chenhall and Homulos, 1978
  France. Ministère de la Culture et de la Communication, 1981a and b
  Light and Roberts, 1981
  Museum Documentation Association, 1980
  North American Planning Conference, 1980
  Vance, 1975
New technology
  Art Museum Association, 1982
  Chenhall, 1975
  Chenhall, 1978b
  Light and Roberts, 1984
  Museum, 1971
  Museum, 1978
  Roberts, in press (a)
  Sarasan and Neuner, 1983
Conference reports
  Metropolitan Museum of Art, 1968
  Cutbill, 1971a
  Brenan, Ross and Williams, 1975
  International Conference on Automatic Processing of Art History Data
  and Documents, 1978
  North American Planning Conference 1980
  Computerized Inventory Standards for Works of Art, 1981
  International Seminar on Information Problems in Art History, 1982
  International Seminar on Museum Documentation, 1983
National developments
  Museum, 1971
  Museum, 1978
  Roberts and Light, 1980
Specialist newsletters
  MDA Information (quarterly) (Museum Documentation Association,
  Duxford, Cambridge, UK, CB2 4QR)
  Spectra (quarterly) (Museum Computer Network, State University of
  New York, Stony Brook, N.Y., USA, 11794)

References

Aarts, H.J., 1979. *MARDOC-onderzoek inventarisatie maritieme collecties.* (MARDOC publicatie, 2.) Vlaardingen: MARDOC. 72p.

Abell Seddon, B., 1982. A natural history computer-based catalogue. *Museums Journal*, *82*(2), 93-97.

Allan, D.A., Owen, D.E. and Wallis, F.S., 1960. *Handbook for museum curators. Part A. Section I. Administration.* London: Museums Association. 51p.

American Association of Museums, 1981. *The official museum directory 1982.* Skokie, Ill.: National Register Publishing Co., Inc. 1177p.

Anon., 1975. The Borden system of site identification. *Oracle* (National Museum of Man), 8.

Anon., 1978. Compact computer speeds access to accession, exhibition and other museum data. *Technology and Conservation*, *3*(4), 9.

Anon., 1981. Editor's note. *DIA: DARIS Newsletter* (Detroit Institute of Arts), 1.

Anon., 1982. Canadian museums to go online for posterity. *Computerworld*, November 29, 27.

Arlazarov, V.L. et al, 1979. Informatsionaya sistema INES. *Automatika i telemechanika*, 6, 109-121.

Art Museum Association, 1982. *Technology in museum environments.* A national survey of current and anticipated computer use in art museums. San Francisco, Ca.: The Association. 59p.

Aseyev, U.A., Podnozova, E.P. and Sher, J.A., 1980. Katalogizatsaya muzeinich kollektsii i informatika — Sovremenyi tchudozhestvenyi muzyei. *Problemyi deyatelnosti i perspechtivy razvitia*, L, 16-37.

Atkinson, R.J.C., 1955. A national index of archaeological collections. *Museums Journal*, *54*(10), 255-259.

Bamberry, A., 1982. The use of MDS decorative arts cards at Sheffield City Museums. *MDA Information*, *6*(2), 26-28.

Bán, A., 1980. A múzeum memoriája. (The memory of the museum.) *Müvészet*, 6, 12-13.

Barker, W.R., 1906. *The Bristol Museum and Art Gallery. The development of the Institution during a hundred and thirty four years.* Bristol: Arrowsmith.

Bezeczky, T., 1980. Számitógépes múzeumi nyilvántartás. (Computer registration in museums.) *Múzeumi Közlemények, 1*, 24-29.

Birukov, B.V. and Heller, E.S., 1973. Kibernetika v humanitarnych Naukach. M.

Boot, C., Van de Voort, J.P. and Wander, B., 1982. *Handleiding voor de beschrijving van historische voorwerpen.* (SIMIN-publikatie, 2.) Rotterdam: SIMIN. 33p.

Booth, A.V., 1972. An inventory for the art researcher. *Museum News*, *51*(4), 37-39.

Borden, C.E., 1952. A uniform site designation scheme for Canada. *Anthropology in British Columbia* (Victoria), *3*, 44-48.

Bowles, E.A., 1968. Introduction to the work of the conference. *In* Metropolitan Museum of Art, 1968. Pages xv-xx.

Brailsford, J., 1967. Indexing techniques in the Department of British and Medieval Antiquities, British Museum. *Museums Journal*, *67*(2), 105-106.

Brenan, J.P.M., Ross, R. and Williams, J.T. (eds.), 1975. *Computers in botanical collections.* (Proceedings of an international conference, sponsored by NATO, on the use of electronic data processing: major plant taxonomic collections, Kew, October 1973.) London: Plenum Press. x, 216p.

Brill, R.C., 1978. *The TAXIR primer.* 3rd ed. Ann Arbor, Mich.: University of Michigan. Computing Center. 179p.

Brunton, C.H.C., 1979. The development of a computer-based curatorial system for palaeontology at the British Museum (Natural History). *In* Bassett, M.G. (ed.). Curation of palaeontological collections. (Special Papers in Palaeontology, 22.) London: The Palaeontological Association. Pages 159-173.

Brunton, C.H.C., 1980. The use of a computer based curatorial system in the Dept. of Palaeontology B.M. (N.H.). *Geological Curator, 2*(9/10), 624-628.

Burnett, J. and Wright, D., 1982. Practical problems in cataloguing the Wellcome Collection. *Museums Journal, 82*(2), 86-88.

Canada. Department of Communication, 1982. *Report of the Federal Cultural Policy Review Committee.* Ottawa, Ont.: Minister of Supply and Services. 406p.

Canada. National Museums of Canada, 1982. *Introducing the Canadian Heritage Information Network/PARIS system.* Ottawa: NMC. 8p.

Castillo-Tejero, N., 1978. Keeping a record of the cultural heritage in the National Museum of Anthropology, Mexico City. *Museum, 30*(3/4), 179-184.

Castillo-Tejero, N. and Flores García, L., 1975. *Diccionario básico para describer las colecciones arqueológicas del Instituto Nacional de Antropología e Historia.* (Antropología Matemática, 29.) México: MNA. Sección de Máquinas Electrónicas.

Castillo-Tejero, N., Garza, S. and Piña Chán, R., 1972. *Diccionario de términos básicos para describir y catalogar las colecciones arqueológicas del Museo Nacional de Antropología de México.* (Antropología Matemática, 21.) México: MNA. Sección de Máquinas Electrónicas.

Chaldecott, J., 1967. The automatic typewriter for computer input. *Museums Journal, 67*(2), 97-105.

Chalmers-Hunt, J.M., 1976. *Natural history sales 1700-1972. A register of sales in the British Isles.* London: Sotheby, Parke, Bernet. 189p.

Chenhall, R.G., 1969. Editor's note. *Newsletter of Computer Archaeology, 5*(1), 1.

Chenhall, R.G., 1971. The archaeological data bank conference. *Newsletter of Computer Archaeology, 6*(4), 1-2.

Chenhall, R.G., 1975. *Museum cataloguing in the computer age.* Nashville, Tenn.: American Association for State and Local History. viii, 261p.

Chenhall, R.G., 1978a. *Nomenclature for museum cataloguing: a system for classifying man-made objects.* Nashville, Tenn.: American Association for State and Local History. viii, 512p.

Chenhall, R.G., 1978b. Computer use in museums today. *Museum, 30*(3/4), 139-145.

Chenhall, R.G. and Homulos, P., 1978. Museum data standards. *Museum News, 56*(6), 43-48. (Also *Museum, 30*(3/4), 205-212 and *Gazette, 11*(3), 12-18.).

Chere, Y.A. and Polyakov, A.O., 1978. *Museum cataloguing and the*

318

computer. ICOM Committee for Conservation, 5th Triennial Meeting. Zagreb.

Cleevely, R.J., 1982. *World palaeontological collections.* London: Mansell/British Museum Natural History.

Codrington, K. de B., 1931. A suggested system of museum registration. *Museums Journal, 31*(4), 126-136.

Computerized Inventory Standards for Works of Art, Nov 1-3, 1979, 1981. *Conference proceedings.* Collection of papers prepared under the direction of Raymond Vézina. Montreal: Éditions Fides. 287p.

Conybeare, W.D., 1836. A general memoir of the Institution from its commencement. *Proceedings of the thirteenth Annual Meeting. Bristol Institution.* Pages i-xvi.

Cooper, J.D., Phillips, P.W., Sedman, K.W. and Stanley, M.F., 1980. *Geological record centre handbook.* Duxford, Cambridgeshire: Museum Documentation Association. vii, 65p.

Crane, M.D., 1981a. Arthur Broughton, a late eighteenth century botanist in Bristol and Jamaica. *Archives of Natural History, 10*(2), 317-330.

Crane, M.D., 1981b. Catalogue of type, figured and cited fossils in the City of Bristol Museum and Art Gallery. *Geological Curator, 2*(8), supplement. iv, 17p.

Creighton, R.A. and Crockett, J.J., 1971. SELGEM: a system for collections management. *Smithsonian Institution. Information Systems Innovations, 2*(3), 1-24, appendix.

Creighton, R.A. and Parsons, M., 1977. Origins and goals of MESH. *Curator, 20*(1), 23-31.

Cutbill, J.L. (ed.), 1971a. *Data processing in biology and geology.* (Systematics Association Special Volume, 3.) London: Academic Press. xv, 346p.

Cutbill, J.L., 1971b. *Cambridge research on data processing in geology.* Reports 1-6. (OSTI Report, 5109.) London: Office for Scientific and Technical Information. Various pagination.

Cutbill, J.L., Hallan, A.J. and Lewis, G.D., 1971. A format for the machine exchange of museum data. *In* Cutbill, J.L. (ed.)., 1971a. Pages 255-274.

Dauterman, C.C., 1968. Sevrès incised marks and the computer. *In* Metropolitan Museum of Art, 1968. Pages 177-194.

Davis, P., 1978. A new gallery on a limited budget — 'Local Wildlife' at Sunderland Museum. *Museums Journal, 78*(2), 70-72.

Davis, P. and Hebron, J., 1982. Computer cataloguing at the Hancock Museum, Newcastle upon Tyne: a review of progress to date. *Museums Journal, 82*(2), 89-91.

Dawes, C.C., 1982. Pictorial representation cataloguing in Stevenage Museum. *MDA Information, 6*(2), 20-23.

Dudley, D.H. and Wilkinson, I.B. (eds.), 1979. *Museum registration methods.* 3rd ed. Washington, D.C.: American Association of Museums. ix, 437p.

Elkin, P., 1975. Treasures in store: the Bristol Museum storage project 1975. *Museums Journal, 75*(2), 57-60.

Éri, I., 1971. A múzeumi nyilvántartás, tájékoztatás és a számitógépek. (Registration in museums, information and computers.) *Múzeumi Közlemények, 3,* 42-48.

Etchells-Butler, S.H., 1982. From matchbox to computer or the computerization of the Philip Cambridge Collection at the Sedgwick Museum. *Geological Curator, 3*(5), 300-310.

Fabritius, E., 1982. *Registrering af kunstvaerker. SMN/Informationsblad.* Copenhagen: Statens Museumsnaevn. 8p.

Fédération Internationale des Archives du Film. Cataloguing Commission, 1979a. *Film cataloging.* New York: Burt Franklin and Co. 198p.

Fédération Internationale des Archives du Film. Cataloguing Commission, 1979b. *Study on the usage of computers for film cataloguing.* Brussels: FIAF. 60p.

Feinberg, E.L., 1981. Kibernetika, Logika, Iskusstvo. M.

Flood, S. and Perring, F., 1978. *A handbook for local biological record centres.* : Biology Curators Group and Biological Records Centre. Unpaginated.

Forbes, C.L., Harland, W.B. and Cutbill, J.L., 1971. A uniform cataloguing system in the Department of Geology at Cambridge. *In* Cutbill (ed.), 1971. Pages 311-320.

France. Ministère de la Culture et de la Communication. Direction des Musées de France, 1981a. *Système descriptif des peintures.* Paris: Bureau Informatique. 108p.

France. Ministère de la Culture et de la Communication. Direction des Musées de France, 1981b. *Système descriptif des sculptures.* Paris: Bureau Informatique. 126p.

Fraser, S., 1982. Recent experience at the Hunterian Museum. *MDA Information, 6*(3), 39-41.

Freundlich, A.L., 1966. Museum registration by computer. *Museum News, 44*(6), 18-20.

Gardin, J.-C., 1955. Problèmes de la documentation. *Diogène,* II.

Gardin, J.-C., 1975. Logical effects of data bases on the study of historical sources. *Intern. Soc. Sciences Journal,* 27.

Gautier, T.G., 1978. Automated collection documentation system at the National Museum of Natural History, Smithsonian Institution, Washington, D.C. *Museum, 30*(3/4), 160-168.

Glaister, J., 1981. The Turner Collection at the Hunterian Museum, University of Glasgow. *Museum Ethnographers' Group Newsletter, 11,* 12-15.

Gomez de Mendez, G., 1975. *Glosario básico para inventariar las colecciones históricas del Instituto Nacional de Antropología e Historia.* (Antropología Matemática, 30.) México: MNA. Sección de Máquinas Electrónicas.

Grassl, C.O., 1936. Visualising our herbaria by the application of mechanical methods of tabulation and indexing. *Museums Journal, 36*(9), 373-384.

Great Britain. Department of Education and Science, 1973a. *Provincial museums and galleries. A report of a committee appointed by the Paymaster General.* [Chairman, C.W. Wright.] London: HMSO. vii, 92p.

Great Britain. Department of Education and Science, 1973b. *Local Government Act, 1972. Reorganisation of local government: museums and galleries and the arts.* (Circular 9/73.) London: DES. 5p.

Great Britain. Parliament. House of Commons. Committee of Public

Accounts, 1981. *Tenth report from the Committee of Public Accounts ... Session 1980-81.* London: HMSO. Pages x-xiii and 20-36.

Group for Regional Studies in Museums. SHIC Working Party, 1983. *Social History and Industrial Classification (SHIC).* A subject classification for museum collections. Volume 1: the classification; volume 2: index. Sheffield: University of Sheffield (available from the MDA). xiv, 96p and v, 74p.

Gutchin, E.B., 1969. Kibernetitcheskie Modeli Tvortchestva. M.

Hackmann, W.D., 1973. *The evaluation of a museum communication format. Part I — collection of input data.* (OSTI Report, 5154) London: Office for Scientific and Technical Information. 99p.

Hall, M., 1983. Practical implications of implementing the MDA documentation system at Mutare Museum, Zimbabwe. *MDA Information,* 6(5), 82-85.

Hancock, E.G. and Pettitt, C.W. (eds.), 1981. *Register of natural science collections in North West England.* Manchester: Manchester Museum for North West Collection Research Unit. 188p.

Harrison, R.K. and Sabine, P.A. (eds.), 1970. *A petrological-mineralogical code for computer use.* (Institute of Geological Sciences, Report 70/6.) London: HMSO for Institute of Geological Sciences. vii, 134p.

Heller, J., 1968. The value of a computerised data bank as an adjunct to a museum card catalogue. *In* Metropolitan Museum of Art, 1968. Pages 307-322.

Hellman, G.T., 1964. Profile of a museum. *Art in America, 52*(1).

Hiley, M.D. and Wallis, F.S., 1936. A suggested scheme for museum records. *Museums Journal, 36*(4), 134-140.

Hislop, R., 1967. Information retrieval and computer printed indexes. *Museums Journal, 67*(2), 91-97.

Hogenboom, J. and Van de Voort, J.P. (eds.), 1982. *MARDOC-Handleiding voor de beschrijving van afbeeldingen.* (MARDOC-publicatie, 4.) Rotterdam: MARDOC. 220p.

Holm, S., 1982. SHIC — a new subject classification for museum collections. *MDA Information, 6*(3), 44-49.

Homulos, P., 1978. The Canadian National Inventory Programme. *Museum, 30*(3/4), 153-159.

Hoyle, W.R., 1891. The registration and cataloguing of museum specimens, *In* Museums Association. Second Annual Report. London: Museums Association. Pages 59-67.

Humphrey, P.S. and Clausen, A.C., 1977. *Automated cataloguing for museum collections: a model for decision making and a guide to implementation.* Lawrence, Kan.: Association of Systematics Collections. 79p.

International Conference on Automatic Processing of Art History Data and Documents. 1st, Pisa, 1978. *Conference transactions.* Edited by Paola Barocchi and Fabio Bisogni with the assistance of Laura Corti. Vols I and II. Pisa: Scuola Normale Superiore.

International Seminar on Information Problems in Art History, Oxford, 1982. *Proceedings.* Compiled and co-edited by Jill Heberden and Michael Doran. *Art Libraries Journal, 7*(2), 5-99.

International Seminar on Museum Documentation, August 1982, Sydney,

1983. *Report of the seminar on museum documentation*. Canberra, ACT: Australian National Committee of ICOM. iv, 60p.

Irwin, H.S., 1973. Flora North America: austerity casualty? *Bioscience, 23*, 215.

Italy. Ministero per i Beni Culturali e Ambientali. Istituto Centrale per il Catalogo e la Documentazione, 1980. *Materiali dell' età del Bronzo finale e della prima età del Ferro*. (Dizionari Terminologici, 1.) [ed. Franca Parise Badoni.] Firenze: Centro di. 230p.

Italy. Ministero per i Beni Culturali e Ambientali. Istituto Centrale per il Catalogo e la Documentazione, 1982. *Armi difensive dal Medioevo all' Età Moderna*. (Dizionari Terminologici, 2.) [ed. L.G. Boccia.] Firenze: Centro di. 230p.

Kamenetskii, E.S., Marshak, B.E. and Sher, J.A., 1975. Analiz Archeologicheskich Istochnikov Vozhmozhnostu Formaliz vannogo Podhoda. M.

Kirk, J.J., 1979. Using a computer in Brighton's museums. *Museums Journal, 79*(1), 17-20.

Kovalchenko, E.D. (ed.), 1977. Matematicheskie Metody v Historiko. Ekonomicheskich y Historiko — Kultunyich Issledobanyach. M.

Lewis, G.D., 1965. Obtaining information from museum collections and thoughts on a national index. *Museums Journal, 65*(1), 12-22.

Lewis, G.D., 1967. Information retrieval for museums. *Museums Journal, 67*(2), 88-91.

Lewis, G.D., 1971. An interdisciplinary communication format for museums in the United Kingdom. *Museum, 23*(1), 24-26.

Lewis, R.H., 1976. *Manual for museums*. Washington, D.C.: US Department of the Interior. National Park Service. xiii, 412p.

Light, R.B., 1979. Computer-based cataloguing in British museums. *In* Bassett, M.G. (ed.), 1979. Curation of palaeontological collections. (Special Papers in Palaeontology, 22). London: The Palaeontological Association. Pages 149-157.

Light, R.B., 1982. Today's microcomputers for museum documentation? *Museums Journal, 82*(2), 77-78.

Light, R.B., 1983. Proceedings of the MDA microcomputer workshop, Leicester University, 12-13 April, 1983. *MDA Information, 7*(1), 1-14.

Light, R B. and Roberts, D.A., 1981. *International museum data standards and experiments In data transfer*. (MDA Occasional Paper, 5.) Duxford, Cambridgeshire: Museum Documentation Association. iv, 100p.

Light, R.B. and Roberts, D.A. (eds.), 1984. *Microcomputers in museums*. (MDA Occasional Paper, 7.) Duxford, Cambridgeshire: MDA. v, 78p.

Litvak, J. Castillo-Tejero, N. and Thomas, F., 1964. *Lista de conceptos que servirá como base de un programa para la dosificación y acumulación de datos sobre piezas de la colección de arqueología del Museo Nacional de Antropología*. México: MNA. Seccion de Máquinas Electrónicas.

Locke, P. and Pellatt, J., 1983. Adoption of the MDS by the National Museums and Monuments of Zimbabwe and their proposed documentation procedure for historical artefacts. *MDA Information, 6*(5), 74-81.

Lowe, E.E., 1903. The registration and numeration of museum specimens. *Museums Journal, 2*, 258-266.

Loy, T.H., 1982. Experience with the National Inventory Programme of

Canada. *Computer Applications in Archaeology* (University of Birmingham), 1982. Pages 114-116.

Loy, T.H. and Powell, G.R., 1977. *Archaeological data recording guide.* (Heritage Record Series, 3.) Victoria, B.C.: British Columbia Provincial Museum. 88p, figures.

McInnes, G., 1978. The Hunterian IRGMA geology vocabulary and grammar. *MDA Information*, 2(2), 11-17.

MacKie, E.W., 1978. A hierarchy of artifact names for the MDA cards. *MDA Information*, 2(6), 55-79 and 2(7), 66-69.

MacKie, E.W., 1980. Using the MDA cards in the Hunterian Museum. *Museums Journal*, 80(2), 86-88.

MARDOC-Handleiding, 1977. *MARDOC-Handleiding voor de beschrijving van scheepsmodellen.* (MARDOC publicatie, 1.) Vlaardingen: MARDOC. 35p.

Mayhew, W., 1980. *Inexpensive computerized museum cataloguing.* Boston: Children's Museum. 47p.

Metropolitan Museum of Art, 1968. *Computers and their potential applications in museums.* New York, N.Y.: Arno Press. xx, 402p.

Mironov, B.N. and Stepanov, Z.V., 1975. Istorik i matematika. M.

Mollo, B., 1982. Use of ADP cataloguing at the National Army Museum. *MDA Information*, 6(3), 42-43.

Murdock, G.P., Ford, C.S., Hudson, A.E., Kennedy, R., Simmons, L.W. and Whiting, J.W.A., 1961. *Outline of cultural materials.* 4th revised edition. New Haven, Conn.: Human Relations Area Files. xxv, 164p.

Murtfeldt, L., 1974. International species inventory system (ISIS). *ASC Newsletter*, 2(4), 9-10.

Museum, 1971. Museums and computers (whole issue). *Museum, 23*(1).

Museum, 1978. Museums and computers (whole issue). *Museum, 30*(3/4).

Museum Documentation Association, 1980. *Data definition language and data standard.* Duxford, Cambridgeshire: MDA. v, 144p.

Museum Documentation Association, 1981a. *Guide to the museum documentation system.* 2nd edition. Duxford, Cambridgeshire: MDA. iv, 42p, forms.

Museum Documentation Association, 1981b. *Practical museum documentation.* 2nd edition. Duxford, Cambridgeshire: MDA. viii, 188p.

Museum Documentation Association, 1981c. *Guide to GOS.* Duxford, Cambridgeshire: MDA. iv, 26p.

Museum Documentation Association. Development Committee, 1982. The future development of the Museum Documentation Association. *Museums Journal*, 82(2), 72-76.

Museums Association, 1982. *Museums yearbook.* London: Museum Association. 176p.

Museums Association. Information Retrieval Group, 1969. *Draft proposals for an interdisciplinary museum cataloguing system.* London: Imperial War Museum for IRGMA. 46p.

Museums Association. Information Retrieval Group. Standards Subcommittee, 1977. Ten years of IRGMA, 1967-1977. *Museums Journal*, 77(1), 11-14.

Nalimov, V.V., 1979. Veroyatnostnye Modyel i Yazika. O Soothoshenii Estestvennych i iskusstvennych Yazikov. M.

Neufeld, S.D., 1981. *The MDA systems and services: a user's view*. (MDA Occasional Paper, 6.) Duxford, Cambridgeshire: MDA. v, 115p.

Neuner, A.M., 1976. *SELGEM manual*. Lawrence, Kan.: Association of Systematics Collections. 104p.

Norgate, M., 1982. Museum record. *Museums Journal*, 82(2), 83-85.

North American Planning Conference, Stony Brook, June 1980, 1980. Final report. *Spectra*, 7(2/3), 1-4.

Nyerges, A.L., 1982. Museums and the videodisc revolution: cautious involvement. *Videodisc/Videotex*, 2(4), 267-274.

Oddon, Y., 1967. Information retrieval and ICOM. *Museums Journal*, 67(2), 115-120.

Oddon, Y., 1968. *Elements of museum documentation*. Jos, Nigeria: Jos Museum. 68p.

Olive, A. de V.M. and López Rivas, G., 1964. *Datos para la clasificación de objetos etnográficos*. México: MNA. Sección de Máquinas Electrónicas.

Orna, E., 1982. Information management in museums: there's more to it than documentation and computers. *Museums Journal*, 82(2), 79-82.

Orna, E. and Pettitt, C.W., 1980. *Information handling in museums*. London: Clive Bingley. 190p.

Peebles, C.S. and Galloway, P., 1981. Notes from underground: archaeological data management from excavation to curation. *Curator*, 24(4), 225-252.

Perry, K.D. (ed.)., 1980. *The museum forms book*. Austin, Tx.: Texas Association of Museums. xii, 380p.

Petersen, T., 1981. Computer-aided indexing in the arts: the case for a thesaurus of terms. *Art Libraries Journal*, 6(3), 6-11.

Pettigrew. T.H. and Holden, J., 1978. Internal conventions used with the IRGMA geology and mineral specimen cards in the documentation of the geology collections of Tyne and Wear County Council Museums. *Newsletter of the Geological Curators Group*, 2(3), supplement. 26p.

Pettitt, C.W., 1981a. The Manchester Museum Computer Cataloguing Unit: a STEP in the right direction? *Museums Journal*, 80(4), 187-191.

Pettitt, C.W. (ed.), 1981b. *MANDATA. How to obtain information from the Manchester Museum databases*. Manchester: Manchester Museum. 10p.

Pettitt, C.W. and Hancock, E.G., 1981. Natural science collection research units, their origin, aims and current status. *Museums Journal*, 81(2), 73-74.

Platnauer, H.M. and Howarth, E. (eds.), 1890. *Report of Proceedings*. Museums Association. First Annual Report. London: Museums Association. 1-10.

Pole, L.M., 1983. Saffron Walden Museum. *MDA Information*, 6(4), 67-69.

Porta, E., Montserrat, R.M. and Morral, E., 1982. *Sistema di documentación para museos*. Barcelona: Departamento de Cultura de la Generalitat de Catalunya. 84p.

Porter, M.F., 1978. Establishing a museum documentation system in the United Kingdom. *Museum*, 30(3/4), 169-178.

Porter, M.F., 1981. *GOS reference manual*. Duxford, Cambridgeshire: MDA. vi, 214p.

Porter, M.F., 1982. GOS: a package for making catalogues. *Information Technology: Research and Development*, 1, 113-129.

Porter, M.F., Light, R.B. and Roberts, D.A., 1976. *A unified approach to the computerization of museum catalogues.* (British Library. Research and Development Reports, Report 5338HC.) London: British Library. v, 75p.

Rauschenbach, B.V., 1980. Prostranstvennye Postroenia v Zhivopisi. M.

Reibel, D.B., 1978. *Registration methods for the small museum. A guide for historical collections.* Nashville, Tenn.: American Association for State and Local History. 160p.

Rensberger, J.M. and Berry, W.B., 1967. An automated system for retrieval of museum data. *Curator, 10*(4), 297-317.

Ricciardelli, A.F., 1968. Inventorying ethnological collections in museums. *In* Metropolitan Museum of Art, 1968. Pages 81-100.

Roads, C.H., 1968. Data recording, retrieval and presentation in the Imperial War Museum. *Museums Journal, 67,* 277-283.

Roberts, D.A., 1974. *Proposals for a national survey of museum cataloguing practice.* London: The City University. Centre for Information Science. 198p.

Roberts, D.A., 1975. Proposals for a survey of cataloguing practice in British museums. *Museums Journal, 75*(2), 78-80.

Roberts, D.A., 1976. *Introduction to the IRGMA documentation system.* London: Museums Association. 29p.

Roberts, D.A., 1982. Computerized inventories, catalogues and indexes of museum collections. *Art Libraries Journal, 7*(2), 33-40.

Roberts, D.A., in press(a). *Planning the documentation of museum collections.* Duxford, Cambridgeshire: MDA.

Roberts, D.A., in press(b). The development of computer-based documentation in United Kingdom museums. In Museums Association. Manual of curatorship: a guide to museum practice. London: Butterworths.

Roberts, D.A. and Light, R.B., 1980. Progress in documentation. Museum documentation. *Journal of Documentation, 36*(1), 42-84.

Roberts, D.A., Light, R.B. and Stewart, J.D., 1980. The Museum Documentation Association. *Museums Journal, 80*(2), 81-85.

Rolfe, W.D.I., Ingham, J.K., Currie, E.D., Neville, S., Brannan, J. and Campbell, E., 1981. *Type specimens of fossils from the Hunterian Museum and Glasgow Art Gallery and Museum.* Glasgow: Hunterian Museum. 12p and 5 microfiche.

Royal Ontario Museum, 1982. *The Royal Ontario Museum. Statement of principles and policies on ethics and conduct.* Toronto, Ont.: ROM. xi, 130p.

Sarasan, L., 1979. An economical approach to computerization. *Museum News, 57*(4), 61-64.

Sarasan, L., 1981. Why museum computer projects fail. *Museum News, 59*(4), 40-49.

Sarasan, L. and Neuner, A.M. (compilers), 1983. *Museum collections and computers.* Lawrence, Kan.: Association of Systematics Collections. viii, 292p.

Schneider, M.J., 1970. *A guide to inventorying ethnological collections.* Columbia, Mo.: University of Missouri. Museum of Anthropology. Unpaginated.

Schulman, J.L., in press. The Detroit Art Registration Information System DARIS. *In* Encyclopedia of information systems and services, 6th edition. Chicago, Ill.: Gale Research.

Seaborne, M.J. and Neufeld, S., 1982. Historic photograph collection management at the Museum of London. *Museums Journal, 82*(2), 99-103.

Sharpe, T., 1983. *Geology in museums: a bibliography and index.* Cardiff: National Museum of Wales. 128p.

Sher, J.A., 1978. The use of computers in museums: present situation and problems. *Museum, 30*(3/4), 132-138.

Sherborne, C.D., 1940. *Where is the — collection?* Cambridge: CUP. 148p.

Shetler, S.G., 1975. *The Flora North America generalized system for describing the morphology of organisms.* (Museum Data Bank Report, 4.) Rochester, N.Y.: Museum Data Bank Committee. 4p.

Shetler, S.G. and Read, R.W. (eds.), 1973. *International index of current research projects in plant systematics, no.7.* (FNA Report, 71.) Washington, D.C.: Smithsonian Institution. Department of Botany. xxii, 118p.

Sinclair, N., 1979. Monkwearmouth Station: the development of a transport museum for Tyne and Wear. *Museums Journal, 79*(1), 6-10.

Smith, J.F., 1983. Stamford Museum. *MDA Information, 6*(4), 61-65.

Smither, R.B.N., 1979. Using APPARAT: cataloguing film and sound recordings at the Imperial War Museum. *Aslib Proceedings, 31*, 170-179.

Smither, R.B.N., 1980. The film archive of the Imperial War Museum: a case history. *Computer Bulletin, 2*(26), 24-26.

Smither, R.B.N. with Penn, D.J., 1976. *Film cataloguing handbook.* London: Imperial War Museum. 58p.

Squires, D.F., 1966. Data processing and museum collections: a problem for the present. *Curator, 9*(3), 211-221.

Stewart, J.D., 1980a. *Environmental record centres: a decade of progress?* (MDA Occasional Paper, 3.) Duxford, Cambridgeshire: MDA. vi, 44p

Stewart, J.D., 1980b. A summary of local environmental record centres in Britain. *Museums Journal, 80*(3), 161-164.

Stewart, J.D., 1983. Museum documentation in Britain — a review of some recent developments. *Museums Journal, 83*(1), 61-63.

Stone, S.M., 1978. St Albans Museums documentation project. *Museums Journal, 78*(3), 117-119.

Stone, S.M., 1979. MDA user experience — St Albans Museums. *MDA Information, 3*(7), 49-54.

Stradling, S., 1983. Countywide documentation in Suffolk. *MDA Information, 6*(5), 86-88.

Sunderland, J. and Geyer, G., 1982. A traditional art museum — modern inventory control. *Perspectives* (IBM), *2*(3), 32-41.

Sustik, J.M., 1981. *Art history interactive videodisc project at the University of Iowa.* Iowa City, Iowa: University of Iowa. Weeg Computing Center. 12p.

Sweeney, J.W., 1970. *A feasibility study of a nationwide system to catolog ethnological collections.* Norman, Okla.: University of Oklahoma. Research Institute. Unpaginated.

Thornton, C.E., 1983. Williamson Art Gallery and Museum. *MDA Information, 6*(4), 58-61.

Turner, S. and Robson, P., 1979. Computer controlled data bank system at the Hancock Museum. *GCG Newsletter, 2*(7), 443-447.

Unesco, 1977. *Meeting of experts on modern methods of inventory of movable cultural property.* (Barcelona, Spain, 4 to 8 October 1976). Final report. [CO/CH/76/CONF.648/1.] Paris: Unesco. 9p.

Ustinov, V.A. and Fellinger, A.F., 1977. Istoriko — Sozialnye Issledovania, EVM u Matematika. M.

Van de Voort, J.P., 1974. VISDOC, een documentatieproject voor de Nederlandse zeevisserij in het verleden. *Open, 6,* 218-220.

Van de Voort, J.P., 1980. *Van model naar werkelijkheid. MARDOC voortgangsrapport.* (MARDOC publicatie, 3.) Vlaardingen: MARDOC. 73p.

Van de Voort, J.P. (ed.), 1981. *Museumregistratie en ontsluiting van gegevens, tevens een aanzet tot automatisering.* (SIMIN publicatie, 1.) Enkhuizen: Nederlandse Museum Vereniging. 36p.

Vance, D., 1970. Museum data banks. *Information Storage and Retrieval, 5,* 203-211.

Vance, D., 1975. *Manual for Museum Computer Network data preparation.* Stony Brook, N.Y.: State University of New York. Center for Contemporary Arts and Letters. 33p, ix, 76p.

Vance, D., 1977. *GRIPHOS.* Stony Brook, N.Y.: State University of New York. Center for Contemporary Arts and Letters. 55p.

Vance, D. and Heller, J., 1971. Structure and content of a museum data bank. *Computers and the Humanities, 6*(2), 67-84.

Varveris, T., 1978. Using the computer for Australia's art museums. *In* International Conference on Automatic Processing of Art History, Volume I.

Varveris, T., 1980. *Cataloguer's manual for the visual arts.* Sydney: Australian Gallery Directors' Council. 107p.

Varveris, T., 1981. A cataloguing manual for Australia. *Art Libraries Journal, 6*(2), 15-19.

Varveris, T., 1983a. Accessioning paintings and drawings. *In* International Seminar on Museum Documentation, 1983. Pages 25-32.

Varveris, T., 1983b. Conversion from manual catalogue systems to computers. *In* International Seminar on Museum Documentation, 1983. Pages 43-47.

Walton, K.M., 1980. *Bristol Art Gallery, 1905-1980.* Bristol: City of Bristol Museum and Art Gallery.

Wilcox, U.V., 1980. Collections management with the computer. *Curator, 23*(1), 43-54.

Will, L., 1982. Computerisation of museum records at the Science Museum. *MDA Information, 6*(3), 36-39.

Williams, D.W., 1981. How museums can use information management systems. *History News, 36*(6), 37-40.

Williams, I.J., 1919. The preservation, cataloguing and educational value of print collections. *Museums Journal, 18*(8), 125-129.

Zavipov, R.X., 1971. Kibernetika i Musika. M.

Index

332